Urban America

Politics and Policy

Urban America

Politics and Policy

Second Edition

Eugene Lewis

Provost
and Professor of Political Science
New College
University of South Florida

Frank Anechiarico

Assistant Professor of Government
Hamilton College

Holt, Rinehart and Winston

New York   Chicago   San Francisco   Dallas
Montreal   Toronto   London   Sydney

Library of Congress Cataloging in Publication Data

Lewis, Eugene.
  Urban America.

  First ed. (1973) published under title: The urban
political system.
  Bibliography: p.
  Includes index.
  1. Municipal government—United States. 2. Community
power. I. Anechiarico, Frank, joint author. II. Lewis,
Eugene. Urban political system. III. Title.
JS341.L43 1981   306'.2   80-25592

ISBN 0-03-050391-4

To Maren Donaldson Lewis and
C. Michael and Linda Sassano Anechiarico

Preface

This book provides a general introduction to some significant aspects of the politics, economics, and social life of cities and suburbs. Although substantial revisions and additions have been made, the central tenet of the first edition—*The Urban Political System*—continues as the dominant theme of the present text. The claim of a fundamental shift in political power from simple elites or pluralistic democracies to functionally defined urban bureaucracies and their constituent and clientele networks is, we believe, strengthened in this new edition.

The new material reflects changes in the object of study as well as in the way in which one might profitably understand the urban political system. The discipline of public economics directs new light on the policies, programs, and effects of local, state, and national attempts to solve urban problems. This new edition compares and contrasts policies and programs in five empirical settings. It also traces the impact of demographic change and intergovernmental relations on the key questions of resource allocation, service distribution, and equity.

We have retained the original historical emphasis, combined the discussion and analysis of the community power debate, and strengthened the framework of the central concept having to do with the urban policy process. We have also retained and amplified the interdisciplinary tone that we believe essential to any introduction to a phenomenon as complex as the urban political system. Our concern with public finance reflects what we consider to be a long-run and increasingly significant matter of political choices for cities and suburbs in the 1980s.

There has never been anything approaching a generally agreed upon framework for the description and analysis of the urban political system. Certainly this text does not imply that it offers such a framework. It does offer several different ways of studying the complexity that is contemporary urban America. This text depends upon the work of historians, political scientists, sociologists, and economists, and we acknowledge our indebtedness to them here and in the pages that follow. Errors of descriptions and analysis we of course acknowledge as our own.

Maren Donaldson Lewis contributed vital assistance as editor, copy editor, and proofreader without portfolio or compensation. We gratefully acknowledge her effort. Professor Charles H. Levine offered useful criticism, as did Professors Alphonse Sallett and R. P. Suttmeier of Hamilton College and Patrick Powers of Holt, Rinehart and Winston. We were also fortunate in enlisting the research assistance of Jonathan B. Fellows, Lee E. Berner, and Candace Paris. Among others whose presence and support we found invaluable we include Katherine Martin and Charles Henry Lewis, and David Anechiarico, fellow students of society.

E. L.
Sarasota, Florida

F. M. A.
Clinton, New York

September 1980

List of
Figures
and Tables

Contents

Urban America

Politics and Policy

Part I

The Evolution of Urban Politics in America

Chapter 1
In Search
of the City

The Chaotic and the Pathetic: Social Scientists
in Search of Theory

Not too many years ago, social scientists felt reasonably secure in offering courses which dealt with a series of matters somehow readily bounded by the term "urban." In our discipline, political science, professors taught courses on state and local government, city politics, and, more recently, urban government and politics. These academic enterprises left students feeling comfortable about a body of ideas and facts circumscribed by clear-cut legal entities. One studied towns, cities, counties, and states according to their institutions and the limits of their political systems. As time passed, the object of study became something called the urban area or region, in submission to a set of social facts, not the least of which was the general recognition that the concept of SMSA (Standard Metropolitan Statistical Areas) developed by the Bureau of the Census in 1950 made more than just statistical sense.

Our colleagues in economics, sociology, planning, and allied disciplines similarly became concerned with a more expanded view of matters urban. One can now study economics, sociology, and a host of related disciplines according to the urban perspective. Each discipline tended to define "urban" according to its own theoretical disposition. There was rough and imprecise agreement about the ordinary language meaning of the term. Then, about twenty years ago, there began a series of events which threw the students of cities into a turmoil that continues to the present day. The boundaries of our thought collapsed as the social, political, and economic life of cities changed and changed again.

Millions of black Americans migrated to cities from rural areas in search of the immigrant's dream: a better life for themselves and their families.[1] Others sought fulfillment of this dream in the suburbs, the new American frontier, during the middle decades of the century, for the rising expectations of the predomi-

[1]For more on black migration see Gilbert Osofsky, *Harlem: The Making of a Ghetto* (New York: Harper & Row, 1966); Gunnar Myrdal, *An American Dilemma* (New York: Harper & Row, 1944); and Herbert Gutman, *The Black Family in Slavery and Freedom, 1750–1825* (New York: Pantheon, 1976).

nantly white middle classes. Almost immediately thereafter new populations began to migrate in ways unforeseen and little comprehended by social scientists. The aged began to leave cities and suburbs in the colder climates and to move to the "sunbelt" cities stretching from southern Florida across the continent to southern California. For the first time in world history, a nation began to develop cities for the older members of the society. Tampa and Miami are two large urban areas rapidly filling up with older citizens, many of whom are fortunate enough to retire with sufficient pension income to move into the sun for their "golden years."

Left behind by the relatively affluent, white, employed middle class were the poor, the blacks, and the nonaffluent elderly. If these changes in population characteristics were all that had happened in the past two decades of urban history, the job of the social scientist would still have been a difficult one. But these changes were not the only ones that have left us confused over basic concepts.

Deteriorating industrial plants in northern and eastern regions of the nation were usually not replaced by new plants in the old locations. Managers moved them to the South where labor and energy were cheaper.[2] The mills of New England and upstate New York became silent, remains of a bustling past. The same story holds true for the increasingly significant retail trade sector. The center-city department store is today becoming a relic akin to the mills of yesterday. Shopping centers, seemingly endless in number and imitative of what their center-city predecessors sold, sprang up rapidly in the late 1950s and through the next decade as well, only to be superseded by enclosed malls of intimidating size. The foundation for such growth and physical change was financed by the national and state highway programs, which had created physical and economic conditions sympathetic to the development of the "spread city." So, too, could rural "industrial parks," airports and whole towns be rapidly erected.

As suburbanization progressed, outworn buildings in the central city were not usually replaced except when large amounts of public funds were obtained to finance construction. Most major cities spent those urban renewal dollars on revitalization schemes that were partially justified on the grounds that revitalization would bring white, middle-class professionals back to the cities they had abandoned for the rustic joys of the suburbs. Inexplicably and suddenly, the generally peaceful conditions of city life were shattered in the middle and late 1960s by widespread rioting by blacks enraged by years of neglect and by the failure of the urban dream. The term "ghetto" was transformed from its original sense—the urban confinement of Jews in European cities—to a new one: neighborhoods of black and Hispanic citizens of the United States. The cities and their surrounding areas thus became *the* focal point of domestic problems and politics in America. The relatively simple view of city politics, or even urban politics,

[2]The shift to the South is considered generally· by Kirkpatrick Sale in *Power Shift* (New York: Random House, 1975).

began to crumble seriously, and by the early 1970s, the pitiable condition of the city and the chaos of its many governmental and political agencies seriously damaged many of the implicit theories of local politics.

The Objects of Study: People, Places, and Policies

To understand how and why this damage to implicit theory took place, it is useful to consider what it is that students of urban politics study. City politics was normally studied in two ways. The first and most popular way acquainted the student through a guided tour of the different offices, optional forms of government, and legal aspects of city government.[3] A bit of this may be found in Chapter 4 of the present volume. A second approach, usually addressed very differently, was taken by those who studied bosses, elections, and political parties and elites.[4] Seldom were the two approaches combined.

Most of the interesting work done on cities historically came from the discipline of sociology, where concerns for description and analysis were strong. This was particularly true of the Chicago School of Robert Park and the political scientists Charles Merriam and Harold Gosnell.[5] The discipline of sociology developed, moreover, a tradition of studying community power; a tradition which differed greatly from that of the political scientists. Those differences contributed to a battle that has ebbed and flowed for nearly fifty years and to which we devote some time in Chapter 5. As useful as the debate between elitists and pluralists has been, there is good reason, we think, to believe that the whole conflict has become somewhat distant from the material realities of present-day urban America. Our reasons for affirming this are spelled out at some length as a central theme of this text.

At this introductory point, it will suffice to point out a few things about the objects of study. City residents are now among the most studied population in world history. They have been analyzed and described in great detail by all of the social science disciplines and by government agencies, as well as in movies, plays, and poems. Predictably enough, the term "urban dweller" now is associated with a "problem." Our contemporary view of the city resident vacillates between "problem" and "stranger." This comes about in part because of the vast publicity and dollar expenditure by government agencies to "solve" such "problems" and

[3]Arthur Bromage, *Introduction to Municipal Government* (New York: Appleton, 1957).
[4]Edward Banfield and James Q. Wilson, *City Politics* (Cambridge, Mass.: Harvard University Press, 1965).
[5]Some examples of work of the Chicago School are Robert Park, *The City* (Chicago: University of Chicago Press, 1925) and *Human Communities* (Glencoe, Ill.: Free Press, 1952); Harold Gosnell, *Machine Politics* (Chicago: University of Chicago Press, 1968); and Charles Merriam, *Chicago* (New York: Macmillan, 1929).

because the press insistently deals with urban citizens as though they were either wards of the state or inhabitants of a foreign nation.

Cities are viewed as a concentration of human problems. As people moved to suburbs or migrated to sun cities, the central cities became segregated from the suburbs by more than race and political boundaries. Cities also became class, age, health, and crime "ghettoes." Americans left a concentration of such distinctions behind for a new life in the class, age, and race "ghettoes" of the suburbs. The stratification, segregation, and economic differentiation characteristic of the central city became commonplace throughout the urban area. Thus one must look to what had been a city society, vertically integrated and differentiated by social and economic class. Today the city is spread horizontally, but in no way is it less differentiated, stratified, or segregated. Social, economic, and political distance tends to equal physical distance in the new spread city. Instead of looking for the wealthy in the "best part" of town, one now looks to the suburbs to find the upper-crust stronghold.

While the great cities of America continue as always to exhibit the contrast between the very rich and the very poor, the large white-collar classes have tended to drift toward the geographic outer edge. The peculiarly American pattern of physical separation between the haves and the have-nots now encompasses huge geographic distances, particularly in the West. Certainly the automobile has made this continuing pattern of geographic dispersion and social distance relatively easy to create and maintain. Social distance is further increased by the concept of the "walled suburb" which makes possible the virtual isolation of crucial services particularly related to future social structure. Educational opportunity for children of the affluent can be (and is) readily maintained by the remnants of "local self-determination" preserved by the semiautonomous character of the suburb.

Physical place, then, becomes a serious matter economically, socially, and politically. Economically, the move to the suburbs of the 1950s and 1960s by largely white middle-class and white-collar families was followed by a tendency to locate factories and administrative headquarters of large companies outside city limits. The simple notion of the bedroom suburb is complicated by the fact that shopping and then business centers have been built away from their former locations in the urban core. Transportation opportunities, both for companies and for their employees, have made such relocations possible, and the tax differences between city and suburb served as a further incentive for such physical moves.

In the face of such movement and change, the student of urban politics tends to lose his focus. Simply including the suburbs or the SMSA as a new unit of analysis does not solve the social scientist's problem; our theoretical understanding of what constitutes, say, an urban polity does not automatically expand to include the new urban society being created over shockingly short periods of time. The ties that bind people to their city have tended to disappear rapidly in recent urban history. The city itself seems indistinct even as it moves through an ordinary day. One commonly notices a great difference between the daytime city and its nighttime counterpart. Hordes of office and managerial workers invade the city in the early hours and recede in the late afternoon. Such conveniences as restaurants, theaters, and bars are rather strictly segregated by urban/suburban differences, so that one may find the suburban population in one specific area of the city while the rest of the city is either depopulated or left to cater to the local resident population.

Just as people have come to put physical distance between where they work and where they live, so, too, have the policies of the many "urban"-oriented government agencies tended to become dispersed. If we wished to study "urban public policy" or the urban "policy process," where should we look to discover such a body of actions? Wherever we were to look, and however we were to look, we would be hard pressed to locate a systematically consistent set of social, political, or economic objects clustered conveniently within the city proper. Housing, health care, police, education, and a multitude of other policy areas with which all three levels of government are in some way concerned are themselves so scattered, inconsistent, and confusing that the concept of the city itself tends to disappear. One is left with a hodgepodge of policies and practices which seldom integrate, and a general notion of "city" that rests on the complexity and interdependence of urban life traditionally associated with the idea. In some ways, the concern of this book is to describe, analyze, and untangle this pattern of confusion and disjointed incrementalism.

The Units of Analysis

If the legal boundaries of the city and the traditional separation of responsibilities of the American federal system are confused and confusing units for coming to grips with the urban political system, how might study best proceed? In other words, what ought a student of urban politics look to for insights necessary for thoughtful analysis? Americans, particularly, are fond of viewing the natural world as an "environment" to be manipulated according to the latest set of prescriptions.

Our cultural habit of observation has been very much influenced by an architectonic, or engineering, point of view. That is, as scholars, students, and policy analysts, we tend to view urban sociological, political, and economic variables as "problems" and thereby to infer the possibilities of "solutions." Such a frame of mind tends to ignore both the geographical truths of urban existence and the historical events which led us to the present condition.

We are similarly trapped in our political thought when, for instance, we view urban political parties, bosses, and elections as though they were carbon copies of their ancestors or as though they didn't exist at all. We are a nation of designers, reformers, and interveners. In the past generation the politics of urban areas has more often than not tended toward the creation of systems of power and control. But the designs for those systems have been uninformed about or indifferent to the historical circumstances responsible for the "problem" in the first place.

For instance, the history of the American city is, to a great extent, the history of American economic development. From the days when cities were the cores of American commerce and industry, created as much by technological capabilities as by geographic location, to the present era, which reflects to some extent the emerging crisis of late capitalism, there lie sets of patterns worthy of study and contemplation.[6] These patterns are as important for those who wish to work in the city of the future as they are for those who would simply like some insights into an increasingly complex social reality.

The contemporary period has witnessed great changes in the willingness of government to redistribute wealth and help society's less fortunate members. Cities have increasingly become the land of the hopeless and the destitute, as well as the site where multiple public sector interests attempt to cope with a key historical process. This process involves the migration of wealth, capital, and capital-producing skills away from cities and the accompanying centralization of social ills in a physical and political location unable to deal with those ills. We are in danger of becoming a nation which has cities, towns, and suburbs for specific elements in the economic class structure. Perhaps equally dangerous is our inclination to consider the world out of context and with a view to categorizing and theorizing, a tendency that might lead us to conclude either that it was "ever thus" or that yet another "system" must be designed for the "solution" of a set of peculiar problems. We attempt here to combat these particularly American tendencies by addressing the historical city with the contemporary city in mind, to show as often as possible some of the linkages between a past all too quickly forgotten and a present that often seems to have come out of yesterday's television news.

Because of the division of intellectual and scholarly labor and attention, there is an understandable but deplorable habit for each of us to "see" a different city. By this we do not refer to the subjectively different experiences people might have of the city. We refer, rather, to the habit of writing as though the city were *just* a political system or *just* an economic component, much as guidebooks might convince the unsuspecting that cities were little more than concentrations of restaurants, hotels, and tourist attractions. It is precisely this search for an encompassing notion of the contemporary city that social scientists and others seem to have little interest in, despite the admitted interdependence and complexity of nearly everything concerning cities and urban areas.

We have not gone very far in overcoming the division of labor which tends to create and depict as many cities as there are analysts. Despite our failure of integration, we do recognize that *the city itself as an object of study and as a unit of political, economic, and social analysis has declined in at least partial reflection of the changing ways people create and use the urban place.* Geography, an

---

[6]For a broad set of perspectives on the city and commerce see Harold M. Hochman, ed., *The Urban Economy* (New York: Norton, 1976).

incredible investment in transportation systems to overcome geographical limitations, and a deep historical ambivalence about the place of the city in American life have "diffused" throughout the countryside that which had been characteristically "urban." Theater, entertainment, parks, zoos, museums, movie houses, stores and shops, banks, ethnic restaurants, and dozens of other "urban" luxuries have either moved to the suburbs, are in decline in the city, or are experiencing fitful recoveries through massive interventions from government agencies and philanthropical foundations. Billions of dollars have been spent by agencies of the state in attempts to recreate core areas that might attract the more "desirable" middle-class sophisticates "back" to the city. Such taxpayers and potential taxpayers are, it has been argued, urgently needed if the "revitalization" of the city is to take place. All of this occurs as the industrial Midwest and Northeast experience hardening of their economic arteries; capital has migrated to new investment elsewhere, and meanwhile there is great unwillingness to invest in replacing the old and tired industrial plants, now in serious danger of being shut down.

Because the city itself has spread beyond the traditional bounds of its existence and because we are now faced with both a physical and intellectual reality of great complexity, the question of units of analysis can reasonably be associated with the notion of opportunity costs. Opportunity costs are those costs related to any choice that eliminates an alternative. Thus to study city politics usually means not studying suburban politics or urban economics or cultural matters and so on. To sacrifice any of these is to reduce the possibility of conveying the totality (or, more properly, models of totality). Our problem would be a simple and familiar one were it not compounded by one more fundamental—the disappearance of widespread social agreement as to what a city is. Surely most people can and will identify a city in terms of its greater density and its absolute numbers of people. Its physical properties and unique services and conveniences also might be noted, but in the end, the point of having cities in the first place and the reasons for improving them hold no firm place in public thought.

One might argue that such blurriness results from the persistent political and literary association of cities with "problems," as suggested above. It might also be pointed out that cities have been different things to different generations and that the role of the modern city has yet to be interpreted or described adequately. In any event, we argue that no single unit or sets of units of analysis have been developed to command the attention of the student in such a way that the city as a whole, as a psychological, physical, social and political entity, is readily perceived or perceivable.

A Design for Comprehension

Keeping in mind, then, our disclaimers about competing "models" and/or units of analysis that yield an overall portrait, we proceed to identify some parts of the urban forest which we believe to be of significant and enduring concern for students of urban politics. We divide our approach into three major kinds of concern and have organized the text accordingly.

The Evolution of Political Structure

The following three chapters trace some of the significant themes of political, social, and economic urban history. Our central focus is, of course, on governmental and political structures. Our purposes are to provide a framework for contemporary analyses so that the student may get a sense of evolutionary change; to account for the presence of what otherwise might be unexplained aspects of modern urban politics; and finally, to illustrate some of the interdependencies between society, economy, and government within the evolutionary framework.

The peculiar historical evolution of American cities must be at least superficially comprehended if much sense is to be made out of the urban political system as we find it today. The fact that our first cities were created and governed under seventeenth- and eighteenth-century British law and custom (the most notable exception being New Orleans) ought not be forgotten, especially when thinking about intergovernmental relations and the traditional "police power" (health, welfare, and safety) role. The American variety of federalism, the idea of states rights, and, finally, Dillon's Rule, solidifying the legal domination of the states over their municipalities, are extremely important to an understanding of contemporary urban political systems.

Of equal or greater significance is a comprehension of the traditional importance of cities as economic artifacts. The historical centrality of cities to economic development and to major social change cannot be easily overstated. The location and function of cities as economic institutions mirror the growth of capitalism. The first 250 years of American history can be understood as dominated by the settlers' struggle to overcome the limitations imposed by the physical world and by the technologies available to do so. Port cities were the nodes of commerce and industry, first on the Atlantic seacoast and later on inland rivers, that helped to overcome the isolation of the producers and the consumers essential to the growth of a great agricultural state. The cities involved in that first great developmental era remain with us. Some were transformed by the next great economic change, others declined as their premium location on waterways became less valuable in the face of improved land transportation.

The watershed of American cities came in the nineteenth century when early capitalism and industrialization amplified their transportation and commercial function. Cities of the Northeast and then those of the Midwest became factories that absorbed unprecedented amounts of labor and capital. Transportation hubs like Pittsburgh and Chicago became economic powerhouses as raw materials poured into them from the industrial and agricultural outer regions. Whole new cities like Minneapolis were created when the railroads defeated the limitations of distance and time, once seemingly permanent boundaries for remote farms and mines. The labor needs of an industrializing century caused shifts and expansions in population. Internal and foreign immigration brought about a "population explosion" that altered the character of every city and town.

Radical economic change and the population explosion fostered by industrialization permanently changed the political systems of American cities. The magnitude of the transformations was matched by alterations in the color and texture of cities. America had been profoundly a nation of white, English-speaking farmers, shopkeepers, and craftsmen until the last twenty-five or so years of the nineteenth century. Politics reflected the previous age, from the patriarchal elites of the Federalists to the Jacksonian structures of democracy. Party and faction were local fixtures, as were local governmental structures of dubious efficiency and clarity of purpose. The structure of urban government in the nineteenth century was, in general, utterly inappropriate to the needs of capitalism and to those of the ever-increasing immigrants.

The nature of the political system was transformed by the appearance of a relatively new creation, one which arose in the nineteenth century and died in the twentieth. The ghost of the machine form of political organization can still be seen.[7] The effects of the form are still with us in multiple ways. The key functions of linking immigration, capitalism, industrialization, and the dictates of social welfare and universal male suffrage are to be discovered in the machine form of organization and its leader, the boss. Bosses occupy a special place in the hall of fame of American heroes and antiheroes, a place which lives on to the present day, perhaps last and best exemplified in the life and times of the late Mayor Richard Daley of Chicago.

In general, we live today in cities and towns whose governmental structures were created in reaction to the greed, corruption, and power of the machine form and its many bosses. This legacy of a struggle now beyond the memory of most of us is profoundly important to an understanding of the urban political system as we find it today. The next three chapters trace this and other inheritances which we believe are vital to an understanding of the contemporary urban political system.

Political Power: Its Meaning, Structure, and Consequences

In Part II we take up the question of the structure of power in urban political systems. The questions "who has power?" and "power to do what?" are dealt with in several ways. We survey the questions as they relate to the scholarly schools of thought normally associated with the disciplines of sociology and political

[7]An engaging description of the machine's ghost is provided in Mike Royko, *Boss* (New York: Dutton, 1971).

science, particularly in regard to the conflicting claims of "elitists" and "pluralists." This debate has raged on in one form or another almost since the two
disciplines were established in late nineteenth- and early twentieth-century
American universities.

The general question of who or what controls the crucial processes of political decision-making was answered by some sociologists in their discovery and
description of local socioeconomic elites. On the other hand, political scientists,
with some exceptions, tended to ask not "who has power?" but rather "does
anyone have power?" They tended to emphasize the importance of elections and
parties and to discover the fragmentation of power and its diffusion throughout
the urban political system. We describe and analyze these competing theoretical
traditions in order to introduce the student to the major questions involved in the
debate.

We also employ these descriptions and analyses as a basis for the introduction of a synthesized alternative. This alternative, grounded in the two traditional
approaches, argues that beyond local socioeconomic elites or the manifest political structure of pluralist politics lies a newly emergent pattern of power that is
a potential successor to previous theoretical models. Instead of local elites or
openly political decision-makers and processes, we look to an emerging bureaucratic presence for the contemporary evolution of the structure of political power.

We suggest that the presence of large, complex, and extremely powerful
public agencies representing several levels of government is unaccounted for in
most political thought about urban politics. We go on to argue that the norms
and values of modern bureaucracy are very much reflective of a new age in
American urban politics, one resting on the power of expertise, the increasing
weakness of the localities to fund their own needs and wants, and the modern
tendency of urban problems to become national issues. The nationalization of
welfare during the Depression of 1929–39 dealt a deadly blow to the machine
form of political organization. The nationalization of transportation, housing,
and other economic and social areas, traditionally defined as local matters, has
added to the earlier takeover by federal and state agencies.

Changes in the structure of the American economy and its support services
of transportation and communication have dealt yet another blow to the conventional wisdom about the centrality of the urban place. The elites have moved on
to supraurban concerns as the centrality of the city has declined in late capitalism.
The amount and the nature of the resources available to local mayors and other
elected politicians no longer even approximate "solutions" to urban problems as
the number and variety of urban claimants have increased. Indeed, we propose
a new look at the very basic structural aspect of urban citizenship and suggest
a classification which we believe more accurately reflects the kinds of ways people
interact with their government.

In the final chapter of Part II, we offer a description and an analysis of the
processes whereby the allocation of scarce public resources becomes policy. Politics is here understood to be conflict and cooperation over the allocation of scarce

public resources, and we focus attention on the multiple structural environments from which policies arise. Of particular interest are the characteristics of public organizations and their interactions with other elements of the political system. We believe that the products of such organizations and their constituency networks are central to any understanding of contemporary urban politics. These products are, of course, mainly services. Their quality, quantity, and distribution approximate the modern coinage of urban politics, just as patronage and payoffs once functioned in the machine systems.

The Urban Service State

The final section of the text deals with some of the ideas and concrete instances of service creation, distribution, and impact. We address some of the major questions we believe face the modern urban political system and use as examples the development and modern service problems of five metropolitan areas. Our approach begins with some of the theoretical apparatus developed from the discipline of economics and here identified as "public economics." This framework allows us to specify a number of "macrovariables" that serve as architectural elements, expanding or constraining the design of urban services. The use of public economics also allows us to illustrate questions of magnitude, appropriateness, and distribution as key matters of political choice and retains our focus on the urban political system both as a metropolitan entity and as an evolving set of political processes and structures.

The point of this section is to highlight certain key value questions, such as fairness and the democratic nature of urban political institutions. Discussion of these questions will lead us inevitably into a consideration of the city of the future. The matter of costs and benefits and the relationships between levels and structures of politics and government, taxation and location are amplified by consideration of the ancient question which echoes from every corner of the city— "Where's mine?" Finally, we address ourselves to the place of the city in modern political thought and its possible future direction.

In Search of the City

The idea of the city has been at the heart of much political thought since the rise of ancient Greece. It has since that time often been at the core not only of political thought and action, but also of culture as reflected in the arts, the university, legal institutions, commerce, industry, and trade. The central ideas of urban citizenship and governance, in both democratic and nondemocratic cities throughout western history, have been an important key to any understanding of the development of the modern nation-state, capitalism, and socialism.

American cities have until quite recently reflected these traditional concepts in many ways and to varying degrees. Yet today the city is at the center of an intellectual crisis as profound as any aspect of the urban "crises" so loudly proclaimed over the last two decades. This intellectual crisis affects not only students of the city, but its citizens and rulers as well. To attempt to sum up the intellectual and other crises of the city in a single phrase (or even in a book) is a risky enterprise, one that we take up only to set the tone of the text which follows.

The lack of shaped views about what cities ought to be has never, perhaps, been so important in American history as it is now. In the past, cities grew and elaborated according to the waves and tides of immigration, economic and artistic movement, and political thought. Cities were vital aspects of the American political system whose voters chose presidents, bosses, and political parties in colorful profusion. The history of American politics at the national level has often been determined and has always been influenced by the potent political force of organized urban party-based organizations. But the passing of Mayor Richard Daley of Chicago probably marks the end of an era. The last dinosaur departed this world a curiosity and a wonder of the past somehow preserved.

The very rich, the very poor, and most people in between lived within central city boundaries as recently as thirty years ago. Every conceivable racial and ethnic group lived cheek to jowl in a small area of great cultural, religious, and artistic diversity. Rich men dominated emerging industrial capitalism from cosmopolitan cities. They built monuments to their success in the forms of universities, museums, hospitals, and parks. Poor people achieved a measure of possibility in American cities that was not often available to their European, Asian, and African ancestors.

Wealth, vulgarity, poverty, beauty, and ugliness together presented an urban image of vitality, change, and uncertainty to juxtapose against the quiet of tree-lined residential neighborhoods as rustic and peaceful as any small town. The cities were thriving microcosms of America at each point in its historical progress. Millions of domestic and foreign immigrants poured into them seeking fortune, freedom, and the possibility of a new life for themselves "and their posterity."

The city, therefore, while not providing an identical vision of itself politically, economically, socially, and culturally, at least provided sufficient psychological space for a wide variety of human hopes and needs. Diversity, complexity, and change in the physical and social setting marked a place of both corruption and high moral possibility for at least the last century of American history. Today, however, the city seems to be thought of as little more than a warehouse of social, economic, and political problems. How and why has this come about? If we cannot readily answer the question in its totality, at a minimum we can consider some plausible notions that help to explain some of these changes, which we summarize with the general question: "What is the city for?"

We begin as did our revered Greek ancestors by presenting some paradoxes that arise out of that all-important relationship in Athenian and American democracy, the relationship of the citizen to the polis.

No matter what indicator one chooses, one is not likely to find an increase in the rate of political participation in any American city. The acts of registering to vote, voting, and other political behaviors traditionally associated with general self-government and representation are in severe decline in the American city.[8] The idea of citizenship has been changed into consumership, particularly as it relates to the services and benefits provided by the state writ large (i.e., all levels and divisions of government). As more citizens become dependent upon more state agencies for services subjectively indispensable to their everyday lives, how can these citizens simultaneously control, alter, or destroy the very architecture of the state which holds them in bondage? To be a citizen of the city is to be either a recipient of needed service, including all the possibilities from welfare to bridge maintenance, and/or to be an outraged, alienated homeowner, strained to the point of economic trouble by systems of taxation over which one has little control.

The question, however, is not only the relationship between those who produce wealth for the city and those who consume it. The paradox of self-government is compounded further by the seemingly permanent structures of public agencies whose force and presence depend very little on the vote or other legitimate political actions of urban citizens. A generation ago, the cities for good and ill represented the idea of local control over that which was locally important. In other words, policemen, teachers, garbagemen, social workers, librarians, and the host of other urban service workers entered the urban political system subject to the mandates and electoral shifts of the locality. Today the dominant political actors, those who conflict and cooperate over the allocation of scarce public resources, are "outsiders." Federal, state, and special district, professionalized bureaus and bureaucrats exercise growing influence and control over previously local matters, such as housing codes, welfare and other transfer payments, urban renewal, highways, and sanitation. The citizen votes for councilmen, mayors, and other elected local officials who have relatively little or no influence on the conduct of urban public policy or on the future of the city.

The political destiny of the American city is increasingly out of the hands of its residents, including those who are its elected politicians. The citizen has had his classical role modified, usually without his knowledge and always without his consent. While this diffusion of political power away from the city and its citizens to structures of national and regional power has proceeded, a chorus of pious cries and programs have been instituted (usually by agencies outside of the cities' legal or political influence) to try to create in the individual and the collectivity a concern for the participatory power of which he has been deprived.

The paradox should be clear. *Public organizations and their particularistic constituent groups at multiple levels of government have by their acts reduced the control local citizens have over their communities. The same (public organizations) simultaneously attempt to provide "new channels of community input."*

[8]Norman Nie, Sidney Verba, and John Petrocik, *The Changing American Voter* (Cambridge: Harvard University Press, 1976).

The power to allocate scarce public resources has been diffused to agencies of nonlocal political structure, including the states, national government, and special districts. This diffusion of local political power has aggravated the tendency in the national political system toward what Theodore Lowi calls "interest group liberalism."[9] Thus the tendency is toward the creation of groups which directly benefit from the agencies upon whom the lion's share of urban policymaking has devolved.

For instance, real estate developers, HUD, and the state or local urban renewal and public housing agency, along with contractors, construction workers, and financial institutions, have developed a series of relationships often determinative of the physical future of the city. Local politicians become petitioners to such structures of power. Similar examples can be found in such areas as elementary and secondary education, police services, health services, and transportation policy, especially as the latter concerns roads, highways, and mass transit. The citizen, therefore, is best understood as a consumer of services. More precisely, he is constituent, client, or victim of the acts of public agencies that are relatively distant from the general systems of representation and accountability natural to the tradition of local control.

The partial result of this devolution is the paradox of governance as management. In other words, as public bureaucracy divides the citizenry into different kinds of consumers, the meaning of government is altered significantly. *Proper management according to the norms of administrative practice—hierarchy, efficiency, specialization, and professional conduct—are in contradiction with the norms of democratic political control, such as representation and accountability.* To manage is not to govern, but management is the role public agencies must and do take. Diversity, disagreement, public debate, and issue-oriented electoral processes determinative of policy change are the province of politics. Local governments cannot long afford to engage in such processes so long as the resources necessary to the city's survival come from agencies that are beyond local control.

The diminution of local governance has resulted from multiple causes, not the least of which has been the interpretation by the judiciary (at several levels of government) that all citizens must have equality of access to services provided at the local level. Equity demands that citizens have equal access to the traditional means of local democratic self-determination, including city council seats, the mayoralty, and representation on boards and commissions.[10] Similarly, educational services must provide equality of access. Court-ordered redistricting, intraurban busing to achieve desegregation, and a host of other decisions have further removed the play of local political actors from the determination of local policy. Of course one of the great ironies of recent history has been that as courts and other agencies of the national and state governments have mandated equal

[9]Theodore Lowi, *The End of Liberalism,* 2d ed. (New York: W.W. Norton, 1979).
[10]The involvement of the federal judiciary in local decision making is discussed in detail in Chapter 11.

access to local structures of control, these very structures are losing domain over their traditional local jurisdictions. Thus the reflection of black voting strength in city councils and mayors' offices has been accompanied by a simultaneous diminution of the significance of those offices.

It is easy to overstate the significance of the changes in the structure of political power in the city. There is still a great range of power left to the cities. Our point is that these powers have eroded over time and in areas of particular importance to the city. But even within the city, political institutions such as the machines, parties, and councils have lost significance in the face of emerging local patterns of extreme interest-group politics. Local politics has tended toward a system which favors organized petitioners for the products of service bureaucracies. Thus functionally structured interest groups like municipal unions or downtown business associations have tended to dominate in their areas of concern, and this domination has often been to the detriment of the traditional politics of neighborhood or other geographic/population elements.

Hence our final paradox: *as multiple forces of society, economy, and polity bring about the "withering away of the city," a great "search for community" intensifies.* [11] Beginning in the 1960s and proceeding with ever-greater emphasis, several movements characteristically derived from the political left have attempted to create both a sense and a practice of community within cities and towns. By the end of the 1960s, national bureaucratic actors had added to the movement. In the past decade the ideas of those concerned generally with the allegedly alienated life of the individual and specifically interested in small technologies and systems also have tended to focus on the idea of community.

Paradoxically, all of the talk of community has coexisted with the routinized destruction of neighborhoods that had been flourishing, natural communities. They were not "sources of community" nor were they the products of "community organization" efforts. On the contrary, they were naturally evolved aggregations of people, commonly of the same or similar class and ethnic or racial heritage. Repeatedly, policies of national and state governments enticed or chased the populations of these neighborhoods to the suburbs or to other, unfamiliar areas. Highways destroyed their homes, high-rise housing projects overwhelmed their schools and other services, factories and other places of employment migrated. Mortgage policies sent millions to the suburbs on federally constructed highways. Social change, fueled by national and state policies, undermined such natural communities and has left us with the irony of government trying to create community with one hand while it destroys it with the other.

The "search for the city" is not simply a rhetorical exercise; the *idea* of the city, beyond the simple aggregation of ever more statistics about one problem or another, seems to have escaped many who study and think about the city. We know a great deal about what cities have been. In America we have (with few

[11]Credit for use of the former phrase goes to York Wilbern, *The Withering Away of the City* (Bloomington: Indiana University Press, 1966).

notable exceptions) tended to permit the city to become the unplanned physical, social, and economic result of great immigrations and emigrations. Each swing has been followed by political response in the form of an increase in the provision of services. (For instance, Atlantic seaboard cities subject to great foreign immigration built enormous public school systems in the early twentieth century.)

The American "idea" of the city has had many proclaimers since the founding of the Republic. The "idea" was really a set of notions that encouraged social, economic, and political diversity while maintaining a core of shared pride and even chauvinism. Places like Brooklyn, Pittsburgh, and even newer cities like Phoenix and Denver somehow were something more than just the sum of their residents and their institutions. Pride of place, loyalty to whatever its alleged virtues might be (foods, sports teams, neighborhoods), and a sense of the permanency which is summed up in the phrase "my hometown" are not readily perceptible today. Yet the longing for community, the desire to experience shared emotional associations in a particular urban or other space, has not departed us as a society. Perhaps the historical and contemporary discussions and analyses which compose the remainder of this book will help by providing some groundwork for a consideration of the reader's idea of the city.

We view the paradoxes discussed above as summarizing a long list of questions and problems to which we now turn.

Suggested Readings

Banfield, Edward C., and James Q. Wilson, *City Politics* (Cambridge, Mass.: Harvard University Press, 1965).

Hochman, Harold M., ed., *The Urban Economy* (New York: Norton, 1976).

Osofsky, Gilbert, *Harlem: The Making of a Ghetto* (New York: Harper & Row, 1966).

Sale, Kirkpatrick, *Power Shift* (New York: Random House, 1975).

Wilbern, York, *The Withering Away of the City* (Bloomington: Indiana University Press, 1966).

Chapter 2
American Cities in the Nineteenth Century: Parties, Politics, and Economic Growth

The Colonial Legacy

Cities of two hundred years ago were unlike present-day cities in their outward appearances. They were also radically different in their politics, social systems, and economies. Colonial cities and those founded after the Revolution inherited certain legal and customary arrangements from the mother country that were to have profound effect on their futures. The formal relationship between the sovereign states and any cities and towns that might be established under state jurisdiction was a carry-over from British practice.

The power to establish cities and their governmental form passed directly from Parliament to the newly independent states. This fact of eighteenth-century life has been the single most significant legal relationship in American urban political history. It established a relationship between city and state that has been modified but never radically altered, one that is still in force after nearly two centuries of strain. Arthur Bromage summarizes the essence of the relationship between city and state in his discussion of Dillon's Rule. (J. F. Dillon was an eminent jurist whose *Commentaries on the Law of the Municipal Corporation* defined the powers of municipalities for many generations of lawyers and judges.[1]) Bromage says:

> The state legislature, except for limitations specified by the state constitution, may create and dissolve municipal corporations; may grant, enlarge, or curtail their powers; and may exercise administrative supervision over their affairs. Thousands of cases have demonstrated that any reasonable doubt with reference to the author-

[1] J. F. Dillon, *Commentaries on the Law of the Municipal Corporation,* 5th ed. (Boston: 1911).

ity of the city will be resolved against the city. The municipal corporation remains a creature of the state. . . .[2]

It was not until America had begun its second century of independence that some cities were able to regulate simple "house-keeping" activities without specific acts of the state legislatures. Every municipal function, from garbage collection to traffic control, derives from the powers of the state. Legal powers are delegated from the states, but cannot be and are not "given away" for good. The exercise of any degree of delegated authority is subject to being overridden, not only by courts but also by state legislatures, even in many states where "home rule" charters have been granted to some cities. The significance of all of this must not have been great to those who lived in the early part of the last century.

Cities and large towns of the early nineteenth century had fairly stratified societies dominated by local "gentry," who often served in the state legislature as well as on the town or city council. Domination by state legislatures could not have been particularly burdensome so long as high social, economic, and political status in urban society continued to be vested in the same people. Early election laws permitted only property holders to vote in municipal elections. Despite the American Revolution, there seemed to be a general acceptance of the propriety of "aristocratic" rule in cities and towns. Important local offices such as alderman and mayor continued to be held by members of "old" families for generations, and waves of social change in America did not particularly seem to be reflected in the urban political system. Even well into the nineteenth century the "closed corporations" with their city councils seemingly appointed for life persisted in some areas. In some cases councilmen could choose their successors. It took many years for the changes reflected in the new federal Constitution to find their way into the charter documents granted localities by the state legislatures.

The formal structures of city governments slowly began to approximate a rough outline of the national government. Popularly elected councilmen, bicameral councils, and independently elected mayors began to appear during the first twenty-five years of the nineteenth century. Many of the "checks and balances" ideas reflecting traditional American distrust of government characterized, indeed still characterize, the formal structure of city government. But even with new charters and new prerogatives, the cities were still "creatures of the state." Indeed, it could be argued that for many a city, the county of which it was a part was a more important governmental unit than the city itself. Home rule for cities and towns was simply not within the political consciousness of the early nineteenth-century politician.

Until the creation of national political parties in the 1830s and 40s, the very existence and function of city government appears to have been a matter of

[2] Arthur W. Bromage, *Introduction to Municipal Government and Administration* (New York: Appleton-Century-Crofts, 1957), p. 109.

indifference to most people. Glaab and Brown point out the apparent significance of urban government in the following about New York:

> ... In 1810, New York City, with a population of around 100,000, spent only $100,000: a dollar per capita. Voluntary associations took care of poor relief and shared in such an important matter as fire protection. It would be thirty years before there was a uniformed police force in the United States. To many Americans, it was by no means clear that theirs was to be an urban destiny. In the circumstances what one student has called "the petty house keeping of such small urban communities" held little intrinsic interest for contemporaries. . . . [3]

The governmental apparatus of nineteenth-century cities, the political ideology of the era, and the legal relationships between states and cities created a system ill-suited to the demands that were to be placed upon it. The checks and balances ideal coupled with the Jacksonian spoils system were in part responsible for bringing about a structural division of labor and personnel procedures that were as confused as they were colorful.

Rather than consolidate governmental functions into some sort of cohesive authority-linked hierarchy, a variety of complex, independently elected governmental entities were created. There are many examples of so-called "long ballots." Nearly every new function that became a part of the city's responsibility became the responsibility of some independently elected official or board. Thus, it was not uncommon for a city charter to call for the election of a bicameral council, a mayor, a sheriff, a fire commissioner, a city clerk, a treasurer, an auditor, a board of education, a board of health, and countless other individuals and groups. Judges and prosecutors were also normally elected officials. According to Glaab and Brown, New York City in the late 1860s had four different agencies with power to tear up the streets while there was no agency with clear responsibility for repaving them. [4] This blizzard of boards, commissions, and agencies, many with independent powers of taxation and many more with powers of disbursement, created an ideal atmosphere for a newly emergent class of entrepreneurial politicians.

Immigration and Industrialization

Probably the most discussed phenomenon in American history has been immigration. The oft-repeated themes of in-migrants looking for a better life and the pursuit of the frontier need no elaboration here. What must be understood is that the character of immigration changed radically sometime during the 1840s from what it had been in the eighteenth century. Most eighteenth-century immigrants

[3]Charles N. Glaab and Theodore A. Brown, *A History of Urban America* (New York: Macmillan, 1967), p. 171.
[4]*Ibid.*, p. 172.

used the established cities of the eastern seaboard either as starting points for the westward trek or as points of settlement into the variety of jobs to be found in the preindustrial urban economy. These occupations were normally in commerce or in the service "industries" providing the conveniences of life—bakers, teamsters, carpenters, and so forth.

The bulk of immigrants were from Great Britain, and English was well established as the language of American life, despite substantial numbers of immigrants from other countries. As the colonies grew and different ethnic and religious groups arrived, new agricultural communities were created. The numbers of people arriving were small and the country was enormous. The city was a relatively simple, comprehensible place. Town social, economic, and political patterns remained relatively stable and an immigrant arriving from England or Scotland, for instance, must have rather quickly "known his place" in society. The vast social and economic ills of the big cities of the British Isles were not to be found in the budding metropolises of the eastern seaboard or in the new cities of what we today call the Middle West. While it would be misleading to suggest that life for all in American cities prior to the 1840s was peaceful it is true that the urban place was transformed beyond imagination in the century following 1840. The development of cities during the first two hundred years of the Republic bears little resemblance to what occurred during its third century; immigration must be viewed as one of the chief reasons for the discontinuity.

The first great "wave" consisted mainly of rural Irish peasants who were faced with religious and economic discrimination at home. Upon their arrival in the great port cities of New York and Boston in particular, they received similarly poor treatment. They were Catholics in a Protestant country. They were unskilled, cheap labor crowded into segregated housing. The discrimination against them was blatant. They had high crime and illegitimacy rates. They, like most of the people who followed in later years, were primarily rural folk, uneducated, suspicious, and frightened. Irish women found work as domestics; the men, when they could find work, labored at society's most menial tasks. In short, the Irish were a despised mass of people treated in many ways like a subhuman species.[5]

But the Irish and to some extent their successors had opportunities for changing their miserable social and economic state. American egalitarianism, the social patterns of life on the "Oulde Sod," and a relatively disorganized urban political system presented these opportunities. The Irish seized them with a vengeance. To some extent their fellow immigrants, the Germans, the Scandinavians, and later, to a lesser extent, the Italians, Jews, and Poles, involved themselves seriously in American politics, but the Irish were one of the more important molders of the urban political system.

The political culture of the old country and that of the new blended for the Irish in some ways. Irish social life, which revolved around the church, the pub,

[5]See Carl Wittke, *The Irish in America* (Baton Rouge: Louisiana State University Press, 1956) and William V. Shannon, *The American Irish* (New York: Macmillan, 1963).

and the family, adapted well to the evolving political forms of urban America in the nineteenth century. It ought not be forgotten that the Irish were a distinct, visible minority that multiplied at a rate quite alarming to the Yankees. In 1850 the Irish constituted nearly 43 percent of the foreign-born population of the entire country. By 1910 approximately 81 percent of the American Irish lived in towns and cities with a population of 2,500 or more. The urban strongholds of the Irish were New York, Philadelphia, Chicago, Boston, San Francisco, and St. Louis.

The reason most immigrants left their homes and traveled to America was to find a better life. The "better life" awaiting most nineteenth-century immigrants was to be found in the industrializing city. By the middle of the century, new cities had grown up in the Midwest. River cities, regional marketplaces, and new factory towns swelled with the industrial growth of a developing nation. The growth of industrial production, the investment in economic infrastructure (railroad lines, telegraph lines, roads, and canals)—all of these required millions of labor-intensive man-hours. This labor was required at minimal cost and was used simply as another resource.

The business of housing, feeding, and transporting this labor fell to the city. The task of providing the roads, power, and other physical services needed by developing industry fell to the city. The traditional job, frequently called the police power (the health, welfare, and safety functions), fell to the city and began to expand beyond the wildest notions of the nineteenth century. Municipal gaslight systems, public transportation, free public education, water and sewerage systems—all of these had been at least imagined by some brilliant eighteenth-century city fathers such as Benjamin Franklin. But one doubts that even Franklin dreamed of his City of Brotherly Love becoming host to over a half million immigrants in a fifty-year period, all of whom were to be provided with at least the services enumerated above.

Housing had to be built, streets and water mains laid, factories constructed. Municipal services had to support this industrial growth if it was to continue. How was all of this to be done? Who would satisfy this demand? The only answer Americans can be said to have given to the question "who will create the economic environment which supports and encourages industrial development?" is "government." Nineteenth-century city government was, for the most part, publicly "uninvolved" with socioeconomic matters in the sense that we understand "socioeconomic." That is, city government expanded functions in areas that tended to benefit middle-class taxpayers and manufacturing or commercial enterprises. Thus, if gaslighting was to be installed, it frequently made "better sense" to begin installation in front of better homes and shops.

The introduction of new industrial technologies, the expansion of the factory system, the creation of new markets for heavy industrial products, and the introduction of vast amounts of domestic and foreign capital served to make the American city of the nineteenth century the locus of economic development. Cities serving specialized needs, such as St. Louis, Minneapolis, and Pittsburgh, grew enormously because of their vital role in the developing national economy of the United States. Cities in the nineteenth century became the vital junctures where labor, capital, raw materials, and transportation could be brought together for industrial production and commercial profit. They were not particularly places of luxury and culture (although some of the wealthy tried to make them that), but were instead places of utility to be employed to further economic entrepreneurship.

Governmental assistance to the expanding economy was of the most expensive kind: the consequences of industrialization were ignored. The city was a thing to be used; and limitations on industrial activities that had actual or potential danger for society are not easily found in nineteenth-century legislation. Long-range costs figured in lives; billions of dollars spent for such activities as slum clearance and control of air and water pollution were simply not part of the equation of governmental assistance. As we discover *post hoc,* this failure to regulate was the most costly form of government assistance one can readily imagine.

The physical presence of nineteenth-century American cities must have been an exciting contrast of vulgarity, rot, clanging noises of construction, and dozens of smells to delight and assail the senses. Wooden tenements packed with thousands of men, women, and children speaking different languages and wearing odd clothing, the first "skyscrapers" (some made with iron facades!) rising around the magnificent invention of Mr. Otis, and streetcars pulled by horses through gaslit streets must have turned the head of every hayseed come to find his fortune. It should be remembered that as many of the immigrants who jammed into cities were from the agricultural fringe of America as were from Europe. Their problems of adjustment were often as severe as those of Europeans. Conditions resulting from a near criminal density of population and from an unregulated developing industry, coupled with the eighteenth-century governmental structures that persisted throughout the era, are descriptive of that modern cliche—the urban crisis. A series of complex social and economic factors, coming into simultaneous operation during the nineteenth century, made the possibility of clearly rational direction, control, and regulation an impossibility. In this sense what is popularly called the urban crisis has been with us for at least a hundred years.

Political Parties

The development of the modern party system in America was in large part an urban phenomenon. The Jacksonian era produced political parties and electoral ties in urban areas that were to become identified with the Democratic party for generations. Binkley discusses the Workingmen's party, an eastern urban political party which developed in the late 1820s.

> ... It [the Workingmen's Party] represented a revolt against the Regency-dominated Tammany organization of New York City, and alarmed conservatives

with its virulent attacks on bankers and especially their paper money, the ruinous depression to which it was subject proving particularly disastrous to wage-earners. When the new party astounded old politicians by polling 6000 votes in a New York municipal election and then spread to other cities, anti-Regency, anti-Van Buren, anti-Masonic and other political factions began to bid for the now politically conscious labor vote. By 1832, the Workingmen's Party had spread so widely that a convention at Albany had delegates from every New England state except Vermont. The delegates discussed the effect of banks and monopolies on labor, the abolition of imprisonment for debt, the workingman's lien, factory conditions, and free public schools.[6]

The Workingmen's party in time became the Equal Rights party, or Locofocos. The Locofocos and their positions on issues eventually became part of the "regular" Democratic party. A partisanship deeply involved with national issues took root in the cities in this era. By the middle of the nineteenth century the electoral reforms and practices typified by the Jacksonian era made the existence of urban political parties possible. The newer cities of the Midwest also developed continuing electoral parties. Yet another structural change that enlarged the significance of urban parties was the more or less continuous expansion of the physical boundaries of the cities and the consolidation of what had been outlying towns and boroughs. Groups of towns and areas, which we today simply think of as naturally part of the city, were independent jurisdictions during most of the nineteenth century. The movement toward consolidation (at least east of the Mississippi) ended around the turn of the century.

The political significance of the size and nature of the immigration that began around 1840 cannot easily be overstated. American politics in general changed greatly over time, and city politics in particular took on some new aspects almost immediately. For the first time, politicians had vast numbers of supporters (or potential supporters) concentrated in places relatively easy to reach. For the first time, public political splits and partisanship might be based on class, occupational, or ethnic differences rather than simply on regional differences, the "classic" American issue. Political parties, interest groups, and other associations that failed to adapt to the needs of the new residents died out. New groups developed that catered to or reflected the demands of the immigrants.

The federal system, the diversity of interests, and the complications of tripartite governmental structures might very well have turned this ill-organized complexity into a multiparty system. Indeed, until the Civil War, American political parties seldom managed to appear as orderly, disciplined, or stable as some of their European counterparts. Since the Civil War, American national parties have been loose clusters of often conflicting groups that (usually) vote the same way in presidential elections. Binkley gives a charming description of the origin of the Republican party and also asks one of the hard questions involved in the analysis of parties.

[6]Wilfred Ellsworth Binkley, *American Political Parties, Their Natural History* (2d ed., rev.; New York: Knopf, 1958), p. 141.

> Inevitably a new party must constitute an opposition. So every one of our major parties began as a party of the opposition. The antis to the government of the Confederation became the Federalists; the anti-Federalists became the Jeffersonian Republicans; the anti-Adams men, the Jacksonian Democrats; the anti-Jacksonians, the Whigs; and now we are to find the anti-Nebraska men about to become the new Republican Party. Our problem is to ascertain how this aggregation of Free-Soilers, Independent Democrats, Conscience Whigs, Know-Nothings, Barnburners, abolitionists, teetotalers, Germans, and others combined into a well-integrated party, developed a positive program interpreted in terms of national welfare, and pushed it to triumphant reality with the conviction of militant crusaders.[7]

The diversity, magnitude, and confusion of demands suggested by Binkley's list imply only a slice of the political apple of the post-Civil War urban place. Political parties became purposive social organizations insofar as they began to fulfill linkage and brokerage functions between the widely varied interests of urban society and the formal structures of government and the economy. The functions of linking social demand with political and economic supply and of mediating between eighteenth-century American political and legal structures and immigrant cultures became more vital as the century wore on. The costs of such discontinuities to the populace and to the political system were enormous. Pollution, ignorance, crime, and disease are plagues of an unenlightened social and political era, and they continue to haunt us.

Yet for all the social costs incurred and heaped on future generations, the nineteenth century was an exciting era. It was a time ripe for politics. As state and local governments' aloofness to changes in the social and economic life of the city became more inappropriate, the possibility of the remaining elements of the political system growing in importance became very real. Municipal contracts for new and/or expanded services became rather profitable even while city government remained legally "above it all." A lively series of informal governments developed in practically every city in the nation. Based on party, patronage, and industrialization as well as on immigration, overcrowding, and social blight, the new politics of the cities was as brutal and colorful as the environment in which it existed.

Political parties, machines, and movements in American cities in the nineteenth century developed in response to a number of complex demands and sociological events of great significance. In part, the changes in the political system can be understood by examining changes in the occupants of leadership roles. That is, one might view change in an urban political system by examining the socioeconomic and occupational backgrounds of the holders of important political office. Robert Dahl, in his classic study of New Haven, describes the political history of that city in terms of succeeding waves of people from different backgrounds winning political office.[8] Thus in New Haven, as in many other

---

[7] *Ibid.,* p. 206.
[8] Robert A. Dahl, *Who Governs? Democracy and Power in an American City* (New Haven: Yale University Press, 1961), chaps. 1-6.

"old" American cities, a tiny elite of socially and economically powerful "patricians" ruled the city until some time during the first half of the nineteenth century. The patricians were succeeded by "entrepreneurs," men of "wealth and industry" rather than men of "social standing and education." The entrepreneurs were followed by what Dahl calls the "explebes," men who rose from the "urban proletariat" and from recently arrived ethnic groups and who capitalized on their popularity with the "new" masses.

Nineteenth-century America underwent greater changes in a shorter period of time than any other society ever had. A small, underdeveloped, agricultural nation living on the edge of a vast wilderness transformed itself into a huge, powerful, industrial and urbanized giant in a hundred years. To accomplish this task, millions of people were imported to force natural resources into usable, profitable form. Where tiny outposts had been, metropolises arose. Money, power, renown, and the possibility of living a decent, healthy, and long life lured people into movements and organizations that were unprecedented in history.

The political system of the cities and of the nation might be viewed as simply the creature produced by these forces or as the benign superintendent watching over the pushing and pulling of the political actors. One suspects that the political system and the governments that were a part of it managed to be a bit of both during this period. The ideas of what politics was for in America changed considerably during the nineteenth century. There were many people in public life who looked upon the political system as a structure that ought mainly to have been devoted to the furtherance of industrial development. Others, while not completely objecting to that view, believed that the political system was best employed in benefiting the city in general and political actors in particular. Still others saw politics as a means of ensuring political and social justice for "little people" faced with tremendous concentrations of social and economic power. A thousand other, more specific "oughts" might be said to be characteristic of as many interests in American urban society in the nineteenth century. The urban political system, no matter how it responded, would, because of the multiplicity of demands placed upon it, never again resemble the moderately placid, rather sleepy town governments that had served so well during the previous century.

The expansion of city services, both in degree and in kind, required two things that were the "meat and potatoes" of politics—money and jobs. Unprecedented amounts of money were spent after the Civil War on municipal construction of streets and on such public buildings as hospitals, libraries, schools, and police stations. Franchise licenses and an ever-growing number of contracts were awarded. Hundreds of thousands of laborers were needed to dig subway tunnels, build foundations, and to do every other conceivable construction job. New services meant that the city government needed new people to staff new or expanded organizations.

The resources and the demands for their employment in the construction of the city were there. Other demands were being expressed as a result of the swell in population from off the farm and from over the sea. Education, health, housing, sanitation, street lighting, police protection, and decent recreational facilities were lacking in most cities, despite attempts by private ethnic and religious charitable organizations to help. It was said that at least 10,000 homeless children roamed the streets of New York in the period immediately after the Civil War. The growth in demand for social services was tremendous. Nineteenth-century social philosophy and eighteenth-century government prevented the formal, legitimate governmental apparatus from responding significantly. Into the chasm between people desperately in need of social services and a creaky city government unable or unwilling to respond, there stepped a new form of political organization—the machine.

Perhaps it is a bit too deterministic to talk about a particular form of political organization as if it were the "inevitable" consequence of the social, political, and economic forces discussed above. Yet, as we shall see in the following chapter, the machine form of organization was pervasive in American city politics from the end of the Civil War to the end of the Great Depression. We have briefly surveyed some of the major historical facts that are essential to an understanding of the early development of urban political systems. We have suggested that the post-Revolutionary city's relationship to the state was a crucial step in the development of the kinds of city governments that were ultimately created. Political parties, immigration, and industrialization are other factors that must be accounted for in any understanding of city politics. We will explore these phenomena even more carefully with reference to the growth of the machines.

In sum, cities of the nineteenth century were places of unimagined change and diversity. Many of those born in pastoral settings lived to see those settings turned into concrete canyons upon whose cliffs were perched thousands of people, most of them very different from the "old residents." Life became complicated and confused. Buildings went up daily in the big cities. There was constant disruption of the streets and waterways. The city teemed with people. Entire new industries and services were created out of the rush of nineteenth-century technological inventiveness. Elevators, electrified railways, trolley cars, electric lights, and a thousand other technological blessings and curses were visited on nineteenth-century citizens.

Political life was as rich, confused, and vital as the city itself. It reflected the era and becomes important to our understanding of contemporary urban political systems to the extent that it bequeaths distinct traditions, myths, and structures to us that are part of the present urban political system.

Suggested Readings

Binkley, Wilfred Ellsworth, *American Political Parties, Their Natural History,* 2d ed., rev.
      (New York: Knopf, 1958) p. 141.

Cook, Ann et al., eds., *City Life 1865–1900: Views of Urban America* (New York: Praeger, 1973).

Glaab, Charles N. and A. Theodore Brown, *A History of Urban America* (New York: Macmillan, 1967).

Green, Constance McLaughlin, *The Rise of Urban America* (New York: Harper & Row, 1965).

Jones, Maldwyn Allen, *American Immigration* (Chicago: University of Chicago Press, 1962).

McKelvey, Blake, *American Urbanization: A Comparative History* (Glenview, Ill.: Scott, Foresman, 1973).

Teaford, John C., *The Municipal Revolution in America: Origins of Modern Urban Government 1650–1825* (Chicago: University of Chicago Press, 1975).

Weber, Adna, *The Growth of Cities in the 19th Century* (Ithaca, N. Y.: Cornell University Press, 1963). Originally published in 1899.

Chapter 3
The Machine

If Mayor Daley was alive this never would have happened. (Anonymous, 1979)

Introduction

The comment above was made on a national newscast featuring the difficulties faced by Chicagoans during their worst winter in living memory. Daley's successor, Michael A. Bilandic, was barraged with charges of corruption and inadequacy of the snow-removal effort. It seemed to many that the snow crisis was the sign of a great man's passing. Richard J. Daley would not have allowed this kind of weather.

The Daley Machine had a distinct character—even a mystique—among American governments.[1] Chicago may have been tightly governed during Daley's incumbency, it is argued, but at least it was governed. Maybe patronage and under-the-table deals characterized the Chicago public economy, but it was a healthy public economy.[2] The fact that the Daley Machine (which has not survived him in strength or scope) is looked back upon with nostalgia is a good indicator of just how bad things have gotten elsewhere. It should be clear, however, that whatever its faults or accomplishments, the Chicago political system during the Daley administration was not a *machine* in the sense that the term will be used here.

As we argue in this chapter, the classic, nineteenth-century political machine was both the product and engine of newly industrialized cities with large immigrant populations. While the Chicago machine retained the political form of the classic machine—patronage, ward heelers, and party hierarchy—the social and economic functions of the classic machine have been taken over in modern Chicago by federal and state welfare programs and by industrial corporate and

[1]The development and mystique of the Daley Machine is explored by Mike Royko, *Boss: Richard J. Daley of Chicago* (New York: Dutton, 1971); Milton Rakove, *Don't Make No Waves—Don't Back No Losers* (Bloomington: Indiana University Press, 1975), and Thomas M. Gutterbock, *Machine Politics in Transition: Party and Community in Chicago* (Chicago: University of Chicago Press, 1980).
[2]For a description of the relative efficiency of the Daley organization, see J. David Greenstone and Paul E. Peterson, "Reformers, Machines and the War on Poverty," in James Q. Wilson, ed., *City Politics and Public Policy* (New York: Wiley, 1968), pp. 267–292.

banking interests.[3] Several other American cities, like Albany, New York, also have remnants of the machine form in their governments. Our point here, however, is that the machine was more than the sum of these remnants. The machine was a well-integrated social, political, and economic structure that must be brought into focus before we can consider what urban governments have become.

There are two essential points to be made about understanding the machine. First, the machine era directly affected the culture and form of the urban political system handed down to the present generation. Much that is puzzling about contemporary urban governmental apparatus can be understood in terms of the legacy of the machine era or the reaction to it. Thus, if we are to understand the system, we must know where it came from.

Secondly, the machine form of political organization was a solution, however imperfect, to the complex problem of relating governmental power to society in general. The machine, as we shall see, rose and adapted itself in the face of the most overwhelming and complicated transitions ever undergone in any prior urban civilization. It was an organizational creation that managed to sustain itself over time with the assent (either unspoken or public) of nearly all segments of urban society. The question must arise: How did this happen? One hundred years ago, the political mechanisms of the cities of the United States *functioned.* To say simply that circumstances differed in those days is to ignore the possibility of examining the workings of a sociopolitical phenomenon that dealt with problems similar to those that face present systems.

Nineteenth-century America was a horror for many of its urban citizens. Slums in the large cities were worse than they are today. There was incredible overcrowding and disease; crime and poverty characterized every urban center. Starvation was frighteningly common. Millions of people arrived in America poor, hungry, diseased, and completely unable to cope with life in the New World. Millions could neither speak, nor read, nor write the language common to their new home. Epidemics related to poor or nonexistent sewers were regular seasonal occurrences. Crimes against person and property by juveniles soared during the late nineteenth century. Gangs of roving teenagers terrorized many streets and sections of the cities. There were whole sections of New York City that the police, by common understanding, would not enter. Social disintegration was everywhere. Fatherless families and illegitimacy were commonplace among nearly all of the immigrant and native poor. All of this and more was characteristic of the cities of the last century. It sounds depressingly familiar. Many circumstances were different, yet some of the core social problems of the time are still

---

[3]The replacement of the machine with governmental and corporate structures, the "new machine," is described by Theodore J. Lowi, *The End of Liberalism: The Second Republic of the United States,* 2d ed. (New York: Norton, 1979), pp. 177–185.

with us. Social disintegration and alienation from public institutions were root problems for urban dwellers—both old and new.[4]

An important question was (and is): How is such a social system to be governed? Further, how are diverse interests to be represented and served? How are problems to be solved? How is the danger of open conflict to be avoided? The politicians of the last century were faced with these questions in the cities. One of the answers they provided was the machine, an organization with many roots and antecedents, but one that ended up being a peculiarly American creation. One of the unfortunate facts of this creation is that its name has been most frequently employed as a disparagement. The term "machine," as used in these pages, does not imply disapproval. It will be used to specify a particular phenomenon that is defined by the remainder of this chapter.

Another difficulty that arises in any discussion of machines is that, while they were a general characteristic of American cities and states, there were specific instances that would tend to contradict general propositions about them. Because of the impossibility of discussing every case, it is necessary to talk about some general propositions that describe and analyze this complicated system. With these cautions and disclaimers in mind, let us proceed to a consideration of some of the socioeconomic foundations of the machine.

The Socioeconomic Environment of the Machine

An understanding of the machine must be based on a comprehension of the social and economic environment that presumably supported and sustained it. Clearly, the relationship is somewhat reciprocal. That is, the machine form of political organization helped to create and sustain the social and economic structures that, in turn, supported its maintenance. But in the main, the machine was a political structure that evolved in response to changes in the social and economic fabric of the city. Of what, in general, did that fabric consist? What seem to have been the social and economic foundations of the machine?

Population Density

The increasing density of the urban population enhanced the possibility for the political machine to develop and perpetuate itself. Universal male suffrage enabled organized politicians to garner the most valuable resource in a democracy —the vote. The number of voters increased dramatically after the Civil War as a function of the natural increase in the population, the beginnings of the move-

---

[4]*See* Charles N. Glaab and Theodore A. Brown, *A History of Urban America* (New York: Macmillan, 1967); Blake McKelvey, *The Urbanization of America, 1860-1915* (New Brunswick: Rutgers University Press, 1963); and Alexander B. Callow, Jr., ed., *American Urban History* (New York: Oxford University Press, 1969).

ment from the farm to the city, and immigration. He who could organize this mass of voters so that it would consistently perform at the polls in a predictable fashion would have one kind of power. Not only did the total number of voters increase, but particular segments of the potential voting population began to become much more numerous during the period.

Growth of a Working Class

A large urban working class began to develop in America before the Civil War. Clear and massive divisions in the population along economic class lines were an obvious characteristic of late nineteenth-century urban America. The tenement, which had once been thought to be the housing salvation of the "decent working-class poor," multiplied greatly in some cities. Francesco Cordasco, in his introduction to the work of Jacob Riis, critic of the tenement system of New York City, writes about conditions in 1855.

> ... The tenement-house population had swelled to half a million souls by that time, and on the East Side, in what is still the most densely populated district in all the world, China not excluded, it was packed at the rate of 290,000 per square mile, a state of affairs wholly unexampled. The utmost cupidity of other lands and other days had never contrived to herd much more than half that number within that space. The greatest crowding of Old London was at a rate of 175,816. Swine roamed the streets and gutters as their principal scavengers. ... [5]

Public welfare, health, and housing codes were simply nonexistent. Tenements were located near docks, warehouses, and factories, where there was easy access for the laboring classes. The working classes in nineteenth-century America were physically wedged into dangerously overcrowded housing. They suffered common social deprivation. Neighborhoods that had previously housed the burghers of the city became slums. In short, workers were a highly visible, easily identified class. They had common desires and needs, and only one legal resource that could satisfy those desires. That resource was the vote.

Ethnicity: The Case of the Irish

Distinctions other than class divide people. One of the very important points of division in American cities was, and still is, ethnicity. People of widely different cultures came to America and many got stuck in the big cities for lack of funds to go elsewhere. The cities were flooded with millions of immigrants who had borrowed, saved, or stolen every penny they could to get to the "promised land."

[5]Francesco Cordasco, ed., *Jacob Riis Revisited: Poverty and the Slum in Another Era* (New York: Doubleday, 1968), p. 10.

When they arrived, they were herded into vile tenements. When they could find work, it was the most menial. Almost invariably the job did not pay enough to sustain a family. Wives and children were put to work. The slums expanded as the immigrant population grew. Because of a natural desire to live with neighbors who spoke the same language and because there were simply no other options, ethnic slums became "urban villages."

Typically, the Irish were rural peasants totally unfamiliar with urban ways in Ireland, let alone in a new country. They were Catholics who were "prisoners in their own land." English domination of Ireland was harsh and repressive. The court system, the political system, and the manorial economy of the country all conspired to make life miserable for the farm worker who happened to be Irish *and* Catholic.

The Irish developed a number of political behavior patterns which, it has been argued, enabled them to survive under English rule.[6] Avoidance of governmental authority of any kind has long been a peasant trait useful in the face of overwhelming and repressive power. The Irish by the nineteenth century had learned how to bamboozle the tax collector, confuse the judge with blarney, and overwhelm policemen with good humor. The Irish led a bleak life, leavened only by humor and guile, the only weapons available in the face of English repression. The great failure of the potato crops in the 1840s was the straw that broke the back of the Irish farmer. Thousands of Irish died of starvation. Thousands more indentured themselves and their families to make the steerage passage to America.

Suspicious, parochial, illiterate were some of the more charitable terms used to describe the Irish when they landed in the big coastal cities. Each wave of new immigrants was looked down upon by the natives as well as many of the slightly older, second generation that had sprung from immigrants. The Irish had it especially hard in that they represented not only a different cultural and religious background, but also were the first to seriously threaten the rather fixed relationships in the stable societies of the "big towns."

The pre-Civil War history of the urban Irish is very reminiscent of some of the contemporary experiences of blacks. Such comparisons are risky, but it is of more than passing interest to note how a maligned minority such as the Irish came to gain power in the cities. The "newer" Irish of the 1840s and '50s represented not only a religious and cultural threat to the established Protestant, teetotaling society of the cities, but were also viewed as a menace to native labor. The old system of apprentice, journeyman, and master was threatened by cheap, unskilled labor employed in the rapidly growing field of industrial manufacturing. The Irish were cheap labor threatening the poorest natives. The Irish, with their ever-multiplying families and their tremendous immigration, filled up all the inexpensive housing, displacing the old working poor. Fences were erected to wall off Irish sections. So-called "nativist" and Know-Nothing political parties, some of the first superpatriotic bigots to organize in America, did their best to make

---

[6] *See* William V. Shannon, *The American Irish* (1st rev. ed.; New York: Macmillan, 1966).

the lives of the Irish miserable. The term "Know-Nothing" comes from the answer given when a member of the secret nativist group called the Order of the Star-Spangled Banner was asked by an outsider about the organization. The Know-Nothing Party survived through the 1840s and '50s. It was dead by the Civil War. But before it died it contributed some of the most wretched examples of organized bigotry in urban political history.

A native mob burned a convent in Charlestown, Massachusetts, in 1831. In 1846 a mob sacked the St. Philip de Neri Church in what is now South Philadelphia. The militia was called, and gangs of nativists roamed Penn's City of Brotherly Love in search of Irish heads to smash. Thousands of Irish Catholics fled the city. The burning of churches in Philadelphia and the bombing of churches in Birmingham three generations later bear comparison. The militia (today called the National Guard), which must rush to a city to keep open warfare from breaking out, is also part of our heritage. The riot in Philadelphia in 1846 resulted in thirteen dead and dozens wounded. For at least a generation, priests really needed bodyguards of parishioners as they walked many of the streets of Boston, New York, and Philadelphia. Fistfights between Irish "bhoys" and nativists were commonplace, as were the notice in the newspapers and the signs on the fences, "No Irish Need Apply."

The Irish burst on the American political scene at the right moment in history. The old Federalist political beliefs of an intelligent informed citizenry participating in government were in the process of being forsaken for a laissez-faire view of things favorable to the entrepreneurs. After the Founding Fathers, the Irish were the great innovators of American politics. They were the main creators of the style and form of urban politics in this country. The reasons for this lie not only in the inventiveness of the Irish, which was considerable, but also in the nearly absolute impotence of the existing political system of the cities to deal with the needs of millions of new urban residents crammed into tenements. Government was simply not geared to meet the needs or satisfy the demands of these new urban dwellers.

The needs of the laboring urban masses were to be satisfied by themselves; the railroads, canal companies, and others managed to obtain government aid and assistance in a variety of ways. Such distinctions were not lost on the Irish who were used to the hypocrisy of the English government. The Irish and their successors made use of this ideological peculiarity of nineteenth-century American government. The political innovations of the Irish were reactions to existing governmental structures and behavior. The forms created were adaptations of the old political structures of the city.

Law and Custom

To a great extent, the political innovations of the Irish were inherited by other immigrant groups that followed. Many of the innovations involved recognizing the difference between the way things were in society and the way the law and government said they were, or ought to be. One example of how the "new" urban politics of the immigrants and the bosses differed from the stated norms of government is to be found in the important area of representation. The Lockean notion of representative assemblies freely elected on the basis of citizenship and geography was firmly implanted in American political culture by 1850. Yet another area of basic importance was the common law system of England, which required government and its instrument, the courts, to treat only individuals. Thus, a case might arise called People of the Commonwealth of Pennsylvania versus Jones, Smith, and Green, each of whom is being prosecuted and judged as an individual. A case could not arise titled People versus The Jones Family. Each member of a family could be prosecuted, but never the family as a unit.

These two basic principles of American law and government had very little to do with life in the cities. The significant thing about urban populations is their diversity. Thus, under the accepted practice, an area of 100,000 people might be entitled to a city councilman or two, a few state legislators, and perhaps a congressman. This statement represents a legalistic view of representation, one taken by government throughout the nineteenth century and most of the twentieth. What if further investigation revealed that this population of 100,000 people consisted of 35,000 Italian immigrants, 50,000 Irish-Americans, and 15,000 Jews? What if we also knew that the area was working class and that unemployment was high? The facts of social life could be recited endlessly, but would not alter how the 100,000 were represented by government. But the ethnic, economic, and social conditions *did* matter indeed. This the Irish politician and his successors realized. They frequently tried and succeeded in giving formal recognition to these differences in the population. Systems of incentives and rewards, specialized methods of communication, public demonstrations of respect, and tolerance of different customs and religions—all these were devices to alter the nature of representation.

In Ireland, in Italy, in Poland, and in nearly all the places in the world that gave America its nineteenth-century immigrants, life was family centered. Grandparents often lived with children and grandchildren. Young men and women rarely married without the family's permission. Businesses, professions, and crafts were centered in the family. Farming, until very recently, was always a family-centered affair. When individuals got into trouble, it became a family matter automatically. The notion of family in most immigrant cultures extended broadly to include uncles, cousins, and aunts as well as great-aunts, great-uncles, and cousins-by-marriage. People who came from the same country settled in the same general area. The pattern of settlement was frequently even more refined, for families tried to live as closely together as they possibly could. Thus, five or six families from the same village would assemble in a few city blocks. After a time, whole neighborhoods might be made up of people who themselves came from a particular village or region in "the old country." Their children often stayed on in the "old neighborhood," thus extending the life of the original urban village.[7]

The law and customs of the new country said that people were to be treated as individuals, not as families. Strong familial ties were a conspicuous feature of urban ethnic life and the politicians whose existence depended upon the "bloc" votes of such families were quick to adapt. One dealt with the top of the family hierarchy first before one approached any other level. The authority of the head of the clan was never called into question by the politician who wished to continue to operate. Papa, no matter how poor or incompetent, was not just another individual in the eyes of the smart ward politician, and when members of the family (usually youthful) ran afoul of the law, the politician frequently assisted papa in "talking to the judge." There were many ways that the machine politicians gave special recognition to the primacy of the family as the unit of social life.

Industrialization and City Services

High population density, ethnicity, and the existence of a large working class were some of the social foundations of the machine. The economic foundations were the industrialization of the urban centers and the expansion of municipal services. In a sense, the machine is an outgrowth of nineteenth-century industrialization. Obviously, the tremendous growth of manufacturing industry created a working class and stimulated immigration. But manufacturing also brought on some social conditions that may have been of great significance to the creation of a person-centered sociopolitical organization such as the machine. If "depersonalization" or "anomie" has to be ascribed to one source (which it ought not be), that source would probably be industrialization. The assembly line enforced a series of split occupational roles. Instead of simply being a street sweeper or a butcher's helper, men and women became screw turners, or the "person who lifts this piece of steel and dumps it in this bin." The residential surroundings of industrial laborers in the city were likely to be tenement buildings that had all the warmth and charm of the factory that employed them. Industrialization in the nineteenth century was harmful to family stability in other ways. Women and children worked in mills and factories in and around cities and towns all over the country.

The growth of the industrial base of the cities required the acquiescence, if not the direct support, of government. Rights-of-way for rail lines, water mains for factories, and municipal docks and warehousing facilities were provided to the growing industries of the cities. Industry needed assistance and cooperation from government. This it usually got at a small price, usually an annual "campaign" fund contribution to the local machine. New industries with specifically urban-oriented services to sell grew like weeds in the city garden. Natural gas for street

[7]Herbert J. Gans, *The Urban Villagers* (New York: Free Press, 1962).

lighting and cooking was a miracle of the era, soon to be followed by a greater miracle, electricity. Horsecars pulled on rimmed wheels along steel tracks gave way to electrified trolley cars. Indoor plumbing and the consequent installation of citywide underground sewers were further wonders of the nineteenth-century city. Franchises, licenses, permits, contracts, and bids—all of the legal paraphernalia making public service improvement possible—lay in the hands of elected or appointed politicians. By limiting competition through the grant of exclusive franchises for municipal services, the politicians served their own needs as well as those of the contractor or operator. Industrialization and the expansion of municipal services meant increased opportunity for the politicians and the industrial owners and managers to find common, mutually profitable ground.

Social Organization

The final socioeconomic "foundation" of the machine lies in the type and character of social organization commonly found in most American cities in the nineteenth century. The city, as we have suggested, was far from being homogeneous. Indeed, as time passed, cities became more heterogeneous. The problem facing a political organization was: How do we organize such complexity so that we can sustain ourselves in office over time? In a sense, this is an unfair statement giving a conscious rationality to a "natural" social phenomenon, the machine. The machine grew out of the confused diversity of the city because those who populated the organization understood urban social structure in a very personal way. Almost without exception, machine politicians came from and seldom lost contact with one of the basic social institutions of the city, the neighborhood.

The neighborhood was a basic unit of social organization. Some neighborhoods derived their names from either physical characteristics ("the hill"), historical structures ("the Battery"), antiquated ethnicity ("Germantown"), or the presumed occupational characteristics of the environs ("red light district"). The definition of "neighborhood" is a difficult problem for social analysts. At this point we may simply say that the neighborhood consisted of people who were economically and socially similar and who lived in the same geographical area. Working-class neighborhoods, silk stocking neighborhoods, ethnic neighborhoods, "old" neighborhoods and new ones, formed a patchwork covering the city. Human ecologists have theorized about how people have formed communities and organized themselves into rough residential, industrial, and commercial patterns. The politician of the last century was not very much interested in how the neighborhood came into existence. Rather, he was concerned with its potential power in elections and in servicing the needs of the people who inhabited it.

Below the neighborhood level were to be found the social organizations larger than families to which the politician had to relate. Some of the more important of these were the church, the saloon, the gang, and the public service organization or club. In areas where the population was church-going, the tolerance, if not the best wishes, of the minister or priest, was helpful to the health of the political organization. Particularly in Catholic areas and in places where there was a language or cultural barrier, the ward politician had to avoid running afoul of the local cleric. Often this was done by making substantial contributions to church projects. Many of the famous bosses of the late nineteenth and early twentieth centuries were big donors to the churches, particularly the Catholic church.[8]

Saloons were a focal point of nineteenth-century social life for urban workingmen. There were thousands of saloons in Manhattan, for instance, and hundreds of political careers began in them. The saloon was the place where men gathered after work to argue about politics, engage in minor contests of athletic skill, and generally to enjoy the fruits of the grain. It was in saloons that politicians could gain access to the leaders of the neighborhood, and nearly every neighborhood had a saloon. Until laws were passed against the practice, the saloon was the "marshaling yard" for the precinct workers, clerks, bully boys, and "repeaters."[9] The saloon's bottles and taps provided payment for many. It was in the saloon that public issues, both national and local, were discussed, and often organizations grew and were sustained out of such discussions.

In many cities of the last century, voluntary fire departments were formed to fill a void in public services. The voluntary clubs took on many of the aspects of fraternal military organizations, complete with uniformed bands, initiation rites, and gaily colored uniforms. Money was raised to purchase equipment, and competition between organizations was keen. Competing brigades would race to the fire, try to put it out, and all too frequently end up in a brawl with the opposition. Such tightly organized, multipurpose organizations were "natural" environments for the growth of political groups.

Another "natural" kind of social organization that formed the basis for the development of political groupings was the gang. Groups of young men in the impoverished neighborhoods of the cities gathered informally for purposes of comraderie and petty crime. Members of such gangs frequently were employed as repeaters and as political "workers" at the polls. They were also called upon from time to time to make fistic contributions. The gangs held social events in clubhouses and often asserted peculiar forms of territorial rights in their wards. Gang leaders quite often became political leaders. An insightful description of the social processes underlying ward-level political organization has been provided by M. Ostrogorski, a brilliant Russian analyst of American parties and politics.

> . . . In the popular wards of the large cities the small politician has no need to create the political following which he forms around him; he finds it ready to hand in social

---

[8]Harold Zink, *City Bosses in the United States* (Durham, N.C.: Duke University Press, 1930), pp. 30–31.

[9]"Repeaters" were those who voted "repeatedly" in the same election for a slight fee. The frequently used preregistered names of occupants of the cemetery were particularly useful in primaries.

life, in which neighbourly ties, and above all common tastes and mutual sympathies, give rise to small sets, groups of people who meet regularly to enjoy the pleasures of sociability and friendship. The street corner serves them as a rendezvous as long as they are in the youthful stage. Then, when they grow older and have a few cents to spend, they meet in a drinking-saloon or in a room hired for the purpose with their modest contributions. Several "gangs" unite to found a sort of club, in which they give small parties, balls or simply smoke, drink, and amuse themselves. This merry crew is a latent political force; when the elections come around it may furnish a compact band of voters. The small politician has but to lay his hand on it. Often he himself has grown up in the gang and with it; the stirring life of the gang, with its escapades, its quarrels, and its brawls with the members of rival gangs, frequently gave him an opportunity of displaying his superior faculties of command and of organization; his companions got into the habit of following him in everything. . . .[10]

Ostrogorski's commentary, written in 1908, is but one of a number of accounts of how the machine grew and was sustained.[11] Some hellfire and damnation sermonizing characterized this kind of writing. A close examination of the scholarly literature of the era reveals at least one point: the machine was created and sustained by people living in cities. It was the result of no plot. How did the machine function? Throughout the following description and analysis it should be kept in mind that the machine existed in a social context, as all political institutions must.

A Structural-Functional View of the Machine

In a now-classic section of his book, *Social Theory and Social Structure,* Robert Merton described the "latent functions of the machine."[12] Merton's general point was that the "functional deficiencies of the official structure generate an alternative (unofficial) structure to fulfill existing needs somewhat more effectively." As we have suggested, formal nineteenth-century government was a creature of eighteenth-century traditionalism and nineteenth-century Social Darwinism. This combination was further complicated by the relationship of the city to the state. Merton suggests that the machine successfully fulfilled three distinctive functions. It provided needed social services in a form acceptable to people. That is, a local politician who also was in effect a neighbor personally provided help. The "deprived classes" thus were one subgroup in urban society whose demands, or at least some of them, were satisfied by the machine. A second function of the machine, notes Merton, is to serve "business corporations, among

---

[10]Moisei Ostrogorski, *Democracy and the Organization of Political Parties* (London: Macmillan, 1908) II, pp. 368–69.

[11]*See* William L. Riordan, *Plunkitt of Tammany Hall* (New York: Dutton, 1963); James Bryce, *The American Commonwealth* (New York: Commonwealth, 1908); Zink, *City Bosses in the United States;* and Ostrogorski, *Democracy and the Organization of Political Parties.*

[12]Robert K. Merton, *Social Theory and Social Structure* (rev. enl. ed.; New York: Free Press, 1957), pp. 71–75.

which the public utilities (railroads, local transportation and electric light companies, communications corporations), ... simply the most conspicuous in this regard, seek special political dispensations which will enable them to stabilize their situation and to near their objective of maximizing profits."

Finally, Merton suggests that the machine provided "alternative channels of social mobility for those otherwise excluded from the more conventional avenues for personal 'advancement.' " This argument is an old and respected one. From the testimony of and research done on old bosses and ward politicians, it seems clear that the enhancement of the possibility for upward mobility was a significant machine reward.[13]

A question that may have particular significance for contemporary urban politics is: How was the machine organized to fulfill its functions? The structure of machines was nearly always similar to the formal structure of the political party or representational system. It was decidedly hierarchical. The lowest level of organization was the precinct. A number of precincts made up the next unit, the ward. Ward organizations were represented by party committees that usually consisted of the more powerful ward leaders. One of these was usually the city boss. Party structure varied to an extent in the cities, but the basic pattern was the same.

The fundamental coin of the machine was the vote. The vote permitted the machine to capture the formal reins of government. The governmental apparatus was then employed to maintain the machine and enhance its possibility of winning the next election. The precinct leader (or captain) functioned as an arm of the ward leader. The role is described by those who filled it in two extraordinary books.[14] The ward-level politician lived in the neighborhood and was most likely born there. He typically started out as poor as his neighbors and seldom ended up living much better. He was available day and night and characteristically held "open house" in his clubhouse or living room at least once a week. He dealt with any request that came before him. In general, he functioned as the liaison man between citizens and impersonal governmental and economic institutions. His service was personal and face to face. He was in the business of doing favors. He dealt in patronage jobs, petty bribery, and manipulation of judicial proceedings, among other things. Families burned out of their houses got help in finding someplace to live. Perhaps some furniture and clothing also could be obtained. The Christmas turkey and the sack of coal in the winter were part of the ward heeler's stock in trade. The troublesome adolescent faced with court proceedings could, with the precinct man's assistance, find leniency. The ordinary citizen unable to obtain a peddler's license or faced with some other petty bureaucratic problem that seemed large to him, could find quick and effective aid at the door of the ward leader. Merchants and small businessmen who were in violation of

[13]See John T. Salter, *Boss Rule: Portraits in City Politics* (New York: McGraw-Hill, 1935); Riordan, *Plunkitt of Tammany Hall;* and Zink, *City Bosses in the United States.*
[14]See Salter, *Boss Rule: Portraits in City Politics* and Riordan, *Plunkitt of Tammany Hall.*

some municipal ordinance or other often simply paid a small fee to the ward leader or precinct captain to avoid penalty.

The jobless, the homeless, and people with lesser problems were treated as people, not as "clients." Rarely was any overt demand made on their political loyalties, but the expectations of the politicians were well known. A professor of political science recorded the following precinct-level action in the early 1930s in Philadelphia.

> While I observed, 177 men and women voted. Of that number, 11 people voted without assistance; the 166 were assisted—partly because the machines were new to these people, but more truly because Nick (the machine politician) was their friend, and they wanted to show him that their vote was his. Voting was almost continuous while I was there. A voter would come in and Nick would call him by name—not once did he fail in this. While the clerk was writing down the name, someone would ask for help—say that he or she could not work the machine. The judge of elections would look at Nick and say, "Who would you like to assist you?" Sometimes the person would point to Nick, and other times he would call him by name. . . .[15]

If American politics ever had "grass roots" political organization, it was to be found in the cities during the machine era. The clubhouses of the neighborhood politicians were open and available to people with all kinds of needs. Political leaders rose from the most humble surroundings. Indeed, one of the important consequences of the machine-type local organization was that it offered open access to people with political ambitions. The precinct level was the place where young men found their apprenticeship if their vocation was politics. In Harold Zink's study of twenty important city bosses he notes that all twenty began at the lowest level and that their apprenticeships in the rise to the top took anywhere from ten to twenty-four years.[16]

Ward politics was a hard game requiring large amounts of time and energy. The ward leader was normally a man who did not have time for employment outside of politics. Of course, many of the occupations of ward politicians, like saloon-keeping, simply amplified political activity. Many, if not all, ward leaders held patronage jobs that amounted to positions requiring no work. In the absence of civil service regulations, appointive offices paying reasonable salaries often had incumbents who appeared only on payday. While it is impossible to obtain national figures on the number of patronage jobs, we can find some valuable illustrative examples:

> These men who held sinecures and recieved presents from Boss Tweed were known as the "Shiny Hat Brigade," and they could be seen on fair afternoons—for they never rose early—on the sunny side of Broadway or Fifth Avenue, smoking their cigars and discussing horses, women, politics and prize fighting. It was said by a

[15]Salter, *Boss Rule: Portraits in City Politics*, pp. 149–50.
[16]Zink, *City Bosses in the United States*, p. 43.

contemporary observer, Matthew P. Breen, that from twelve to fifteen thousand of these men occupied the street corners of New York during the reign of Tweed.[17]

Not all of the jobs controlled by the bosses were governmental. Part of the "kickback" exacted from contractors might very well include the provision that the ward leader be allowed to name laborers. Public utility construction and operation might also provide a powerful patronage component. The infamous Republican "gas ring" of Philadelphia, which operated under the direction of James McManes during the last century, was in some ways as prototypical as its famous brother to the north.

> This army of jobs (5,630 Gas Commission employees) provided the very best fuel for the political organization which "King" McManes created. Few bosses have had more skillful lieutenants or supervised all with more vigilance than he. Every one of the more than seven hundred precincts of the city had organizations manned by leaders who represented them on the thirty-one ward committees. The ward committees held each local leader responsible for getting out the vote and in turn sent a ward representative to the central committee. Mr. McManes for many years occupied a place as leader of the Seventeenth Ward and its representative on the city central committee.[18]

In most machine organizations the ward was the crucial link between the diverse neighborhoods of the city and any central authority. The city boss normally came from the ranks of the ward bosses and, while many city bosses seemed to rule as "kings" or "czars," the fact of the matter was contrary to that impression. Bosses ruled by and with the consent of the ward leaders. Any attempt by the boss to deprive the ward leaders of their "just" rewards and prerogatives was likely to be met by revolt. It was seldom that even a strong city boss could successfully name his successor. A serious falling-out among ward leaders often meant that the machine would lose an election.

Although much about the internal operations of the machine remains a mystery, some things of interest are known. The ward system functioned like a cross between baronial and legislative organizations. A system of mutual dependence developed between the city boss and the ward bosses. Each "scratched the other's back" so long as the relationship proved mutually advantageous. Strong bosses could and did enforce discipline ruthlessly on deviants, and the ward system in most machine cities remained stable through generations of bosses. The most famous of all urban political machines, Tammany Hall, was a political force of varying importance for over a century and a half. Throughout that time, the basic units of organization and some of the rules of conduct remained relatively stable. Tammany was founded as a social club or fraternity. By 1800, it was deeply

[17]Morris Robert Werner, *Tammany Hall* (Garden City, N.Y.: Doubleday, Doran and Company, 1928), p.170.
[18]Zink, *City Bosses in the United States*, p. 202.

involved in trying to get Aaron Burr elected president. It followed no political party for the first several decades of its political involvement. It finally "adopted" the Democratic party of New York City and dominated it off and on (mostly on) until quite recently. By 1865 Tammany had come to be dominated by the Irish immigrants who had pushed most of the old Yankees out of power. One of those few Yankees who remained, William Marcy "Boss" Tweed, became the stereotype for all political bosses when he was immortalized in the cartoons of Thomas Nast.[19]

Tweed's great-grandfather emigrated from the town of Kelso on the river Tweed in Scotland. The great-grandson was a native American if ever there was one. Born with few political resources, a son of the respectable "commercial" class, Tweed molded Tammany into a true political machine; one that controlled city and state. His own downfall and disgrace did little to damage the monument he constructed. His rise to power was classic. He began as a foreman of the fire department, rose to alderman, congressman, and finally boss.

> . . . Judges rendered decisions dictated by Tweed. The Legislature passed or defeated measures as he willed. The Governor carried out his orders. The taxpayers filled the city treasury that Tweed might loot it. From this one source alone Tweed stole in excess of $30,000,000 in cash in less than three years—the total peculations of the Ring are not less than $45,000,000 and have been put at $200,000,000—and yet he was not satisfied . . .[20]

During the period of the Tweed domination of Tammany, an alliance was forged with the powerful as well as with the poor. Tweed actually managed to persuade John Jacob Astor and five other millionaires to sign a document attesting to his character and saying that Tweed had not taken a cent from the city treasury! Jim Fisk and Jay Gould happily supplied the unprecedented $1 million bail set when Tweed was arrested. Tweed's opponents finally cornered him and he landed in jail. But his end was uncharacteristic of bosses in general.

Ward politicians who could reach and hold the position of city boss seldom spent any time in jail. They were as tough and clever as the nineteenth-century capitalists they so admired. Few ever attained the public notice that Tweed did and few wanted it. Most bosses held minor public office if they held any at all and few ever stole directly from the treasury. Many bosses became rich men, others apparently worked mainly for power. Almost inevitably, city bosses came from modest backgrounds and climbed the only social or economic ladder available to them—the political ladder.

Lord Bryce, writing in 1889, described a path of upward mobility for the machine politician that is reminiscent of the Protestant Ethic. A poor, but hardworking lad gathers some votes for the local precinct captain from his friends and

[19]See Werner, *Tammany Hall* and Dennis Tilden Lynch, *"Boss" Tweed: The Story of a Grim Generation* (New York: Boni and Liveright, 1927).
[20]Lynch, *"Boss" Tweed: The Story of a Grim Generation,* p. 16.

neighbors. He regularly attends meetings and votes in primaries and general elections. He works at the polls. He has entered the class of general political workers. Continued hard work and loyal service bring appointment to some petty city office. Eventually he may be nominated for some minor elective office. By this time, he has found his way to membership on the ward committee and finally becomes a member of the central committee. He surrounds himself with a group of local supporters who follow his orders in hopes of "something good." Such men, called "heelers," help by their actions in primaries to sustain the leader. Eventually, he (the leader) discovers, by his membership on the central committee, "what everybody who gets on in the world discovers sooner or later; by how few persons the world is governed."[21] The hypothetical leader becomes part of a "knot" consisting of men who are most powerful on the central committee.

> ... Each can command some primaries, each has attached to himself a group of dependents who owe some place to him, or hope for some place from him. The aim of the knot is not only to get good posts for themselves, but to rivet their yoke upon the city by garrisoning the departments with their own creatures, and so controlling elections to the State legislature that they can procure such statutes as they desire, and prevent the passing of statutes likely to expose or injure them. They cement their dominion by combination, each placing his influence at the disposal of the others, and settle all important measures in secret conclave.[22]

The upward progression is in many respects a parody of the corporate climb to the top, a process glamorized in the popular literature of the era. It might be argued that politics was one of the few avenues upward really open to highly motivated sons of the poor. Whatever the variety of reasons, the process described took place in practically every city in the country. New Orleans, San Francisco, New York, and Chicago as well as hundreds of smaller cities had bosses and machines. The machine dominated Republican and Democratic parties. Big city bosses, despite newspaper accounts to the contrary, were pervasive not because of a particular governmental structure, but because they fulfilled needs and met demands left unattended by other social and governmental structures. In what follows we take an overview of how the machine was structured, how it functioned, and how it related to the society of which it was a part. In a summary model, Figure 3.1, we deal with historical information, first for its own sake, and secondly for whatever insights it may provide about contemporary urban political systems.

The Machine in Urban Society: A Paradox

Figure 3.1 illustrates the interdependent and reciprocal nature of some important relationships between the machine and social and economic structures. The pyra-

[21]Bryce, *The American Commonwealth*, p.75.
[22]*Ibid.*

48

Figure 3.1
The Machine and Urban Society

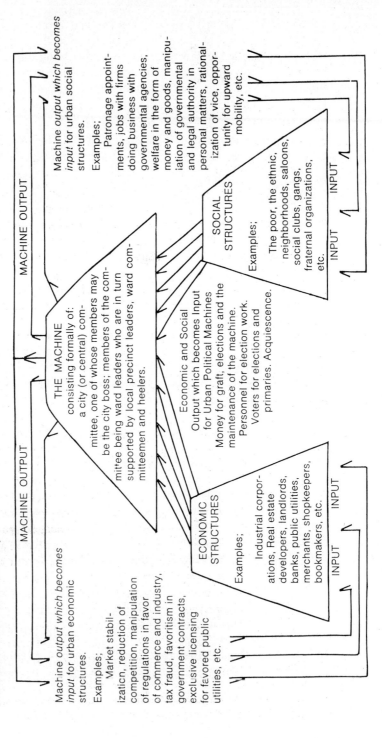

mids symbolize the stratified and hierarchical nature of the machine, social structures and economic structures. Machine outputs are converted to usable inputs by other elements of society. So long as the illustrated functions continue to be provided adequately and without serious competition, the stability and future of the machine is more or less assured.

It is easy to draw oversimplified conclusions from Figure 3.1. One conclusion that ought not be drawn is that such a series of societal relationships constitute a plot. On the contrary, many of the "Outputs" of the machine created "end states" that made short-run circumstances for some segments of society more convenient. Thus, the model presented should not be read as implying that industrialization of the cities would not have occurred without the assistance of the machine. The form it took and the more or less "public be damned" behavior of industrial corporations were aspects assisted by the machine, not created by it. This is a most important point: the machine, for all its greed and color, was a conservative and stabilizing institution. It provided equilibrium and continuity.

The machine was conservative in that it tended to preserve and stabilize existing divisions in society. It soothed the poor with turkeys, bags of coal, and occasionally jobs, but did not change their long-run prospects. It served the city to the extent that the needs of urban society matched those of the politicians. The machine reacted to and was purchased by public utility companies and industrial corporations. Where some segments of public belief or hope coincided with practices that either benefited the machine as a whole or some of its members, then it became an "instrument of progress," providing urban masses with new sewers, new lighting systems, or new streets. All these were built at considerable cost to the taxpayer who not only paid real costs, but also paid the costs of bribes, kickbacks, and poor construction of streets and public buildings. While one might applaud the personalized, almost dignified social welfare function of the machine, it should never be forgotten that such generosity was at the cost of an independent electorate and possibly the development of a true social welfare system.

The tenements and the miserable social conditions discussed at some length earlier were taken as a "given" by the machine. Poverty and social deprivation similarly were considered to be facts of life to be turned to the advantage of the machine. It was simply not in the character of a stabilizing institution like the machine to suffer any institutional costs in an attempt to eliminate such conditions. The machine, as suggested in Figure 3.1, was the great intermediary and communicator between segments of society. It was a creature of the society that created it. As long as some urban social institutions remained chaotic and fluid, the machine could well function to stabilize others.

The macrofunctions of the machine appear to have provided some of the social cement that kept nineteenth-century and early twentieth-century cities from internal warfare. It must be remembered that what we today would call the middle classes was a smaller part of the population during the past century and into the present one. Thus, a Dickensian or Marxist set of conditions prevailed: a very large proletariat and *lumpen* proletariat were employed at slave wages and in wretched conditions by a tiny-but-greedy gang of capitalists. Labor unions were forbidden. Neither political party was particularly concerned about social problems until the end of the century when two-party competition on the national level and the introduction of special-purpose third parties caused a few politicians to awaken to the lure of social justice as an issue. In the gulf between the two classes, the very poor and the very rich, who mediated and stabilized so that the radical kind of urban workers' revolts of Europe never were very serious in America? The machine helped to serve this macrofunction. The large distance between the citizenry and a government that was supposed to be responsive to it might not have remained so large so long had not an obliging form of organization been created as an informal link between the two.

Who, in the main, performed the crucial function of linking government and the governed? The machine, of course, managed to involve itself where profitable in every conceivable kind of relationship between government and citizen. Thus, at the societal level it became a rather effective means of social control. The machine functioned as a "shadow government" in that its hierarchy paralleled that of formal government. Ultimately, it was the most paradoxical of complex political organizations. In light of most of the public values of the last generation, the machine could be accounted for as some kind of a cancerous growth on the corporate democratic corpus. It was criminal, in the narrow sense that its members stole money from the public, corrupted elected officials, and encouraged monstrous inefficiencies and public personnel practices.

In light of some more recently trumpeted values, however, these evils might be counterbalanced by what we today would consider virtues. Participation in politics was not only open, but conceivably could be meaningful in an easily observed way. Indeed, one needed special qualifications to become a machine politician, but none of them served as tickets of admission, neither education, wealth, nor high social status. The question of citizen effectiveness in mass, impersonal surroundings was almost as prominent in nineteenth-century urban America as it is today. The machine provided knowable, workable, and accessible routes for bringing about some change in one's immediate environment through governmental action. While the machine was utterly inappropriate as an institution for *mass* social change, it was exceedingly useful as a means of achieving personal ends. Millions of ignorant, illiterate immigrants became citizens and voters almost immediately after leaving the steerage of their ship. A central canon of democracy—an informed electorate independently choosing among candidates —was thus violated. The impartiality of judges and juries was destroyed countless times. The police forces of almost all major cities were corrupted. Public vices such as prostitution (in those days a public vice; in these days apparently a private enterprise), gambling, and policy games or numbers were centralized, tithed, and kept orderly by the machine. In sum, the machine fought to maintain stable relations between all segments of society which were vulnerable to manipulation, or which were likely to be profitable in money or votes. Stability and continuity are two words used often here, yet we have presented socioeconomic evidence that would seem to belie any chance of stability. How did the machine form of political organization maintain control, service its clientele, and invest sufficiently in itself to ensure its own viability? Lord Bryce provided one set of answers in 1889:

> In large cities the results are different because the circumstances are different. We find there, besides the conditions previously enumerated, viz. numerous offices, frequent elections, universal suffrage, an absence of stimulating issues, three others of great moment—a vast population of ignorant immigrants—the leading men all occupied with business—communities so large that people know little of one another, and that the interest of each individual in good government is comparatively small . . .[23]

The problems of formal governmental structure mentioned by Bryce were discussed earlier—the long ballot, the "blizzard of boards," universal manhood suffrage, and the rest of the catalogue of Jacksonian and state-house-related structural problems. But the most important part of Bryce's analysis lies, we would argue, in the ignorance-apathy question. Either through some kind of rough calculus ("interest of each individual is comparatively small") or because of private preoccupation ("leading men engaged in business") or because of ignorance ("vast population of immigrants"), Bryce argues, the machine had its way and dominated the political system. Bryce traveled from city to city listing machine faults yet never once did he conceive of the public wanting the machine. Perhaps it would be more accurate to say that certain publics demanded particular kinds of public services.

Such a view radically differs from Bryce and his successors. Part of reform thought, then as now, has included a certain neo-Platonic loftiness. Thus, only ignorant immigrants, preoccupied businessmen, and honest-but-alienated citizens would put up with the machine. Even an informed electorate became bored and because of its boredom, the argument seems to go, it allowed the rascals back into office. For whatever reason, the machine is viewed as an aberration to be corrected when an informed public finds out about it. Such a view is not consistent with a history suggesting that the most characteristic form of urban political organization from the 1840s to the 1940s was the machine. Machines were to be found in large and middle-sized cities throughout the country. They were created and sustained by the activities of large groups of citizens who regularly depended upon the organization for the satisfaction of needs, real or imagined.

It would be foolhardy to try to sum up the machine experience by attempting to draw up a balance sheet that recorded social debits and credits. The American experience with the machine form of organization is far from over.

What ought not be forgotten about the machine and its era is that the machine form of organization represents one of the few coherent political forms ever devised in the United States. Machine organization reflected and represented social and economic differences in the population as no other institution has.

[23]*Ibid.*, p. 67.

Suggested Readings

Bryce, James, *The American Commonwealth* (New York: Commonwealth, 1908).

Callow, Alexander B., *The City Boss in America: An Interpretive Reader* (New York: Oxford University Press, 1976).

Gardiner, John A. and David J. Olson, eds., *Theft of the City* (Bloomington: Indiana University Press, 1974).

Kennedy, Eugene, *Himself! The Life and Times of Mayor Richard J. Daley* (New York: Viking, 1978).

Lynch, Dennis Tilden, *"Boss" Tweed: The Story of a Grim Generation* (New York: Boni and Liveright, 1927).

Rakove, Milton, *Don't Make No Waves—Don't Back No Losers* (Bloomington: Indiana University Press, 1975).

Riordan, William L., *Plunkitt of Tammany Hall* (New York: Dutton, 1963).

Royko, Mike, *Boss: Richard J. Daley of Chicago* (New York: Dutton, 1971).

Salter, John T., *Boss Rule: Portraits in City Politics* (New York: McGraw-Hill, 1935).

Shannon, William V., *The American Irish,* 1st rev. ed. (New York: Macmillan, 1966).

Zink, Harold, *City Bosses in the U.S.* (Durham: Duke University, 1930).

Chapter 4
Reform and the Development of Modern Urban Government

Introduction

Migration to the cities from rural America and from Europe accelerated after 1900. As the machine grew more powerful in the cities, a counterforce began to develop that would eventually change the face of municipal government and politics.

This was the reform movement. The reform movement was a phenomenon that encompassed much of American life, one that came to overshadow political parties and eventually the structure of American political thought. Reform ideology was concerned with all aspects of political, social, and economic life which seemed to pervert the ideals of American democracy. Especially in the 1890s, political parties were created to carry the banner of reform throughout the nation. The Populist party and the Progressive party succeeded in electing candidates to some national and many state offices. More importantly, reformist principles were legitimized in the platforms and programs of the major parties. Theodore Roosevelt utilized the reform movement rhetoric, and ultimately that became the basis for the actions of his cousin Franklin. Many reformist notions now are fixed concepts in American government. It is our intention to discuss some of the broad philosophical and political ideas of the reform movement, and then to concentrate on the conflict between the reformers and the machine.

The Roots of Reform

The turn of the century brought even greater change to the urban place. Millions of people left farms and small towns in rural America to come to the city to find better ways of life. The giant cities grew, but it was the "Akrons, the Duluths, the Tacomas that were bursting at the seams; no less than 101 American communities grew by 100 percent or more in the 1880s."[1] By the turn of the century, foreign-born and the children of the first generation born in America outnumbered the "natives" in Boston, Chicago, Cleveland, New York, and Philadelphia. The wave of immigration after the turn of the century was in many ways more frightening to the natives than the Irish immigrations had been sixty or so years before. This later immigration brought people not only of different religion, but also people of different language.

The great deprivations suffered by peasant and minority people in central and southern Europe during the last quarter of the nineteenth century made America, with its open doors, seem like Paradise. Millions of Poles, Italians, Hungarians, Greeks, and others from central and southern Europe quickly inundated the cities of the East and Midwest. By the turn of the century, America had begun to develop a small but articulate and recognizable urban middle class. At the same time, the children of shopkeepers, mechanics, and farmers began to become physically and socially mobile. College and university enrollments rose and the utility of education in the marketplace began to be recognized.

But increasingly, young rural Americans coming to the city were not poor or disoriented. They were American children, not the least bit intimidated by language and custom. They had been trained and educated to a set of beliefs fabricated in the classroom and the church. Their numbers were small, but their influence was enormous. The reform ideology owed much to the evangelical Protestant view of obligation and guilt. But of greater importance were the combined ideals of the informed common man of Jefferson and a sort of Marxist-Darwinian notion of man as an evolving creature constantly being molded while adapting to his environment.

If one accepted the idea that all people are of equal inherent worth and that society (social environment) was created by people rather than being some sort of "natural" creation, then, it was argued, manipulation of that environment could accomplish changes in people. Otis Pease discusses some of the practical conclusions drawn on the basis of these assumptions.

> . . . Therefore, remake your criminals; care for your poor; treat your insane. School your young to use their minds, not their memories. Police your factories. Infuse the business ethos, the competitive tensions, with the spirit of respect for the equal rights of each. Second, the pragmatic vision implied that human nature is for the most part socially conditioned. Man's reason can solve most of his problems if given a chance. If you take steps to reduce the sting of poverty, you may succeed in curbing base passions. If you abolish economic privilege and favoritism, you may make it possible to end poverty altogether. It was at least worth-while to assume so, to believe that a society which supported the eight-hour day, decent housing and spacious parks, the secret ballot, public power, and the scientific administration of the cities was

---

[1]Stephan Thernstrom, "Urbanization, Migration, and Social Mobility in Late Nineteenth Century America," from Barton J. Bernstein, ed., *Towards a New Past: Dissenting Essays in American History* (New York: Pantheon, 1968), pp. 158–175.

creating merely the first essential conditions for a more noble and reasonable race of men . . .[2]

The rural, small-town, Protestant American coming face to face with the city for the first time found what must have been to him a complete perversion of American life. The machine, the corruption, the ethnic, and the general conditions of the city itself must have been a profound shock to the "hayseed." The city in American life suffered, as Elazar has pointed out, from being thought of more as a Biblical city of sin than a European center of culture and enlightenment.[3] Many rural Protestant churches and leading layman of the era, such as William Jennings Bryan, looked upon the city as the ultimate in evil and corruption.

The native Yankee, by this time nearly forgotten (or, as Bryce suggested, "occupied with business"), was also alarmed by what was happening in the city. Many of those who had done business with the machine were undergoing a change of heart that involved concern for the "development" of the city. The objects of the muckrakers—many of the leading capitalists of the day—found it useful and convenient to become part of the reform movement. As was suggested in Chapter 3, the relationships between machine politicians and the business community were important structural links. The growth of industrial capitalism and the machine were interrelated. The accommodation reached between these two powerful forces began to break down when the business community realized that its opportunity for controlling policy-making and reducing the costs brought on by the machine was to be found in such reform devices as city-manager forms of government and at-large elections. Municipal research bureaus, founded to do research as a kind of lever for influence, were funded by wealthy gentlemen, themselves under severe fire from the progressive trustbusters.

Capitalism itself was everywhere under fire. In the popular press and magazines, long devoted to dry recitations of public events and genteel travelogues, a new class of writing appeared. The muckrakers caught the reading public's fancy with exposés of corporate misdeeds and municipal corruption, with human interest stories depicting the seamier sides of urban life. Lincoln Steffens in his *Shame of the Cities* and Lord Bryce's *American Commonwealth* are but two of hundreds of popular books and magazine serials of the era that shocked and spurred educated middle- and upper-class readers. The slums described by Jacob Riis and others exposed what had been hidden to thousands of upstanding, self-satisfied Americans.

Protestantism in its more evangelical forms became increasingly concerned with its mission in the cities. The moral imperative to do good found outlets in creating organizations to aid the poor. The moral dominance of the growing middle classes was felt in all fields in the form of "crusades" and missions of uplift.

[2]Otis A. Pease, ed., *The Progressive Years* (New York: Braziller, 1962), p. 9.
[3]Daniel J. Elazar, "Are We a Nation of Cities?" *The Public Interest,* Summer 1966, 42–58.

Women, freed from old chores by technology, assumed important new ones in social welfare.[4] The obligation of each person to do good works and to "show the way" to the less fortunate became a more or less fixed part of sermons in middle-class churches during the period. Much of the preaching of the era managed to intertwine patriotism, capitalism, and theology.

The reformers faced an issue central to American life. All believed in the virtue of hard work and competition in the pursuit of life, liberty, and property. Yet the ultimate success of competition seemed to involve capturing all the resources in a given field, thus destroying the possibility of "free enterprise" for those who had no resources to speak of. Giant corporations increasingly dominated industrial production and giant machines dominated political life in the cities. The question facing the reformers was: How was one to enjoy the rewards of the large organization and still maintain the cherished autonomy of the individual citizen and worker? The partially successful attack on the machines and the less fruitful assault on the trusts never resolved the problem. The reformers came armed with three beliefs they thought might correct matters.

The first of these was a profound faith in the myth of the American common man. The sturdy farmer who left his plow to read about the issues and then to vote and speak at the town meeting had always been part of American mythology. Like the soldier-farmer at Lexington and Concord and the boy born in a log cabin who became President of the United States, the reformer believed that democracy could work for everybody. The idealization of the citizen and his role in history became an institutional truth in the public schools. The problem facing the nation, the reformers thought, was that it had slipped away from the ideals upheld by the forefathers. If we could simply return to those days in our institutional and personal lives, it was argued, then things would be fine. The idealism of the nineteenth-century reformer was based on a myth that has been carried forward to the present day. The creation of institutions that were to have fulfilled this ideal for the cities was one of the sources of urban reform.

A second article of faith involved the belief that the nineteenth-century economic system was, for all its faults, the best ever created by man. The marvels of the transportation and communications industries, the vast increase in the availability of the amenities once meant only for the wealthy, and the tremendous productivity of industrial agriculture, all tended to make the reformers accept the fundamental rightness of the system. Most of the reformers were themselves the sons and daughters of people who had flourished under capitalism. The fact that they had gone to college or at least had not been consigned for life to a coal mine or plow seemed proof of the possible goodness of the system for all. Thus what the economic system of the nation needed was not radical overhaul or destruction, but *regulation*—regulation ensuring that the hard working and ambitious individual would have the opportunity to compete.

[4]See Seymour Mandelbaum, *Boss Tweed's New York* (New York: John Wiley & Sons, 1965) for an interesting discussion of the role of the churches in nineteenth-century New York City.

The third leg on the reformist stool was science and technology. Many of those who could not put all their faith in the redemption of mankind through God, found a repository for it in science and technology. Early twentieth-century man was surrounded and overwhelmed by the remarkable evidences of this new faith. The skyscraper, rising up to dizzying height braced by a steel skeleton made of girders of a size and quality unimaginable a few years before, was an astounding sight. Hundreds arrived at work in horseless carriages while hundreds of thousands arrived on electrically powered elevated trains—it was an age of mechanical miracles. If men could but muster the right materials and get together to think out a problem, then it was only a matter of time before any problem could be solved. This faith was formalized in a number of ways. Pragmatism, the experimental method, and new principles of organization were all that was needed to solve problems. The men who were to become the high priests of the religion of science and technology came from every field. Medicine, the recently born social sciences, psychology, and, probably most important of all, scientific management were making great advances. Science seemed to be discovering the order of things while technology applied the lessons learned to practical matters. Management became a "science" and the responsibility for running plants and factories began to leave the hands of the crusty old pirates who had founded them. The productive capacity of the nation became the responsibility of professional managers who applied science to the structure and function of their factories.

Frederick Taylor and his notion of scientific management symbolized the new era in management. His *Principles of Scientific Management* appeared in 1911. Taylor's work was not only the basis for the discipline known as industrial engineering, but also was one of the foundations of the modern doctrine of efficiency. The idea of the division of labor fragmented into specialized roles so as to produce a product cheaply was one of the great discoveries of the age. Taylor and his successors with their clipboards and stopwatches conceived not of men, but of their movements in performing a task that contributed to production. Such a task was either efficient or inefficient in terms of the short- or long-term goal of productivity. Efficiency was an input-output relationship to be measured and improved so that productivity increased while cost remained the same or decreased. Taylor's doctrine of efficiency and automation seemed to many to be the application of science to old problems—with remarkable results. There were other brilliant pioneers in the area of industrial management. Their basic idea was that rationality (science) and hardware could solve any problem of management.

Now, what had bigger managerial problems than the giant corporations? What was more inefficient and costly? Why, municipal government, of course. If Ford could produce an enormous number of cars, pay good wages, reduce prices, and still make a huge profit, then why could not a city be run so that more services were provided for less (or the same) taxes? Why indeed?

The myth of the noble citizen, the faith in the basic rightness of capitalism, and a vision of the possible application of science and technology to the problems of society were three important beliefs underlying much of the behavior and thought of the reformers. In some ways their faith was touching; in others it was arrogant. They conceived of the public interest as something discoverable, like radium. Their view of heaven was an enormous small town in which each informed citizen (and all would be informed) would participate in a government run on sound scientific principles. The beliefs and activities of the Progressive movement have been summarized in greater detail (and with more grace) in a number of excellent volumes.[5]

The Objects of Reform

A generation of bright, eager, middle- and upper-middle-class people approached the problems of the cities with the kinds of beliefs summarized above. They were a tremendously active lot. They wrote literally thousands of argumentative tracts exposing their enemies and promoting their causes. What forces in the city stood in the way of their dreams? A number of scholars have argued that one of their primary problems was the immigrant.

The "Immigrant-Yankee" Conflict

Hofstadter has argued that the frame of mind of the immigrant and that of the reformer were almost wholly incompatible.[6] The clash of the two different political cultures is, according to Banfield and Wilson, one of the most significant, enduring conflicts of American urban politics. They speak of modern "patterns of cleavage" which, it is suggested, derive from the immigrant-reformer split.

> . . . These patterns reflect two conceptions of the public interest that are widely held. The first, which derives from the middle-class ethos, favors what the municipal reform movement has always defined as "good government"—namely efficiency, impartiality, honesty, planning, strong executives, no favoritism, model legal codes, and strict enforcement of laws against gambling and vice. The other conception of the public interest (one never explicitly formulated as such, but one all the same) derives from the "immigrant ethos." This is the conception of those people who identify with the ward or neighborhood rather than the city "as a whole," who look to politicians for "help" and "favors," who regard gambling and vice as, at worst, necessary evils, and who are far less interested in the efficiency, impartiality, and honesty of local government than in its readiness to confer material benefits of one sort or another upon them. In the largest, most heterogeneous of our cities, these

[5]See, for instance, Grant McConnell, *Private Power and American Democracy* (New York: Knopf, 1967); Richard Hofstadter, *The Age of Reform: from Bryan to F.D.R.* (New York: Knopf, 1935); and Pease, ed., *The Progressive Years.*
[6]Hofstadter, *The Age of Reform: from Bryan to F.D.R.*, pp. 175–184.

two mentalities stand forth as distinctly as did those which, in another context, caused Disraeli to write of "The Two Nations."[7]

Hofstadter in *The Age of Reform* suggests that one of the early and continuing elements in the reform psyche was a fear and a hostility toward immigrants and their culture. Despite efforts to suppress the public expression of such thoughts, many of the reformers were convinced that the great wave of immigration in the early part of this century was contrary to their notion of democracy. Some of the sentiment was bigotry, some snobbery. The "nativist" distrust of foreigners (immigrants are to this day called "aliens" in governmental jargon) was coupled with an elitism implying that the best educated should run the cities. All too frequently the immigrant was patronized. It was felt that he simply did not understand what was best for him. Such opinions were held by people (reformers) who were not immigrants and who were members of a class that had "made it."

The condescending tone of the reformer and his literature was frequently coupled with an impressive ignorance of immigrant culture. The reformers had some ideas about what was generally wrong with the city in terms of undesirable end-states, but had little interest in or understanding about the supposed dupe of the economic interests, the poor immigrant. They believed that the problem was simply one of educating the immigrant, not of converting him from a very different world view. Yet, as Hofstadter notes:

> ... It would be hard to imagine types of political culture more alien to each other than those of the Yankee reformer and the peasant immigrant. The Yankee's idea of political action assumed a popular democracy with widespread participation and eager civic interest. To him politics was the business, the responsibility, the duty of all men. It was the arena for realization of moral principles of broad application— and even, as in the case of temperance and vice crusades—for the correction of private habits. The immigrant, by contrast, coming from autocratic societies with strong feudal survivals, was totally unaccustomed to the active citizen's role. He expected to be acted upon by the government, but not to be a political agent himself. To him government meant restrictions on personal movement, the arbitrary regulation of life, the inaccessibility of the law and the conscription of the able-bodied. To him government was the instrument of the ruling classes, characteristically acting in their interests, which were indifferent or opposed to his own. Nor was government in his eyes an affair of abstract principles and rules of law: it was the actions of particular men with particular powers. Political relations were not governed by abstract principles; they were profoundly personal.[8]

These distinctions are far from being simply of historical interest. Attitudes about political participation on the part of contemporary Americans do not reflect the

---

[7]Edward C. Banfield and James Q. Wilson, *City Politics* (Cambridge, Mass.: Harvard University Press, 1963). p. 46.
[8]Hofstadter, *The Age of Reform: from Bryan to F.D.R.,* p. 181.

simple dichotomy suggested above, but do reflect a variety of alienated stances despite the rapid disappearance of immigrants.[9] The fact that high socioeconomic status correlates positively with political participation and a sense of political might suggests that simply being a peasant-immigrant is insufficient reason to typify a particular kind of general orientation as being "immigrant" as against being "Yankee." The "subject" and "parochial" categories employed by Almond and Verba in their *Civic Culture* to distinguish between sets of attitudes about government and politics held by people in different political systems are applicable to the American city.[10] The feeling that government is "the man" or "the system" did not pass away with the immigrant.

The Trusts

Steffens, Howe, and others believed that many of the problems of the city could be understood as by-products of the conspiratorial relationship between the machine and the "trusts." By virtue of the tremendous centralization of money and political power, reformers believed, the citizen and the city were denied the possibility of democracy. The archvillain of the drama was the trust. Bigness was badness in that not only was the individual's right to compete demolished, but government itself was incapable of resisting the blandishments of the industrial barons. Thus, the task before the reform movement appeared to be two-fold— the breaking up of the trusts and the restructuring of municipal government so as to make domination by the trusts through their agents, the machine politicians, impossible. A third, highly related task was also undertaken: the social maladies of society became a target for reform action.

Social Welfare

Some of the more visible creations of the general reform action in the cities were the settlement house and the social worker. Social welfare functions in the cities had not improved much since the early part of the century and, it will be recalled, contemporary ideology did not hold with governmental "do-goodism." The gulf that had grown between popular governmental notions of how people should live and how, in fact, they did live was enormous. The great wave of immigrants after the turn of the century aggravated already horrible living conditions. An arm of the reform movement (still with us in slightly different form today) was the settlement movement. Houses in poor neighborhoods were set up as community

[9]See Lester W. Milbrath, *Political Participation: How and Why Do People Get Involved in Politics?* (Chicago: Rand-McNally, 1965).
[10]Gabriel A. Almond and Sidney Verba, *The Civic Culture* (Boston: Little, Brown, 1965), pp. 1–44.

centers, the idea being that the educated, middle-class staff, or "residents," might give aid to the needy. All kinds of social services today associated with government agencies were performed in settlement houses. One of the pioneers of the settlement house movement in the United States wrote a remarkable book describing a settlement career and providing insight into the reformist conception of social justice. Writing about what a settlement house and its staff (residents) should be like, Jane Addams had this to say in 1911:

> ... It [the settlement house]must be grounded in a philosophy whose foundation is on the solidarity of the human race, a philosophy which will not waver when the race happens to be represented by a drunken woman or an idiot boy. Its residents must be emptied of all conceit of opinion and all self-assertion, and ready to arouse and interpret the public opinion of their neighborhood. They must be content to live quietly side by side with their neighbors, until they grow into a sense of relationship and mutual interests. Their neighbors are held apart by differences of race and language which the residents can more easily overcome. They are bound to see the needs of their neighborhood as a whole, to furnish data for legislation, and to use their influence to secure it. In short, residents are pledged to devote themselves to the duties of good citizenship and to the arousing of the social energies which too largely lie dormant in every neighborhood given over to industrialism. They are bound to regard the entire life of the city as organic, to make an effort to unify it, and to protest its over-differentiation.[11]

Miss Addams's view of the purposes of social welfare activity reflected much of the general philosophical stand of the reformers. The call for influencing legislation and the need for reducing differences between neighboring groups, coupled with the implicit demand for "Americanization," is consistent with reform ideology. Also of interest is the suggestion for a professional and detached involvement on the part of the resident, or social worker, in dealing with the public. The professionalized settlement worker stands in sharp contrast to that "enemy of democracy," the machine politician with his personal favors and pay-offs for votes. Government, in the view of the settlement worker, had a responsibility to provide essential social services, rather than leave such activity solely to the politicians who were not only corruptive of civic virtue, but also inadequate to the task of providing properly for the needy.

Conflict between reform ideology and machine ideology was found on many fronts. It, like the battle with the trusts, continues in some interesting forms even today. As we proceed, we shall see how reform ideology and institutions restructured city hall. As we proceed even further, we shall see the efficient, specialized, bureaucratic agencies of government trying to overcome the virtues of impersonality, mass organization, specialization, and expertise in favor of neighborhood representation and personal citizen involvement. But the question before us at the moment is: What did the reformers do to city government and politics?

[11]Jane Addams, *Twenty Years at Hull House* (New York: Macmillan, 1911), pp. 126–127.

The Conquest of City Hall

The single best set of goal statements about municipal reform is to be found in the *Model City Charters* of the National Municipal League. The first of these was published in 1900 and was called *A Municipal Program.* The volume consists of a series of essays by various authors describing significant aspects of the program proposed. The 1900 *Program* was revised in 1916 and the *Model City Charter* with additions and revisions has been available ever since. The *Municipal Program* and its successors contained recommendations for reform of nearly every aspect of government. Some of the more significant changes advocated and widely adopted are reviewed here. A brief assessment of their effects follows.

Parties, Elections, and Representation

Electoral and representational forms constituted one of the primary targets for the reform assault. The reformers wanted at-large elections for city councilmen on a nonpartisan basis. The virtues of this were supposed to be numerous. The narrow interests represented by ward politicians would be destroyed because each candidate would have to run "on citywide issues." Special interest factions, such as ethnic groups and the poor, would have their representation diluted by at-large elections. A second target of the reformers was the political party. The parties were viewed by many reformers as media "for special-interest power; to strike at the special interests themselves involved some kind of change in the party system."[12] The change most often advocated by municipal reformers was nonpartisan elections. Under a nonpartisan electoral system, candidates were chosen in popular primaries and then ran without party label. In a 1952 evaluation of nonpartisan elections, Professor Charles R. Adrian argued that "all elections are partisan in the sense that people and groups take sides and struggle against one another for victory; and offices filled 'without party designation' are partisan enough according to this meaning."[13] Adrian offered a number of propositions about the effects of nonpartisanship based on a large number of existing studies.

> . . . Nonpartisanship serves to weaken the political parties in those areas where it is in effect.
> . . . The voting public views participation in partisan and nonpartisan elections as two different kinds of activities, independent of the other; and the nonpartisan office-holder is normally expected by the voting public to keep any party activity on his part separate from his role in nonpartisan office.
> . . . Channels for recruitment of candidates for partisan office are restricted by nonpartisanship.

[12]McConnell, *Private Power and American Democracy,* p. 42.
[13]C. R. Adrian, "Some General Characteristics of Nonpartisan Elections." *American Political Science Review,* 46 (September 1952), 766–776.

... Channels for recruitment of candidates for nonpartisan office are restricted by nonpartisanship.

... Limited new channels for recruitment of candidates for nonpartisan offices are opened by nonpartisanship.

... Segregation of funds for financing nonpartisan and partisan election campaigns is nearly complete.

... Facilities for fund-raising by candidates for non-partisan offices are restricted by nonpartisanship.

... Nonpartisanship encourages the avoidance of issues of policy in campaigns.

... Nonpartisanship tends to frustrate protest voting.

... Nonpartisanship produces a legislative body with a relatively high percentage of experienced members, making for conservatism.

... There is no collective responsibility in a nonpartisan body.[14]

The truly significant effects are long-range. As Adrian has suggested, the weakening of the party system permitted easier access into public office for "respectable businessmen" and other civic booster types. Strategies for election are dictated by the fact that the candidate does *not* try to please party adherents plus a few middle-of-the-roaders. On the contrary, the logic of the system dictates the blandest possible approach in order to garner as many votes as possible. This is especially true in at-large cities. The whole thrust of nonpartisanship is to lessen the possibility of neighborhoods and ethnic groups controlling legislators while substituting middle-class candidates capable of generating funds and support from private enterprise. Sharp issue orientation, protest voting, and the access provided in the elector-elected relationship suffer severely under nonpartisanship. In making the government official "independent," the system must sacrifice all those institutional points of potential coalition created and sustained by the parties.

Over 60 percent of cities with a population of 5,000 or more have nonpartisan electoral systems. Large cities and small are included in this number. Those cities with council-manager forms typically have at-large nonpartisan elections for council. The use of the term "nonpartisan" might suggest to the reader that no party politics occurs in a city with such a system: urban political systems adapt to nonpartisanship in a number of ways.[15] Adrian has suggested that cities called nonpartisan actually fall into three categories: those cities in which the parties exist on the local level, but fail to participate directly in local elections (Denver, Seattle, Cincinnati, and Kansas City); those in which the parties play no part at all but in which other "parapolitical" organizations either episodically or continually back candidates or issues (San Francisco, Detroit, Dallas, Fort Worth, and Flint); and finally, those cities in which neither parties nor local organizations play a continuing role. Mostly, as Banfield and Wilson suggest, these are small

---

[14] *Ibid.,* pp. 766–776.

[15] The discussion of types of nonpartisan cities relies heavily on C. R. Adrian, "A Typology of Nonpartisan Elections," *Western Political Quarterly* (June 1959), 449–458 and on the interpretation of Adrian in Banfield and Wilson, *City Politics,* pp. 151–152.

cities in which a candidate creates an organization simply for the purpose of his election. Of course, the term nonpartisan may refer to an electoral system that simply fails to show the party designation of the candidate on the ballot. Chicago is such a case and is hardly what one would call a city in which the Democratic party is not influential in local matters.

Nonpartisanship and at-large elections were two devices which, it was argued, would serve to stimulate an enlightened electorate to vote for men who had the best interests of the city as a whole at heart. Another way of looking at the reform efforts at structural revision is frankly Marxist: the actions of reformers in the electoral area served to disenfranchise the poor masses and place the formal powers of government into the hands of the managerial classes. Yet another view dismissed the others as too complicated for the problem at hand. Holders of this particular perspective of urban government argued that the main problems of the city were nonpolitical. The efficient use of resources converted into the most inexpensive services seemed to many to be the solution to the problem. In other words, let us keep politics out of municipal government. This mindless cliché typified (and still typifies) too much thinking about cities. It is reflected in almost all of the structural reforms found in contemporary cities. One version of such nonpolitical clichés is: How can you talk about a Republican or Democratic sewer? The answer suggested here is that any person engaged in the authoritative allocation of scarce public resources is engaged in politics, because resources do not tell people where they wish to be allocated. People tell other people where resources are going to be allocated. Thus Lasswell's question about "who gets what, when, why, where and how" does not become irrelevant at the city line. It does not matter that we call one person a "manager" and another a "politician" when we operate under this definition of politics. We have thus far discussed some of the sources of reform and have considered briefly some of the electoral or "input restructuring" created by the reform movement. But it was on the output end of things that the movement finally concentrated. It was the industrial management-scientific expertise image of government that the reformers were able to sell best.

The Creation of New Governmental Forms

The most general method for enforcing the value-premises of the reform movement involved the installation of new structures for government at the local level.[16] The creaky, confusing structures inherited by urban citizens of the early twentieth century were excellent targets for demolition. The Jacksonian spoils system, the Jeffersonian boards and commissions created out of a mistrust of

[16]A thorough description of the variety of municipal government structure can be found in Arthur W. Bromage, *Introduction to Municipal Government and Administration,* 2d ed. (New York: Appleton, 1957).

government, and a desire to split as many powers as possible—these plus the plundering of the bosses made the very outline of municipal government itself ripe for attack. Before proceeding to a description of the reform programs for governmental organization, we might review briefly the common structure of unreformed municipalities. Figure 4.1 illustrates an hypothetical governmental structure such as might have been found in any city in the early part of the century. (Those to whom Figure 4.1 looks familiar are either rather elderly or are living in a town that has a very old governmental structure).

The Old Structure

As can be readily seen from Figure 4.1, the structure of government is so fragmented that seemingly no single person or group could dominate it. The first built-in conflict is evident at the top of the diagram. Voters, by wards, elect a variety of officers of government on a so-called "long ballot" thus ensuring the "independence" of each elected official from the other. The four offices in the diagram are simply for illustration purposes; in most medium- and large-sized cities the string of offices would go right off the page. Attorney, solicitor, constable, sheriff, and dozens more might be included in weak-mayor cities.

A second problem of the weak-mayor city government is the characteristic overlapping of authority to hire, fire, and confirm, exercised by mayor and council. Administrative personnel as well as various board and commission members were never really certain whether they should fear intervention by the council or mayoral displeasure. The most common solution to problems arising from overlapping and conflicting chains of command is to remain immobile. This urban bureaucrats could do rather well, especially when their loyalty went to the people who got them their job or place on the ballot—the bosses.

If all of these checks and balances were not sufficient to bring about governmental immobility, then the third tier from the top usually was. Boards and commissions appointed by the mayor by and with the consent of the council (which usually had committees that substantively corresponded to the boards) were responsible for hiring, firing, and promoting people on the police force, the fire department, and the streets and public works department. There was little, short of taking court action, that a "clean" mayor could do about a corrupt police chief if the chief was in collusion with the police board.

Complicating matters even further were those boards and commissions that were creatures of the council. Those substantive areas of vital concern to the machine were frequently left to the council, a more predictable governmental organ than the mayoralty. Anything relating to the construction, demolition, or maintenance of buildings and other structures fell directly under the power of the council. It all looks rather cynical. Without knowing the history of America, one would think that Figure 4.1 might have been created by some evil genius intent on governing by default. By default we mean to suggest that such a divided

66

Figure 4.1
Weak-Mayor-and-Council Plan with Wards and Boards*

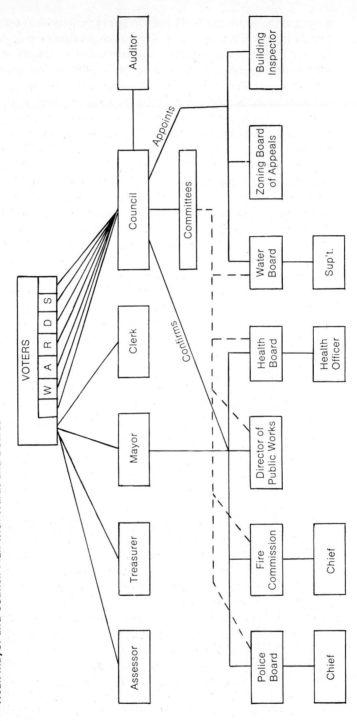

* Arthur W. Bromage, *Introduction to Municipal Government and Administration*, 2d ed. (New York: Appleton-Century-Crofts, 1957), p. 261.

governmental structure is essentially incapable of governing, to the point where central direction and responsibility for most actions are nonexistent. Yet all of the vast powers and prerogatives of government are lodged, however confusedly, within this ungainly structure. Who then could make all this cumbersome machinery work? The men who were responsible for obtaining the offices for the incumbents in the first place—the bosses.

The weak-mayor system perpetuated itself by growing horizontally over time. That is, whenever a new governmental function was to be performed, a new commission or board was created. All too frequently, the board members' terms overlapped the mayor's and often the council's, thus leaving them in the position of not being accountable to those who appointed them. Their allegiances frequently were located out of the governmental structure entirely. Many thought that there was wisdom in appointing leading citizens familiar with the substantive problems facing the board rather than just plain old political hacks. Thus, it might seem smart to appoint large real estate holders and mortgage bankers to zoning boards. Municipal government was a chaotic mess. Responsibility for and central direction of public policy was so hopelessly divided and confused as to be almost impossible to observe. When the system did work, it required an unthinkable amount of delay and discussion. Arthur W. Bromage summarizes one of the responses to this situation:

> Throwing the rascals out once in a city meant that it must be done over again. How to break this encirclement of the democratic process was the question. It was a better system that was needed, and the belief grew that responsibility should center in the mayor and that more power to control administration should be formally assigned to him by charter. An alert electorate would then, presumably, make certain that mayoral candidates should be honest and able. The short ballot, nonpartisan nomination and elections, election at large for councilmen were urged as means to break the grip of the boss.[17]

The Strong Mayor-Council Form

Figure 4.2 illustrates the formal structure of government most commonly found in big cities in the United States. The mayor ("strong mayor") in this scheme of organization is responsible for hiring and firing all operating department heads. The council in this system is weakened. It still controls budgetary approval and other fiscal matters, but it is out of the personnel business. The mayor is given powers analogous to the domestic ones of the president of the United States. He is independently elected and responsible to a constituency that is his alone. Under charters that grant cities a substantial amount of local autonomy ("home rule"), mayors hold strong legal positions that suggest vast power. Many factors limit these powers in practice. A thorough treatment of some of the major constraints

[17] *Ibid.*, p. 264.

Figure 4.2
Strong-Mayor-and-Council Plan with Integrated Administration*

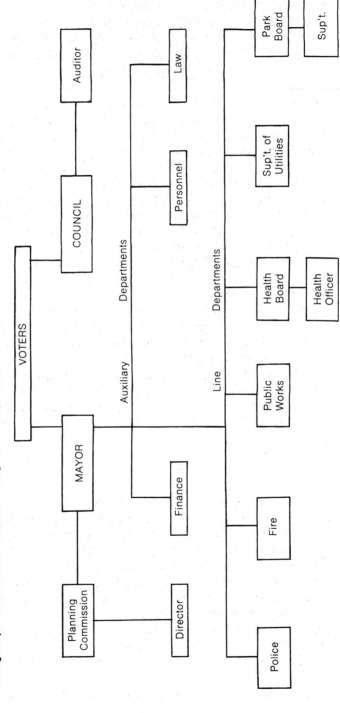

*Bromage, *Introduction to Municipal Government and Administration*, p. 265.

on executive powers in urban areas requires and deserves a more detailed consideration than possible at this point. It should be remembered, however, that the strong mayor reform movement was in many ways the least daring in that it upgraded an old office (the mayor) while maintaining many of the relics of the past.

The Commission Plan

A more unusual set of formal governmental reforms derived in part from the response by leading citizens of Galveston, Texas, to a tidal wave that killed over 6,000 people. The cataclysm occurred in 1900 and the existing governmental apparatus was incapable of reacting to it effectively. Out of the chaos of the disaster and after much fighting in the courts and in the legislature, Galveston set up the first commission plan of government. It seemed to eliminate many of the evils that had so upset reformers while providing the kind of leadership many thought would save municipal government. The commission form at one stroke eliminated the built-in conflicts of the mayor-council forms and established clear functional responsibility in the jobs of generally at-large elected officials, who in the Galveston case were "leading citizens of the community."

The commission form, as illustrated in Figure 4.3, fused administrative and legislative responsibility. Commissioners are elected at-large in most cases and frequently in nonpartisan elections. Commissions retain all the powers of a council, including taxation and budgetary powers as well as ordinance powers. Additionally, each commissioner is assigned a department or departments to supervise. Thus in Figure 4.3, Commissioner Number 3 is responsible for directing and supervising the bureaucracy that oversees street repairs, street lights, traffic signals, and perhaps runs the municipal water works.

The commission idea fused two strains of reformist thought. First, it was anticipated that men of substance and business experience could run governments. Because of the at-large and nonpartisan characteristics of most commission cities and towns, businessmen and professional people not ordinarily involved in ward politics would have an opportunity to compete successfully for office. Secondly, the "apolitical" commissioners would have the power and responsibility to put their managerial skills and public service desires to work. Government would become more efficient and less costly because of the fact that experienced managers would know how to provide the maximum high quality services at the least cost (as they were supposed to do in the business world). Of course, it was further assumed that the patronage and bribery costs of the old forms would be eliminated under the new plan. This latter assumption was borne out. Some of the others are open to question.

The commission form found a home in many small and medium-sized cities. It seems to have succeeded in middle-class cities and suburbs where social conflict has been minimal and one stratum of local society dominates in most areas. In

Figure 4.3
Commission Plan*

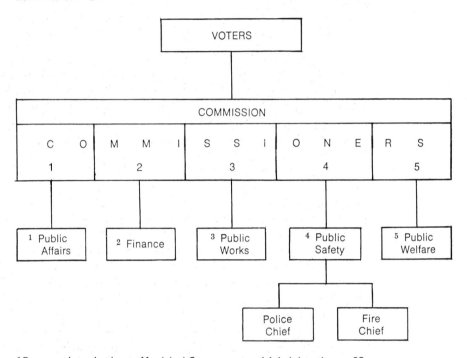

*Bromage, *Introduction to Municipal Government and Administration*, p. 28.

many ways the commission form is the oldest structure of local government in America, for it resembles most closely those governing bodies that prevailed in colonial times. The early councils chose one of their own to be mayor, but his powers were defined by the council and he could be replaced at any time. The real business of legislation and administration was conducted by the city councilmen.

The commission plan suffered from a number of internal defects as well as from problems arising out of the changing urban environment. The number of commissioners, their assigned departments, and the relationship between commissioners posed basic problems. Resting all responsibility in a commission allows for a lateral buck-passing not easily accomplished in other forms. Thus, while Commissioner Number 3 might be responsible for public works, the entire commission is responsible for his appropriation. Such an arrangement often led to coalition formation to the detriment of some departments and the benefit of others. Without central direction and responsibility for the budget, it was possible for whole areas, such as public welfare, to be ignored. Another difficulty arises when all of governmental responsibility is to be vested in a small number of commissioners (usually five). It is difficult to divide functions evenly. The result frequently left some commissioners more to do than others.

Factionalism, blurred responsibilities, and lack of coordination make the commission form of government difficult to operate, especially on a large scale. But the central problem of the commission form is one that affects all local and urban government. How, given the increasing complexity of governmental operations, can government by amateurs be sustained? One of the enduring myths of American government is that any reasonable, honest, well-informed person can, with similiar people, run a government. The commission plan seemed to be a return to that old and powerful notion. At the same time (paradoxically) it stood in seeming opposition to another belief that is very important in American society —the specialist-expert myth. This article of popular faith suggests that if we simply train enough experts in the complex business of government, then "politics" and "inefficiency" will disappear. The commission plan as described here runs right at that argument in that it implicitly suggests that talented amateurs are the best people to run governments. It seems clear at this point that many of those who had great hopes for the commission plan as a managerial or administrative system have been disappointed. The talented amateurs were simply not up to confronting the technical problems of growing urban areas. Most commissioners were not and could not become expert in such fields as health, sanitation, engineering, and other areas requiring specialized education and training. The commissioners simply could not be familiar enough with these fields to act as true administrative managers. As the tasks of government grew more various and specialized, the most talented amateur had to be left behind. The commission plan was simply one reform proposal that served to dramatize the conflict between our belief in the informed citizen and our faith in specialization and expertise. That basic problem is still with us and appears to be arising in the urban areas with ever greater ferocity.

The Manager

One of the important structural ways of dealing with this and other problems of government is to be found in yet another reform innovation—the manager. The manager is a professional administrative generalist charged with the supervision of all the executive functions of government. He is a professional who is hired by the council. He has no political identification and is normally expected not to be tied to the city or town by previous residence or other past connection. The International City Managers Association functions as a professional base for the manager. His loyalty is to his profession, not to a particular local political system. He serves at the pleasure of the council that contracts for his services.

The manager plan seemed to be the answer to many of the problems of boss dominated, weak-mayor systems. It also appeared to correct some of the faults apparently inherent in the commission form. The role of the manager is supposed to be strictly construed. He is not supposed to be a policy maker, although how to define that term may not be as simple a matter as Bromage suggests it is:

> As a major function, the manager advises the council on policies in process of formulation or revision. Ordinances are usually prepared for the council by the legal staff after consultation with departments under the manager's eye. In financial matters, the manager is charged with preparation of the annual budget for presentation to the council, and he depends upon the budget director, who may be responsible directly to him or to the head of the finance department. The manager keeps the council aware through regular and special reports of the general condition of affairs in the city.
> Because the manager lays alternative suggestions before the council does not mean that he makes policy. He is doing the necessary staff work, and if he does not underline a proposed policy with facts and figures, councilmen are not likely to be favorably disposed. They can always modify or reject any proposition he submits. He advises, but they establish policy. A manager's proposed budget gives the outline for the ensuing fiscal year, yet decision on that budget is up to the council. If a manager appeals to voters over the heads of councilmen or in actual opposition to them, then he is attempting to make policy; but an adept executive may, without transgressing, push a council forward. The initiative of the one to propose is as important as the authority of the other to accept or reject.[18]

As Figure 4.4 indicates, the manager is responsible for running the city. He functions much as a mayor would in a strong-mayor system, with the exception that he has no constituency other than the council that contracted for his services. It is sometimes suggested that the relationship between council and manager is analogous to that of a board of directors and the president of a corporation. In some ways the analogy fits. In most council-manager cities all formal powers of policy making are concentrated in the council, avoiding the divisions found in the old weak-mayor system. The pitfalls of centralizing legislative and administrative roles, found in the commission plan, are avoided by the creation of the manager's job. Nonpartisanship, at-large voting, and the short ballot are almost always found in council-manager cities. The idea of a nonpolitical manager running the day-to-day operations of the city has also been adapted to large cities that operate under a strong-mayor system. Philadelphia's Home Rule Charter of 1952, for instance, establishes a strong-mayor system with a "managing director" appointed by the mayor. He is responsible for managing the day-to-day operations of the "line" departments of the city.

The manager plan has been one of the enduring successes of the reform movement. It, and the procedural details associated with reform, proved effective against the old machines. The governmental mechanisms created and sustained by the move to "nonpolitical" bureaucracies may not be quite as relevant to

[18] *Ibid.,* pp. 296–297.

Figure 4.4
The Council-Manager Plan*

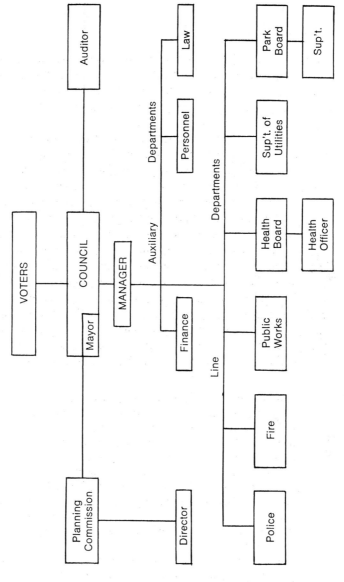

* Bromage, *Introduction to Municipal Government and Administration*, p. 295.

modern urban society as the reformers would have hoped. Table 4.1 illustrates the wide extent of the new reform structures. In form, they dominate American urban government.

The reform movement succeeded in changing the overall shape of government in urban areas. The forms of government under which we live in contemporary cities and suburbs can in large measure be explained as products of the reform movement. As such, many of these structures, and the procedural changes that went along with them, put formal governmental powers into the hands of the rising middle classes of the early twentieth century. These formal powers were taken from a political system based on a conspiratorial relationship between some of the very wealthy and a hierarchically arranged mass of politicians organized

Table 4.1
Form of Government in Cities over 5,000 Population

Classification	No. of Cities Reporting	Mayor-Council Number	Percent	Council-Manager Number	Percent	Commission Number	Percent
Population Group	27	22[1]	81.5	5	18.5	. . .	. . .
Over 500,000	27	11	40.7	13	48.2	3	11.1
250,000 to 500,000	93	33	35.5	50	53.8	10	10.7
100,000 to 250,000	215	83	38.6	116	54.0	16	7.4
50,000 to 100,000	439	166	38.2	233	53.6	40	9.2
25,000 to 50,000	1,072	511	47.7	488	45.5	73	6.8
10,000 to 25,000	1,112	686	61.7	378	34.0	48	4.3
5,000 to 10,000							
Type of City							
Central	266	111[1]	41.7	126	47.4	29	10.9
Suburban	1,385	717	51.8	605	43.7	63	4.5
Independent	1,334	684	51.3	552	41.4	98	7.3
Geographic Division							
New England	138	80	58.0	56	40.6	2	1.4
Middle Atlantic	598	387	64.7	155	25.9	56	9.4
East North Central	647	432	66.8	190	29.4	25	3.8
West North Central	308	175	56.8	100	32.5	33	10.7
South Atlantic	352	117[1]	33.2	225	63.9	10	2.9
East South Central	170	108	63.5	29	17.1	33	19.4
West South Central	305	109	35.7	180	59.0	16	5.3
Mountain	137	62	45.3	70	51.1	5	3.3
Pacific	330	42	12.7	278	84.3	10	3.0
No. cities over 5,000	2,985[2]	1,513[1]	50.6	1,283	43.0	190	6.4

[1] Includes the District of Columbia.
[2] Not included in this table are 89 places with town meeting government and 38 with representative town meeting government.
SOURCE: International City Managers' Association, *Municipal Yearbook 1968*, p. 54.

into a "machine." We have reviewed some of the devices employed by the reformers to change government to conform to their views of "proper" political relations. What were some of the important events associated with the downfall of the machine and the victory of reform structure?

Three "Handmaidens" of Reform

Three major events are discussed here which, it is argued, are central to an explanation of the crumbling of the machine. These are: the tremendous growth of upwardly mobile "respectables," the children of the immigrant population; the destruction of the "informal welfare system" of the bosses and the subsequent nationalization of welfare; and finally, the creation of urban "meritocracies" to replace the patronage structures so vital to the machine.

The Americanization of the Immigrant

The Americanization of the first and second generation children of the immigrant population took place rapidly. While ethnic identity lasted much longer in politics than almost any one had anticipated,[19] a pattern of upward mobility closely associated with physical mobility took place.[20] The school systems of the cities were in the hands of reformers or teachers sympathetic to reform. Civic books, histories, and the general content of magazines and newspapers associated the machine with ignorance, criminality, and "dirty politics." In short, machines, machine politicians, and the old neighborhood reminded many a recently minted Yankee of things about his past he might not have wished to remember. The machine failed to attract young people while the reformers were able to convince millions that respectability, moral rightness, and the American way were on their side.

As the offspring of the immigrants moved up to a better economic position in the country, they more or less naturally assumed many of the values of their superiors, those who had "made it." Such moves upward usually involved physical moves away from "the ghetto" or "little Italy" into new neighborhoods quickly abandoned by the previous occupants. Changes in occupation, education, income, and residence occurred rapidly for the children and grandchildren of the immigrants. These changes, for many people, were accompanied by changes in dress, custom, language, and values. The machine politician had nothing but

---

[19]See Nathan Glazer and Daniel P. Moynihan, *Beyond the Melting Pot: The Negroes, Puerto Ricans, Jews, Italians and Irish of New York City* (2d ed.; Cambridge, Mass.: M.I.T. Press. 1970) for an argument sustaining this point.
[20]See Samuel Lubell, *The Future of American Politics* (New York: Harper & Row, 1952), pp. 75–80 for the "Jacob's Ladder" argument.

embarrassment to offer the children of his supporters. The leadership of the urban machines aged and was not replaced by a new generation.

Despite this gradual loss of support, the machines were not particularly disturbed by the activities of the reformers. Reformers could only occasionally ignite enough righteous indignation in voters to cause them to throw the rascals out. They usually remained out for only a few years and returned easily when things cooled off. The battle between the reformers and the machine politicians was an off and on affair in many of the big cities. Machines did rather well during the 1920s despite growing reform activity and a failure to replace old pols with young pols. Time was on the side of the reformers, especially after the events of 1929.

The Nationalization of Welfare

No governmental structure was prepared for anything like the Great Depression. Welfare systems were predicated on eighteenth-century poorhouse legislation. The federal government had no welfare to speak of. The consequences of unemployment and hard times were the province of the local settlement houses, charitable organizations, and most importantly, the machine politician. At first the machines were able to meet the demands of rising unemployment. By the first few years of the decade, however, the disaster that had befallen the nation in general hit the machines particularly hard. Tax revenues could barely support city employees and there was no money to let contracts. There were no jobs, favors, or money to be had. The sack of coal, the bag of groceries once so freely given, now were not to be found at all. The small-time ward politician was as much a victim as was his neighborhood. The machines foundered as badly as the governments that normally hosted them.

The New Deal Democrats of 1933 set about the job of recovery without much concern for the bosses. Franklin D. Roosevelt created national bureaucracies that co-opted some of the traditional roles of machines and governments. Millions of jobs were provided by the federal government, usually without consultation of the local bosses. A national system of social security providing retirement benefits, burial insurance, and unemployment compensation was created, thus undercutting some of the basic social functions of the ward politician. At the same time, the New Deal Democrats legitimized and encouraged organized labor to such a degree that the leverage of the local machine was barely on a par with the UAW or the gentlemen from the Building Trades Union. The unions told the contractors how many men were needed. If they did not quite do that, they at least designated *which* men were to work on which job under what conditions and for what pay. The machines were faced with new competitors who could simply overrun them. The primacy of mass issues and mass politics at the national level became apparent in the 1930s. The New Deal Democrats did more to destroy the machines (mainly Democratic) than all the reformers and Progressives put together. They simply outbid the machines in providing services to the urban masses.

The federal presence in the cities has continued to grow since the New Deal era. The Community Action Program of the War on Poverty, a case of major importance to understanding contemporary urban politics, is in many ways an extension of the pattern begun in 1933. Urban political systems themselves appear to be (at least to some officials in Washington) stumbling blocks in the way to a series of true national urban policies. The matter of relations between the various political systems affecting urban political life is discussed more thoroughly in succeeding chapters. The point here is that as systems become more interdependent, unanticipated consequences and instabilities result. Relations between cities, suburbs, and Washington since 1933 have continued to alter the basic structure of all three political systems.

Meritocracy

Civil service reform had been one of the great successes of the reform movement at the national level. The Pendleton Act of 1883 was followed by similar legislation in New York State in 1894. With varying effects, civil service reform spread throughout municipalities until by World War II, few towns and cities of any size were without local civil service commissions. Today the urban centers of the country have very few jobs not under civil service regulations. There are roughly 1.5 million municipal employees covered by civil service systems. Those patronage jobs left are usually so menial and financially unrewarding as to be more like penalties than benefits.

The urban bureaucracies grew as the functions of government expanded and became more complex. The era when any amateur could be expected to operate in any governmental capacity has given way to a time of increasing specialization of task. Modern government at any level is administrative. This is particularly so in a service-oriented governmental unit. The whole thrust of late nineteenth- as well as twentieth-century culture leads in the direction of specialization and expertise. Civil service reform in the urban areas fulfilled reformers' faith in the rightness of these two requisites for "good government." There is today, with the development of personnel departments acting as the administrative organs of civil service commissions, a specific description and entrance requirement for nearly every job imaginable. The business of classifying jobs and creating tests for admission and promotion has become an important subfunction of government.

The significance of urban bureaucracy grows almost daily as more and more governmental tasks are assumed by permanent civil servants. The point here is that civil service reform and the development of permanent urban bureaucracies staffed by people who do not "relate" to the machine politician destroyed yet another structure of machine support.

Battles Won, Wars Lost: The Reformers and the Machines

Slowly at first, and then in the late 1930s very quickly, the machines lost some of the principal foundations of their support. The 1920s saw the beginning of a trend that would ultimately have great effect on all of city life, especially urban political life. The automobile and the trolley line brought the country to the city. Mass suburbia was born, and after the disastrous decade of the 1930s it began to blossom with exurbanites. Potential political leaders left for the suburbs, upwardly mobile machine supporters became reform-minded or indifferent, money and jobs dried up or went into more powerful hands (the state and national governments), and finally the machine simply failed to keep up with the needs of a changing society. Neighborhoods that seemed always to have been stable changed overnight. New people arrived and departed almost before politicians could find them. Anonymity grew despite an informal political structure dedicated to personal relationships. Thus, in part, the "victory" of the reformers over the machines was as much a function of inevitable social change as anything else.

How is the long war between reformers and the machine to be summarized? Indeed, it might well be asked, "Is the fight over?" If one were to look only at the laws and charters of American cities and suburbs, one might conclude that the reformers won, insofar as their aim was to change the structure of government. Yet, it must be remembered that one of the reform aims was to foster widespread participation in the local political process. This has not come about and does not appear to be in the offing, at least in the traditional sense understood by the reformers.[21] Is government less corrupt? All in all, local government is probably as honest as the reformers had any reason to hope it could be. Widespread municipal corruption is pretty much a thing of the past, although organized crime (a phenomenon more or less unknown to the old reformers) still probably enjoys a more comfortable relationship with local government than one would hope for. While traditional kinds of vice in their centralized forms may be disappearing (the house of prostitution, gambling dens, and so on), crime in the cities is still with us. The social ills to be remedied show few signs of disappearing under the new governments.

Machines died hard in some cities. Traces of their structure and of their functions still may be found in some supposedly "reformed" cities. Some of the old politicians were able to weather the reform era and adapt successfully to the modern conditions of urban political life. Mayor Daley's Chicago was the outstanding example of this. The traditional forms of political organization in the big cities have successfully resisted reform efforts at "democratization."[22] In some cities, old functions of the machine were adopted by the new governments.

[21]Robert R. Alford and Eugene C. Lee, "Voting Turnout in American Cities." *American Political Science Review*, 62 (September 1968), 796–814.
[22]See James Q. Wilson, *The Amateur Democrat* (Chicago: University of Chicago Press, 1962) for a description and analysis of reform political clubs in the three largest cities.

In Philadelphia, the new city charter, adopted in 1952 after six or seven decades of Republican machine rule, had to be amended to create an agency to meet some of the needs formerly satisfied by the old ward politicians. A "Mayor's Office for Information and Complaints" attempts to provide some of the services formerly handled as favors by precinct and ward politicians. Traces of machine forms still exist but they are only shadows of their ancestors. Can we conclude from this that urban government in the traditional sense dominates urban political life? Almost without exception, the answer is "no."

A long report in a popular magazine a while ago dealt with the reasons mayors leave city hall.[23] The author interviewed four big-city mayors who were leaving office after beginning their incumbency as "new" strong mayors. The gist of what really drove them out of their "reformed" governmental positions is summarized by Jerome Cavanagh, former Mayor of Detroit:

> It is expected that the mayor deal with crisis day after day. And this is one of the major factors contributing to the tremendous physical and mental frustration which eventually wears guys down in these jobs after eight years. You can't sit and think about what you should be doing in this city five years from now, or ten years from now, because you're dealing with the politics of confrontation constantly. It's the only political job in America in which that's true. That's the job. It's fine to deal with crisis and confrontation if you have resources to meet them. But when all you have is a limited amount of money and a few programs, and you're on rhetoric, that just isn't enough.[24]

Perhaps with some ironic understatement one could fairly conclude that while reformed governmental structure effectively dealt with some of the perceived evils of the past, it has been less than perceptive in dealing with and anticipating present difficulties. Put in stronger language, there is a growing feeling that urban governmental structure is barely relevant to the systemic changes confronting it. The reformers won by their own efforts and with the luck provided them by the Great Depression. Ultimately the conditions of life to which the machine related so successfully changed. The world envisioned by the reform movement never came to be. Modern urban government, despite numerous efforts to impose rationality upon it, is more confused in some very basic ways than the old hodgepodge of municipal government of the nineteenth century.

Government has grown laterally in a manner very much reminiscent of the nineteenth century. Boards, commissions, and semiautonomous bureaucracies, usually created by and responsible to nonlocal governments, bypass local government. As we shall see in following chapters, the cities in a sense have become too important to be left to the complete control of their residents. The problems of the central cities and their surrounding surburbs are *the* domestic problems of the American political system. It is easy to paint a picture of such confusion and

---

[23]Fred Powledge, "The Flight from City Hall," *Harper's*, November 1969, pp. 69–86.
[24]*Ibid.*, pp. 69–70.

diffusion of power, responsibility, and authority that the study of urban politics becomes either an exercise in futility or a series of human interest stories. Such resignation may be tempting, but it begs some of the important questions about political systems that may lead to insights about cities.

Throughout our description of urban political systems of the past, common themes occur that are of more than passing interest for the contemporary social scientist. Groups conflict over the values of society. The instruments of power are real and their use has demonstrable effect on the physical character of the city as well as on the conduct of our everyday "apolitical" life. The machine was founded on and sustained by one set of social mechanisms. It helped to maintain a set of relationships in society and to set a course for the development of the modern American city. The reformers had similar effects. Both the reformers and the machine left a substantial inheritance that permeates contemporary political culture and thought. Our study of the machines and the reformers suggests that the formal organization charts governments and civics books employ to describe governments and political systems impart only one kind of knowledge—knowledge of how a government says it works. All of us know, though, that it is a popular American pastime to guess at how things really work. Who really runs the city? Who has *real* power and how is it employed? Indeed, what do we mean by power?

The social sciences have been trying to provide answers to these and related questions of interest for about fifty years. In the next section of this book, three models are presented in the attempt to recombine the variety of answers to the question: "Who really runs things in town?" The significance of the question cannot be easily overestimated. This is an age in which those who control the powers of the state control increasing portions of our daily lives.

Suggested Readings

Bromage, Arthur W., *Introduction to Municipal Government and Administration* (New York: Appleton, 1957).

Hofstadter, Richard, *The Age of Reform from Bryan to FDR* (New York: Knopf, 1955).

Kolko, Gabriel, *The Triumph of Conservatism: A Reinterpretation of American History 1900–1916* (New York: Free Press, 1963).

McConnell, Grant, *Private Power and American Democracy* (New York: Knopf, 1967).

Pease, Otis A., ed., *The Progressive Years* (New York: G. Braziller, 1962).

Schiesl, Martin, *The Politics of Efficiency: Municipal Administration and Reform in America, 1800–1920* (Berkeley, University of California Press, 1977).

Steffens, Lincoln, *The Shame of the Cities* (New York: Hill & Wang, 1957).

Part II

The Structure of Political Power in Urban Systems

Chapter 5

Locating Power
in Urban Areas

Introduction

The central concern of Part II in this text is the question: "Who has power in the urban political system?" Unfortunately for students of politics who thought that they at last had a direct and straightforward question with which to deal, things are not so simple. The concept of power itself as well as its location in cities and towns has been (and continues to be) a subject of intense discussion and controversy among social scientists.

The term "power" is one that is employed in everyday usage with common understandings so vague and variable as to make an effort at a specific definition necessary at this point. There is an impressive and lengthy literature on the subject which we cannot even briefly summarize here.[1] Our own definition however relies upon much of this literature.

We define political power as *conflict and cooperation over the allocation of scarce public resources. Such conflict and cooperation takes place between actors who are understood to be individuals, groups, organizations, and institutions. Scarce public resources are those objects of competition and cooperation that give their possessor(s) the ability to direct some part or all of the political system in accordance with their desires.*

Examples of scarce public resources are votes, money, formal status and symbolic goods including loyalties and selflessness. Laws, regulations, customs, or procedures that inhibit, expand, or in some way define the boundaries of the decision-making that affects the allocation of scarce public resources are themselves scarce and therefore *valuable.* To control or direct the employment of these public resources directly or indirectly is to have that capability we call political power.

The search for the meaning and location of political power is of course an

---

[1]On the definition of political power see generally: Robert A. Dahl, *Modern Political Analysis* (Englewood Cliffs, N.J.: Prentice-Hall, 1963); David Easton, *A Systems Analysis of Political Life* (New York: John Wiley & Sons, 1965); Harold D. Lasswell, *Power and Society* (New Haven: Yale University Press, 1950); Andrew S. McFarland, *Power and Leadership in Pluralist Systems* (Stanford, Cal.: Stanford University Press, 1969).

ancient one and we do not imply that our definition makes any great contribution to that endeavor. It is however justifiable and, more importantly, leads us into a consideration of two schools of thought which traditionally have dominated the search for political power in the urban political system.

It is too easy for the student of politics to assume that the conflict between elitists and pluralists outlined in this chapter is a product of scholastic confusion. It is not. Indeed, the analysis of power and its location and distribution is one of the key debates implicitly carried on by political actors in everyday life. The outcome of such implicit debates materially affects all of us in a variety of ways. Our own contribution to the discussion, contained in the last two chapters of this section, recombines some aspects of elitist and pluralist thought according to what we believe to be the practical conditions of modern urban political systems. First however, we turn to a graphic example of the importance of locating community power.

The Location of Political Power and the Decline of New York City

The critical question about American cities is no longer simply "Who governs?" but more to the point in many cities, "Who would want to govern?" Apparently there will always be a sufficient number of public-spirited and egoistic men and women to fill municipal posts, but *control of the city* (if the phrase can still be used) is no longer the shining prize it once was. Figures 5.1a, b, and c show in unfortunate detail the formidable problems facing the leaders of one major city, New York. The odds do not seem to favor even the best-equipped, most virtuous mayor or council member in a city with problems such as New York's.[2]

But New York, for one, was not always so wretched. At one time it had an unemployment rate lower than the rest of the United States and the lion's share of the Fortune "500" companies. Certainly, its decline is not due in any significant way to a particular leader or elite. The massive migrations of the poor from the South and from the Caribbean had little to do with policies made locally. However, New York is not unique in being influenced by pressures beyond its own control. What is unique about New York is its scale. We chose New York to consider the question of power location because its scale allows a view of events and crises that few other cities afford. There is more reportage, documentation,

---

[2]The impact of the fiscal crisis on various aspects of urban politics is the concern of an expanding body of literature. In this volume, the question of fiscal constraint is discussed in terms of community power in the case of New York City and more extensively in the consideration of intergovernmental relations in chap. 10 and in each of the metropolitan case studies in chap. 11. Among works examining the fiscal crisis are the following: Roy Bahl, ed., *The Fiscal Outlook for Cities* (Syracuse, N.Y.: Syracuse University Press, 1978); David Mermelstein and Roger Alcaly, *The Fiscal Crisis of American Cities* (New York: Random House, 1977); Thomas Muller, *Growing and Declining Urban Areas: A Fiscal Comparison* (Washington, D.C.: Urban Institute, 1975); Jack Newfield and Paul A. Dubrul, *The Abuse of Power* (New York: Penguin, 1978); and Robert B. Pettengill and J.S. Uppal, *Can Cities Survive?* (New York: St. Martin's Press, 1974).

and scrutiny of formal and informal public activity in New York than in any other American city. If the exercise of power is centered anywhere, it should be apparent in New York. Did anyone, any leader or group, guide New York toward bankruptcy? And more important to our discussion, how much political power over municipal affairs have the people of New York had and how much have they retained?

There are a variety of potential explanations for any fiscal crisis (shortfall of spendable revenue). The crisis in New York filled volumes of newsprint with speculation, charges, and countercharges. The crisis was variously caused by greedy, self-interested bankers, unreasonable unions, departing corporate leaders, or incompetent public officials. Out of the sound and fury came a few clear voices; one belongs to Martin Shefter who provides an analysis of the general causes of municipal fiscal decline. As Shefter describes the circumstances of decline, they combine elements of elite dominance together with increasing interest-group pressure and a large measure of uncertainty. The most important circumstances are the following:

Figure 5.1 a–c
The Decline of the New York City Public Economy*

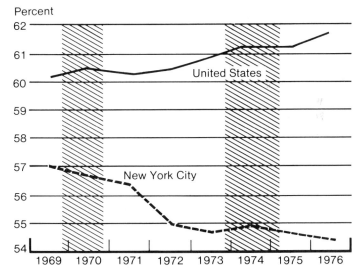

Figure 5.1a Civilian Labor Force Participation Rates

Shaded areas represent periods of recession as defined by the National Bureau of Economic Research.

Source: United States Bureau of Labor Statistics.

*Rona B. Stein, "New York City's Economy: A Perspective on Its Problems," *Federal Reserve New York*, Summer 1977, pp. 49–59.

Figure 5.1b Retail Sales

Seasonally adjusted; * 1973 = 100

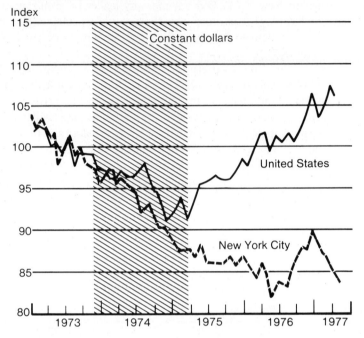

Shaded area represents the latest period of recession as defined by the National Bureau of Economic Research.

*New York City data were seasonally adjusted by the Federal Reserve Bank of New York.

Sources: Retail sales from the United States Department of Commerce. Sales were converted to constant dollars by using the commodity sectors of the consumer price indexes issued by the United States Bureau of Labor Statistics for the United States and for the New York – Northeastern New Jersey area.

1. A social group that has recently gained political power begins to assert claims upon the government for greater public benefits.
2. The government responds to these claims either because it is allied with the group in question or because it cannot withstand its opposition.
3. The government is too weak politically to finance these new claims by reducing the flow of benefits to other groups, or by raising taxes.[3]

[3]Martin Shefter, "New York City's Fiscal Crisis: The Politics of Inflation and Retrenchment," *The Public Interest* (1977), p. 99; much of this section relies upon Shefter's insightful analysis.

Figure 5.1c Unemployment Rates

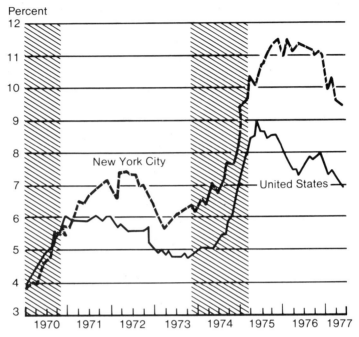

Seasonally adjusted *

Percent

Shaded areas represent periods of recession as defined by the
National Bureau of Economic Research.

*New York City data were seasonally adjusted by the Federal
Reserve Bank of New York.

Sources: United States Bureau of Labor Statistics and New York
State Department of Labor.

Events leading up to the crisis in New York followed this pattern fairly
closely. What Shefter shows us is that the loose coalition of ethnic and business
interests that was held together by Tammany Hall for over a century is as close
to a "locus" (or seat) of power as New York has ever had. The balance, however,
was very fragile and had come apart several times before; first, during the 1870s
when the Tweed Ring's corruption surpassed its ability to govern, and second,
during the Great Depression when a fragmented Tammany leadership declared
"open-season" on the city treasury. In both cases we find that a crisis is sparked
by one or another of the coalition who are not benefiting from the contemporary
distribution of benefits. In 1870 the out-group was the city's creditors who got
tired of financing the Tweed Ring. In the 1930s the out-group was the upwardly
mobile ethnics who called themselves reformers and came into power with Fi-

orello LaGuardia in 1933. This odd combination of ethnic groups, banks, business leaders, and municipal bureaucrats does not easily fit into either of the two categories of community power that we will discuss further on. From some angles it appears as if a small group of anxious bankers call the shots, but from other angles it looks as if ambitious ethnics have the upper hand. What the New York example shows is that the major schools of thought on the location of community power are largely matters of perspective—change your angle of vision and the location of power will change as well.

By the late 1950s the game in New York City was to get an angle on the center of power by building up credit with the incumbent mayor or a likely challenger. The game caught on, and Mayor Robert Wagner found that in order to win reelection in 1961 he would have to make promises to the traditional Democratic coalition and also to the school integration movement and the new movement to unionize city employees. As Wagner found out quite soon, these promises could be kept only by overspending the city budget, which he did in 1961 and in each subsequent year of his third term.

The administration of John Lindsay brought several additional groups into the coalition; most prominently, blacks and the generally disadvantaged. For the period 1966 to 1971, so many high-demand groups were in the coalition that there evolved spending increases of 251 percent for higher education, 225 percent for welfare, and 123 percent for public hospitals.[4] The entire public economy had grown enormously, very quickly, and the first serious challenge it had to face, the national economic recession of the mid-1970s, nearly proved fatal. The demand of coalition members did not abate and there seemed no easy place to *start* cutting the budget that would not result in charges of broken faith. So city officials went to the state legislature for increased taxing authority and to the banks for extension and expansion of bonding authority. Shefter summarizes what happened next:

> The Republican state senators for New York City banded together in May 1975, and agreed to present a common front against the pressure from their party leaders and colleagues to vote for legislation granting additional taxing authority to the city. The refusal of these spokesmen for the city's taxpayers to consent to any new taxes increased the city's demand for credit, and thereby weakened the market for New York City securities. Later that month, the major New York banks refused to underwrite or purchase any more New York City notes and bonds, and thereby drove the city to the verge of bankruptcy.[5]

These events have changed the location of power in New York considerably. In fact, it may no longer be accurate to speak of power being located in New York. State budget reviews and congressional loan guarantees have replaced the old coalition. The inescapable conclusion is that whether elitist or pluralist, the local

[4]*Ibid.,* p. 107.
[5]*Ibid.,* pp. 110–111.

power base—the connection between taxpayers and tax spenders—is gone. Political power in New York City has reached a postcommunity stage, since critical spending decisions are no longer purely local matters.

But until the eleventh hour, New York was not considered to be in terribly serious trouble. A major study of the city's governance by Wallace Sayre and Herbert Kaufman—published in 1960—found a functioning, pluralistic system, and thereafter an expanding coalition was taken as a sign of improved urban democracy.[6] The way the city is considered—the angle that is used to study it —can have an influence on the way it is governed. If life can imitate art, it can also verify scholarship. We now turn to the two major schools of community power scholarship as they have become perspectives on the American city.

The Status of the Debate on Community Power

The debate between elitists and pluralists that has waxed and waned now for a generation has, in several important ways, become either sterile or irrelevant— or so thoroughly qualified as to make the distinctions blur in the eyes of those new to the conflict. C. Wright Mills, a prominent elite theorist, was reinterpreted and suitably qualified by Prewitt and Stone in 1973:

> In using the term "political elite", we do not imply that the members of this elite are all-powerful. The decisions they make may regularly reflect the preferences of the broad public as those preferences have been expressed through the democratic channels of elections, individual petitioning, and organized pressure. The amount of power in the hands of the elite is a matter of analysis, not definition. Neither do we imply that the political elite is a cohesive group and like-minded on all major issues. . . . Conflicting career ambitions necessarily lessen the cohesion of any elite group. Just as the "power" of the elites is an issue for empirical investigation, so is the "cohesion" of elites. *What is assumed in our analysis is the presence of an elite.* The power to influence political, social, economic, religious, artistic, and educational events is not equally distributed across the entire society. Some citizens have enormously more powers than do other citizens.[7] [Emphasis added]

Thus elites vary in power as to sphere or realm and as to intensity as well. They also may accurately reflect broad public preferences from time to time. Their degree of internal cohesion as well as their power to allocate scarce public resources varies between elites contemporaneously as well as over time. But in the end, the basic assumption is that some citizens, by virtue of birth, merit, or luck, have access to substantially greater resources than do others. Furthermore, these resources (when employed in concert with others similarly placed) provide a source of political power unrivaled by any other structure of state and society.

[6]Wallace S. Sayre and Herbert Kaufman, *Governing New York City: Politics in the Metropolis* (New York: Russell Sage Foundation, 1960).
[7]Kenneth Prewitt and Alan Stone, *The Ruling Elites; Elite Theory, Power and American Democracy* (New York: Harper & Row, 1973), p. 132.

Although it is important to know of Hunter's work in Atlanta and of the great and sophisticated defense of the ideological beliefs and beliefs about research made by Robert Dahl and his followers at Yale University, there is now a sense in which the political world has outdistanced the debate. This is not to suggest that the two schools of thought are not worth understanding, but rather that one think in terms of combination and areas of overlap. Some of this is reflected in the quotation above. It is also emphasized in chapters 6 and 7.

The view of Prewitt and Stone, as well as some of the second-generation pluralists, suggest that the object of study has itself shifted and that social scientists must heed that shift or be left hopelessly arguing about material conditions that have vanished. The Muncie of the Lynds is no more, and the Atlanta of today (however described) bears little relation to the Atlanta of nearly thirty years ago. Dahl's New Haven has similarly been transformed. Although we have something to say about these classics in the pages that follow, it must be kept in mind that there is a set of common questions which transcends the specifics of the arguments while still being very much rooted in them.

The questions are not only definitional and specific. They are also politically contested matters of great importance to people in the social world. The concepts of power, representation, influence, legitimacy, responsiveness, and participation are much more than mere symbols to be variously defined by social scientists in order to strengthen a particular thesis. Such terms and their authoritative "ownership" by political actors constitute potent resources. To define a situation as "unrepresentative and unresponsive" in a political context tells both the audience and the participants something about the drama that is about to unfold. That drama, we will argue, occurs daily in courts, legislatures, boardrooms, and on the streets in front of television cameras. So we tread carefully when, for instructive and analytical purposes, we define political power as a *relationship latent or manifest, which involves the allocation of scarce public resources or private resources which affect some public action or enterprise.* Clearly we wish to focus as much as possible on the *conflict and cooperation over the allocation of scarce public resources which takes place between powerful political actors,* because this constitutes a definition of politics for us. We are, moreover, left unconstrained to limit the place of political action to the traditional institutions and functions of the state.

It is particularly important not to limit the physical or conceptual scope of one's idea of politics and political power when thinking about urban politics. This is so for a number of reasons, not the least of which is the material fact that as time passes, more and more supposedly external forces become crucial political actors in the urban political system. By supposedly external, we do not suggest only such actors as local bankers and the PTA. We also mean the President of the United States (e.g. the case of the New York City fiscal crisis), or the horde of federal and state agencies with jurisdictions that overlap and conflict with local political and administrative agencies. We will make clear, moreover, that the concepts mentioned above and many of the ideas of the elitists and the pluralists are helpful in analysis of what we argue is the true heir to the mantle of urban political power: complexly interdependent urban-centered public bureaucracies and their constituent and clientele networks. With this as introduction, let us return to the "elitist" perspective as reflected in the early studies of cities and towns.

Elitism and the Urban Political System

An important formulation of the elitist argument comes out of the trend-setting work of Floyd Hunter on Atlanta in the early 1950s and published as *Community Power Structure* in 1953. It is an imposing work, one which has been much discussed and criticized on methodological and substantive grounds. Despite such criticisms and despite the age of the study, Hunter's work remains an excellent example of elitist hypotheses applied to a large and complex American city. *Community Power Structure* will be used as a prime illustrative example of what we have been calling the elitist position.

Hunter begins his study of Atlanta with some explicitly formulated premises that seem to him to be self-evident. He argues that "power is structured socially, in the United States, into a dual relationship between governmental and economic authorities on national, state, and local levels." Further, "Power is a relatively constant factor in social relationships with policies as variables . . . and . . . wealth, social status, and prestige are factors in the power constant." Hunter hypothesizes that "power is exercised as a necessary function in social relationships . . . and that . . . the exercise of power is limited and directed by the formulation and extension of social policy within a framework of socially sanctioned authority." Hunter's final hypothesis is that "in a given power unit (organization) a smaller number of individuals will be found formulating and extending policy than those exercising power."[8]

Hunter's study of Regional City (Atlanta) comes to conclusions that are in no way ambiguous. Institutions of society in general and of the political system in particular are subordinate to that small band of economic policy makers. Hunter says, ". . . Businessmen are the community leaders in Regional City as they are in other cities. Wealth, social prestige, and political machinery are functional to the wielding of power by the business leaders of the community."[9] He comes to these conclusions by describing the structure of Atlanta society as being essentially a series of pyramids representing the various institutions and associations that were subordinate to a grander pyramid made up of policy makers and "upper level power personnel." Several immediate questions arise from these notions and the elitists are helpful in answering some of them.

[8]Floyd Hunter, *Community Power Structure* (Garden City, N.Y.: Doubleday, 1953), pp. 6, 7.
[9]*Ibid.*, p. 81.

Leadership, Representation, Responsiveness, and Participation in Elitist Systems

A first question might be: "Who are the members of the elite and where do they come from?" In Hunter's study practically all of the policy makers were Atlanta-born and well-to-do members of the "best" families of the city. They were well educated and devoted to the enterprises they headed, such as banks, utility companies, and industrial firms. They were, as one might expect, concerned with the economic development of the region. Further, the powerful were much concerned with the redevelopment of the city proper and anxious to give it a cosmopolitan tone. One did not belong among forty or so men isolated by Hunter as powerful simply by being wealthy, socially prestigious, and interested in civic improvement. Those who had these attributes but who simply did not bother to participate were not part of the group Hunter describes. People rose in the community power structure through effort, given the proper social and economic prerequisites. After studying smaller towns and cities of the past, some researchers have concluded that a single family dominated all of the social, economic, and political life of the community, and that this domination was a facet of the family's existence from generation to generation. The Lynds found this true of the famous Ball family in Muncie, Indiana, in their well-known *Middletown* and *Middletown in Transition.* The historical fact of aristocratic oligarchs running colonial and post-Revolutionary American cities is a familiar one to most students. Whichever elitist writer one cites as evidence, it seems fair to say that entrance into the elite was difficult if not nearly impossible and that elite membership and structure were modified only under the most serious conditions of historical change.

If an elite does, in fact, run the significant aspects of community life, then it might be asked; "How is this leadership accomplished?" Hunter argues that the top forty are themselves divided by interest and competences that suggest *who* at the top might formulate policy. Following his distinction, cited above, about people with power and people who have power *and* policy-making capacities, leadership may, in an elite, take a variety of forms, including communication and mobilization of the substructures for purposes of implementation. Probably of equal importance is the capacity of the power structure leadership to set "the rules of the game" or those constraints under which people may propose programs or struggle for power. Peter Bachrach and Morton Baratz support the significance of this particular point in a well-known article written a decade ago.

Bachrach and Baratz quote E. E. Schattschneider, who in his *Semi-Sovereign People* said: "All forms of political organization have a bias in favor of the exploitation of some kinds of conflict and the suppression of others because *organization is the mobilization of bias.*" In support of this point Bachrach and Baratz ask the following question: ". . . Can the researcher overlook the chance that some person or association could limit decision-making to relatively noncontroversial matters, by influencing community values and political procedures and rituals, notwithstanding that there are in the community serious but latent power conflicts?"[10] This important observation of a phenomenon not easily verifiable through objective means suggests some interesting possibilities to be more carefully considered in chapter 6. For the moment, we may say that leadership may come in the form of (as Bachrach and Baratz suggested) *nondecision-making.* In other words, the conditions for the exercise of political power may have been quietly and authoritatively set in an informal manner so that the top of the elite seldom have to say anything at all so long as lesser men of power continue to enforce the elite's rules of the game.

A third question of some importance is suggested by the answers to the first two. If an elite does exist and does in fact exercise leadership (overtly and covertly), then how are the multiplicity of interests normally found in cities and towns represented? It seems clear that the traditional democratic forms of representation mean little or nothing if the elitist arguments are correct. Yet if urban society is as complex and fragmented as we have thus far argued, then interests must be represented in some manner. The elitist response to this is likely to be something that looks like the organization chart of a large corporation.

A corporatist political system is one that divides society by function. Unions, for instance, would be structured into one "unionist hierarchy," or pyramid, stratified and in turn subordinate to a larger community or state hierarchy. Churches, political organizations, ethnic subcommunities, regions or neighborhoods—all of these categories of human organization are conceived of as being subordinate and hierarchically arranged so that society, economy, and polity might be managed and policy made from above. Citizenship, as commonly understood in democratic terms, is forgotten. Group membership becomes the true representational unit. For the ambitious, upward mobility is possible within the group, institution, or associational structure. Power, however, is gained as one would gain it in a large organization rather than in the traditional democratic way of mobilizing mass support through election campaigns and so forth.

Representation, then, approximates an employer-employee relationship between the governed and the governors rather than the more unpredictable relationship imagined when elections take place. No one elects the power structure. It exists and the extent to which its members represent the public interest probably depends in large part on the extent to which that interest overlaps with their own. Requests for change do come from the lower strata and one suspects they are met on (a) the criterion mentioned above and on (b) the possible effect a negative response might have on the continued stability of the system. Representation in elitist systems is always paternalistic, if not thoroughly authoritarian and repressive. The individual actor in an elitist system must first consider his personal well-being and place in the community before he can begin to think seriously of making representations about change. Thus, the very way in which the totality of an individual's roles may be invested in the system seriously influences

[10]Peter Bachrach and Morton S. Baratz, "Two Faces of Power," *American Political Science Review,* 56 (December 1962), p. 949; E. E. Schattschneider, *The Semi-Sovereign People* (New York: Holt, Rinehart and Winston, 1960).

the kinds of "demands" that he conceivably might be able to make on that system.

In a truly elitist system the distinctions between public and private power, leadership and representation tend to blur because power is structured hierarchically in service to the economic elite. Thus representation really is the odd coincidence of interests of the elite and of the general community. Hunter describes generally how he discovered representation to work in Regional City:

> . . . The interests of economic power groups are often of necessity coincidental with the larger interests of the general community welfare. The men who hold the power structure intact through policy decisions are firmly convinced that their decisions are correct more times than incorrect, and that their decisions are made with the whole community and the nation, for that matter, in mind. That the system holds together and that the interests continue to dominate the political situation is the pragmatic test of the policy-making group's ability to meet the minimum requirement for satisfying all interests in the community.[11]

Elite responsiveness seems dependent upon a number of significant variables. First, the external presence of demand must filter through the elaborate "corporate" structure in order for it to be noticed. Second, the strength and source of the demand must be perceived. Most issues can, in an elitist system, be ignored because they lack support from significant numbers of citizens or members of power groups in the community. Third, the quality of the demand must be "filtered" through the decisional precedents and customs of the top policy group. Demands considered illegitimate or inappropriate are either ignored or their supporters are punished through the variety of sanctions available under such a system. Most major policy decisions (usually those involving large sums of money) do not come about through the hierarchy, but are initiated within the upper policy strata.

Some Implications of Elitism

How then, one might ask, does all of this relate to the manifest structure of politics and political organization? If what Hunter has to say about Atlanta is true, then voting, as well as city councils and mayors, is the dog that is wagged by its own tail. Other structures such as political parties, community organizations, and school boards would seem also to have a sham quality. Even organized interest and pressure groups, "those protectors of the public interest," appear to be noisemakers rather than policy makers. In sum, the entire structure of community political life in America is at least something of a fraud if the elitists are correct in their analysis.

To suggest that all manifestations of public political activity are fraudulent is seriously to misrepresent what we generally take to be the elitist position.

[11]Hunter, *Community Power Structure,* pp. 166–167.

Within certain interest groups or institutional associations there are to be found representatives of the elite and functionaries who carry the "message" of the leadership. Elected officials operate independently of the elite except insofar as they may perceive themselves entering upon a sensitive issue or uncharted waters. The operations of the elite, while not clandestine, certainly are not so clearly public as to cause a complete affront to the democratic mythology.

A question raised by the existence of an elite and its substructure is: Who participates? Clearly, an answer is provided by the elitist when questions of major policy are raised. But what of all of those day-to-day problems that require immediate decision or which, because of a lack of elite interest, may involve debate or political competition? It would appear at this point that the traditional forms of political democracy begin to assume significance.

Those who wish to participate in their own governance must, according to Hunter, be within an organized group. The machinery of democratic structure as the means for self government, or at least participation, does not receive much mention. Hunter says,

> ... The leaders of the policy-making realm are not going to open doors of participa-
> tion with charitable graciousness. It has been noted that they may even use police
> power and the power of governmental machinery to keep back criticism and threat-
> ening political elements ...[12]

What might we conclude from this general reading of those who perceive the urban political system as being essentially elitist in structure and operation? One thing suggested by the elitist position is that certain kinds of values might be expected to dominate in the urban political system thus structured. Order, predictable individual and collective relationships, systemic stability, and measured, anticipated, indeed even planned change—values such as these would, one might guess, be maximized. Economic growth and measured socioeconomic upward mobility with accompanying suburbanization and human homogenization might also be inferred. An elite-dominated urban system might also be expected deliberately to ignore those who could safely be ignored, including blacks and the poor. The entire notion of externally generated legitimate demands is alien to the elitist concept. Requests may be made, but demands backed by threat of legitimate sanction (votes, withdrawal of support), *never.* Power is not dispersed throughout competing hierarchies in the political system. It is to be found in the upper strata and one draws horizontal, not vertical, lines between the powerful.

What kinds of things would one not expect to see in an elite-dominated urban political system? Political power separated from wealth and social standing would be impossible. The elite would not permit the existence of conflicting centers of power organized along a variety of lines and exercising differing amounts of influence according to history, issue, significance, and circumstance. Political party activity involving the distribution and employment of resources indepen-

[12] *Ibid.,* pp. 251–252.

dent of the direction of the elite would be unthinkable. Any form of random, unapproved mobilization of resources that fell outside of the dominant elite values would be crushed.

Minority group representation and influence in a nonelite system would have significance where electoral competition had meaning. In other words, one would not expect "permissive" values to be maximized in an elite-dominated urban political system. Significant questions of public policy would have answers, answers more or less the same over time. One might not be able to ascertain such answers by looking at a public document, but fairly careful research would be likely to reveal them if they did, in fact, exist, as Hunter claimed for Atlanta. What of the intellectual perspective reviewed thus far? The elitist view is far from being the accepted view of urban political power in the literature of political science today.

Elitism and Its Critics

As McFarland suggests in his excellent *Power and Leadership in Pluralist Systems:* "an elitist system . . . is a simple political system, having simple causation."[13] By simple causation, McFarland suggests that power is a central capacity of only certain actors and those actors tend to remain few in number and durable over time. If we summarize the elitist notion at its most fundamental level, we can say that social, economic, and political power are aspects of the stratification of urban society. Thus the richest man in town is likely to be socially prominent and politically powerful. Indeed, he and a small group of his peers will dominate all significant matters of their local society. These kinds of notions are demonstrable in nature (or can be made so with sufficient definitional specification), and one should be able to demonstrate their truth or falsity through investigation. As mentioned above, a substantial effort has been made at discovering the structure of power in American communities. What has been presented thus far has been a brief and general summary of the conclusions of those whom we have labeled "elitist" in orientation. Much criticism has been made about those conclusions and about the hypotheses and methodologies that underly them. These are summarized and evaluated below, but it may be worthwhile at this point to remind those interested in the study of community power that the debate is far from over.[14]

---

[13]McFarland, *Power and Leadership in Pluralist Systems,* p. 222.

[14]One day a scholar of the history of knowledge may discover the roots of a fascinating dichotomy between the sister social science disciplines of sociology and political science. This dichotomy is illuminated by the discussion at hand. In general, sociologists who go forth to study community power arrive at elitist conclusions, while political scientists usually can be found in the nonelitist or "pluralist" camp. The reasons for this are not entirely obscure, but they are not, alas, germane to the present discussion. Suffice it to say that the critics of elitism are mainly political scientists who have been writing in reaction to the large body of elitist literature on community power produced mainly during the first five decades of the present century.

Robert Dahl, probably the most distinguished pluralist critic of the elitist approach, argued in an oft-quoted article that:

> ... whatever else it may be, a theory that cannot even in principle be controverted by empirical evidence is not a scientific theory. The least that we can demand of any ruling elite theory that purports to be more than a metaphysical or polemical doctrine is, first that the burden of proof be on the proponents of the theory and not on its critics; and, second, that there be clear criteria according to which the theory could be disproved.[15]

In part what Dahl objected to in the elitist literature (Hunter and C. Wright Mills are specifically mentioned) was the capacity of the elite notion to "infinitely regress" in the face of empirical evidence to the contrary. In other words, if one set of leaders did not constitute an elite, then it is assumed that the "real" leaders are elsewhere. At no point can one test for the existence of an elite within the whole community. One apparently must keep looking until one finds it, for given the elitist's assumptions, *it must be there somewhere.* Nelson W. Polsby, upholding the pluralist cause and attacking the elitists two years after Dahl in a *Journal of Politics* article, puts the matter in colorful terms:

> Nothing categorical can be assumed about power in any community. . . . If anything, there seems to be an unspoken notion among pluralist researchers that at bottom nobody dominates in a town, so that their first question is not likely to be, "Who runs this community?" but rather, "Does anyone at all run this community?" The first query is somewhat like, "Have you stopped beating your wife?" in that virtually any response short of total unwillingness to answer will supply the researchers with a "power elite" along the lines presupposed by the stratification theory.[16]

So a first criticism of the elitist argument regarding power in communities is that it has (1) a tendency to avoid verification, and (2) what Robert Merton called a "self-fulfilling prophecy" such that the way in which the question is asked brings about the result anticipated by the questioner.

Yet another objection raised concerns the elitist notion about the essential permanence of the domination of the top power structure over time. The problem of change is simply not a problem in a "simple" elite argument. This unsupported proposition suffers from the difficulty that the one commonly observable aspect about life in American cities, towns, and suburbs is change. Change of all types, in all realms and at what appears to be an ever increasing rate is the distinguishing characteristic of the American urban place. Particularly variable is the change in the social makeup of urban areas, a phenomenon that tends to vitiate the elitist argument that power/socioeconomic elites remain relatively stable over time.

Dahl, Polsby, and others have raised objections to the way in which the

[15]Robert A. Dahl, "A Critique of the Ruling Elite Model," *American Political Science Review,* 51 (June 1958), p. 463.
[16]Nelson W. Polsby, "How to Study Community Power: The Pluralist Alternative," *Journal of Politics* (August 1960), p. 476.

elitists have conceived of power. They have criticized Hunter and others on several distinct points in the elitist idea of power. First is the elitists' alleged failure to distinguish between actual and reputed power. In other words, because a person or group is reputed to have power, it does not necessarily follow that such power is used. The alleged capacity of, say, an economic elite to prevent the election of a given candidate does not constitute a useful definition of power until (in our terminology) something is actually done. Yet another criticism of elitism is that it fails to account for any situational aspect of power.

Central to Hunter's argument, for instance, is the idea that power is "lumped" within the elite and is a constant aspect of social structure exercised in relation to an endless variety of matters of concern. Yet the question might be asked: "What about important matters about which the elite does not care?" A response might be, "The elite cares about all important matters." This leaves one in the awkward position of having his prophecy fulfilled since we logically end up with the elite defining all matters of importance. We may deduce from this that all matters of society that do not concern the elite are unimportant—a proposition not easily defended. Critics of elitism argue that power is situational and that coalitions are formed and resources mobilized when groups are threatened or perceive opportunities for self-serving. Further, the critics argue that power becomes a function of awareness, energy, organization, and coalitional strategies in pursuit of the allocation of resources. As we shall see in our consideration of the pluralist alternative to the study of community power, the idea of a single group consciously concerned with every significant public issue (however "significant" is defined) and able authoritatively to allocate resources in every area of public life, is impossible to support by observation.

The methodological problems involved in the study of community power lie, as most do, in the very first question asked. If one proceeds from the "who has power?" perspective, one is likely to come to conclusions different from those of the researcher who asks "Where is power exercised?" The controversy over how one goes about studying community power has been somewhat bitter. Hunter's "reputational" techniques have been criticized as have those of the pluralists.[17] It is not appropriate to go into these methodological differences here, but those interested in the debate are well-advised to see in this literature a prime example of the proposition that "the question is more important than the answer." The ideological as well as the methodological presuppositions of the elitist writers contributed much to the conclusions they reached, one suspects. Most of the political ideology of the European and American sociologists (to the extent to

[17]For instance, criticizing the elitists: Norton Long, "The Local Community as an Ecology of Games," *American Journal of Sociology,* 64 (1958), pp. 251–261; Dahl, "A Critique of the Ruling Elite Model;" Raymond Wolfinger, Reputation and Reality in the Study of 'Community Power,' " *American Sociological Review,* 25 (1960), pp. 636–644; Nelson W. Polsby, "Three Problems in the Analysis of Community Power," *American Sociological Review,* 24 (1959), pp. 796–803. Criticizing the pluralists: Bachrach and Baratz, "Two Faces of Power;" William E. Connolly, "The Challenge to Pluralist Theory," *The Bias of Pluralism,* ed. William E. Connolly (New York: Atherton Press, 1969); Theodore Lowi, "The Public Philosophy: Interest-Group Liberalism," *American Political Science Review,* 61 (March 1967), pp. 5–24.

which it was manifest) revolved around economic theory. The great issues and thinkers of the first part of the century were concerned with capitalism and socialism.

The elitist position on community power, as thus far presented, is essentially based on a general notion of economic determinism. Such a notion, as employed here, implies that the distribution of economic wealth in a community determines the structure and operation of political power (Figure 5.2). In other words, once the economic order is understood, the social and political order is easily knowable. There is more than a bit of truth in such a statement, one suspects, but the difficulty lies in defining it in such a manner that it can be observed in operation. The elitists have, as we have noted, been severely criticized for failing to do just this. They have also been criticized for carrying this general argument about economic stratification even further, to the point of claiming the existence of a "power elite" or "power structure" that operates in a self-aware manner.

These criticisms seem valid. But before one dismisses the entire matter, it might be well worth considering some variations on the elitist theme that may be fruitfully employed in looking at the urban political system. One of the effects of Hunter's work in Atlanta has been to raise the question of the difference between the observed formal structure of political power and the "real" situation. In arguing as he did about Atlanta, Hunter threatened several conceptions of political power. First and most obviously dismissed was the structure represented by the artifacts of popular democracy. Elections, elected officials, political parties, and the like were viewed as window dressing at best and as instruments of the power structure at worst. Secondly, the notions that had come to serve "informed" people in place of the details of democracy suffered a severe blow in Hunter's work. Hunter strongly contradicted those who argued that the primacy of "interests" and the groups created to preserve them actually maintained a more or less democratic equilibrium that prevented elitist domination.

The reaction to Hunter, and on the national level to C. Wright Mills, was to employ the new scientific methodologies of political science to demonstrate the truth of a complex and interrelated series of ideas. This collection of ideas is generally called pluralism, and it has formed the conventional wisdom of political science for several decades.

Pluralism and Urban Politics

An important premise of pluralists was carefully stated in a small volume that appeared in the mid-1950s and which had significant impact on subsequent pluralist thinking. In *A Preface to Democratic Theory,* Robert A. Dahl, the dominant pluralist scholar of recent times, made the following argument:

> Prior to politics, beneath it, enveloping it, restricting it, conditioning it, is the underlying consensus on policy that usually exists in the society among a predominant portion of the politically active members. Without such a consensus no democratic system will survive the endless irritations and frustrations of elections and

**Figure 5.2
An Elitist Model**

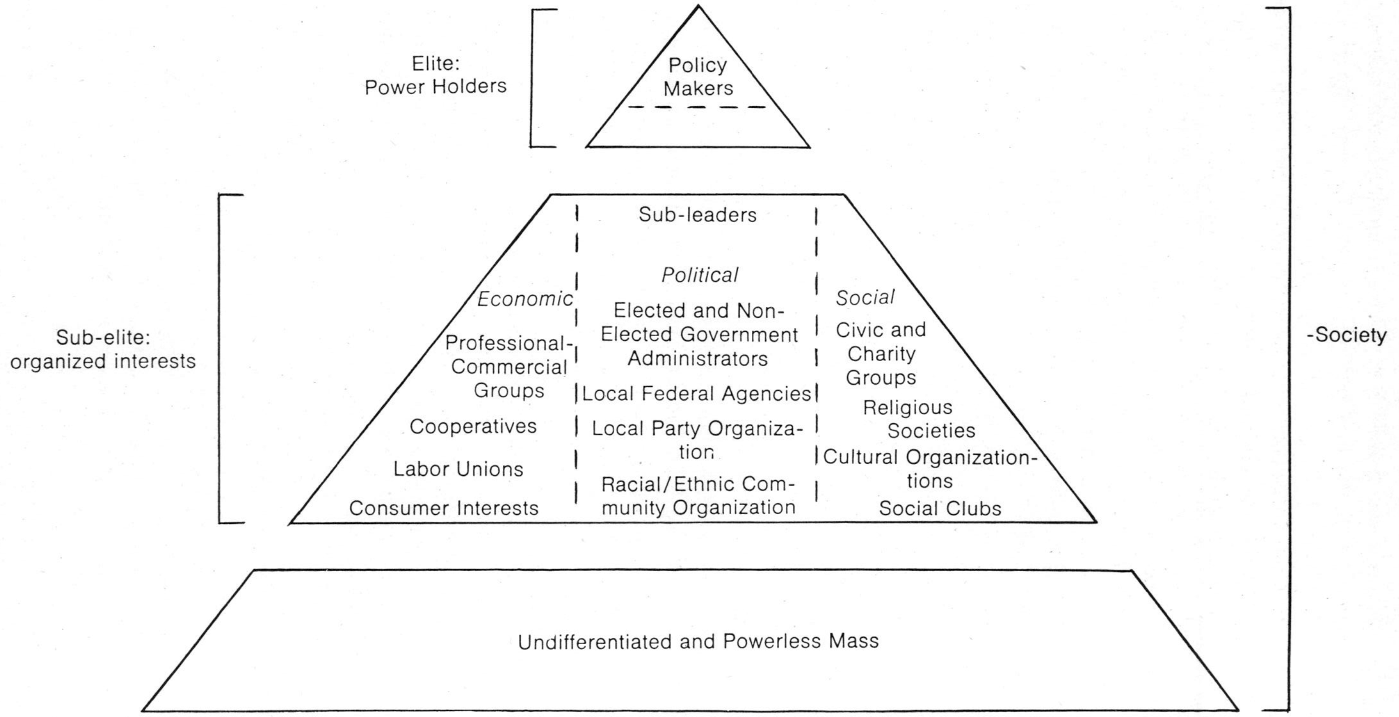

Elite:
Power Holders

Policy
Makers

Sub-leaders

Economic

Professional-
Commercial
Groups

Cooperatives

Labor Unions

Consumer Interests

Political

Elected and Non-
Elected Government
Administrators

Local Federal Agencies

Local Party Organiza-
tion

Racial/Ethnic Com-
munity Organization

Social

Civic and
Charity
Groups

Religious
Societies

Cultural Organization-
tions

Social Clubs

Sub-elite:
organized interests

Undifferentiated and Powerless Mass

Society

party competition. With such a consensus the disputes over policy alternatives are nearly always winnowed to those within the broad area of basic agreement.[18]

A broad consensus among the politically active about what? Some might reply: "About the rules of the game, of course." Others might respond that such a consensus depended on more than just agreement about the rules, that it would include basic agreement about the proper and legitimate role of government vis à vis basic economic and social phenomena. The key to Dahl's statement seems to have an elitist ring to it, for he really is only talking about the "politically active." One may perhaps legitimately infer that the "politically active" make demands according to "the rules of the game." Survey research has indicated that participation beyond voting is to be found among a tiny portion of the total possible participants.[19] Events of the past decade, beginning with the civil rights demonstrations, have raised some questions about the amount of real consensus.

Pluralism, then, is an idea about political reality and has ideological components as well. As we noted in our discussion of elitism, the scholarly approach one takes in the study of politics is not always free of one's ideological preferences. In general, one might argue that the pluralists believed in liberal democracy and tended to discover it when they addressed themselves to questions of community power. Much of the introductory passages about pluralism above could just as well have been about Liberalism. Without presuming to attack the problem of defining that much-abused term, we can note that pluralist writers frequently conclude that the political system as they discover it is a just and reasonable device that provides adequate amounts of representation, responsiveness, and participation opportunities. The existing system provides fairly open access to new inputs and achieves remarkable stability. The pluralists are in total disagreement with the elitists, it would appear.

Robert Dahl's *Who Governs?* is subtitled "Democracy and Power in an American City," and it deals with New Haven, Connecticut, from colonial days to the late 1950s. It is the most famous pluralist work relating to American cities, despite some flaws and deficiencies to be discussed below. The first matter to be dealt with involves Dahl's conception of power as he employed it in his work on New Haven.

Probably the most significant difference regarding power between Dahl and Hunter was that the former did not come to his work with the belief that power was necessarily an attribute of social or economic standing. Indeed, in a long historical section he makes the point that New Haven went from a system of "cumulative inequalities" to one of "dispersed inequalities." The former refers to a system in which social prestige, economic well-being, and political power were synonymous. Thus, where one found a holder of high political office, one would

[18]Robert A. Dahl, *A Preface to Democratic Theory* (Chicago: University of Chicago Press, 1956), pp. 132–133.
[19]Lester W. Milbrath, *Political Participation: How and Why Do People Get Involved in Politics?* (Chicago: Rand-McNally, 1965).

find in that same person a member of the elite, or "oligarchy" as Dahl uses the term. Such a system, Dahl argues, was characteristic of eighteenth- and early nineteenth-century New Haven. What happened over time, Dahl suggests, is that the system evolved into one of dispersed inequalities. Thus, people who became wealthy did not automatically achieve high social status and political power. The push of upward mobility caused the dispersion of inequalities and Dahl traces that push and subsequent entry of the "newly arrived" into positions of power, influence, and wealth. As a first point of contrast, Dahl admits the existence of an elite in the colonial era, but argues that resources were captured from the elite over time to the point where that elite was no longer discernible. If power was not a characteristic of those who had high social standing and wealth, then where was it to be discovered? How was it to be conceptualized?

Dahl emphasized what he believed to be the crucial difference between actual and potential power. The difference is between ascription and description. The pluralists argue that simply because a person possesses a great many resources that could place him in a position to exercise a disproportionate amount of influence, this does not mean that he actually does exercise it. Power employed, power in reference to something, power in an observable condition of exercise— this is how Dahl and company chose to use the concept in New Haven. Such a step logically led Dahl to a study of decisions. In focusing on decisions, Dahl explicitly rejected two central assumptions of elitist writers. First, a person's reputed power was ignored, as we have suggested. The second rather common idea to be rejected was the positional assumption made by some elitists. The positional assumption holds that a high formal position within an institution necessarily involves the exercise of great power. The pluralists, particularly Dahl, Polsby, and Wolfinger, explicitly reject any *a priori* assumption about the distribution of power, either by reputation or by position.

In *Community Power and Political Theory,* Polsby asks the central question: "How can one tell, after all, whether or not an actor is powerful unless some sequence or event, competently observed, attests to his power?"[20] Repeatedly Dahl emphasizes this point in *Who Governs?* Dahl and his associates were very much concerned with developing significant hypotheses about power in New Haven that could be empirically verified through the examination of concrete decisions of far-ranging significance.

The question of "key decisions" is of great significance to the pluralist arguments about power in the urban political system. Polsby enumerated four criteria used in identifying decisions of major importance.[21] The number of people affected by the decision and the benefits that result are the first two. Presumably, the latter criterion would also involve an estimate of the costs

[20]Nelson W. Polsby, *Community Power and Political Theory* (New Haven: Yale University Press, 1963), p. 60.
[21]*Ibid.,* pp. 95–96.

accruing as the result of a major decision. The third criterion involves the breadth of the distribution of benefits and the fourth rests on a consideration of the extent to which existing patterns of resource distribution within the community are altered. As reasonable as these criteria seem, they do raise some rather important questions about community decision-making Dahl and his associates do not always answer explicitly. We return to this question in some detail below and in the ensuing chapter, but perhaps it is worthwhile at this point to consider the argument that Polsby failed to mention concerning a more general criterion.

David Ricci argues rather persuasively that Dahl and his associates in selecting decisions indeed employed a fifth criterion which is of great significance.[22] Ricci suggests that the pluralists define community power always in terms of the political arena. Of course, Dahl makes it clear that in general he believes that the significant question is the domination of public structures, not private institutions. Such a belief defines more narrowly the scope of community power than the elitists prefer. Indeed, it centers attention on the explicitly political rather than viewing the social and economic aspects of community life as central. Accordingly, the New Haven study considers decisions relating to public education, urban renewal, and political nominations as being among the "key" decisional areas in the city.

A careful study of the decision-makers involved in these three areas was undertaken. A political elite of active participants was discovered to dominate in the three issue-areas, but Dahl's elite differed from Hunter's in two very important aspects. The first aspect is the dissociation of the possession of political power and socioeconomic elite membership. In fact, little overlap, except in the urban renewal area, was discovered between the holders of economic power and the people who predominated in political decision-making. A second major finding that tended to refute the findings of Hunter was that the politically powerful (with the notable exception of Mayor Lee) were not powerful in reference to more than one issue-area. Thus a powerful position in reference to public education decision-making meant nothing at all in the urban renewal area. Dahl sees a very different form of political elite, then, than the one Hunter and other elitists describe. Leaders exercise power in a narrow area. According to the pluralists, they are limited by this fact and by their personal lack of cumulative resources. This contrasts directly with the elitist view of a monolithic socioeconomic elite dominating *all* aspects of community life.

If power is so constrained and narrowly exercisable within the upper political strata, then what kind of an urban political system might we expect to result? One might logically extrapolate some characteristics. In order to dominate successfully, or even influence more than a narrow range of decisions, leaders must compromise, negotiate, and bargain. In this necessity to bargain lies one of the

[22]David M. Ricci, *Community Power and Democratic Theory* (New York: Random House, 1971), p. 130.

keys to the pluralist faith. As suggested more generally above, the balance and integrity of the political system in part derives from the requirement that leaders must compete for political support in order to maintain themselves and to have their way. If we take this motive as given, then it is easy to concede that leaders must bargain for the support of nonleaders. It is in this enduring tension that leaders must take account of the desires of some of the electorate, according to pluralist lights.

One of the central sources of conflict between elitists and pluralists lies in the very question of whether or not this built-in system of competition and tension really does work. A crucial component of any answer lies in the notion of resources. As we have noted, the elitists define resources rather narrowly in terms of position or socioeconomic status. Dahl defines resources in much broader terms. He concedes that wealth, social status, and high position are indeed resources, but would disagree about their primacy and the exclusivity of the list. This is particularly so given the six characteristics Dahl believes typical of a system of dispersed inequalities or noncumulative resources. These characteristics are:

1. Many different kinds of resources for influencing officials are available to different citizens.
2. With few exceptions, these resources are unequally distributed.
3. Individuals best off in their access to one kind of resource are often badly off with respect to many other resources.
4. No one influence resource dominates all the others in all or even in most key decisions.
5. With some exceptions, an influence resource is effective in some issue-areas or in some specific decisions but not in all.
6. Virtually no one, and certainly no group of more than a few individuals, is entirely lacking in some influence resource.[23]

Dahl proceeds to discuss three broad groupings of resources in some detail.[24] He includes social standing, access to cash, credit, wealth, and access to resources at the disposal of public officials, such as legal powers, patronage and popularity, and control over information.

As described thus far, pluralist ideas might lead one to the conclusion that while a kind of democracy different from the textbook variety prevails in the urban political system, the governance of that system (given all of those dispersed inequalities) must be chaotic. It is not chaotic partly because of the activities of some fairly distinct categories of participants and non-participants. The first and most populous of Dahl's categories was the class *homo civicus,* which included

[23]Robert A. Dahl, *Who Governs? Democracy and Power in an American City* (New Haven: Yale University Press, 1961), p. 228.
[24]The discussion in these pages is a summary of what we see as the significant part in *Who Governs?* Needless to say, much more is to be found in the original.

the great mass of the citizens of New Haven who simply had no interest in politics. The small minority of people who joined political clubs or engaged in active campaigning were dubbed *homo politicus.*

From these two kinds of people, Dahl hypothesized the existence of two general strata of society—the apolitical and the political strata. The apolitical stratum represented a formless mass that showed no continuing interest in public affairs. Despite this general condition of apathy, the apolitical stratum holds a key position in the maintenance of the pluralist system. If, as Dahl argues, political resources are dispersed and have the attribute of potentiality discussed above, then the apolitical stratum constitutes a threat to any group of leaders who might dominate the city. This occurs in two ways. The first involves the possibility of the mobilization of the "slack" or potential power available in the apolitical stratum because of the failure of the leadership to satisfy the demands of the general community. Thus political leaders and city officials would always have to design policies that would satisfy the general community and would never encourage slack power to be mobilized in an unstable (or disruptive) way. A second possibility involves the availability of people in the apolitical stratum for conversion to active participation in politics through increased competition between groups in the political stratum. Serious conflict over policies might drive less powerful groups to stimulate parts of the apolitical stratum to action, thus upsetting the equilibrium.

This argument was in general supported by Dahl's findings in New Haven. He concludes from this that the apolitical stratum does in fact influence decisions in an important way that is perhaps not obvious. In the very anticipation of community demands and probable community dissatisfaction over a particular policy decision, a kind of influence is exerted. This Dahl calls indirect influence. Elections become crucial to this line of argument since Dahl insists on the primary significance of the manifestly political. For it is in anticipation of winning the election that both the "ins" and the "outs" try to estimate probable community reaction and thus modify their (the competitors') behavior accordingly. This tension, leading to a kind of moderation and stability, is a central aspect of representation and responsiveness, and leads Dahl to the conclusion that democratic norms are operating in New Haven. Significantly, Dahl also argues that the widespread belief in the legitimacy of these practices among the political strata tended to reinforce those norms.

It is in precisely the degree to which both strata hold to what Dahl calls "the democratic creed" that one may or may not discover the "social glue" of pluralism. Dahl makes two arguments in support of the primary significance of the democratic creed as a deeply held belief of both the political and the apolitical strata. The political stratum finds the democratic creed—civility in debate, toleration of dissent, the legitimacy of bargaining, and reasonable use of the electoral machinery—to be a practical and workable framework for politics. The democratic creed is predictable, knowable, and fair in the eyes of the political stratum and thus its preservation is in the self-interest of people in politics. A second source of support for the democratic creed is to be found in the widespread consensus Dahl believes to be present in the apolitical stratum. This makes itself felt episodically at the polls, particularly when some violation of the creed is believed to have taken place in officialdom.

By way of concluding this summary of the leading pluralist work on community power, one might repeat the original question: Who governs? Dahl answers that in New Haven one particular form of political order dominated at the time of his study, although this did not mean that this one pattern of influence was the only one in operation. Dahl concludes after much analysis that an "executive-centered grand coalition of coalitions" predominated, having evolved from a system of "independent sovereignties" with spheres of influence. He includes the entire political system of the city with the exception of the political parties which, he argues, exhibit a different pattern called "rival sovereignties fighting it out."

The existence and operation of the executive-centered coalition is explained through Dahl's study of the three significant issue areas—urban renewal, public education, and political nominations. In all three, Mayor Richard Lee was found to be a central presence able to bring rival structures of power into agreement if not harmony. The narrowly defined spheres of influence remained primary, although as Lee became more powerful, his ability to coordinate the demands and satisfactions of different groups tended to overshadow any single group's influence. Despite the central role of the mayor, politics in New Haven remained, according to Dahl, open and accessible to anyone with the interest and motivation to mobilize those resources available. Membership in the political strata was voluntary and the very top leadership structure was relatively open to would-be members.

Some Implications of Pluralism

What kind of place do we find the American urban political system to be when we look at it through pluralist eyes? In general, it conforms to what many would view as a "realistic" statement of what actually happens. What we discover actually happening in New Haven is democratic government—perhaps not the government pictured in secondary school textbooks, but a government that realistically matches the way society is with the ideals of liberal democracy. How does this come to pass? This state of democratic equilibrium comes about as a function of balances and counterbalances. The former is active, the latter normally passive. This activity-passivity permits the orderly running of the city, while still keeping the holders of power within certain "rules of the game" or the democratic creed.

We have discussed potential power and actual power, cumulative resources and noncumulative resources, direct influence and indirect influence, political strata and apolitical strata. In all of these concepts, as well as others Dahl employs, seem to lie either the notion of balance or of potentiality. For almost every tendency toward oligarchy, Dahl offers a countervailing force that tends toward democracy. For every holder of power there seems to be a potential check which that power-holder must calculate. Dahl, Polsby, and other pluralist writers offer these ideas as hypotheses and proceed to attempt to demonstrate the truth or falsity of them through work in the field. The New Haven study attempted to do just that. The contrast between *Who Governs?* and *Community Power Structure* extends to more than differences in hypotheses and conclusions. We have discussed some of the methodological aspects of both works very briefly. Further, it has been suggested that of essential importance is the kind of question with which both the elitists and the pluralists begin their studies. The ideological-philosophical context and implications of the elitist view of community power have been explored briefly. The same kind of exploration of pluralism deserves a bit more discussion, since pluralism remains the dominant ideology not only of political scientists, but of the practitioners of politics.

We asked about power, representation, responsiveness, and participation. The elitists would argue that power is a function of socioeconomic status and/or reputation. The pluralists (Dahl) talk of a system of dispersed inequalities, slack, and potential power, thus dissociating structure from the stratification of society and creating the impression of fluidity and openness within the various "patterns of influence." Power, it will be recalled, is situational and not very constant within the pluralist system. The idea of power makes the most sense to Dahl when it is made operational by observation of concrete decisions of community significance. It is at that point and that point only that one's notion of who has power begins to have validity. That some people exercise more influence over one area of public policy than another is to be expected and anticipated, given a system where the inequalities of resources that are influence or power-creating are dispersed rather than cumulative. Thus caste and class are not the controlling variables of the political system, because to be deficient in wealth and social status and position is not to be without resources entirely. Potentially, by hard work and intelligent planning, those with few resources could mobilize and carry the day against those with many resources.

Representation, interpreted here as "making present"[25] demands of constituencies, occurs in the pluralist form in a variety of institutional settings. The interests of functional, ethnic, religious, as well as geographical constituencies, gain representation not only through the formal structures of political representation, but also through the multitude of boards, committees, and institutionalized pressure groups. The demands of these constituencies must be represented if the top leadership of the community is to retain its position. Representation also takes place in a form the elitists and the pluralists might find compatible with their conflicting views of political power. This possible overlap of viewpoints concerns the representation of interests that occurs when policy makers take into account the probable reactions of one or more constituencies. The pluralist view of representation seems to be that, despite the fact that the traditional, formal democratic

[25]Hanna F. Pitkin, *The Concept of Representation* (Berkeley: University of California Press, 1967).

means of representation through elected officials works, a "second" system provides a truly thorough representational structure.

It is in this "second system" that the pluralists seem to have found the continuation of representative democracy in the face of the deficiencies discovered in the old system. It is through the organization of the various interests in society for purposes of the representation of demand that liberal democratic notions of "making present" are to be found. It is in the balance struck between competing groups and a neutral government refereeing the combat that justice is to be found in the making of public policy. It is of no little importance to the pluralist argument that this institutionalized tension be understood. For without the competition between groups trying to gain some control over the allocation of scarce public resources, the pluralist conception of liberal-democratic representation fails. The elitists are fairly straightforward in this area. They simply do not believe that the conflict between groups has any meaning at all except insofar as the ruling elite condescend to notice it. They are under no compulsion to do so, whereas in a pluralist system the leadership must always be aware of such conflict.

Responsiveness in pluralist systems is entirely related to the system of representation. If the system works as described above, then officials charged with the responsibility of responding must do so or else. This raises an interesting point. If officials must be more or less immediately responsive to legitimate interests that have either been victorious in some struggle with other interests or that have compromised to everyone's satisfaction, then what becomes of the "general public interest?" Worse yet, what if the legitimate imperative demand calls for a stupid, wasteful, or harmful allocation of scarce public resources? The public official who denies such demands not only can be expected to be removed from office, but also denies the effectiveness of the system of representation and the resultant responsiveness of the "referee."

Participation, according to the pluralists, is very much a matter of individual preference, talent, and resources. The revision of classicial democratic theory, which wrongly held every man born equal, argues that while equality at birth does not exist, the *opportunity* to participate in politics is pretty much equal. The operation of a pluralist system, with its premium on organization and mobilization of numbers in contrast to just the mobilization of wealth and position, provides a real contrast with the elitist view. The variety of groups and the viability of the party system makes participation a simple matter. Indeed, Dahl argues in *Who Governs?* that access to leadership roles in certain areas like political nominations and public education is relatively free of any qualifications of birth or wealth or social-positional status. The failure of large numbers of the population to participate simply reveals a lack of interest in politics and a general satisfaction with the ways things are going. Much of this tolerance, passivity, and apathy is explained in terms of an underlying consensus said to be characteristic of most of the population.

What has thus far been presented is a general discussion of the doctrine called pluralism and a brief examination of pluralist hypotheses tested in an

American city. Until quite recently pluralist doctrine in the study of urban political systems was the received wisdom of political scientists. If one had to guess, it would probably be true to say that most students of American politics today still view pluralist ideas somewhat uncritically. A critical nonpluralist, nonelitist literature has appeared in the past ten years and the remainder of this chapter will deal with some of those criticisms. Some of the criticism is directed at pluralism in general. Much of it has been directed specifically at pluralist studies of community power.

Some Criticisms of Pluralism

A key methodological component of *Who Governs?* was the selection of significant issue-areas for study. This choice presumably demonstrated that leaders were powerful only in relation to specific and rather narrow areas. Bachrach and Baratz criticized Dahl rather revealingly on this point, arguing that the Social Notables (elite) of New Haven displayed an apparent lack of interest in two of the three important issue-areas selected for study. They point out that Dahl himself suggests that business leaders, the vast majority of whom lived in the suburbs, could conveniently ignore both issues of public education and of political party nominations. This is so because most of these "Notables" sent their children to private schools and were not eligible for elected office in the city proper.

Bachrach and Baratz then proceed to argue:

> . . . Thus, if one believes—as Professor Dahl did when he wrote his critique of the ruling elite model—that an issue, to be considered as important, "should involve actual disagreement in preferences among two or more groups," then clearly he has for all practical purposes written off public education and party nominations as key "issue-areas." But this point aside, it appears somewhat dubious at best that "the relative influence over public officials wielded by the Social Notables" can be revealed by an examination of their nonparticipation in areas in which they were not interested.[26]

Bachrach and Baratz do not argue that the "Notables" in New Haven lack power in most significant matters, but that Dahl simply did not make his case. He does make his case in regard to the area of urban renewal, and in this Bachrach and Baratz find the most basic weakness in Dahl's approach. Dahl measured relative influence completely on the basis of an actor's ability to initiate and veto proposals. According to these critics, Dahl fails to recognize *the power to limit the scope of initiation.* In other words, if a powerful actor like Mayor Lee precensors his possible course of action because of his view of what would or would not "cause trouble," then as Bachrach and Baratz suggest, one "face of power" may be being ignored at the cost of a more thorough understanding of community power.

[26]Peter Bachrach and Morton S. Baratz, "Two Faces of Power," *The Bias of Pluralism,* ed. William E. Connolly (New York: Atherton Press, 1969), p. 59.

Bachrach and Baratz make some further proposals for the future study of community power which, with some independent interpretation, might be understood to be general criticisms of the findings as well as the methodology of pluralism. Their suggestion for a new approach to community power:

> Under this approach the researcher would begin—not, as does the sociologist who asks, "Does anyone have power?"—but by investigating the particular "mobilization of bias" in the institution under scrutiny. Then, having analyzed the dominant values, the myths and the established political procedures and rules of the game, he would make a careful inquiry in which persons or groups, if any, gain from the existing bias and which, if any, are handicapped by it. Next, he would investigate the dynamics of *non-decision-making,* that is, he would examine the extent to which and the manner in which the status quo oriented persons and groups influence those community values and those political institutions . . . which tend to limit the scope of actual decision-making to safe issues. . . .[27]

This methodological suggestion carries with it certain kinds of implications for a broader critique of pluralism, one which focuses on an aspect of the subject only briefly touched on thus far. Pluralism has been discussed in this chapter almost entirely as a series of hypotheses and conclusions worked out by scholars to explain the workings of the American political system at different levels. It also may be viewed as an apology for the existing political configuration found in the United States. Such a view would be essentially committed to the preservation of existing patterns of political life that seem to maximize certain aspects of liberal democratic doctrine, although in a way not entirely consistent with the dreams and visions of the Founders. In what ways would the processes and institutions described as important to the pluralist view of things be supportive of the *status quo ante?*

As has been pointed out, pluralists tend to take the existing system as given, including, as Bachrach and Baratz suggest, the "mobilization of bias." What of the processes that ensure the possibility for people to capture control of some of the authoritative allocative capacity? Dahl and others attach a meaning to the nonparticipation of the masses (as they used to be called), which is at least debatable. The argument about the "apolitical strata" 's capacity to punish violators of the democratic creed at the polls is open to some question. What survey research we have does not suggest a widespread feeling of political efficacy among those who do not participate in politics.[28] (By political efficacy, we mean the feeling on the part of individuals that they can by their efforts influence political leaders so as to bring about a change which they believe to be desirable.) Dahl's

---

[27] *Ibid.,* p. 61.

[28] For instance: Gabriel Almond and Sidney Verba, *The Civic Culture* (Boston: Little, Brown, 1965) find that just 48 percent of the U.S. polity expect serious consideration for a private point of view . . . from bureaucracy, p. 72; and 49 percent think an ordinary person should be less than active in his or her local community, p. 127. See also: Norman H. Nie et al., *The Changing American Voter* (Cambridge: Harvard University Press, 1976).

book about New Haven fails to notice a black community almost totally estranged from the political life of the city. Mayor Lee and his "coalition of coalitions" brought more per capita expenditure for urban renewal to New Haven than had been received by any other city in the country, but was shocked into a different perspective when riots hit New Haven's black neighborhoods several years after the publication of *Who Governs?*[29]

The riots in New Haven, as elsewhere in America during the 1960s, raised some serious doubts about the other aspects of the pluralist view. The idea of intergroup competition for allocative control over some portion of governmental resources bringing a sort of balance to public policy rests on some questionable assumptions. First, one must assume the possibility of mobilizing sufficient organizational resources to do battle in the "political arena." Secondly, an assumption must, it seems, be made about the possibility that any given group can more or less permanently dominate a "pattern of influence" so thoroughly over time that combat is merely ritual. There is much to suggest that the poor, the blacks, and other "ethnics" have generally lacked such organizational resources or have for generations been faced with odds so overwhelming as to make any conflict they may cause simply ritualistic. In other words, the contest is so unequal as to be meaningless in terms of modifying significantly the existing patterns of influence. The blueprint for the achievement of political power which might be inferred from a reading of the pluralist literature leaves much to be desired.

A central part of "the pluralist blueprint" is usually a working, dominant political system. By "working political system" we suggest a restricted, traditional notion that implies a series of elected legislative and executive officials who represent competitive political parties that regularly fight it out at the ballot box (Figure 5.3). Whatever may be the case nationally, growing interparty competition within American cities and towns is hard to find over the past twenty-five years. We have documented the golden days of the political party in the urban political system and have discussed at length some of the causes of its decline. The prizes available in American cities and towns are not to be found in the electoral arena, at least not to the extent that they once were. Capturing the mayoralty, according to the testimony of recent occupants of that office in some of the larger cities, is far from providing the kind of payoffs expected by those who read pluralist literature.[30] There are some strong probable causes for the continuing progressive illness of the electoral system in cities. At this point it is sufficient to note that the central role of the traditionally defined political structure of cities that appears to be so important to the pluralist perspective is, if not near collapse, in deep trouble.

Pluralism is a series of occasionally rather complicated hypotheses, rules, and myths that to some extent function independently of any clear explanatory

[29]Bernard Asbell, "Dick Lee Discovers How Much Is Not Enough," *New York Times Magazine,* September 3, 1967, p. 6.
[30]Fred Powledge, "The Flight from City Hall," *Harper's* magazine, November 1969, pp. 69–70.

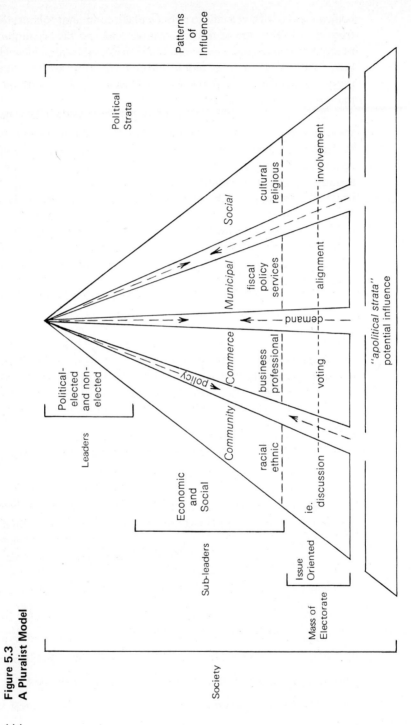

Figure 5.3
A Pluralist Model

purpose. One could venture a guess about the central bias of pluralism. It attempts to explain away the deficiencies of liberal democracy as descriptive political theory. The analysis of the existing political structure is usually in terms of liberal value premises. Pluralism becomes a hindrance to politically induced social change when it functions as an ideology. As an ideology, pluralism tends to maximize system maintenance functions in a self-conscious manner. As a theoretical scheme written in the language of modern social science, pluralistic research, despite the criticism leveled here and elsewhere, still provides much of the most useful information available about the politics of urban areas.

Community Power and the "New" Urban Political System

The debate between elitists and pluralists over the methodology and substance of the study of political power on the local level was, in some ways, very important for the development of new ideas about cities and towns. Unfortunately, there have been costs. The debate quieted at just about the time in the late 1960s when the term "urban crisis" began to be heard. All at once, it seemed the stability and regularity of city political life were disturbed from unexpected quarters. Blacks appear subordinate and fully segregated from the elite in Hunter's Atlanta. They do not even warrant analysis in Dahl's New Haven. Federal and state agencies appear distant or totally irrelevant to the stories told by elite theorists, and hold positions of marginal relevance for pluralists who studied community power. Courts likewise appear to be either marginal artifacts of elite power, or simply another channel for the expression of demand in the pluralist scheme.

No social scientist writing of community power in the 1950s imagined a federal judge running the school system of the City of Boston.[31] The relative physical permanence of the elite, its association with a more comprehensible past, and its potential for internal disruption and external intervention, were, we think it now fair to say, miscalculated. White flight, the riots of the 1960s and early 1970s, and, as if to add to the unpredictable confusion, a massive series of population movements which were to undermine the very best theories of us all, left the community power debate behind in something of a mess. If the corporate giants move their middle-level, middle-class, managerial talent around the country every five years, what happens to the participation base upon which both elitist and pluralist writers so depend? This group is a key participant in either formulation of political power, it would seem.[32]

Even a vision of a single clump of economic elites (expanding on Hunter's more massive conception) gets dimmer and dimmer. This is not because there has

[31]For a survey of court-ordered school desegregation, see *The New York Times,* September 6, 1976, p. 1.
[32]For example, between 1965 and 1970, 41.8 percent of the population over five years of age changed residence; U.S. Department of Commerce, Bureau of the Census, Census of Population, 1970, PC (2)-2B, "Mobility for States and the Nation."

been a pluralistic dispersion of wealth and political power. Rather, the era of local enterprise, locally owned and operated by people who live in the city or in the suburb, seems to be rapidly coming to an end. America has become a nation of multinational corporations, interlocking financial institutions, retail chain stores, restaurants, and movie houses. The day of the mill or mine or factory owner who also owns the town and all the people in it is by and large over. The people who manage such local operations are not the replacement for the oligarchs of old. Their destiny, and that of their children particularly, lies not in the city or town in which they reside; it lies in national organizations of vast economic and political power. Ownership of wealth, rooted in a given locality, is supplanted by highly mobile managers of resources, typically deployed on a national level.

The point, then, is that while elites or pluralist groups may in fact dominate important areas of political life in many cities, the actors and the structures described by Hunter and Dahl have probably been supplanted nearly everywhere one looks. (Of course, the state and federal officials who control New York City's finances are an elite in some senses.)

This is not to suggest that there are not still powerful local socioeconomic associational groups who can bring influence to bear in certain kinds of situations. Rather, it is being argued that local socioeconomic elites have been detached, first from their old property ownership, and then from their political ties, as their wealth gets progressively more diversified in the general economy. In addition, Dahl's interest group coalitions have lost their clout. Even in those cases where management and ownership are, for locational reasons, still attached to some city or another, the local political system itself is only rarely a source of uncertainty sufficient to make political control an organizational problem. There is a new source of uncertainty, of course, located in the cities and towns, and this source may, in fact, cause or stimulate a kind of elite that supplants the traditional ownership-wealth-high social status structure. That source is "intergovernmental aid" and the new elite may well be "the emergency financial management team."

If Judge Gary were alive today and thinking of running an enormous steel mill in some small or medium-sized city, it wouldn't be the locals who needed controlling so that the judge could conduct his business. No, the old judge (after whom Gary, Indiana, was not so coincidentally named) would have to worry about some new elites and coalitions with names like OSHA (Occupational Safety and Health Administration), EPA (Environmental Protection Agency), and the Department of Energy, to name just a few powerful political actors with enormous local significance. From pension reform to environmental impact statements, and going back to national highway, urban renewal, and home mortgage policies, the problems and opportunities for local economic elites increasingly have come from state and federal bureaucratic actors. These actors, taken together with *their* constituent and client networks, constitute an elite of power and wealth at least equal to the oligarchs of Hunter or Dahl. Nearly every aspect of political life discussed in the classics of community power study now has a national or state administrative organization designed to regulate it, encourage it, or destroy it. HUD, the Housing and Urban Development Department (yet another agency not in existence when Hunter wrote), now owns more housing in more cities and towns than any old-time robber baron or slum lord ever dreamed of. Perhaps we could say that as the capitalist elite moved its physical investment to more profitable national ventures, it was supplanted by the new oligarchs of state and national control.

In any event, as a broad generalization, the simplistic notions of a single power elite or a pluralistic, grand coalition do not apply, if ever they did. To compound the dilemma, there was a movement of population in the 1970s that threatened to rival the great black migrations of the post-World War II era and the suburbanization period that may only now be tapering off. Affluent, potential local leaders have been moving out of the midwest and northeast in astonishing numbers. This so-called elite, as well as the old leaders of New Haven and New York, are moving to the "sunbelt" cities as rapidly as their offspring take off for new challenges when they complete college training.

The influence and control of scarce private and public resources which seriously affect allocation and allocative structure lies in the hands of a distinct numerical minority. Political power remains concentrated in the hands of relatively few people, almost none of whom are even symbolically elected or otherwise legally acknowledged through democratic ceremony. Wealth, education, associations, and contacts still matter, but in some new and different ways. Clusters of federal and state bureaucracies and their local constituencies have tended to supplant the older, more simply understood elites. Such "aggregates" consist of structures like the regional HUD bureaucracies, the banks, the national insurance groups, and the major national construction firms. These structures, with their patterns of continuous collaboration, form "policy area" elites which happen to be local.

Such clusters of control do not exist because of the characteristics of their members or because of the local interest groups to which they belong. They are not based in a past rooted in the locality. The individuals may or may not belong to the same social club or be alumni of the same elite colleges. They are brought together by coinciding and occasionally conflicting patterns of organizational interest and personal ambition. The leaders of the city of today are, like most of the rest of us and unlike our grandfathers, strongly fashioned and directed by large, complex organizations that tend to be labeled apolitical. Corporations, colleges, schools, unions, fraternities, and the thousands of suborganizational units of which they are composed, create and define the possibility of a new urban elite. Not rooted by tradition or memory to the city, not obliged to respond, the new elitist sometimes appears to us as the neutral manager simply doing his job. He stands in sharp contrast to the Balls of Muncie, or their more historically distinguished counterparts in the East.[33]

[33]Even the Balls have changed. The family firm went public in 1974 and has diversified. In addition to the famous jar, the company now produces hardware for the aerospace industry; see *The New York Times,* August 10, 1979, p. D–1.

If the maldistribution of political power and the resources that create it still hold promise for understanding, despite some alterations suggested above, what else is there to remember from the elitist-pluralist debate? Perhaps one might fruitfully raise the question of self-interest, because to change the characters in the leadership group might well be to alter the patterns of reward said to be most valued by the "top people."

No political scientist ever went broke betting on self-interest (enlightened or otherwise) as part of the incentive pattern of any political actor. One thinks of the development of municipal unions, as an example, since Hunter (and Dahl for that matter) wrote, and wonders whether this clearly powerful new elite strains for rewards different from those sought by their upper-crust predecessors. Municipal unions must ensure a continued level of urban service provision if they are to survive and flourish. Obviously, union leadership has many more people to please than did its counterparts in the old local economic elites.

In other words, city councils, mayors, and the like seldom have the long-term political power to effectively checkmate municipal union demands. Nor do they have the long-term ability to stretch their taxation levels to a point that readily satisfies the unions, bankers, and organized taxpayers groups. State and federal agencies become involved as mediators, funders, and brokers in order to settle strikes by teachers, policemen, firemen, sanitation workers, and other municipal employees. The cumulative outcome of the growth of municipal union power is unclear. Whatever the outcome, there is little dispute that municipal unions are extremely powerful in many cities and that they will figure prominently in many political processes in the future. Their self-interest lies in part in creating some conditions nearly identical with the incentive patterns of the old elites. They need stable, predictable, positive political processes in order to consolidate their position over time. They must have ready and predictable amounts of tax dollars guaranteed beyond the often overmortgaged tax base of most central cities and many suburbs.

This means that the municipal unions must reduce uncertainty in at least two ways. First, they must be able to predict local political institutional outcomes by controlling local political institutions, just as machine bosses, elites, and pluralist coalition-builders once did. If the local apparatus, despite their control, fails to provide for their needs, the municipal unions must look beyond the city. As did the corporate moguls, as did the bosses, so the unions must control some leverage in state and national political arenas—and they do. Municipal unions are but one example of the new urban elite, and although they differ in many ways from the elite of Hunter's Atlanta, some of the ideas of the elite theorists still point us in useful directions.

Conclusion

The simpler ideas of the community power debate have, at the least, been qualified by material changes in the urban world. We conclude that the cities are in the process of being dominated by what we have called "new elites." These elites represent interests that typically arise outside of the city or even the urban area. Rather than being elites of a homogeneous nature, rooted in family and enterprise, historically nested in a given locale, the new heterogeneous elites circulate around the nation, often cut off from a collective past based on a "hometown."

We have suggested that the composition of such elites tends to reflect organizational facts rather than social facts. High position in a state or national enterprise, public or private, which is decentralized for local operational purposes now rivals ages-old partial ownership of the local bank as criteria for our identification of elite membership. Clearly, we reject the simpler aspects of the deterministic arguments. Moreover, the simpler determinisms of social class and economic clout continue to be suspect. But the notion of leadership, elitist or pluralist, is not to be excluded from our analysis of political power in the urban political system. On the contrary, we may say that the many continue to be governed by the nonelected few and that the "new few" may be every bit as powerful politically as any predecessor.

We can also note that the city or the urban area as a unit of analysis suffers greatly as we move away from the traditional conceptions of local leaders. This is so not only because of our modification of elite theorists' ideas and our criticisms of the pluralists. Rather, the entire question of what a city is has been called into question by virtue of the fact that more and more of those who determine the life of the city have no personal attachment to it. Even the very worst of the traditional local elites could at least be said to have tied some aspects of their collective futures to the locality, as had their ancestors. Today it is hard to find such embeddedness among the class of professionals who tend to dominate the new elites. We return to these themes in the chapters that follow.

Suggested Readings

Bachrach, Peter and Morton Baratz, *Power and Poverty* (New York: Oxford University Press, 1970).

Connolly, William E., *The Bias of Pluralism* (New York: Atherton Press, 1969).

Dahl, Robert A., "A Critique of the Ruling Elite Model," *American Political Science Review,* 52 (June 1958), p. 463. *Who Governs?* (New Haven: Yale University Press, 1961).

Domhoff, G. William, *Who Really Rules?* (New Brunswick: Transaction Books, 1978).

Hunter, Robert, *Community Power Structure* (Chapel Hill; University of North Carolina, 1953).

Polsby, Nelson W., *Community Power and Political Theory,* 2d ed. (New Haven: Yale University Press, 1980).

Chapter 6
Bureaucracy and Political Power

Introduction

Some social scientists believe that the modern city is an inadequate and incomplete unit of political analysis. Such analysts look upon the urban area or SMSA as more appropriate for description and understanding of what constitutes the urban political system. Certainly we have no quarrel with such spatial expansions. What such expansions tend to do, however, is to count suburban and urban politics as part of a *metropolitan* political system, thereby necessarily introducing subjects for analysis not typically included in studies of politics in cities and towns. The metropolitan focus rightly brings to our attention problems, issues, and situations that otherwise might have gone unmentioned or unnoticed in the multiple battles of the elitist and pluralist thinkers. Although such a focus was (and is) all to the good in altering our attention, it unfortunately did not often bring with it the intense methodological and politically interesting kinds of questions raised by earlier analysts of city politics.

The study of metropolitan regions, while coming to grips with the vital material facts of suburbanization and renewing interest in intergovernmental and interjurisdictional politics, commented little on the community power debate. The metropolitan focus was (and in general still is) determinedly concerned with outputs or the provision of public services, a vital set of matters to which we devote one-third of this book. Such an emphasis has tended to produce economic models while ignoring political ones, perhaps because there are so few satisfying ones for those who look to the urban region's service distribution as central to understanding the urban political system.

We contend that the attention of modern students of urban politics should be on the explicitly *urban,* the city and suburb.[1] The community power debate, moreover, should not be discarded simply because the traditional unit of analysis

[1]For an example of the literature on suburbanization see: *Annals of the AAPSS,* 422, (November 1975).

has been the town or the city as more or less self-contained entities. Rather, it seems appropriate to recombine some useful elements of both elitist and pluralist thought with some of the implications for political theory in urban settings brought about by the more recent stress on the metropolis.

What kinds of elements for political analysis arise when we look at the material conditions of cities and their environs in, say, the past quarter century or so? Certainly the human ecology of movement, economic activity, social life, and the like must be part of any political ideas which might build on the foundations of elitist and pluralist theory. Black immigration to northern cities peaked in the past twenty-five years while white emigration to the suburbs intensified. The suburbs no longer could be stereotyped as simply white, middle-class bedrooms. Rather they became more clearly "class ghettoes" for some, "age ghettoes" for others, and shopping centers for all. They were no longer simply the rural settings for the dreams of the upwardly mobile. Drugs became hot items in suburban high schools; traffic congestion, air pollution, high property taxes, and many social ills previously identified with core cities were "discovered" in the suburbs.

Citizenship in Cities and Towns

A matter of political significance, appropriate to theories of elite or plural domination, seems worth raising at this point. A root concept of both theoretical perspectives is the role of the individual in relation to the political system. In other words, the status of citizenship in either elitist or pluralist formulations is central to many of the key arguments. In the elitist's eyes, citizenship is a necessary imitation of acceptance. The pluralists generally hold citizenship to be relevant as a general support of the manifest political system and a potential resource in the struggles of interest and "interested" groups and potential groups.

But one must ask, given the altered material conditions discussed above, what do economic elites or democratically elected mayors, councils, and the like have to do with the everyday life of citizens of the urban area? Although it is relatively simple to identify the major holders of land, labor, capital, and other resources that determine the quality of life locally, it is improbable that such concentrations of economic power *themselves* ever become a recurrent local issue. Nor have the elite theorists ever demonstrated that such elites concern themselves with the multiplicity of issues that arise, even those they directly cause. The migration of thousands of mill jobs from the North to the South left some urban areas with terrible unemployment levels, for example. Alternatively, the many elected boards, panels, councils, executives, and judges who hold nominal and highly limited powers over local matters are hard for the citizen to interpret as either the cause of or the solution to his needs and problems.

What are some of those problems and where does one look for their solution or improvement? Reasonably inexpensive services in the expanded areas of education, police, fire, health, highways, welfare, and recreation are some of the places one might look to for the satisfaction of citizen want or need. Certainly some significant adjustments in a given service for a given person might be obtainable from an interested local member of an economic elite or from an elected city, county, or town official. But in the overall scheme of his existence as it pertains to government and to most of his public interactions, the citizen must confront public bureaucracies staffed by civil servants who often act with the authority of the state and of their profession. It is true, moreover, that such bureaucrats are more than likely responsible to hierarchical authorities with absolutely no significant local accountability under the law.

It is striking that as the era of "1,400 governments" moves into the epoch of "2,800 national, state, and local bureaucracies," few attempts have been made to suggest that the community power battles of the past be brought into this present reality.[2] For the purposes of his interest representation, the citizen is now factored into as many roles in relation to the state as an ever-refining division of bureaucratic labor can manage. What do we mean by citizen interest representation? Simple things such as getting a pothole repaired or having a traffic light installed at a dangerous intersection come to mind. A truant child, a family illness, financing a new home, or some other set of more urgent personal problems are similarly associated with local solutions.

Yet time and again citizenship has become identified in vital ways with public organizations whose centers of control are far distant from the physical locality of the wants and needs of the person. Each example of a "local" problem cited above has potentially two governmental agencies involved in its solution. Some have even more, and the connection between electoral outcomes, administrative responsiveness, and accountability becomes ever more tenuous. In the things that matter individually and collectively to citizens of the urban area, the most common and serious problems are generally within the mandates of public organizations over which individuals and collectivities have little effective control.

Such flat statements solve no analytical problems. Rather they point us in directions previously dealt with outside of the pluralist-elitist debate. How might one profitably think of citizenship if one were to include this argument about the significance of public bureaucracy? A first conclusion might be a sigh of relief that, despite what appears to be a "new" pattern of political domination, at least we are in theory *all* citizens again rather than subordinate blockheads of the elite. Nor are we "potential" resources to be employed by the multiple hierarchs of the pluralist "nonelites." Unfortunately, a quick glance at the material conditions of our daily lives tells us that such is far from the case. On the contrary, the emergence of complex, professionalized, unionized, functional public organizations not only provides us with a new and formidable political actor to compete with the elitist and pluralist views. They also control aspects of the allocation of

[2]Robert Wood, *1400 Governments* (Garden City, N.Y.: Doubleday, 1964).

scarce public resources. The consequences of this are so profound politically that a rough classification of citizen interaction with the state is necessary if our discussion is to proceed.

First we must specify that for the person, the significant interactions he has with the state are with its administrative agents, be they policemen, schoolteachers, nurses, firemen or clerks, not to mention forms, tax bills, and the other debris of everyday civic life. Occasionally, a numerical minority of eligible voters will appear to vote on some of those who are said to set the policies and practices of the administrative agencies with whom the citizen must interact. In general, however, the citizen finds it difficult to see the connection between what he faces when he meets that state and his vote or other political activity.

The key differences between citizens, particularly at the local level, lie in the degree of their dependency upon a state agency for services which are differentially determinative of important aspects of their lives. Those who live on welfare checks or who must stay in a public hospital's poor ward are the same sort of citizen only in a legal sense as the one who sits on that hospital's board. And with the exceptions of certain kinds of court decisions, the distinction is (following the elitist implication) as trivial as it is legal. If we look back to our discussions of the pluralist and elitist positions, we can see that the designations of citizens as either *constituents, clients,* or *victims* might be useful in analyzing the connections that matter when citizens meet the state in their city or suburb.[3]

Constituents

The idea of citizens as constituents draws upon the thinking of the pluralist writers initially, but then diverges with analysis. Certainly we are all represented by some group or other to which we belong. This proposition, however, encompasses too many different situations to serve as a satisfactory generalization. One is represented by both ascriptive and descriptive groups, such as "the blacks" and the NAACP. I have little choice about my inclusion and "representation" in the former, while the latter usually implies that I have taken some voluntary step in becoming a group member. Constituent groups are, then, at least partially defined by the supposedly voluntary nature of their membership.[4]

We may move farther down the pluralist road by stipulating that constituent groups represent the interests of their members to appropriate elements in the political system. This last phrase is meant to be understood in a very specific way. Constituency thus defined suggests that the student look to the actual place in

---

[3]For a more extensive discussion of the constituent, client, victim typology, see Eugene Lewis, *American Politics in a Bureaucratic Age* (Cambridge, Mass.: Winthrop, 1976).

[4]The voluntary nature of interest group membership has been challenged in Theodore J. Lowi, *The End of Liberalism* (New York: W. W. Norton, 1969) and, especially, in Mancur Olson, *The Logic of Collective Action* (Cambridge, Mass.: Harvard University Press, 1971).

the political system where the representatives of the constituency "make present" the demands of the group.[5] We may further specify that such groups are minimally interdependent with the appropriate element of the political system, where interdependence implies mutual power to channel the desired flow of scarce public resources. Thus a constituent group could be a "veto" group quietly presenting a policy alternative to one which they think potentially injurious to their interests. Typically, however, such constituent groups can be considered as similar to the active elites of Hunter or the interests of Dahl which pursue carefully limited spheres of policy domination. Builders, savings and loan associations, and construction unions form a cluster of groups around a set of interests. Such interests always have at least one institutional focal point within the political system. Often, as in this example, such constituent groups have multiple focal points, particularly in the urban political system.

This is so because most of the significant questions for such clusters of constituent groups today arise simultaneously in local, state, and national agencies. The issues are also divided into the obviously political (such as elections and referenda) and the potentially political (such as regulatory policy, judicial decisions, and, most importantly, bureaucratic discretion). The simple idea, then, of legislative representation of a geographical distribution of population is in our view not descriptive of the constituency-type of relationship we find in the urban political system. If one accepts these modifications of the interest group theorists, then have we any idea where power truly rests in the urban political system?

Probably not, for we have not quite dealt with the initial question of the citizen. If I have a few shares of the local bank stock and belong to the plumbers' union, does this mean my interests are being represented? Not necessarily. Constituent groups are, as a rule, not run exclusively in their members' interests. The PTA, the Teamster local, the local savings and loan association, and the local chapter of the American Federation of Teachers are as liable to oligarchical domination as is any other group. In other words, group membership in a constituency thus defined does not necessarily imply the representation, much less the satisfaction, of the rank-and-file membership.

What distinguishes such groups is their relative interdependence with some aspect of governmental power, the generally voluntary nature of their membership, and their relatively marginal dependency on a public agency for their survival. This latter is most important, for it suggests that the constituency has alternative routes of action should the interdependent relationship somehow fail. The constituent organization as defined has alternative resources upon which to depend should the scope of conflict expand beyond normal bargaining. Strikes, strike funds, friends in the higher levels of the political system, money to defeat candidates, and more are among some of the independent resources held by constituency groups.

[5]Hanna Pitkin, *The Concept of Representation* (Berkeley: University of California Press, 1967).

Such resources seldom have to be applied, however. The whole idea of constituency, as represented here, is to reduce uncertainty in the political system by cooperating with agencies needed for the continued health of the constituent organization. It must be stressed that constituencies, as defined here, are almost always organized. They frequently are formal organizations, usually collecting fees, dues, or contributions from their membership through voluntary or coercive methods. Equally important is our stress on the point that such groups are not only involved with representation in legislative bodies. Our concept of representation includes not only the geographic space of the urban area, but also the intellectual space which takes into account multiple levels of public bureaucracies, boards, and courts of one sort or another. It is in these arenas that most of the significant acts of public policy for urban areas take place.

For at least a generation, public organizations at the three levels of American government have dominated most of the public policy landscape of the urban area. Urban renewal, public education, welfare, police and fire services, and highways and roads are to ever-increasing degrees funded in large part outside of the specific location in the urban area. Thus the police of a given city or town look not only to the police union, city council, and the like, but must now attend to what the LEAA (Law Enforcement Assistance Administration) is up to. Urban renewal has long been the child of HUD, local (often semiautonomous) authorities, and state agencies. The examples are endless. The point is that when we speak of constituent groups in the urban political system, we are increasingly referring to bureaucratic constituencies. We also speak of members of constituencies as being represented by their leaders according to the dominant values of the usual oligarchy controlling the constituent group. The power of the citizen who is a bureaucratic constituent is relatively weak compared with the influence he has over group leaders. The leadership can, however, pose a potential threat and offer potential benefits to political actors who recommend and implement public policy within the sphere of the constituent group's interest.

The idea of a constituent much resembles the pluralist notion of interest group membership in that it suggests the possibility of another representational system operating above and below the waterline of public democratic structure. This traditional idea has been discussed, criticized, and modified for more than a half-century. We bring it into the present analysis and point to the differences in the material conditions of the political system and of those who are constituency group members. These differences lie in the area of structure; i.e., bureaucratic and regulatory constituencies dominate their field of policy interest at multiple levels within the federal system which have significant primary and secondary effects on the lives of urban citizens. Secondly, we have suggested that the complex elaboration of such systems of power and representation effectively shields much of the making of public policy in cities and towns from the members of the traditional political world of mayors and councils. Finally, we have repeated the argument, begun with Michels and brought up to date by many writers, that even though the citizen is a member of such a constituency group, the chances of his effectively exercising "voice" in the operation of the organization are minimal.[6]

The kind of interdependence involved in agency-constituency relationships could be conveniently called mutual cooption. Historically, organized groups "captured" agencies created to regulate and/or stimulate them.[7] The great regulatory commissions and all manner of local boards and councils somehow ended up being run by people who came from the private sector interest that was to be regulated. This results in a series of policy or regulatory decisions likely to be favorable to the powers that be. The repetition of such cooption throughout the structure of American federalism is a fact noted by many pluralist and antipluralist writers. Dahl's discussion of the urban renewal program in New Haven is a nice example of this sort of "classical cooption." Many organized constituencies, such as the banks and the unions, met the federal bureaucrats at the point of policy initiation to work out plans for New Haven's urban renewal program under the guidance of Mayor Lee.

The picture is undoubtedly a reasonably familiar one to students of American government. There is a "contemporary cooption" that begins to tell us to look for citizens who are not quite as potentially independent as their constituent fellows. It must be remembered that in a "classical cooption" situation organized interests band together to capture or dominate some aspect of public policy-making structure, as in the New Haven example. But what about agencies who have no political, economic, or social group to become their constituents? Recall that the agency that possesses a powerful constituency has a vital resource in dealing with its competitors or potential competitors in the struggle over the allocation of scarce public resources. Since the New Deal, government agencies providing services to unorganized, labeled groups have grown enormously at all levels of the federal system, particularly in urban areas. Thus the common example of organized agricultural constituencies creating and capturing the Agriculture Department has to be contrasted with an HEW whose constituents were few while their agency's resources were potentially great. As more services of a social nature are provided and fewer direct economic benefits are perceived, the chances of classical cooption are reduced and the contemporary version enhanced.

The idea is for the agency to develop a group of citizen-backers whom it presumes to represent. The problem is that the objects of social service provision

[6]Robert Michels, *Political Parties,* trans. Eden and Cedar Paul (Glencoe, Ill.: The Free Press, 1958); the exercise of "voice" is discussed in Albert O. Hirshman, *Exit, Voice, and Loyalty* (Cambridge, Mass.: Harvard University Press, 1970).
[7]"Capture" and "mutual cooption" are described and illustrated in, especially: Phillip Selznick, *TVA and the Grass Roots* (New York: Harper & Row, 1966); Grant McConnell, *The Decline of Agrarian Democracy* (Berkeley: University of California Press, 1953); and, also by McConnell, *Private Power and American Democracy* (New York: Knopf, 1966).

are themselves far from being politically powerful or economically independent. There often is a class of professionals, employed by the public organization and who are its main financial beneficiaries as well. Schoolteachers, social workers, policemen, and public hospital employees provide services to those who are normally incapable of creating true constituencies. Clearly, they serve such groups as pupils, welfare mothers, and the sick or infirm. Such service recipients tend not to resemble the constituent in many ways, yet they are used to create the basis for a form of bureaucratic representation which we label "contemporary cooption" and which depends upon what has been described as the client form of citizen-state interaction.

Clients

A client is the object of a public policy who has little or no potential, much less actual, influence over the political processes that create that policy. Clients are typically "represented" by those professionals whose livelihood depends upon the existence of the client population. In cities this is a substantial and growing population. Welfare recipients, AFDC mothers, schoolchildren (with some exceptions), "urban renewed" neighbors, "red-lined" property owners, and many other service recipients are clients. They are distinguished by the degree of their dependency upon public agencies for their continued receipt of the service. They ordinarily are members of the vast working class and impoverished population visually and statistically concentrated in the center of most large urban areas.

While the constituent is to be "worked for" by the organization supposedly in existence to serve him, the client gets "worked on," or, in the more pleasant expression of domination-subordination relationships, "worked with." The mediating force between clients and the allocative processes that so greatly affect their fate is the growing army of professionals who are the truly powerful representatives of their clients. Indeed, "contemporary cooption" often involves professional service workers, professors, and relevant bureaucrats in the construction of a seemingly representative system that mimics that of the bureaucratic constituency. The point is that the organizers are those public employees and others who dominate the clientele and define the limits of its thought and action. How is this possible in a city where all are citizens? The answer is as simple as it is chilling. For purposes of action, the person who meets the state to receive a service becomes, however momentarily, an object of administrative action. I am a client without much recourse to an alternative when I apply and submit myself to a procedure for obtaining a driver's license. For those trivial moments, I allow myself to be treated as simply another unit in the efficient process of driver-license production. My will is suspended insofar as I accede to the demands of those who are imposing the rules upon me. In return for this temporary suspension of will, the public agency provides me with the legal means to drive a car.

What if my relationship were extended over time? The act of defining me in rule-bound, objectified terms might be somewhat similar if I were a public school pupil or a welfare recipient, but the duration of my powerlessness would, we argue, create, along with the initial authoritative labeling by professional social worker or school administrator, a relatively permanent state of dependency. Typically, clients live in a state of dependency for the service provided and that service is often the only way possible for the recipient to live a normal life. In some cases, of course, the dependency sustains life itself. This is particularly true among the very young, the indigent sick, and of course, the poor in general. It must be stressed that such people are not only "dollar poor," but are more often than not "resource poor." One's parents might be able to keep one in minimal food, fiber, and shelter, but without public education, chances of an economically successful life are utterly dim. The client, then, is usually "resource poor" and is gathered by the public agency into a clientele that is simply ascriptive. The political significance of a clientele lies almost totally in the hands of those who operate the bureaucratic system that dominates clients' lives. Those who seek to maintain and enhance agency power are paid to act as if they represented a constituent group capable of mobilization in the streets or polling booths.

Yet clientele groups are generally a mockery. The professional who meets the client at the door often has defined him into a role which is at best subordinate and inferior. The social world similarly views welfare recipients and schoolchildren as somehow less able to speak for themselves than those who are responsible for them. Essentially, the relationship is paternalistic and cooptive. To return to the citizen mode, no matter how idealized, is a difficult sociopolitical jump not often seen. The state and the professionalized wisdom of its employees therefore become the representatives of the ascriptively labeled. Those who would label are always careful to label only those who tend not to fight back. A great and pathetic attempt to overcome this client relationship came with the passage of the U.S. Government's Community Action Program of the Economic Opportunity Act of 1964. The Office of Economic Opportunity tried to organize the urban poor into a constituency that would compete with the existing structes of urban government. The government was to pay and supervise such "representatives" who were to be duly elected and responsive to "the needs of the community."[8] As sad and ill-thought-out as this program was, it did provide an insight into the changing role of the citizen and the state in urban areas. The program is long dead. Its clients and potential clients are still among us. Their dependency has not decreased, nor has the growth of powerful bureaucratic actors allocating scarce public resources in their interest abated.

[8]*See* J. David Greenstone and Paul E. Peterson, *Race and Authority in Urban Politics* (New York: Russell Sage Foundation, 1973).

Victims

We turn now to the final, general variety of citizen interaction. The victim category is a leftover one, derived from the idealized citizen through the bureaucratic constituent to the client and climaxing in a class of the citizenry lacking in even the minimal resources of the client. The victim is created by the state in at least two different ways. The powerless objects of state classification form one group of victims. Mental patients, criminals, juvenile delinquents, derelicts, and social deviants of all sorts form a small but substantial group of citizens who for good reasons or bad are excluded from most forms of political participation. The abject, the hopeless, the confused, and the utterly useless are visible and troublesome in cities as they seldom are in the countryside. This does not mean that the rural population has fewer victims: it suggests only that victims are more visible in cities and far less tolerated in suburbs. Former mental patients, prisoners, drunks, drug addicts, prostitutes, runaways, and drifters constitute a class of citizens who are the objects of attention of various government agencies, partly because, in general, the society will have nothing whatever to do with them.

Such people and the "dollar poor" receive "warehousing" treatment from the professional groups operating public jails, prisons, reformatories, hospitals, and various other "total institutions." It is hard to portray people in this condition as citizens who possess slack or potential resources with which to oppose public policies that affect their lives. Unlike the client, who at least has the potential for disruption through organized action or because of an occasional advantage created by conflict between agencies for his possession, the victim has no such glimmer of hope. The aged poor and the very young are too often victims of the social world, and public organizations simply become the "last stop" for them. Nonfunctioning people who do not possess material resources, family, or friends often become—not victims of the state—but victims of the social world. They drift into a terminal dependency upon agencies physically located in the spot of their greatest concentration, the city.

Whether victimized by public agencies or by the social world in general, the people in this first class of the victim category at least have minimal knowledge of the government and its actions. There is a final group of citizens which doesn't admit of even this small bit of comprehension. These are the millions of urban citizens vitally affected by policies made beyond their sight or knowledge. These policies may be made in Washington and have to do with macroeconomic policy, or they may involve a tiny increase in the sales tax in the city or state. Whatever the source, whatever the distance in time and space, victims are created by distant policy decisions which, say, effectively reduce the number of weekly family meals from 21 to 20 or compel people by the thousands to move out of their homes to make way for a turnpike toll plaza or a bridge approach.

Bureaucratic constituency groups may have had a great deal to do with the site location, planning, and financing of such a project as a new bridge or a toll plaza. The public employment service may even have gotten some of their clients a little bit of work on the project. Nobody spends a great deal of time or money, despite claims to the contrary, on relocation programs for the displaced.[9] The anticipation of such construction normally leads to the dispersion of the population as speculators typically buy up the buildings in which the potential victims rent space. The stage is thus set for a high turnover migration, a severe reduction in landlord services to new and remaining tenants, and eventually a lucrative settlement when the real estate speculator "cleans up" following formal condemnation proceedings needed to raze the building. The owner collects handsomely; the construction contractors, union members, and bankers make money; and the former tenants move on to more expensive but qualitatively inferior housing.[10]

This tale was (and is) repeated in city after city in America. There are not a lot of words to describe what happens to such citizens who are displaced after futile protest. "Victim" is useful in this context. It ought to be stressed that victimization by the state in its multiple and federal forms does not come from the vindictive desire to inflict pain and suffering. Victimization is usually manifest in the mindless carrying out of a plan or responsibility by some functionary who has little to fear from the human object affected by his act.

From the deliberate prejudicial annoying of minority and socially deviant populations by police to the senseless damage done to family and community by urban renewers, there is a continuum. The acts may vary, but the effect is the same: victims either are utterly dependent upon some agency of the state for life itself or they are turned into victims by the mindless, unplanned incremental changes implemented by a many-headed public bureaucracy. In any event, to view victims as citizens who have a sense and a reality of efficacy in civic affairs is absurd. Unlike clients, who at least are partial beneficiaries of the absolute need of professionalized agents of the state to have clientele, victims approximate garbage whose number makes relatively little difference to the human refuse collectors of the state.

In terms of resources, interdependence and dependence, and civic effectiveness, there seems ample reason for splitting the urban citizenry into these three modes of interaction. They lead us to a series of unanswered questions however. They contrast in several ways with the citizenry of the pluralists and the stratified minions of an elite. Our citizens live in a more complex political world, one populated with multiple organizations of state and private interests. One central question which proceeds from our classification of interaction modes concerns the geography and history of the particular form of political power identified as being worthy of conceptual competition with the ideas of the elitists and the pluralists. It is to this geography and history that we now turn.

[9]The lack of planning in neighborhood relocation is documented in a legal suit brought to the federal courts by the black community in Norwalk, Conn.: *Norwalk Core* v. *Norwalk Redevelopment Agency*, 395 F, 2d 108 (1968).

[10]Scott Greer, *Urban Renewal and American Cities* (Indianapolis: Bobbs-Merrill, 1966).

The Political History and Geography of Urban Bureaucratic Power

The Reform Movement, Neutral Competence, and Expertise

In Chapter 5, we identified "meritocracy" as being one of the three "handmaidens" of the urban reform movement. Certainly the effective reduction of patronage jobs to bare minima helped to destroy the machine form of political organization. What has yet to be adequately described and discussed are the historical ramifications of the introduction of meritocracy and its contemporary meaning. The core notions of competitive entry examination, effective tenure (guarantee of long-term retention except for cause) and open examinations for promotion derive from a cluster of beliefs best expressed in this country by Woodrow Wilson during his career as a political scientist.[11] Wilson symbolized the progressive idea that bureaucracy was a potentially vital tool for good in the hands of politicians. It could summon the best techniques and wisdom of business management, of scientific procedure and substance, and of the British higher civil service to bring American values to their fullest realization. This idealism must be understood in the context of a crusading reform movement out to destroy the twin antidemocratic forces of political machines and economic cartels.

As we suggested earlier, there was a root belief among the reformers that not only would efficiency and honesty be served by such public organizations, but civic virtue itself would be enhanced. This was to come about by the replacement of party hacks by college-trained professionals whose only concern would be the efficient and effective deployment of organizational structures in service to the highest ideals of democracy and civilization. A key value conflict can be seen in this early stage, one which grows over the decades and continues to cause problems for many who study urban politics.

Wilson and his many successors persisted in claiming that bureaucracy was itself a neutral instrument in service of the values given it by the politicians responsible to the electorate for their policy choices. A paradox is thus concealed. Public administrators cannot hold political beliefs that vary from those of their policy-making, elected (or appointed) superiors if the Wilsonian scheme is to work. Yet it is part and parcel of the democratic concept that *all* citizens have such values. The Wilsonian prescription also holds with the notion that self-interest for the individual and for the organization is to be eliminated in service to the people whose government the bureaucrats managed. There was, in short, to be an army of professional managers and experts at the disposal of town, city, and nation, dedicated to implementing the policies of their political superiors no matter what were their own wishes, wants, or needs. Separation between some-

[11] Woodrow Wilson, "The Study of Administration," *Political Science Quarterly,* 2 (June 1887).

thing called "policy" and something else called "administration" was to be the essential condition of the new urban public bureaucracies.

Superiority over the lazy, corruptible laborers of the machine period was to be demonstrated not only by the personal and professional qualities of the new public administrators. The reformers put at least as much stock in neutral competence through "scientific" training and in organizational design as they did in individual integrity.

A particularly important value, in our view, was the reformer's belief in the separation of expert knowledge from the conditions of its creation and more importantly from its imposition.[12] What the new public administrators did was to bring efficiency, effectiveness, and legal honesty to the enterprise of administering and governing, under the appearance of a disinterest which was sold as neutrality. By "sold" we mean to suggest that the public, the politicians, and the administrators themselves were "educated" to a belief that there was "one best way" for most policies concerning localities. There was no partisan garbage, only garbage; and there was only a technical problem in getting it cleaned up at the least cost to the public. The "one best way" always contained (and still does) the assumption of superior insight on the part of the person and process which brought it to our attentions. There could be no public or political debate about education, crime, sanitation, welfare, penology, and delinquency once such matters were attended to by experts schooled in the proper policies and procedures.

The appeal of such arguments in a technology and science-worshipping culture must have been compelling. The idea of applying the very successful managerial forms of capitalist enterprise must have been equally alluring to those who were acutely embarrassed by the incompetent and corrupt buffoons conducting the public business under the thumb of illiterate political bosses. Our belief in rationalistic solutions to our problems is matched only by our touching faith in the magic done to human nature through the imposition of formal structure. The "new" bureaucrat was no doubt a great improvement over his predecessor. But the problem was (and is) that public organization remains, to paraphrase Max Weber, a power instrument of the first order, and it was the control of this instrument from within and without that the reformers had not adequately considered.[13]

Federalism

If bureaucratic power, expertise, and the idea of neutral competence were to become problematic over time, the question of federalism itself had to intensify.

[12]The historical separation of politics from administration is analyzed in detail in: Vincent Ostrom, *The Intellectual Crisis in American Public Administration* (University, Ala.: University of Alabama Press, 1973).
[13]Max Weber "On Bureaucracy," in K. De Schweinitz and K. W. Thompson, eds., *Man and Modern Society* (New York: Holt, 1953), pp. 501–509. Also on this point: Jacques Ellul, *The Technological Society* (New York: Knopf, 1964).

The three *levels* of government, matched by the balance of power doctrine that gives us three *branches* at each level, has caused one sort of problem or another throughout American history. In the nineteenth century, the role and relative autonomy of the states came into question repeatedly in political and economic areas. But the Civil War and the growth of the trusts, while perhaps settling some questions of great magnitude for the states, left little direction for those who would understand the relative powers of government in relation to the locality.

The states, it will be recalled, possessed what used to be called in legal jargon "the police powers." These normally included health, welfare, and safety (or morality.) As explained in Chapter 2, cities and towns are legal creatures of the states that create them. Their functions and powers come about because *and only because* a state legislature and a governor grant them. Traditionally, the "house-keeping" functions of road maintenance, sanitation, police and fire protection, recreation, and the like have been delegated to the cities and towns. Sometimes these clusters of functions are put together in the form of a "home rule" charter, approved by state government and given to the town's citizens through referendum. Local power to tax is similarly delegated, and some municipalities have excise taxes and income taxes in addition to the traditional property tax.

To further complicate matters, Americans have a tradition of creating special taxing districts, giving their directors powers not often delegated in other parts of the world. The local school board is perhaps the best and oldest example. Most cities and towns place school tax and administration completely outside of the municipality. Today one can easily find water, sewage, lighting, and other special districts with taxing powers. All of this careful division of responsibility and power in states and cities makes for a rich and complex system of government, enabling the citizen, by the relatively simple device of moving, a choice as to who will govern him and tax him, at least in some matters.

As a system of hierarchical power resembling an organization, federalism leaves a great deal to be desired. Because we are speaking of *levels of government* with sovereign powers, traditional functions with great affective clout (local school boards *locally* elected) and sets of relatively autonomous political actors capable of causing problems, the idea of federalism as a fruitful ground for complex bureaucratic domination seems dumb. After all, one might argue, with all of those governments and elected officials, how could bureaucratic organizations ever influence outputs and therefore outcomes? Whatever happened to those local elites dominating the urban political landscape, and what about those pluralistic, skillful, self-interested aggregations of specific interests? Certainly each of these formulations of local political power would encompass the "true powers" to allocate scarce public resources in cities and towns!

To begin to answer the questions posed above, we must conceive of federalism not as a governmental system, but as a set of problems for public organizations designed to deal with a particular element in the mix of problems. Thus we might go back to the era of Franklin D. Roosevelt and note that the vast unemployment of the Depression years was wholly beyond the capacities of the states and localities, despite the fact that they, and they alone, had the legal and traditional authority to deal with welfare. The New Deal simply created multiple districts and proceeded to design organizations with national goals whose local managers commanded the districts thus established. Cities and towns in America are still fitted out with the fruits of such labors. The federal government, by law, created vast public works programs to provide jobs and wages for the unemployed. Repeatedly, the state governments were ignored and the local ones not even noticed as the New Dealers designed formal organization after formal organization to deal with one problem area or another.

But this was, as they say, only the beginning. Federal structure could be looked at as simply an archaic obstruction, plentifully supplied with elected officialdom standing in the way of the unyielding growth and complex elaboration of bureaucratic organization. This is too strong a statement. What seems really to have happened is bureaucratization of state and local systems, perhaps in response to the nationalization of social welfare, highway construction, and the like. The vast elaboration of private corporate organization and the increasing complexity of their own territories contributed as well. The political point of local control, autonomy, and other aspects of federal governmental organization seems to have been lost and a new focus substituted. This "new focus" was probably provided first by the New Dealers, but it was significantly elaborated by its successors at all levels.

The idea is that, rather than looking upon America as a set of semisovereign instrumentalities called states and localities, one might best conceive of the nation as a set of problems located in a geographically dispersed fashion requiring a decentralized form of administrative organization. If one adopts such a view (implicitly reflected in the organization charts of thousands of federal, state, and local organizations), then the problem of urban politics is to effectively relate the decentralized component to local conditions. This is in sharp contrast to the common view attributed to the Founding Fathers, which holds that states are sovereign political entities and that people should, to the greatest extent possible, govern themselves. Federalism in the modern era is rapidly becoming administrative decentralization at the cost of the traditional model of political decentralization.

It is important to note that this is far from simply the ancient conservative wheeze about the "feds" taking over everything. On the contrary, the states and cities since the early 1950s have followed suit with a vengeance. Few large cities are without highly refined special districts of their own bureaucratic organizations. Fire, health, police (the precinct is an ancient political-administrative unit), and most other services are provided through geographically dispersed special districts wholly unrelated to the traditional political representational districts like wards. The states, for their part, divide themselves in a similar manner. The point is that the *problem* (mental health, welfare, etc.) has become the significant jurisdiction and seems to be replacing simple representational districts as the crucial element in the urban political system.

Certainly this is not universally so, and no implication is being made here that federal organization of government is no longer significant. Nor is it being argued that legislators and elected executives lack power. The federal form of political organization is being replaced by administratively decentralized problem areas (functional). The organizations which represent these problem areas are large and control vast amounts of scarce public resources. Most such organizations are beyond the control, if not the influence, of most elected politicians most of the time.

National Problems, Local Solutions

If we pause for a moment to consider what the great problems of urban areas have been for the past two generations, what do we find? Without carefully specifying, one can at least identify the following with a "buzz word" or two: poverty, racism, unemployment, transportation, pollution, energy, health care. Certainly there are others, and our list could be expanded and more highly detailed. The point of the list, however, is to suggest that nearly all the problems of domestic politics have one thing in common: a strikingly urban location. If we were to push the point to include tempestuous issues such as busing and "crime in the streets" or rioting, then there probably would be little doubt that most people would identify even more strongly with the notion that we are talking about a cluster of *urban* problems.

Yet because of their scope or their magnitude or both, all the issues of American domestic politics mentioned above have federal, state, and local agencies devoted to their "solution" or improvement. The great division of responsibilities between the levels of government is no more. Most recently, this claim came into dramatic highlight when New York City became effectively bankrupt and nearly brought down the state of New York with it. It required the federal government's intervention to "stabilize" the financial situation. There are other sets of problem or issue clusters that are less dramatic but far more significant for our general point, which is that *the significant matters of urban politics have increasingly become the "property" of public bureaucracies and their constituency and clientele networks which extend far beyond any given locale.* By "property," we mean to suggest that the major urban problems have long since become the mandates for the powerful national, state, and local agencies and their constituents and clients. Such mandates are, of course, vital and valuable resources for the agencies, for they constitute the agencies' reason for being and to lose them would likely mean organizational death.

Let us consider some examples. Forty years or so ago, the problems of housing and transportation were largely matters of private-sector investment and public-sector regulation on the local level. Cities inspected housing for fire, sanitation, and health violations. Landlords were fined, buildings were razed, and the public/private distinction was not particularly complex. Cities taxed property and used some of the revenues to pay inspectors to enforce state, county, or city laws and ordinances. In the matter of transportation, cities and towns owned, leased, or simply regulated the vast networks of trolley lines, elevated subways, commuter railroads, interurban tram lines, and bus, taxi, and truck operations that constituted urban transport infrastructure. Taxes paid for road construction and maintenance, and the cities, towns, counties, and states haggled over who was to pay for what repair on what particular road.

In many ways this routinized conflict over who is to pay for what continues today as though it were still 1940. But nearly everything else has changed. There are no more trolley lines, and the interurban train has gone the way of all railed flesh—to the scrap heap or to the federal receiver. Private enterprise no longer has much interest in public mass transit. The local elites who once profited greatly by owning shares in the local transit line are increasingly difficult to locate. Indeed, many of the local patricians allegedly running Philadelphia from its suburban Main Line (named after the main line of the Pennsylvania Railroad, the largest railroad in America forty years ago) have disappeared. The Pennsylvania Railroad went broke, and many of its respected owners and managers barely avoided jail—a nasty and unforeseen fate for such eminent oligarchs. But who runs the Pennsylvania Railroad today? National government corporations called Conrail and Amtrak.

National and, to a lesser extent, state bureaucratic agencies created a continental system of limited access freeways that has transformed the face of the nation's cities. The constituencies of such agencies included bankers, unions, local elites of one sort or another, politicians of every stripe and from every level, and contractors of every conceivable variety. The question of national highways was too large and too important to leave up to localities. Indeed, it was to such experts as Robert Moses and thousands of engineers and planners that the multiple governments involved turned. Cities were cut into bits by intersecting limited-access freeways. Neighborhoods were devastated and displaced to God knows where. Automobile traffic into, around, and through cities, towns, and suburbs was, of course, vastly increased by the construction of such superhighways. Superpollution, supergasoline consumption, and supermaintenance costs followed as the day follows the night. These became the problem of the cities, but they also aggregated themselves into the need to create yet more agencies and even cabinet-level departments. Again the problem has an urban locus, but national and state bureaucratic agencies are given the mandates and other scarce public resources needed to "solve" them. Perhaps the word "given" should be considered as problematic at this point.

Housing, like transportation, used to be largely a matter for local economies, private investment, and government regulation supplemented by generally ineffective, politically naive planning efforts. Planning commissions are perhaps a bit less ineffective and a mite less naive, but nearly everything else has changed. Bankers now are "covered" by various national programs to ensure that they lend money to home buyers and builders without much risk to them or their profits.

Larger projects now have national and state agencies as full partners or guarantors of the builder's risk. As much as the roads and expressways, the urban renewal programs begun after World War II have changed the character and face of our cities. Before HUD there was HHFA (Housing and Home Finance Administration), but before HHFA there was virtually nothing. Today real estate speculators, bankers, contractors, and unions are on the sidelines, awaiting the next grand expenditure of public monies for the renewal of the cities. They are not likely to look for local initiatives, nor are they likely to be lobbying in Congress or the state legislatures without the cooperation and encouragement of the bureaucratic agencies which helped create and maintain the great urban renewal boom of the 1960s and 1970s.

How it is that complex bureaucratic actors and procedures come to dominate policy areas of major concern to localities is something we shall deal with in the pages that follow. At the moment, we wish only to point to the existence of such organizations, to their relative newness on the political scene, and to the possibility that bureaucratic growth and elaboration goes unmentioned, unaccounted for, and certainly not predicted in either the pluralistic or the elitist formulations of political power in communities.

Bureaucratic Political Power: Summary and Conclusion

There is an important set of compatible ideas that bring together some of the different elements for analysis raised in this chapter. These have been macroscopic in focus. Chapter 8 deals with some microscopic aspects of a bureaucratic politics synthesis of certain elements of the elitist/pluralist controversy. At this point, it is worth returning to some of our earlier points by way of summary.

The fabric of American politics is and has been undergoing some important changes that have to do with the increasing tendency to create organizations and mandates that often become almost uncontrollable. In other words, balance of power arguments and counterbalanced notions of federal versus state powers seem not to hold as much water as they once did. We have suggested that there is a cultural tendency to "buy" the truth of expert knowledge over the truth of the traditional political process. Issues seldom are debated by electoral politicians; interest group politics has long been accepted to be a legitimate "supplement" to the electoral process, and the decline in citizen participation in voting and campaigning is seen to be offset by such group affiliations (ascriptive or descriptive) as the individual has.

We dispute such a claim as being naively unconscious of the single, overwhelming fact of the modern age, other than anxiety, and that is the growth and elaboration of complex formal organization.

We identified the values associated with the urban reformers of generations past as primarily and peculiarly adapted from the kinds of industrial organizations so extraordinarily productive during the early days of urban reform. Neutrality in controversial matters and a concern for scientific behavior, without special interest or secular concern, were (and continue to be) very important core values of public organizations and of reformed local governments. The key question at this point is to assess what these characteristics (and some others) have to do with the question of community power dealt with by the elitist and pluralist thinkers.

We began by noting the emergence of a metropolitan focus which moves analysis beyond the city limits. We then suggested a set of interaction modes that might fit the realities of politics as observed in the present space and time. We noted that the noble and global ideas of citizenship found in primary and secondary school textbooks left something to be desired. One might be better served, we argued, by looking at the question of citizenship through the lenses provided by the two schools of thought on community power. The elitists argued that the notion of citizenship in any important participatory democratic sense is nonsense. Pluralists held out more hope for the classical, conventional wisdom which argues that citizenship entails not just voting, but also group membership and hence more representation of people's interests. There was also some idea of potential, which suggested that sufficient provocation could bring out the masses, later called the "silent majority."

We have suggested that important changes in American society have brought about important changes in the core notion of citizenship. Metropolitan sprawl, neutral competence, scientific detachment, the nationalization of what had been local matters, and the structure and consequences of a three-level/branch system have contributed to the development of a new kind of citizenship. This is characterized by a division of the citizen into the relevant roles, problems, or other designation of some agency or another. We have pursued the point by implicitly noting the power and hence resource differences *between* citizens, pointing out that power and organization are inextricably linked. The taxonomy of interaction modes is, we believe, reinforced by the continuing elaboration of complex, professionalized public organizations. They successfully differentiate between groups of citizens according to the degree to which the agency depends upon the particular segment of the public (and *vice versa*) in the long-term struggle over the allocation of scarce public resources.

Our reformulated notion of constituency attempts to highlight the interdependent nature of some groups of citizens with particular agencies such that neither can long dominate the flow of public resources alone, but collectively can probably reduce uncertainty to the point of effective monopoly. As examples, one might point to the fascinating development of municipal unions whose members are interdependent with their employers (the city) who are in turn (according to our understanding of democratic theory) supposedly "owned" by the undifferentiated mass of citizens. The classic interest group aggregation which surrounds urban renewal in a given city rests not so much on influencing legislators as upon striking bargains with HUD bureaucrats whose discretionary power is sufficient to "make or break" any given project. Such policy-making professionals might be "pushable" through Congressional or other pressure once or twice but in the long run hold sufficient control over key processes so that it is normally better to "bargain and broker" than to try to compel.

In Chapter 7 we deal with the internal processes which act to foster and channel such relationships. At this summary point, we wish only to point to the existence of such connections in one subset of citizen/state interactions and to note how nicely these fit with the removal of partisanship from the public business and into the hands of professionals, a consummation devoutly wished for by the reformers of old. Unfortunately, the hopes of those reformers were not fully realized, for the reformers wanted only a benevolent bureaucracy unchained by the mean and low self-interest of the machine politicians and the "interests."

Local "policy elites," politically allied with nationalized bureaucratic organizations of great power and linked to relevant electoral politicians, form a rough constituency relationship. Here the needs and wants of given groups are represented by sets of leaders who claim to be in control of significant scarce resources, including money, numbers of members, symbolic meanings, and the multiplicity of ideas and things which make up scarce resources. So, in some areas of urban politics, we do believe that the ideas of Dahl and Hunter can be synthesized to reveal a corporatelike form of representation and domination of policy areas by groups of people whose behavior we identify as having the characteristic properties of constituencies.

We also introduced a notion of citizenship that implicitly recognizes two facts. First, that as individuals, few of us have significant control over distinct bureaucratic interactions with the state so long as the bureaucratic actor (either an organization or a person) follows rules which are publicly known and knowable. For most of us, such relationships are fleeting. A second class of citizen is far less fortunate. He or she is compelled by circumstance to live a life of prolonged dependency upon public organizations of one sort or another. We have called this group of persons and interactions "client" in an attempt to suggest that the primary aspect of the citizenship of such persons is dependency.

The term suggests, moreover, a relationship that assumes the temporary or highly segmented kind of dominant-subordinate situation one usually experiences as a patient of a physican. His superior knowledge and skill, licensed by the state, causes one to "suspend disbelief" temporarily and to put one's self into the doctor's care. Our example stops short if it becomes impossible to sever the relationship and move on to another doctor. And this is precisely the case with our "citizen as client" category, for the citizen has little or no effective choice in the way in which he is defined by the social worker, teacher, or other professional who acts with the authority of the state. Increasingly, over the past generation or so, such interactions take place in cities. Welfare mothers, juvenile delinquents, reformed drug addicts, as well as small shopkeepers, vendors to the city, or state public agencies and many others, fall into a client relationship with government authority. It is important to reiterate that the interaction in the urban place can be with multiple branches of national, state, or local agencies. Thus a continuing health problem can involve the dependent person with at least the three different levels of government and possibly with several different branches of one level or another.

But in explicitly political terms, clients are most often authoritatively represented by those employed by the state who hold professional qualifications which appear to entitle them to speak for the needs of the citizen who has fallen into their care. Agency leaders will, therefore, without cynicism or malice, attempt to obtain resources (including mandates) which will benefit their clients and (not incidentally) themselves and their organizational members. This is, after all, what agency heads are supposed to do. Our point is that the citizen thus transformed is passively represented as part of a "problem," the solution to which lies in the actions of a particular state agency (or, more likely, cluster of agencies). Thus the possibility of withholding assent, of going into active battle (as constituencies may potentially do), is for practical purposes unavailable to client groups.

The values of the reformers, the segmentation of the person into as many categories of "problems" as the powerful can create, and the violent transitions of the historical urban place provided us with some of the bases for our final category. The bottom of the social and political world received little description or analysis from most of the community power writers. Yet to describe anything about the powerful, however defined, is necessarily to imply something about the powerless. Victims are powerless for all practical purposes. Although clients may protest the misapplication of agency rules or may attempt to convert themselves into a true constituency or may develop some bargaining power when agencies occasionally compete for their numbers, victims enjoy few such hopes.

Victims are the leftovers of our classification and of the social world. We suggested that there are two general sorts of victims, one the descriptively identified and selected, the other a result of unanticipated consequences of some policy action by either public or private sector actors. The former are conceived of by the relevant policemen, jailors, mental health professionals, and others who deal with social deviants as "cases," most of whom cannot (and occasionally should not) exercise much in the way of self-expression, let alone political right to representation. The ideas of the reformers since the early nineteenth century informing much of this attitude have been highly paternalistic. Felons who have served their jail sentences still may not legally vote in the United States.

The vagrants of society have become the special province of cities by virtue of the concentration of population and transportation possibilities. Every large city has an area where winos, drifters, and derelicts are to be found. They commit no offense save living a life repugnant to the rest of us. They are generally treated as something less than a citizen, who, no matter his station in life (according to central guidelines of democratic theory) is not only entitled to rights *but is sovereign.*

So the initial discussion of our modifications and syntheses of the pluralist and elitist writers concludes. The move toward a set of ideas about the modern phenomenon of citizenship in the urban political system was related to some ideological and structural components not normally discussed at length in elite and pluralist formulations. Our next concern is to take these ideas and to more carefully apply them and others to that set of routines, improvisations, and wretched confusions which political scientists, with more than a touch of presumption, call the policy process.

Suggested Readings

Benveniste, Guy, *Bureaucracy* (San Francisco: Boyd & Fraser, 1977).

Jaques, Eliott, *A General Theory of Bureaucracy* (New York: Halsted Press, 1976).

Lewis, Eugene, *American Politics in a Bureaucratic Age* (Cambridge, Mass.: Winthrop, 1976).

Lowi, Theodore, *The End of Liberalism*, 2nd ed. (New York: W. W. Norton, 1979).

McConnell, Grant, *Private Power and American Democracy* (New York: Knopf, 1966).

Olson, Mancur, *The Logic of Collective Action* (Cambridge, Mass.: Harvard University Press, 1971).

Ostrom, Vincent, *The Intellectual Crisis in American Public Administration* (University, Ala.: University of Alabama Press, 1973).

Presthus, Robert, *The Organizational Society* (New York: St. Martin's Press, 1978).

Rourke, Francis, *Bureaucracy, Politics and Public Policy* (Boston: Little, Brown, 1976).

"The Suburban Seventies," *Annals of the AAPSS,* November 1975.

Weber, Max, "On Bureaucracy," in K. De Schweinitz and K. W. Thompson, eds., *Man in Modern Society* (New York: Holt, 1953), pp. 501–509.

Chapter 7

The Urban
Policy Process

Introduction

Nearly every interaction between government and citizen begins and ends with an administrative agency. Nearly every policy proposal begins and ends with an administrative agency. Bureaucrats have created and elaborated the most rapidly expanding area of modern legal practice—administrative law. Different public organizations relate to the citizenry in different ways, but almost always each deals with the public in a manner rooted in its relative capacity to allocate scarce public resources finally and authoritatively.

The "answer" to who holds community power is not thoroughly and unambiguously stated here. The argument introduced holds that political power, as we have defined it, is most concentrated in clusters of administrative agencies and their constituency networks. The role of the traditional political structure in cities and towns has deteriorated, and the balance of pluralism, if it exists at all, must be discovered in a bureaucratic configuration. The whole notion of "system" is itself brought into question in that pluralist and elitist maps of power are displaced by a discontinuous series of relationships between agencies at multiple levels of government, ascriptive and descriptive groups, mayors, legislatures, and courts. An answer to Dahl's question (who governs?) may be as unsatisfying as it is true: nobody governs.

Our task in this confusion is to further argue the case for considering government organizations and their networks of support, dependent, and competitor groups. To do so requires a brief consideration of the structure, or anatomy, of modern bureaucratic organizations and a more lengthy consideration of the key processes that determine policies in the urban political system. Finally, we must deal with the questions of complexity and planning, so as to complete a rough portrait of the emerging successor to what we believe are the two major (and increasingly irrelevant) models of political power in cities and towns.

Anatomy, Physiology, and Pathology of Modern Public Organizations

Bureaucracy is itself a term that describes at least two things: one analytical, the other downgrading and nasty. The former simply refers to a scheme of organization which implies hierarchy, specialization, disinterestedness, routinization, and a generally mechanical, replicable, and above all, predictable flow of actions on the part of persons and the organization taken as a whole.[1] The latter is the more commonly found usage and refers to organizations that are blind to human differences, inefficient and costly in structure and function, unreasonably slow, and, in general, a blight on civilization. Bureaucracies, according to either definition, can be public or private, recent (the Department of Education) or ancient (the Roman Catholic Church), efficient (the Israeli Air Force), or inefficient (the United States Postal Service), and so on.

We have used and will continue to use the term in its analytical sense and employ the terms "agency" and "organization" synonymously, unless there are reasons to do otherwise, in which case they shall be noted. The visible anatomical and physiological facts of bureaucratic description must minimally include hierarchy, specialization, task, and mission or purpose.

Hierarchy refers to a system of subordinate-superordinate roles such that any occupant of any given role is responsible for directing others in the organization to follow legitimate and appropriate orders and directions. This is done and made known to superiors and subordinates through published rules, customs of practice, and psychosocial patterns of expectation developed over a lifetime of subordination to authority (legitimate power) vested in roles and procedures. Formally, hierarchy always implies increasing amounts of risk, uncertainty, and policy-making powers as one proceeds analytically from the lowest official to the highest. Increases of discretion over significant matters are supposed to be highly associated with position in the hierarchy, as are salary and other material and symbolic rewards, including social status and deference.

Nearly every employed adult works in a hierarchical setting within a formally bureaucratic organization. In public organizations, safeguards are built into the patterns of recruitment, promotion, and tenure by creating an elaborate personnel system to insulate the civil servant from the vagaries of patronage. Thus a bureaucrat, whether a schoolteacher or a budget officer, is, after a probationary period, given tenure for life and can be fired only for "cause," usually a very difficult thing to do.

Traditionally, one was to find greater degrees of skill and/or expert knowledge as one gazed upward into the hierarchy. Today there is a conflict in many organizations that makes such a glance more than a little confusing. Knowledge of highly specialized and thoroughly differentiated pockets of essential knowledge

---

[1]On the formal definition of bureaucracy, see Max Weber, *Economy & Society* (Berkeley: University of California Press, 1978) Vol. 2, pp. 956–1006.

does not readily conform to the pattern of hierarchy. This specialization of knowledge, persons, and tasks, of course, constitutes a second traditional characteristic of bureaucratic organizations.

At least three aspects of specialization are typical in formal organizations of the bureaucratic type. At each hierarchical level there is a set of specialized activities, normally called functions, which vary in the degree to which the organization must perform them. Thus, if we conceive of the entire civil service of a city, and view the police department as part of the whole, and if we then look into that department as an example, we can observe some officers out on patrol, others conducting investigations, and still others writing press releases. The hierarchical differentiation is nicely symbolized for us by the uniforms; each displays a symbol of rank denoting hierarchy and some even illustrate specialization by such symbolic devices as arm patches designating the wearer as a traffic cop or a motorcyclist. Thus the division of labor, attention, and knowledge, said to be the very basis for the superiority of bureaucratic organization, is made evident to us. Instead of every policeman being able to do everything that every other policeman can do, the potential overlapping inefficiency is reduced by training people to do a few things commonly and many things specifically, according to organizational design.

As organizations, their environments, and their techniques have become more complex and elaborate, the possibility of any one person (or for that matter, any small group of persons) knowing all there is to know about the organization declines. The principle of superknowledgeability on the part of the top leadership is in conflict with specialization based on expert knowledge.

Specialization of function defines the second major attribute of bureaucratic organization. The police are organized by function (traffic, robbery, homicide, etc.) and geographically (by precinct) as well. A second aspect of specialization today arises from the important distinction between specialization of task and specialization of persons. The specialization of task, which comes from the ancient imperative for a division of labor, should be familiar to students who went to high school and moved from classroom to classroom. The specialization of people, however, is a more recent and, we believe, very important development.

Specialized training, of course, is not a brand new idea. Nor is the development of professions. What is of interest is the complex and enormous elaboration of professions in the modern era.[2] Of particular concern to urban political analy-

[2]See generally: Talcott Parsons, "The Professions and Social Structure," *Social Forces,* 17 (1939), pp. 457–467; Robert K. Merton, George Reader, and P. L. Kendall, eds., *The Student Physician* (Cambridge, Mass.: Harvard University Press, 1957); W. J. Goode, "Community Within a Community: The Professions," *American Sociological Review,* 22 (1957), pp. 194–200; Kenneth S. Lynn, ed., *The Professions in America* (Boston: Houghton Mifflin, 1965); Peter M. Blau and Otis Dudley Duncan, *The American Occupational Structure* (New York: Wiley, 1967); Mark Abrahamson, *The Professional in the Organization* (Chicago: Rand-McNally, 1967); Eliot Friedson, *Professional Dominance: The Social Structure of Medical Care* (New York: Atherton Press, 1970); Mayer N. Zald and Michael A. Berger, "Social Movements in Organizations: Coup d'Etat, Insurgency and Mass Movements," *American Journal of Sociology,* 83 (1978) pp. 823–861.

sis is the historically recent development of a series of professions which acutely affect not only the character of bureaucracy, but which alter the fabric of the political system as well. The diverse multitude of social workers, engineers, planners, and educational technicians, not to mention highly specialized public health, legal, and administrative professionals, constitutes a very different group of organization members than the "bureaucratic drones" of popular culture.

The differences are important for several reasons. First of all, profession itself is a concept that is supposed to be supraorganizational. That is, people are trained, educated, and certified according to a set of standards of conduct and performance independent of the organization they join. In general, a psychiatric social worker in Des Moines does the same thing that a psychiatric social worker does in Des Plaines. Urban political systems nationwide are populated by bureaucrats who owe loyalty to both the organization and the profession. The heart of profession lies in the specialization of personal knowledge (an asset which is transportable, should the local bureaucracy prove uncongenial) and in the respectful patterns normally accorded professionals in an increasingly credentials-oriented society.

If one goes a step further to assess the political significance of professionalization, two immediate points come to mind. Professionals typically have a client or constituent group that "naturally" supports their efforts to obtain leverage in the conflict for scarce public resources. Secondly, professionals tend to get paid more and to enjoy a sheen of the "nonpolitical" that is a significant resource in a day of debased politicians. Professionalism *seems* finally to be as distant from self-interest as it is from politics. The case may have eroded recently for some professions noticeably engaged in strikes in cities and towns, but, in general, Americans are more likely to trust the word of most professionals long before they trust that of traditional politicians.

As we argued in Chapter 6, the linkage function of frontline professionals constitutes an important evolutionary change from pluralist or elitist predecessors. Policemen, teachers, welfare workers, and other public servants who are professionals and who meet the public at the boundaries of state and society are frontline bureaucrats who often presume to represent the best interests of their clients and victims. The true constituency, of course, is the internal one. It represents the wishes and wants of the organization members *themselves,* in addition to their professional representation of the needs and wants of their designated segment of the public. An interesting and somewhat subtle process results. One hears claims of two sorts being made and as the din continues over time, the distinction becomes increasingly unclear.

The distinction is between policy acts and recommendations which refer to the substance of profession (i.e., curriculum for teachers, methods of crowd control for policemen, family-centered therapy for social workers) and demands for changes in the allocation of scarce public resources (i.e., *more* teachers, policemen, social workers, secretaries, automobiles, etc.). Analysts often lose sight of the distinction between the two kinds of claims. It is important for our understanding of the urban policy process to note this distinction and to argue that the claims of professionals operating within the formal structure of government constitute a profoundly important "internal constituency." This constituency was embryonic and nearly invisible when Dahl and, particularly, Hunter did their work on city politics. Today such professionals loom ever larger in multigovernmental management of urban problems.

If hierarchy and specialization thus described constitute a visible anatomical description of the bureaucratic beast, what then might we say about (to continue the metaphor) pathology or disease? The more or less familiar pathological responses to bureaucratic membership and action need little elaboration. Treating others and oneself as objects, stupid adherence to rules in the face of an unusual situation, a disregard for the facts of human sociability needs within the organization, and a rigid determination to avoid change despite reward systems for "innovation" are some of the more familiar types of "bureaupathology." There is another sense in which the metaphor might profitably be employed. Bureaucracy is no substitute at all for governance. Bureaucratic procedural values (those having to do with the way things get done) are largely in conflict with procedural values of democracy, socialism, and communism. One simply does not take majority decisions in formal organizations. To do so would conflict with both of the great anatomical facts of bureaucratic life mentioned above.

Arguments have been made that try to reconcile bureaucratic dominance with democratic values. Several have stated that the proportion of ethnic, regional, and class members in a bureaucratic organization constitutes a rough kind of representation.[3] The central assumption of such arguments seems terribly determinist at best, and racist at worst, because it seems to suggest that people make policy decisions and recommendations on the basis of ascriptive personal attributes. Such a description of representation is utterly perverse to the Lockean and Burkean traditions of American ideology. The point is that government by bureaucracy potentially leads to a kind of corporatism or state socialism in which the ideas of personal autonomy, outside of the particular constituent or clientele niche, is either irrelevant or illegal. Such an outcome to the present state of affairs in urban politics might arguably be identified with the term "pathology."

Incidence of such "pathology" on many levels in the urban political system is particularly serious. If we are correct about the growth and complex elaboration of bureaucratic actors in cities, towns, and urban areas, then the prospects are indeed dim for the place where the state must seem the most responsive to public desires. Recall for a moment the central self-governing notions of democratic ideology, and one sees immediately that a form of "pathology" of some magnitude results when bureaucratic organizations attempt, deliberately or not, to substitute for the predecessor structures discussed in earlier chapters. Machines and reformed structures, even in pluralist or elitist clothing, provided some elements, however perverse, for the expression of popular will. Bureaucratic

[3]Norton E. Long, "Power and Administration," *Public Administration Review,* 9 (Autumn 1949); pp. 257–264.

agencies have attempted to provide for "more open channels of communication" and "feedback." In the end, however, those organizations that can control their own destinies without fear of periodic accounting, even to the relevant public, tend to reduce uncertainty by cooption in rather permanent and insulated ways. As important as these pathological aspects might be in terms of representation, accountability, and leadership, the internal ways in which bureaucratic organizations make policy in the first place are vital.

Policy and Process in Public Organizations

Making Decisions

There is, of course, a very large body of writing in several disciplines which deals with decision-making. We cannot hope to summarize very much of it in a direct fashion, but we will try to bring in salient ideas where appropriate. Our focus is both middle range and macroscopic, leaving much valuable microscopic analysis by the wayside. Our concern is to outline the sequence of events which typifies much of the process of making policy in the urban political system. Such an approach denies us the comfort of the authenticity of the case study and, alternatively, falls far short of a grand and all-encompassing statement of great theoretical richness.

Let us begin with a set of familiar distinctions. As outlined above, we may assume that the more significant a decision appears, the more likely it is that it will be made at the higher levels of the classic pyramid used to characterize hierarchical organizations. We can generally assume, moreover, that a significant decision is one which immediately or prospectively alters, expands, or contracts the existing pattern for allocating scarce public resources. Note that the word "appearing" means just that: decision makers are as prone as the next person to misapprehend the significance of a decision if it does not appear in the context they understand to be appropriate. Lower-level personnel may make on-the-spot choices which commit the agency to policies not contemplated by top management. This is not supposed to happen, of course, but one should be ever aware that public bureaucracy, like love, is a many splendored thing.

Recalling that scarce public resources include everything from cash to symbolic rewards of a selfless nature, as well as mass symbols of patriotism and good feeling, we can move on to the occasion for choice, or the moment of moments —when decisions are made. Organizations make the complex simple, the unusual regular and the qualitative quantitative whenever and wherever possible. This is done not only to make things easier for organization members; it also provides stability, continuity, and predictability by reducing uncertainty and incrementally satisfying external and internal demands. This is accomplished by creating major routines of collective action guided by sets of ever more complex rules and formulae. The centerpiece is the budgetary process, an annual and continuing series of events which provide us with a peek into the true ways in which policies are made or destroyed.

Key insights into the process of public organizational decision-making have been provided by a small number of social scientists who made several important arguments. Herbert Simon won the Nobel Prize, in part for his work identifying the true nature of decision-making. He concluded that people "satisficed" when they made decisions; that is, they choose satisfactory solutions instead of optimal ones and therefore sacrificed maximum benefit.[4] Simon pointed out that the human search for alternatives and the projection of consequences from such a search could never be optimal (i.e., the cost of searching for the *nth* alternative had to logically be more than the decision itself, because alternatives and consequences are infinite). About ten years later, Charles Lindblom differentiated between "root" and "branch" decision-making, noting that most decision-making was bounded, not only by constraints of time and the cost of search, but also by the immediate past.[5] Decision-makers start not from zero, but from a rich and often determinative history in which similar decisions were made. Lindblom noted that decision-making was seldom fundamental (root), but was normally incremental (branch).

Wildavsky added an important theoretical and practical insight when he located the budgetary process as a key example of incremental decision-making.[6] The process of policy making then could be understood as reflecting only slightly new initiatives under normal (i.e., noncrisis) circumstances. The basic notions of pluralistic reasoning could also be nicely applied. For some, the annual struggle for scarce resources reflected the genius of pluralism in that it involved the constant competition between groups and ideas, with rewards distributed in such a fashion that nearly everyone got a piece of the pie.

Any number of models, pictures, fables, and sermons have been written about the policy process, and we have no intention of adding to the already crowded field. Certain kinds of acts and structures must be understood, however, if we are to salvage any useful insights about urban politics. First, we must address ourselves to the question of structure itself, recalling that structure is artificial (that is, man-made), reflective of specific values (if not the value itself, i.e., the mayor wants to look like he cares about, say, juvenile delinquency, so he appoints a commission), and always exclusionary by rule, statute, or custom (i.e., certain kinds of people, problems, and communications are forbidden). Structure, at the very least, reflects past value-choices which often have major and usually unexamined consequences for the present.

Nowhere are the unexamined effects of incremental decision-making about structure more evident than in urban areas. As discussed earlier, the metropolis has long been identified by political scientists, economists, politicians, and bureau-

[4]Herbert A. Simon, *Administrative Behavior* (New York: Free Press, 1976).
[5]Charles E. Lindblom, "The Science of Muddling Through," *Public Administration Review*, 19, (Spring 1958), pp. 79–88.
[6]Aaron Wildavsky, *The Politics of the Budgetary Process* (Boston: Little, Brown, 1974).

crats as an incredible mix of national, state, county, city, and village governments. This is compounded by the immensely complex overlay of special districts created at each governmental level, seemingly to solve some problem or other. These thousands of jurisdictions are minimally "structure" at the macroscopic level. They are also "structure" at other levels of analysis as well, for each has its own organizational mandates and missions, buttressed by specialized subunits, professionalized bureaucrats, and tens of millions of dollars. If we move our glance down to the internal workings of this variety of structures, can we detect some structural similarities such that cautious generalization is possible?

We profoundly hope so, because the alternative is too frightening to contemplate. The ideas of hierarchy, specialization of persons and tasks, incremental decision-making, and an annual budgetary routine provide some clues as do the notions of citizenship and the historical material discussed earlier. Implicit in much of this is a notion of decision-making which is at once linear and apparently pluralistic. A grossly imperfect picture called "A Model of the Urban Policy Process" (Figure 7.1) illustrates some of the structural attributes we have been discussing. It is a reasonably traditional picture of a straight-line progress showing the familiar cross-pressures, structural characteristics, time sequence, and a feedback loop that reflects the possibility of representation of public interests and organizational learning.

Figure 7.1 tells us that at moment X, a decision-maker Y must choose from a bounded set of policy alternatives. These alternatives have been influenced most heavily by what was done last year, by the constituency and clientele networks appropriate to the decision, and by the multiple competing claims on resources made by other decision makers and *their* constituency and clientele networks. If Y is typical, he will decide that a marginal amount of resources will be added or subtracted from the given program(s), thus either encouraging or discouraging the agency and groups in whose domain the decision applies. Therefore, while protest will inevitably follow a cut or a small increment, it is muted, because patterns of conflict and cooperation must continue over time ("wait 'til next year") and because the genius of incrementalism is that it is precisely that: nothing terribly serious is likely to happen to any given program in any given year.

The decision having been made by Y (where Y is as likely to be a small group as an individual), we then see in Figure 7.1 a hopeful arrow denoting something called a "policy outcome," which might also be called the first result of the decision. Let us assume that Y has decided to add 9 percent more teachers to a large high school, receives board of education approval, and then moves to authorize the relevant claimants to advertise for the jobs now made available. It would be easy and restful and would not even require the jargonistic "policy outcome" if matters ended there. But logically we must see that any outcome has consequences which play themselves out in our growing awareness over time. We can see the proximate and obvious impact of the teacher decision. First, we need some figure that multiplies the number of teachers by the staff, supply, and capital

**Figure 7.1
A Model of the Urban Policy Process**

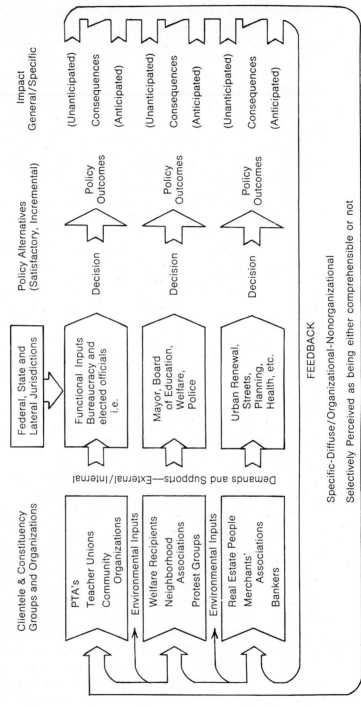

equipment necessary if a new teacher is to be employed. In other words, if I hire a new chemistry teacher, I have to have lab space, chemicals, equipment, and so on. Thus the initial decision is immediately compounded by these additional costs.

The next point of time to think about is represented by the last column which tells us that something called "impact" consists of a series of anticipated and unanticipated consequences. Let us imagine that the teachers are now in the classrooms, the needed support for their activity is provided, and all seems tranquil and tidy. Perhaps because of the improvement in student/faculty ratio, more students register for this high school from different adjacent areas, thus depopulating other schools. A suit is brought that tries to prove that the effect of the teacher addition is to *resegregate* the high schools so carefully desegregated by order of a federal judge in the 1960s. At this point we move our attention to the famous feedback loop or channel from which our decision-maker must gather the fruits of his (or more often, someone else's) decision.

The unanticipated impact of the initial decision is clearly linked to the "resegregation" controversy and the depopulation problem of the other high schools. But the problem of making even weak statements of causality, such as "clearly linked," is that we have no good evidence to prove that the initial decision *caused* the consequence of resegregation. What about changes in local real estate value in the high school area and adjacent ones? Has there been crime or other such problems in the other high schools? In short, how can we readily assume that another set of intervening variables, unnoticed and apparently unrelated at the time of the initial decision, had not reached a point where the resegregation would have happened anyway? Certainly we don't know the answer, nor are we likely to have the time, energy, and resources to even approximate the answer. The decision-making process tends to invest time in the next annual decision, having learned only that the immediate "intervening variable" (i.e., the federal court) should be kept an eye on as we decide next year's budget.

Our example is much too simplified to reflect anything but the grossest aspects of the decision-making process. Yet it illustrates a number of useful themes. Decisions taken incrementally over time have a tendency to "accumulate" into policy rather than to reflect conscious and deliberate policy choices. The nearest end-in-view (the 9 percent teacher increase) is, of course, too short a forecasting limit. One knows this *after the fact* of decision. In our example, the courts, neighboring areas, and probably a half-dozen constituency groups and bureaucrat-represented clientele networks could easily be galvanized into protest action as an unanticipated consequence of an incremental decision whose only purpose was to improve the faculty/student ratio in a high school. If we pushed the example further, we could easily slip into the "everything is related to everything else, so why bother?" school of nonthinking. The desire to know *all* of the probably major consequences of a public policy decision is a potent one in the modern urban political system, in part because it was of such little concern in the past.

The rationalistic temptation is to insist that everything be planned and coordinated before a major decision is taken. Comprehensive versus incremental decisions would have this lovely property, some feel. Yet incremental decision-making with a limited view of the consequences persistently dominates policy-making in and for urban areas, despite claims to the contrary. This persistence is explicable and understandable for excellent organizational and political reasons. Incrementalism is *the* vehicle of compromise, bargaining, and brokering in the system of modern politics. It permits the pull and tug of political forces within time and value boundaries known to all who may participate. There appear to be few permanent winners, and there is always next year for the losers. In organizational terms, the risk of being "caught" by a mistaken decision is substantially reduced if the decision-makers know that they can repair their "errors" next year. Policy-making officials and their constituents can, over time, cement a stable, predictable, and satisfactory set of relationshps and expectations and thereby reduce uncertainty for the entire network. Finally, as the number of participants expands via the multilevel bureaucratic elaboration characteristic of urban politics over the past generation, the importance of knowing what other relevant actors can be expected to do increases significantly.

If incrementalism serves to reinforce pluralistic longings and ideology, if it protects bureaucrats from fatal error, if it allows for the flexibility of annual reevaluation of programs, and if it permits the many actors related to a given policy area to partially predict the actions of their associates and competitors, then what is the problem? The problem is that the diffuse mess that one sees with one's literal and figurative eyes is precisely the result of an excess of *mindlessly* incremental decisions made by officials who were doubtless convinced that what they were doing was valid and beneficial. The American urban area is a monument to such mindless incrementalism. One can look at the unanticipated and interactive consequences of any number of programs in a wide range of policy areas to see the truth of this claim.[7] The more distant the decision-maker, the more horrendous the result. Federal highway construction, state welfare programs, and national, state, and local housing and urban renewal actions combined to transform the urban place in ways totally undreamed of by the people responsible for them. Most of the unanticipated consequences were (need it be said?) negative. Such observations lead some to conclude that what is called for is comprehensive planning underpinned by a structure of authority, willing and able to compel compliance to the dictate of the plan.

Two kinds of objections are made to this line of thought, one logical, the other political. It is to the latter that the next section is devoted, so we shall explore the former by way of conclusion to this aspect of the discussion of decision-making. Planning and allocation of scarce resources according to an agreed-upon design is not unknown in America. Indeed, one could argue that appearances notwithstanding, America has more sophisticated planning than any other country in the world. The problem is that the planning is seldom centralized

---

[7]See Charles E. Lindblom, *The Policy Making Process* (Englewood Cliffs, N.J.: Prentice-Hall, 1968).

in the political system, viewed at any level, and the best examples nearly always occur within the authority confines of large-scale formal organizations. IBM plans, predicts, and manipulates the environment in order to ensure success. It has a brilliant record as a planned and planning organization.

In the public sphere planning is not unknown, particularly in the area of capital improvement, including housing, urban renewal, transportation, and public buildings. The question, of course, is not whether plans are projected over a long period of time, but rather the nature of the process. Planning by government agencies following routines not confined by the annual budgetary cycle involves fundamental decisions which typically are capable of amendment over time. Thus city planning commissions routinely produce long-range physical and other planning documents and have done so over many years. Their plans often lack a vital element for success—the continuing support of other governmental agencies and their constituency networks, including the local community's dominant economic and political groups.[8] In order to be successful, such incursions into the normal process of incremental decision-making must have sustaining networks of support capable of maintaining long-term consensus and enforcement. This point leads us to inquire as to the long-term bases of support seemingly necessary for maintaining a place of dominance or even important participation in the policy process.

Obtaining Resources

For analytical purposes we may separate decisions having to do with incremental changes in an established program area from decisions which create and sustain a given agency and its constituency network(s). The term *analytical* must be stressed for the very good reason that it is seldom clear that a given incremental decision in a given program area is not, at least partially, an investment in the continuing structure of agency support. Our concern at this point is to consider those actions and decisions which tend to increase the agency's ability and capacity to allocate scarce public resources in cooperation with its constituency networks.

Constituency and Clientele Networks

In Chapter 6 we pointed out the constituency and the clientele as potentially great resources. By way of review, let us recall that constituency groups are aggregations of politically powerful organizations and groups interdependent with some agency whose mandate it is to regulate, stimulate, or otherwise support a given set of policies and programs appropriate to the constituency. Constituencies, it will be recalled, include elected politicians, interest groups, elites, and organiza-

---

[8]J. Pressman and Aaron Wildavsky, *Implementation* (Berkeley: University of California Press, 1973.)

tions in and out of government, capable of altering the existing allocative pattern in cooperation with the relevant agencies. Clientele groups enjoy no such power and tend to be authoritatively represented by professionalized agency bureaucrats. The latter are, in our scheme, the "true" constituents of the agency that employs them; they also reflect the professional, altruistic, and other occupational standards that transcend the organization to which they belong. Schoolteachers are an example of such an "internal constituency," while bankers tend to be external constituents of several agencies in most urban areas.

Clearly such aggregations of power are a resource of considerable significance, not only because of their potential to disrupt (bankers withhold capital, teachers strike). Bankers, teachers, real estate developers, doctors, social workers, even tenant groups and landlords are the avenues through which societal needs and wants are now represented in the urban political system. As the great sage of city politics, George Washington Plunkitt, repeatedly pointed out in his famous treatise, it is organization and persistence which win the day in politics.[9] He spoke of party organization and the persistence of machine politics, a system we believe largely replaced by the new forms of constituency and clientele representation discussed above. A primary resource to be obtained, then, is a constituency or, reversing the time sequence to include both "old" and "new" cooptation, a public agency. Thus unaffiliated potential or actual clusters of political power will seek to identify with and at least partially control some public agency or other.

Most often, the great innovations in American politics in this century have been new or restructured public agencies. Indeed, we have a cultural mania about creating new organizations to "solve" specific problems. Dahl's classic pluralist work on New Haven reveals the mayor putting together an *organization* of various interests in order to capture federal urban renewal dollars. As E. E. Schattschneider pointed out so long ago, organization itself may be called the "mobilization of bias."[10] In other words, the creation or modification of a public agency creates an exclusionary principle that not only defines what the organization does or does not do, but also effectively precludes certain kinds of claims from its agenda. More than a decade ago, Bachrach and Baratz identified this phenomenon with "nondecision making" in an attempt to show that certain kinds of claims (usually perceived as not in the self-interest of the agency/constituency) were excluded, not as overt acts of policy choice, but rather as part of the defining characteristics of the agency itself.[11] Public housing programs, for instance, typically regard as outside their mandate the direct participation of potential tenants. Collections of public bureaucrats, real estate people, bankers, construc-

[9]William Riordan, *Plunkitt of Tammany Hall* (New York: Dutton, 1963).
[10]E. E. Schattschneider, *The Semi-Sovereign People* (New York: Holt, Rinehart and Winston, 1960), p. 30.
[11]Peter Bachrach and Morton S. Baratz, "Two Faces of Power," *American Political Science Review,* 61 (December 1962), pp. 947–952.

tion unions, engineers, and architects have then only to deal with each other as they go about planning, financing, and constructing new housing.

Mandates

A second key resource is a series of mandates obtained through the political-legal process which effectively guarantees a monopoly or near monopoly over a given policy area. Once such mandates are obtained, the main job of the agency is to retain them against possible raids from rival structures of political or economic power. This is usually accomplished through bargaining, although one can still find the heat and light of political struggle in urban politics when conflicts arise over which agency has control over which mandates. The many and varied agencies that typically deal with ever-refining divisions of human want and need stand as mute testimony to the results of such struggles. Welfare agencies, particularly, reflect the hodgepodge of past "settlements" of conflicts over who possesses the mandate to "regulate" the poor.[12] One also should not forget the fact that agencies can, if not sufficiently skilled or foresighted, be "stuck" with a mandate they do not want. At the moment, no one wants to represent the "poor," in part because of the diminution of resources directed toward that group.

Mandates may be secured in any number of ways and, remembering the peculiar significance of a federal form of organization, at a variety of levels. Often mandates are obtained by the incremental addition of formal legal power through the legislative process. As often as not, mandates come from the successful interpretation or reinterpretation of existing statute. Such mandates arise out of the fact that almost no legislation is self-enforcing and therefore requires interpretation, which falls under the general heading of administrative discretion. Courts are frequently responsible for the definition and interpretation of mandates at all levels of government. Often the need for a new mandate (or more usually the expansion or reinterpretation of an existing mandate) arises out of practice where the state meets the public. Child abuse, drug and alcohol addiction, and family disturbances are at once part of the mandate of the courts, the police, public health authorities, and other social agencies. As this is written, the multiple actors involved in these matters are attempting to define the proper agency mandates to deal with the problems. Before these kinds of problems can attach themselves to one or another agency, there must be a sufficient "payoff" in order for a struggle to be worthwhile.

Money

This brings us to a third category of resource. Money is, of course, a resource familiar to everyone, yet it is not so readily indicative of political power as is

[12]Francis Piven and Richard A. Cloward, *Regulating the Poor* (New York: Random House, 1971).

frequently assumed. For instance, dollars allocated to cover cost of living increases for clients are undoubtedly a goal of social agencies. But such dollars do not do much to increase the agency's power unless the agency has sufficient discretion over the allocation of the dollars to direct some of them to additional staff and programs. Money which directly or indirectly benefits constituents and clients must also involve increases in agency power and discretion.

Thus, if I wish to increase the number of policemen *and* raise the salaries of patrolmen, I must simultaneously mobilize the internal constituency (the policemen and their union) and the external constituencies (the mayor, city council, crime-fearing neighbors, etc). A balancing act of some significance must take place in distributing the fruits of the agency's labors so as to ensure the cooperation of all concerned when the next budget cycle occurs. If the agency has fewer disposable dollar resources for such discretionary acts as increasing the number of policemen in a given functional or geographic area, then the increment of dollars one sees in the budget represents no true gain in agency power, except perhaps in comparison with other agencies who must live with a lower amount of dollars.

Changes in the amount and variety of services provided over time tell something about the political power of agencies in the urban political system. The sources of those dollars and their potential for regeneration also must figure into one's analysis. In the examples above, federal and state participation has become increasingly significant as the local property tax revenues become inadequate for the provision of services. Thus the source of dollars can be as important a resource, or apparent resource, as the dollars themselves. For instance, one of the ways for police officials to simultaneously raise wages and put more policemen out on patrol has been to use CETA (Comprehensive Employment and Training Act) employees for clerical functions. These employees are in effect provided by the municipality, almost as patronage was distributed in the bad old days. But the significant fact is that they are paid by the federal government. The dollars enabling us to put more policemen on the streets at higher salaries come from a source over which the local police department has little control. This puts such departments at great risk when they include such clerical help as a crucial part of their operational base and is an example of dollars provided on almost a "contingency basis." It will be fascinating to see what happens if and when the CETA program is reduced or eliminated.

As important as the gross amount of dollars is, it is what they purchase and to whose benefit that we should always recur if we are to understand much about urban politics today. Whatever else it may be, the urban political system is in its essence a vast service industry. It produces few consumer goods. Chicago sends treated sewerage down to the farmers in southern Illinois, but it is an exception.

Experts and Expertise

The rule is that urban governments and the political systems in which they are to be found are first and foremost producers of services. This leads us to consider that great companion to dollars, people. Specifically, trained professionals constitute a fourth resource that must be obtained if the agency/constituency or clientele is to grow and prosper.

As public faith in politics and politicians declines, the role of the expert and his expertise becomes increasingly significant. We have traced the development of such positive approbation as it related to the reform movement of the early part of this century. The modern commitment to rational/scientific knowledge is no less firm. Indeed, government has been a major employer and stimulus of the professionalized development of experts to serve the state, particularly since the end of World War II. Universities have cooperated and expanded their roles in training experts appropriate to urban needs for many years. They also function as research arms for a variety of agencies at all levels of government, churning out studies of everything from municipal finance to solid waste disposal to police/community relations. Indeed, urban problems have been a major generator of government-stimulated university programs to train policemen, teachers, social workers, engineers, planners, and administrators.

Such professionally trained people are a vital resource in the struggle for scarce public resources. They provide highly valued technical studies to support claims on state and federal resources vital to any number of local programs. They constitute a legitimating force with some sectors of the public not likely to be sympathetic to the claims of those who need periodically to seek votes, and they represent a crucial link in the policy process under discussion. This is so for a variety of reasons, among the more important of which is the growing control experts now have on a policy process increasingly dependent upon technical knowledge unavailable to layman or politician.

As technical jargon, interdependence, and apparent need has increased, the possibilities for generalist administrators and politicians to make truly independent decisions have decreased. Few politicians can overcome the language and technical detail contained in recommendations from experts whose entire professional lives are spent attending to specific policy areas. The alternatives for decision are enumerated increasingly by experts. Sewage disposal, sanitation, public health, fire fighting equipment, computerized record keeping, and data collection, to name a few, are matters over which politicians have jurisdiction but little technical knowledge. The alternatives presented for choosing a waste-disposal system that will work, be in conformity with various state and federal regulations, and be acceptable to possible funding agencies outside of the immediate urban political system are created by experts.

Up to a point, those alternatives might be thought of in terms of the simple choices of everyday life. If I meet you at the counter of an ice-cream parlor and inquire as to your preference for "chocolate, strawberry, or vanilla," the likelihood is that you will select one of the three. You are not likely to ask for tutti-frutti, even though that is your preference. At the least we can imagine that you might ask for that alternative, because you have long known and loved tutti-frutti. Imagine the same picture, but place yourself in the shoes of an honest and hard-working politician or policy maker of some sort, confronted with three alternatives for a waste disposal system, each of which is costly and each of which has probable assets and liabilities. First, one has no knowledge of a "tutti-frutti" waste-disposal system, else one would be an expert and not a generalist policy maker. Second, the *occasion* for decision in the first place is not likely to be generated by a felt desire, as in the ice cream example, but by external and demanding forces such as state and other government agencies. Third, the possibility of your investment in information and alternative search is unlikely to even compare with that of "your" experts. What would *you* do?

Wiggle and squirm as he might, the policy maker is not likely to be able to defy the experts, because he has not the capability to provide alternatives to their recommendations. A key to understanding all of this is to consider the simple fact of specialization of people and task discussed above. Simply put, one might conceive of expert knowledge as arising not only from professional training, but also from the *prolonged institutional attention span* which is a central characteristic of modern complex bureaucracy. Policy makers at the traditionally political levels are faced with serial problems and decisions. One week may be dominated by a crisis in the schools, drawing attention and energy away from the already overdeadline budget, while the waste plan awaits next week's crisis or time/attention demand. The serially focused policy process itself contributes to the growing power of technical knowledge and those who authoritatively possess it.

The linkages between technical experts at all levels of government are themselves frequently stronger and of longer duration than those binding electoral politicians. Professional journals, societies, and meetings help to foster such links. Politicians who would counter such groupings of attention, interest, and expertise do so at great risk to their programs and possibly to themselves. Expert knowledge dominates not only such newly specialized areas as waste disposal. Finance, taxation, personnel, and other traditionally understood "staff" areas are also becoming professionalized and complex to the point of being beyond the ken of laymen. Certainly there is some serious play acting in all of this. Aggregations of bureaucratic power, bereft of a highly evolved and esoteric technology and knowledge base, are not above trying to appear as if they were so graced. It is the job of the politician and the lay analyst to attempt to make the necessary separation between the "real" and the "not so real." In any event, the growing size, investment, and diversity of experts and expertise in the past generation has become a resource of the first order in the struggle over the allocation of scarce public resources. One ought not forget, either, that the knowledge industry now includes professional experts on the policy making process itself, and they, with their insights and understandings of the complexities of multiheaded, multilevel governments and agencies, may indeed be the power brokers of the future urban political system.

Symbolic Resources

We would be negligent if we failed to conclude this discussion of resources with at least a brief discussion of an ancient and often overlooked resource base. This is the symbolic power of government itself, now most frequently invoked by civil servants, but potent still in the right hands. There can be little doubt that traditional patriotism is in deep trouble in America today. But to be entirely cynical about our tendency to conform to government demands and exhortations is undoubtedly wrong. The key resource that any agency of the state possesses is the probable conformity of the public to its edicts. True, the state still continues to be the crucial possessor of legitimate force and violence, but to simply construe public acceptance of rules, laws, and policies as being totally rooted in this state power is surely to misunderstand the nature of politics in the modern era in America.

Cities and towns are ultimately where we live, send our children to school, and conduct the business of our daily lives. The extent to which we are willing to "suspend disbelief " and abide by laws, rules, and policies about which we have little to say is vital to the notion of "resource" as a power-creating element within the context of any formulation of "obtaining resources" in the urban political system. The conditions under which we are willing to suspend disbelief will define *the public good* in urban areas. These conditions are discussed in detail in the next chapter.

Complexity and Interdependence: Toward a New Model of Political Power in Urban Areas

By way of summary and conclusion to Chapter 7 we will outline some propositions that may be useful to the student of urban politics. It is less a model of urban political power than a skeletal beginning of a description that emerges out of the major schools of thought and from our thinking on the growth of bureaucratic power and intergovernmental relations. The themes clarified here are useful for the analysis of public service policy in urban political systems which follows in Part III.

PROPOSITION 1. *No single explanatory theory of political power adequately describes urban politics today.* The cities are neither places of complete subordination to monolithic elites, nor are they modern reconstructed versions of an Athens. The significance of voters, elections, and the other crucial aspects of

traditional democratic structure is in decline. Fewer turn out to vote and participate in local political affairs than ever before in American history. Similarly, the
decline in local economic elites is evidenced by the increasing centralization of
corporate and commercial power in national organizations untied to any particular locale. Certainly there are exceptions to these generalizations, but there are
fewer and fewer as time goes by.

PROPOSITION 2. *The growth in political power and influence of state and federal
governments over traditional urban problems has accelerated enormously in the
past thirty-five years.* Few would deny this proposition, yet many have ignored
its significance for a model of the urban political system. The growth and development of special districts and state and federal programs and the accompanying
loss of local initiative and control has, of course, been evident in housing, policing,
welfare, and nearly all of the traditional police power areas. This shift has occurred in part as a result of the decline in urban taxable resource bases and
because of radical shifts in the social and economic character of urban areas. In
nearly every instance, the incursion of nonlocal decision-making power has been
through the instrument of bureaucratic organizations.

PROPOSITION 3. *The idea of local citizenship vested in a political process, real* (as
the pluralists would have it) *or imagined* (as argued by the elitist thinkers), *is
being replaced by a new set of interactions that shares aspects of both, but which
is neither.* Our argument is that the citizen now meets the state in its many forms
in an emerging pattern of interactions which we have tried to capture in our
taxonomy. This taxonomy points to the character of the interactions as being
either of a constituent, client, or victim mode. We argue that the growth of the
multiheaded state in the form of bureaucratic agencies tends to create and sustain
such modal interactions; we suggest that by their nature bureaucratic organizations tend to deal with the relevant publics in ways very different than traditional
democratic theory would have it. We argue that differential degrees of public/
agency dependence and interdependence for viability provide a key to these
emerging relationships.

PROPOSITION 4. *Large-scale public bureaucracies operating at national and state
levels are increasingly becoming the competitors to and successors of elites and the
traditional democratic structures of local politics.* For nearly every area of human
endeavor, a public agency now exists for purposes of regulation, stimulation, or
prohibition. Nowhere is this more evident than in urban areas, where most of us
live. Cherished ideas of local control and difference fall before state and national
standards in everything from education to transportation. The weapons used for
domination are money, court decisions, and the legal inferiority of cities and
towns. The resource base of such bureaucratic agencies is enormous and appears
to grow in good economic periods and in bad. The virtuosity of government
agencies is seldom noted as a resource, but as the premium on technical knowledge grows, the overwhelming expertise reservoir of government in general has
become concentrated in public agencies.

PROPOSITION 5. *The physical boundedness of late capitalist organization no longer tends to be the limiting factor it once was, and the elites which control such organizations are no longer long-time residents of given urban areas.* The city is a declining base for the cheap labor supply that industrial organization once demanded. In some cities the giant plants of yesterday still operate, but as those plants are replaced and as local firms are swallowed up by larger organizations, the tendency is toward dispersion into the countryside, where transportation and communication are much more accessible than ever before. The growth of the service component in the gross national product (GNP) has also pushed the need for a centralized place of production into the background. As firms become national in scope and centralized in control, the managerial classes which dominate the firms' policies also tend to become national. By this we mean the prevalent practice of moving managers from plant to plant or office to office in the march toward the top positions of corporate leadership. As this process continues, the bases for local elite domination decline. The capacity for local economic development also rests increasingly with those who live outside of the urban area. Government itself is becoming an absolutely essential provider of economic activity in many areas through its building projects, capital provision for private investors and developers, and, significantly, as a major employer in its numerous offices, military installations, and agencies.

PROPOSITION 6. *New relationships between political, economic, and social groups at multiple levels of society have created an emergent political system of complex interdependencies.* As the urban area reflects the multiple class, ethnic, racial, economic, and political differences once almost wholly contained by the physical boundaries of the city proper, the governmental means for representing the demands that emerge from each has accordingly expanded in scope. In the 1950s the suburbanization of urban areas enhanced class, race, and economic differences, while core cities tended to attract large numbers of in-migrants and retain the older, less affluent populations. Federal housing and transportation policies encouraged this development.

The dominant political interests tended to follow the dispersion of the population which reflected the growing social and economic distance in spatial and geographic terms. The urban area began to display classic core-city problems in a spatially dispersed fashion, revealing a pattern of interest that had both common and dissimilar elements. The transportation needs of the suburb began to differ substantially, for instance, from those of the central city, as did many other needs. Eventually, the overlap of need, the fragmentation of political power, and the painful realization of interdependence will make dominant the national and state presence as a key allocative force. Interdependence costs and needs begin to become apparent when politicians, bureaucrats, and laymen recall that the point of a suburb in the first place was the central city. That place of commerce, transportation, finance, and amenity is in serious decline and reflects the interconnectedness of political and economic life.

Complexity arises in part as a result of the changes noted above and because the consequences of any given policy decision rapidly alter the face of the "problem" and the environment in unanticipated and often negative ways. This is particularly the case in areas like transportation, water and air pollution control, policing, and welfare. The unanticipated negative externalities of past housing and urban renewal programs reflect this claim. Population shifts resulting from such actions have brought about such fundamental alterations in neighborhoods that too many newly displaced residents have themselves become "social problems." Massive investment over the past generation in roadways and highways radiating from central cities has undoubtedly accelerated private automobile purchase and use, thus increasing the scope and magnitude of the energy crisis of the 1980s.

Such complex interdependence can only increase over time, and the only conceivable instruments for managing this condition are formal organizations engaged in large-scale economic, political, and social planning. The new urban political system of the coordination and planning type will, we believe, have an undoubtedly bureaucratic cast and is emerging from Washington and from many state capitals. The role of the traditional political system in urban areas is in decline, and the one which is emerging is as yet unclear in its specific anatomy. In general, however, we may speculate that the ideas of representation, leadership, and the democratic values minimally outlined by pluralist writers are unlikely to continue in their present form.

PROPOSITION 7. *Urban politics is and will increasingly continue to be centered around the provision of services to constituents, clients, and victims.*

The allocation of scarce public resources in American cities and towns revolves around the competition and cooperation of significant actors who seek to control the distribution of *services,* because services account for most of what it is that government does on the local level. The amount, division, distribution, and method of control of services in such key areas as education, welfare, policing, and health care are matters of such financial magnitude that the number and variety of powerful political actors who seek to control them has and will increase. They come from all levels of government as well as from national and locally organized groups.

As a nation, we have expanded the scope of public services greatly in the past generation or so. Many of the services fall to the urban areas simply because that is where the population is. Additionally, the federal government's responses to serious problems, typically found in central cities, have altered the structure of political power in many ways. National, state, and local government agencies have found themselves in conflict over such policies nearly as often as they have agreed. Housing, health care, and police practice and funding, coupled with sporadic attempts to deal with such matters as black teenage unemployment, day care, crime, waste disposal, and dozens of other problems great and small, have left us with a hodgepodge of half-hearted initiatives and programs which some may identify as a national urban plan, strategy, or program. Clearly, we do not. Such attempts have, however, shaken the already crumbling urban political system.

We turn now to a more detailed and careful consideration of urban services, their distribution, politics, and significance.

Suggested Readings

Abrahamson, Mark, *The Professional in the Organization* (Chicago: Rand-McNally, 1967).

Blau, Peter M., and Otis Dudley Duncan, *The American Occupational Structure* (New York: Wiley, 1967).

Friedson, Eliot, *Professional Dominance: The Social Structure of Medical Care* (New York: Atherton Press, 1970).

Kaufman, Herbert, *The Limits of Organizational Change* (University, Ala.: University of Alabama Press, 1971).

Larson, M. S., *The Rise of Professionalism* (Berkeley, University of California Press, 1977).

Lewis, Eugene, *Public Entrepreneurship* (Bloomington, Ind.: Indiana University Press, 1980).

Lindblom, Charles E., *The Policy Making Process* (Englewood Cliffs, N.J.: Prentice-Hall, 1968).

Lynn, Kenneth S., *The Professions in America* (Boston: Houghton Mifflin, 1965).

Piven, Frances, and Richard A. Cloward, *Regulating the Poor* (New York: Random House, 1971).

Pressman, Jeffrey C., *Federal Programs and City Politics* (Berkeley: University of California Press, 1978).

Pressman, Jeffrey C., and Aaron Wildavsky, *Implementation* (Berkeley: University of California Press, 1978).

Simon, Herbert A., *Administrative Behavior* (New York: Free Press, 1976).

Part III

The
Urban
Service
State

Chapter 8
The Public Economy of Urban Life

The Language of Public Economics

Urbanites interact with urban government as constituents, clients, and victims. Some urbanites are locked into one of the three roles for their entire lives, others alternate roles, depending upon the circumstance. Some cities seem to be more congenial to constituency relationships, while others create thousands of victims effortlessly. What is it that allows some cities and individuals to fare better than others? What is it that might support a democratic political environment in urban areas?

The goal of this chapter is to provide a set of tools that can be used to understand the interaction modes of constituent, client, and victim in the context of everyday life in the city. This set of tools will be drawn from the field of public economics, the study of supply and demand in the provision of public goods and services. Public economics is particularly appropriate to the examination of interaction modes because it focuses on the most basic interaction in the urban political system, the exchange between urban government as a producer of public services and the urban citizen as a consumer of public services. The political nature of this economic relationship can be expressed in terms of constituency, clientelism, or victimization. *The producer/consumer relationship between government and urbanite is the economic structure underlying the political interaction modes.*

Like all specialized academic fields, public economics has developed a specialized language. However, public economics is a cross between political science and economics, so many of its basic terms will seem familiar to students with a background in either of these disciplines. Nonetheless, several of the terms have meanings that differ from more conventional definitions. Following are the terms with the greatest potential for confusion:

The Public Good: a subjective standard for judging the quality of collective effort and for establishing social, economic, and political goals.

Externality: the effect of an action or decision on those who had no part in taking the action or making the decision; an externality may be either positive (an external benefit) or negative (an external cost).

Private Goods: those benefits enjoyed separately by individuals so that consumption by one individual excludes consumption by any other.

Public Goods: those benefits enjoyed jointly by individuals so that consumption by one individual cannot exclude consumption by any other.

Public/Private Continuum: the range of possibilities in the provision of public services between complete exclusivity—only private goods provided—and complete nonexclusivity—only public goods provided.

Coercive Assessments: taxation justified by the argument that because all benefit from public services, all must pay for their provision; assumes that public services are public goods.

User Taxes: pay-as-you-go charges for the use of public goods and services; recognizes the private goods generated by governmental effort.

The Urban Public Good

One of the more varied aspects of urban life is the concept of the public good. What should we do as a community? How much should we contribute to the public welfare? Although there seems to be at least some agreement among Americans about the range of urban services that should be provided by the public sector—crime prevention and detection, road construction and maintenance, and perhaps education—it is not wise to argue that any current American perspective on the public good is the "best" or the "most highly evolved." A clear perspective is absent because the *determination of the public good is always subjective.*

To demonstrate the subjective nature of "the good" in urban areas we refer to the experience of those prodigious city makers, the Romans. By the sixth century, B.C., it became apparent that a drainage system was needed for the central area around the Forum due to the construction of public baths and the increased density of population. The public work that was designed to solve this problem, a tunnel called the Cloaca Maxima, was built with such skill and foresight that it has served the Eternal City ever since.[1] However, not all public officials or taxpayers would agree that the resources needed to construct the Cloaca were well spent. A broadly opposite position was taken by the citizens of California in the summer of 1978 when they approved a referendum to *decrease* the resources available for local public works. This action, known by its ballot title, Proposition 13, cut local governmental revenue in the state from $12 billion

[1]J. B. Ward-Perkins, *Cities of Ancient Greece and Italy: Planning in Classical Antiquity* (New York: Braziller, 1974), p. 34.

to only $5 billion.[2] While the latter figure is still a fairly Roman sum, it is the reduction that is significant. Californians, or at least a majority of those voting, decided that the public good may be attained by *less* governmental effort.

The difference between the decision to build the Cloaca and the decision in California to decrease the availability of public resources can be expressed in several different ways. It might be said that such a difference is cultural; that it is a difference in life-style; or that it reflects differences in the moral bases of the societies in question. Culture, life-style, and morality all play a part in a city's definition of the public good. However, since the public good is a subjective combination of elements, we should expect interested individuals to manipulate the definition to their own advantage. In this light, the debate over Proposition 13 can be seen as a battle over the definition of the public good. Supporters of Proposition 13, led by Howard Jarvis, called the measure a "taxpayer's bill of rights" which would return the governance of California's localities to their citizens. Mayor Tom Bradley of Los Angeles, an opponent of the measure, termed it "an invitation to chaos" that would lead only to the erosion of vital urban services.

Where the truth lies in this battle or any similar one is usually irrelevant to the actors involved. What is important is who wins and how much they win. In this case, the winners accomplished a 58 percent decrease in local revenues. Such a victory has profound consequences for the culture and life-style of Californians as they are affected by local government services ranging from libraries and concert halls to police service and hospital costs. The decrease also has moral implications, because it changes the official definition of what it is that's "right" for urban society to produce collectively. Changes in these elements will have an influence on the future of urban life in California. It is important to remember that these particular changes in culture, life-style, and morality did not come about because of a natural disaster or a plague, but because of a political mechanism—in this case the California State Constitution—which allows citizens to reallocate scarce public resources by referendum.

It is through the art of politics that each of the other elements—culture, life-style, and morality—are expressed in everyday urban life. In all societies but Utopia, resources are scarce and either/or choices must be made. Political analysis focuses on the choices and decisions made in allocating scarce resources and in directing society toward certain goals. Such choices are not always well informed, nor do they always appear rational. However, they are extremely important to our understanding of the way things "turn out" in urban society.

What an emphasis on politics boils down to is the need to answer two questions: How does the prevailing concept of the public good influence the allocation of scarce, public resources; and conversely, how does the current allocation of resources influence the public good? There is an implicit assumption

[2]"California Voters Approve a Plan to Cut Property Tax $7 Billion" (*The New York Times,* June 7, 1978) p. 1.

in these questions which should be made clear: the urban public good is not completely shaped by the allocation or non-allocation of resources, nor is it completely determined by ideas or conceptions about the way things *should* be. An accurate picture of the urban public good is a complex mixture of three powerful forces: competition for material resources, the political dynamics of decision making, and the influence of values and beliefs about the city's goals.

No single tradition in the social sciences encompasses these three forces. In order to compose a political picture of the urban public good, a combination of theories is necessary. The most comprehensive approach to both economic competition and the influence of values is provided by the theory of public goods and collective action which has been developed by economists. In order to consider the organizational environment of choice, theories of institutional decision-making will be used as well. By combining these two theoretical approaches it will be possible to explain the political impact of public decisions (good or bad) on the individual urban citizen and on the institutions that provide urban services.[3]

Public Goods

The term "public good," as it has been used so far, is a label for the values and beliefs that citizens and public officials have about the role of the public sector. The concept of *public goods,* as the plural implies, takes the broad notion of the public good and breaks it down into particular conditions and products. However, because of its normative aspect, the public good is always more than the sum of its parts. The sum of all the public goods in a city will seldom fit anyone's vision of the good city. The good or heavenly city, as it was called in an earlier age, will always remain something to seek.

Public goods, the more earthly manifestations of public effort, are those benefits enjoyed jointly by a given segment of society, in this case by urbanites. Public goods may be consciously generated by government, as in recreational facilities and police protection; or they may be products of government regulation, such as the reduction of dog feces on the sidewalks of New York; or they may be altogether uncalculated benefits such as the red-orange sunsets that are seen only through highly polluted air.

Externalities

Some public goods, like the carbon monoxide sunset, are the result of private action. Such goods are called externalities because they have an effect on individuals other than (external to) those that took the private action. In the case of the

---

[3]The combination of theories in this chapter resembles the synthesis in public-choice theory. However, our analysis diverges from both the major premises and prescriptive assumptions of the public choice paradigm. See especially: Vincent and Elinor Ostrom, "Public Choice: A Different Approach to the Study of Public Administration," *Public Administration Review,* (March/April 1971) p. 203.

sunset, pollution, which is usually considered a *negative* externality, has produced an unplanned external benefit. Externalities, anticipated and unanticipated, are at every turn in cities: noisy neighbors, the threat of street crime, clogged storm drains, and the smell of fresh-baked bread. Cities are literal webs of external costs and benefits. The density of urban settlement and the complexity of urban society guarantee external trespasses on almost every action of the city dweller. It is the sum of these external costs and benefits—a blooming, buzzing confusion—that constitutes the excitement and energy of city life for some, and for others, the urban rat race.

The profusion of externalities will be more costly for some individuals than for others. The difference in costs is due in part to differences in individual temperament and in part it is due to differences in wealth, which may be used as a shelter from the environment. Only when an external cost moves individuals to action does it become *politically relevant*. As a number of observers have pointed out, air pollution remained a nonrelevant externality for many years, even though it was recognized as a health hazard.[4] It was not until environmental groups and sympathetic politicians began agitating for regulation that pollution became a politically relevant external cost. The attention focused on an external cost will define its political impact.

Those externalities that have an effect on large segments of the population over time can be considered public goods, whether they are generated by public or private action. Such externalities become public goods when they are so widely diffused that no one individual can be excluded from their enjoyment (or cost, as the case may be). The criterion of nonexclusion is the aspect of a public good that most clearly identifies it. A *pure* public good is one that is enjoyed by everyone equally: no individual's enjoyment of it will decrease anyone else's enjoyment of it. The pure case is usually illustrated by national defense. Although it may be inaccurate to say that everyone "enjoys" national defense, it is true that whatever protection is provided cannot be used individually. This example is primarily useful to show the great difference between such collective use and the use of private goods such as gum drops, shoes, and facial tissue. The point is that others can usually be excluded from the use of a private good.

However, public goods such as national defense are rare (perhaps that is why defense is so often used as an example). It is extremely difficult to find any good or service in urban areas from which someone cannot be excluded. For example, the best analogy to national defense in the city is police protection. Certainly there are some aspects of this service that are not separable. The deterrence provided by the reputation of the police force and the court system may or may not be a critical factor in influencing the behavior of potential criminals. But to the extent that the criminal justice system has any deterrent effect, it will be enjoyed equally by all. There are other goods and services provided by the police that are not so clearly public. As with any other collective effort at the point of congestion or

[4]Matthew A. Crenson, *The Un-Politics of Air Pollution* (Baltimore: Johns Hopkins University Press, 1971).

peak demand, the police have to rank order these demands. This is routinized in some departments by the use of a priorities list for screening calls and dispatching mobile units. More subtly, a whole range of social and psychological factors intervenes when an officer of the law confronts a citizen. These factors also have a screening effect. The outcome of these confrontations and those between judges and citizens is highly variable, so that it is very difficult to claim that justice or protection is enjoyed by all without exclusion or separation.

The Public-Private Continuum

Rather than being either pure public or pure private goods, most urban services have both exclusionary and nonexclusionary aspects. Like police protection, these services provide some separable benefit due to congestion and other environmental factors. If we consider all public services to be arrayed along a continuum (Figure 8.1) from completely exclusionary (pure private) to completely nonexclusionary (pure public), several important political factors come to light. The first factor is *the number of individuals receiving private goods from public services.* In a situation where only a limited portion of a service is separable, a limited portion of society will receive the separable benefit. The distribution of the limited portion of private benefits may very well be random. We would expect this to be the case in the screening of calls for service by police dispatchers. In other cases, characteristics like race and socioeconomic status define that portion of the population that is to receive the separable benefit. Logically, this is what happens in the allocation of low-income public housing. We all may benefit equally from the social good resulting from a well-housed population, but the actual, private benefit of rent subsidy and public maintenance is necessarily unequal. It is a simple political fact of urban life that the distribution of public goods and services is inherently unequal. All legislation classifies, and so do other actions of the state. Once again, it should be understood that most of this inequality is anticipated and is the defining characteristic of the service. Some classification, however, has no compelling state interest behind it and cannot be rationalized as a necessary part of service provision. In either case, the fact to be kept in mind is that inequality in the distribution of separable benefits, whether it be just or unjust, is the *rule rather than the exception* in urban service provision.

The second political aspect of the public-private continuum is the positioning of each service between the extremes of pure public and pure private goods. This aspect determines *which individuals will receive private goods from public service.* The position of each service is political because it can be changed. Because the position of a service along the continuum defines the size of the population that may receive a separable benefit, a change in position means a change of the allocation of a public resource. Such a change is fundamentally political. In many instances, however, urbanites fail to see, or are encouraged not to see, the possibility for changing the position of a service along the continuum. As already argued,

Figure 8.1
The Public-Private Continuum in the Provision of Urban Services

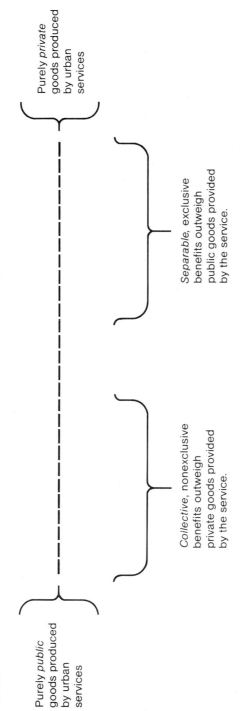

Purely *public* goods produced by urban services

Collective, nonexclusive benefits outweigh private goods provided by the service.

Separable, exclusive benefits outweigh public goods provided by the service.

Purely *private* goods produced by urban services

173

the definition and administration of services in urban areas is increasingly the responsibility of unelected, professional officials. These officials, as service administrators, establish and then defend the position of the service on the continuum. It may then become difficult for the individual citizen to have anything to say about the conduct of public business as it affects him or her. Nonetheless, the position of services along the continuum does occasionally change. Such a change usually involves a redefinition of the group eligible for separable benefits, and redefinition involves a change in one or more of three elements: the *number of beneficiaries;* the *nature of the benefit;* and the *structure of institutions providing the benefit.*

The number of beneficiaries can change in a variety of ways. The amount of resources available can increase—allowing the inclusion of individuals with different characteristics. For example, some urban communities have found it necessary to subsidize middle-income as well as lower-income housing in order to attract the middle class back from the suburbs. In addition, public advocacy programs, which had been reserved for blacks as the most prominent, disadvantaged urban minority, have been expanded to cover discrimination against Chicanos, women, and, in some cases, homosexuals. However, what can increase can also decrease. Tight budgets in a number of cities have justified the complete elimination of rent subsidies and the discontinuation of advocacy programs.

A more subtle shift in the position of a service will result from a change in the nature of the benefit itself. This may involve a change in either the form or the substance of the service. The reintroduction of foot patrols in high-density police precincts would be a change in form of the service. The results of this change cannot be measured exactly, but it might be expected that a foot patrol would be more immediately accessible to citizens and therefore able to provide a greater variety of private benefits. A change in the substance of police service would involve an increase or decrease in police authority or a complete change in the role of the police. The "stop and frisk" procedure once used by the Chicago police increased private costs for many residents of ghetto areas. A change in role, however, is perhaps the most subtle shift in the nature of a benefit, and deserves a more complete illustration.

There have been a large number of suggestions for changing the role of the police in cities. One of the few police adminstrators to implement a major role change is Robert diGrazia, most recently commissioner of police in Montgomery County, Maryland. DiGrazia attempted to change the role of the police in two other major metropolitan areas as well—St. Louis County, Missouri, and the City of Boston. The highly political nature of the police role is indicated by the extraordinary controversy around DiGrazia wherever he has been. The idea that he has come to represent is that the police are, or should be, a service-oriented organization, in contrast to the paramilitary model that had become a big-city style in the late 1960s. The police, then, should not be a fortification against citizen demand, but instead should be sensitive to it. To this end DiGrazia changed the police uniform to a more casual blazer and slacks and changed the point system for promotion to emphasize formal education and training rather than time on the force. Not surprisingly, DiGrazia found these reforms difficult to institute.

In the terms we have been using here, the DiGrazia reforms can be seen as a reaction against the myth of police service as a public good, one that provides an equally beneficial deterrent to crime throughout the city. What DiGrazia proposed was a recognition that police service was really quite different from national defense and that the network of private benefits that had grown up to replace an ineffective deterrent should be brought out into the open and improved. DiGrazia's career is testimony to the political impact of a reform like this. Pointing out that the emperor is naked has its costs, and in December 1978 DiGrazia was asked to resign by the newly elected Montgomery County executive.[5]

A third way in which a service may shift along the public-private continuum is through a change in the structure of the institution providing the service. This may necessitate moving a certain function from one agency to another or making an executive position appointive, rather than elective, or vice versa. However, the most significant example of a change in structure is the introduction of competition into a service area dominated by a monopoly. Competition is theoretically the most direct way to increase private benefit from a service. Competition in postal service, solid waste collection, and security services is usually related to higher consumer satisfaction. With more producers to choose from and with the addition of competitive pricing, the consumer/citizen should be able to pay for the desired level of service (daily or biweekly postal service or garbage pick-up; security patrols by the hour or by the shift) and then hold the producer responsible for delivering it.

A marketplace for urban services is a very attractive idea, but it is not without pitfalls. A major objection to this system is one that is made of all market systems: the benefits from the service will go to those who start out with the most resources. This objection will be taken up in detail in considering the whole question of service equity in Chapter 11. Still, the change in institutional structure from monopoly to market is the most dramatic and most political way to shift the position of a service on the public-private continuum. It represents a fundamental change in the concept of the public good and has become an increasingly popular topic in discussions of "overregulation" or what has lately been called "public sector imperialism."[6] The root of the controversy about public regulation dates to the earliest cities, and it has probably been best expressed by Thomas Hobbes (a strong supporter of regulation). The theory of public goods explains the growth of monopoly public service in terms of the failure of the free market to produce and provide nonexclusionary goods.

[5]"Police Chief Is Dismissed by County in Maryland" (*The New York Times,* December 10, 1978) p. 26.
[6]Norman Macrae, "Towards Smaller Government," *The Economist* (December 23, 1978) p. 46.

The Failure of the Market

A market, according to Francis Bator, is "a more or less idealized system of institutions to sustain 'desirable' activities or to stop 'undesirable' activities."[7] But can such a system be used to sustain desirable *collective* activities like public goods? For a market to sustain the provision of a public good it would have to be possible to set a price for a given public good in terms of its supply and the current demand. "Price" is the defining characteristic of a market system. To use Bator's terminology, it is through a pricing mechanism that both the consumption and the production of any good is sustained.

It is because of the nonexclusionary nature of public goods that the market will not sustain their production. If the individual is aware that he cannot be excluded from enjoying the benefits of a good, he will have little or no incentive to "purchase" it, and setting a price will be impossible. Instead, it becomes rational for the individual to "ride free" on contributions of others, because they will not be able to limit his enjoyment. In spite of all the elegant, economic explanations of the free-rider phenomenon, the best example remains that of the New Testament festival to which all the villagers were to contribute a jug of wine. The wine was to be poured into a large cask from which all would be free to draw during the party. The villager who provides the object lesson in the parable decides that if he contributes a jug of water, no one will be wiser, and he will get the benefit of the slightly diluted wine without paying the price. Of course when the cask is tapped for the party it turns out to be full of water.

Self-interest always counsels the individual to be a cynical villager—to obtain the most benefit for the least cost. In fact, highest-yield-for-lowest-cost is the standard definition of economic efficiency. How can society procure a good, the production of which negates both economic efficiency and individual self-interest? Historically, this question has been answered by the club and the sword. Government traditionally coerces the contribution of the individual. The "reason" for urban government is to employ its monopoly on the use of force toward the attainment of the public good. Without governmental coercion public roads would not be paved, nor would police protection or public recreation be practicable. Most citizens would simply prefer to spend their tax money themselves.

But aren't there some circumstances that will allow individuals to cooperate in achieving the public good without having a sword at their backs? Or will anything short of a public monopoly produce a cask full of water? Answering this question takes us into another tradition in the social sciences, the theory of collective action. This theory is well suited to a discussion of the urban public good since it straddles the disciplines of political science and economics. Collective action theory allows us to consider both the economic production and consumption of collective goods and the political allocation of collective benefits.

[7]Francis M. Bator, "The Anatomy of Market Failure," *Quarterly Journal of Economics* (August 1958) p. 351.

Collective Action and Collective Inaction

The clearest statement of a theory of collective action has been made by Mancur Olson. Olson's study is presented as a critique of the conventional wisdom about the voluntary nature of political organization in the United States. Olson particularly examines the contention of pluralists and interest group theorists that

> . . . participation in voluntary association is virtually universal, and that small groups and large organizations tend to attract members for the same reasons. The casual variant of the theory assumed a propensity to belong to groups without drawing any distinctions between groups of different size. Though the more sophisticated variant may be credited with drawing a distinction between those functions that can best be served by large associations, it nonetheless assumes that, when there is a need for a large association, a large association will tend to emerge and attract members, just as a small group will when there is a need for a small group.[8]

If this contention were an accurate picture of the American political system, our argument about the political dominance of urban public bureaucrats would be an overstatement. We would find instead a citizenry that votes in terms of preferences to which officials readily respond. And when policy does not fulfill the needs of a certain segment of the electorate, a free association of kindred spirits is formed to pursue common interests beyond the election. These associations balance each other, and justice prevails. In such a system, the public good would be a product of the competition between interest groups, rather than being some Platonic Ideal.

As mentioned above, Theodore Lowi, among others, finds pluralist and interest-group theorists inaccurate in their claims about balance and open competition between groups. Instead, Lowi finds a series of closed, noncompetitive policy arenas, dominated by the public and private organizations having the most resources. Mancur Olson looks at another aspect of the picture and finds it to be equally inaccurate; the formation and constitution of the groups themselves. To begin with, Olson argues that it is an error to talk about interest groups in general. Interest groups are of three widely different types, each of which has a distinct effect on the potential participation of the individual and the political character of the group itself. The three are: privileged groups, intermediate groups, and large or latent groups.

Olson's classification is based primarily on differences in size. The first type, the privileged group, is the smallest, and in fact may consist of a single individual. In such a group, a collective benefit will be provided because one or more members of the group desire the good to such an extent that he or they are willing to bear the cost of providing the good to everyone. In this case, free riders are welcomed aboard, or at least tolerated. The privileged group conjures images of great wealth and magnanimity, where the neighborhood big shot hires a police

[8]Mancur Olson, *The Logic of Collective Action* (Cambridge, Mass.: Harvard University Press, 1971), p. 20.

force and installs streetlights to protect himself and the surrounding area. Of course, there are examples of this kind of grand generosity, but a privileged good can result from more modest effort as well. A devoted and energetic parent may clear a path through the snow beyond the limits of his property so that his children can walk to the bus stop, or a neighbor with a fair amount of leisure time may take it upon himself to patrol the block for litter.

In the privileged group and the other two types as well, Olson finds that the individual will voluntarily contribute to the production of the collective good—if he perceives some separable benefit. This is an important finding because it demystifies the process of group politics in urban areas and in the national polity as well. Rather than asking, "What can I do to help the cause toward the attainment of our common goals?" Olson's joiner asks, "What can I do to help attain my own goals through collective effort, and how much will come to me in return?" But do any urbanites participate in civic activities selflessly out of the simple joy of giving? Economists, including Olson, are willing to admit "good feelings" and the "sense of contributing" into their definition of separable benefits. This does not compromise the definition as much as it may seem. Obviously, it is easy to see why someone may drop out of a block association after years of trying unsuccessfully to have a streetlight installed in front of his house. It should not be much harder to identify the separable benefit when an individual joins a good government league in order to "meet people and do something for the community." If the people prove unfriendly and the group proves to be direction-less, we would expect the individual to be disappointed and leave.

The temptation presented by Olson's finding is to try to discover and describe the psychological motives of all joiners. Uncovering the "reason" for any sort of human action is difficult enough for the actor himself, and it is an endeavor fraught with traps and wrong turns for the outsider. "I'm doing it because I want to!" proclaims the volunteer, and the investigator assumes more at his own peril. Instead, the outsider can simply assume that there is *some* motive and *some* separable benefit in view. This will be true, as Peter Blau argues, for all of us except saints and fools.[9]

Separable benefits play a more subtle role in the formation of intermediate groups. These differ from privileged groups in two important ways. Intermediate groups are generally somewhat larger than privileged groups and the nature of the desired benefit requires some organized activity. The need for organized activity becomes more obvious as the complexity and risk involved in obtaining the benefit increase. It would be foolish (or saintly) for one homeowner in a development to bear the cost of installing utility services in the entire area. Similarly, an organized citizens' group is more likely to get results in confronting a hostile and unresponsive police administrator than would an individual citizen. In these cases, the individual has a specific benefit in view (a sewer hook-up or increased police patrol), but it is apparent that his effort alone will not attain it.

Another aspect of intermediate groups involves similarly situated individuals

---

[9]Peter M. Blau, *Exchange and Power in Social Life* (New York: Wiley, 1964), p. 15.

who do not start with the zeal of the organizer. These individuals will participate if they perceive that the collective benefit and their share of it cannot be obtained without their personal effort. The ability of the individual to see a connection between his own time and effort and the attainment of the benefit is crucial to sustaining an intermediate group. The individual must also see, or be persuaded to see, that without his personal effort the success of the enterprise is in grave doubt. A perceived relationship between effort and benefit greatly reduces the incentive to ride free. The incentive is further reduced by the social pressure that can be applied quite effectively in relatively small groups. This factor, known as the mutual threat system (or more informally as the "hairy eye-ball"), loses its power as the size of the group increases and as it becomes more difficult to monitor the behavior of others.

It is the large group that concerns us particularly in this discussion. As city government becomes more complex and policy decisions become remote from the individual citizen, urban democracy comes to depend on the ability of individuals to organize and press their claims against government. However, as we argued in Chapter 7, because of the scale and complexity of urban government, city agencies will respond most readily to groups of similar scale and complexity. Thus, in many cases, the more successful interest groups will probably be the larger ones. As in any other political system, those groups with the resources and support to sustain a demand over time will usually fare the best. None of this should be surprising to even the most casual observer of urban politics. It is simply the repetition of a basic principle of urban politics: the survival of the organized. Surprising or not, Olson's classification should lead us to question the quality of urban democracy.

In a large group, the individual has little incentive to contribute voluntarily. If the group succeeds in obtaining the collective good, the nonparticipant will enjoy it as well as the participant. In the case of a collective good sought by a large group, the individual declines to participate in obtaining the good for the same reason that the market fails to allocate the good: there is no perceived connection between personal effort and personal gain so that a rational strategy for the individual is to do nothing.

It may appear that this perspective on large groups is overly pessimistic. There are, after all, public spirited citizens who work for charities and who would probably pay their taxes voluntarily. Unfortunately, these citizens are the exception. In order for most other citizens to participate in the pursuit of the common good, some element of persuasion or even coercion is often necessary.

It is this coercion that raises a question about the democracy of large groups. The clearest example of the use of coercion in large group organization is the closed union shop. Where allowed by state law, closed-shop contracts prohibit the employment in a unionized work place of any person who is not a union member. This effectively eliminates the free-rider problem from labor organization in large work units. In urban politics there are a number of large or latent groups that have been organized through some measure of coercion. Most special districts providing utilities are capitalized through bonds that are issued against coercive assessments. This technique is also used to fund a variety of other public activities. In St. Louis City and County, for instance, there is a consolidated assessment on each taxpayer for the benefit of the zoo and the St. Louis Museum of Art. Mosquito control and, in some cases, flood control are also supported this way.

There is an important distinction in the ways in which coercive assessments are levied. Utility districts will often include a per capita fee for capital improvements, but the cost of service to the consumer is usually tied to the consumer's level of usage (in terms of gallons of water used per month, for example). Some special districts, such as bridge and highway authorities, are able to limit the assessment only to those who benefit directly from the service on a pay-as-you-go basis by charging a toll. A user tax such as a road toll is indeed coercive, because the problem of the free rider is present. However, it is possible for individuals who are nonusers to be noncontributors. For this reason, the user tax has been lauded by some analysts as a cure for the antidemocratic nature of large group organization. But the user tax is a far from perfect cure. The choice between crossing a toll bridge on the way to work or staying home is not everyone's idea of democracy.

Nonetheless, the user tax is to be preferred in many situations. It takes into account the private benefit received by some from a collective good, and while it does not allow for separate price negotiations with each user, it provides at least a yes-or-no choice. The second and predominant type of assessment, the collective benefit tax, provides no such choice. Theoretically, the imposition of a collective benefit tax indicates the provision of a pure public good. If no one can be excluded from benefit, then no one should be excluded from taxation. Once this argument is successfully made about a particular collective benefit, the provision of it will be removed from the open market. And while there may remain some degree of private benefit from a public good, it will generally be overlooked. Instead, it will be to the advantage of urban governments to stress the collective aspects of the benefit in order to justify the expenditure of general city revenues.

If the definition of "the public good" is subjective, so, too, is the designation of public goods. Because of the "impure" nature of most urban public goods— that is, the provision of private as well as public benefits—urban governments are confronted with a choice. Should a benefit like urban transportation or hospital services be paid for through user taxes which recognize the private benefits involved; or should the collective benefits of good, accessible transportation and health facilities be emphasized to warrant general taxation? The trend in American municipalities has been to emphasize citywide benefits and to tax as broadly as possible. An interesting result of this trend is that once the choice is made to collectivize service provision, it becomes extremely difficult to consider other arrangements, including those that would introduce private or neighborhood provision. While public provision of urban services is not written in a sacred text, it does tend to become entrenched, so much so in many cases that both the service and public provision of it become "subjectively indispensable." A trend toward subjective indispensability of government provision of urban services, together with the often coercive nature of large group organization, raises important doubts about the quality of urban democracy. Two questions should be posed at this point. Why has the public provision of urban services become subjectively indispensable? And, what is the effect of public indispensability on the variety and quality of urban life?

Thinking About the Urban Public Sector

Norman Macrae, the deputy editor of *The Economist,* has considered the problem of public-sector expansion in urban areas in a very interesting and creative way. He examines a variety of difficulties associated with the expansion of municipal control and then presents a tongue-in-cheek prescription that calls for more commercial, private provision of urban services:

> An example of local government functions run by a commerical firm is Disney World. . . . The productivity of local government operations is several hundred per cent higher in private-sector Disney World than it is in the public-sector imperialisms. The reason is that local government in Disney is a customer-oriented, market-dependent, entrepreneurial job carried out with output targets. By contrast, in the public-sector imperialisms local government is a producer-oriented, non-market-checked, bureaucratic job. . . . If Mickey Mouse were everywhere elected mayor on a performance contract, then local government efficiency would everywhere multiply several times over.[10]

There are, in fact, a number of such local governments. The Lakewood cities in Los Angeles County, California, are probably the best-known examples of the "contract city." Under the Lakewood Plan a number of suburban communities incorporated in order to buy services on a performance basis from either private firms or other units of government in the area.[11] This strategy has been used in a number of places and seems to work quite well in relatively affluent small cities and in suburbs. But this is a marketlike arrangement, and like other markets, it will provide the greatest benefit to those with *the most resources regardless of the needs and demands of others.* This is the baldest statement of the inequality that an emphasis on private benefit will produce in the distribution of urban services. However, a number of compromises have been suggested.[12] Most of the compromises provide for some kind of income redistribution (through coercive contribution) or for at least a program of government subsidies for poorer communities. However, even if such a compromise were desirable, what would be the possibility

[10]Macrae, "Towards Smaller Government," p. 49.
[11]Vincent Ostrom, Charles M. Tiebout, and Robert Warren, "The Organization of Government in Metropolitan Areas: A Theoretical Inquiry," *American Political Science Review* (December 1961), p. 839.
[12]Robert L. Bish and Vincent Ostrom, *Understanding Urban Government* (Washington: American Enterprise Institute for Public Policy Research, 1973), pp. 100–101.

in most cities of instituting some marketlike system for distributing urban services?

Municipal Services: The Choice Between Exit, Voice, and Loyalty

If a marketlike system can promise a somewhat more democratic system of service distribution, it should have a large number of supporters. However unfortunate, this is not the case. Those urbanites who have been dissatisfied with coercive contributions or the level of services they receive in the city and who can afford to "purchase a service package" more to their taste have moved to the land of the like-minded, the suburbs. The size and socioeconomic homogeneity of many suburbs allow them to operate as intermediate groups. The suburbs make it possible for the efforts and preferences of citizens to converge so that the product of public effort conforms more closely to private needs than is possible in larger, more diverse political units. The side effect of the migration to the suburbs is that it has drawn off pressure for service diversity in the city. Middle- and upper-income urbanites, those most likely and best able to demand innovation in service provision, have left central cities in large numbers.

According to Albert Hirschman's classification, those who cannot exit from a situation have two main options: voice and loyalty. Loyalty presents no challenge to current arrangements, and voice, in order to have some effect on specialized, urban bureaucracy, must come from an organized group that has expertise and a minimum level of resources.[13] A general protest or outcry against current conditions will be difficult to respond to for program administrators who see the world in terms of their specialty. Of course, elected officials may be sensitive to the demands of their constituents, no matter how diffuse and nonspecific they are. But once in office, elected officials will be confronted with the difficult task of translating dissatisfaction into action. And again, most actions will depend on public bureaucracies and their further interpretation of what should be an appropriate response to any demand.

A classic example of the inevitable gap between promise and action in urban government would be an encounter between a newly elected city councilman and the appointed police commissioner. The councilman has promised to get better police protection for the area he represents. The police commissioner knows that a demand for better service is not unique to the councilman's district, and that at the same time that demand is rising, the mayor's office is making a 10 percent cut in the police budget in order to deliver a promised tax reduction. When rising demand meets scarcity in a situation like this, the appointed official can be expected to carefully guard his allocative authority, or this will be only the first

[13]Albert O. Hirschman, *Exit, Voice, and Loyalty* (Cambridge, Mass.: Harvard University Press, 1970).

of many such meetings with councilmen. At the same time, the commissioner does not need an enemy on the city council. Therefore the councilman is promised immediate action in the form of a study by the department's office of policy and planning and an open meeting between the community and the deputy chief for public affairs. This is action, but it is bureaucratic action, which, it should be clear, is not the same as public service.

For those who choose to stay in the city and for those who cannot leave, the services provided by city governments can become indispensable. This will occur to the extent that urban services are considered public goods and to the extent that they are provided by centralized municipal agencies. The extent has been considerable in both cases, and the urban public economy is still expanding in most cities, Proposition 13 notwithstanding.[14] But the expansion and indispensability of the public economy does not come about by force of arms or cultish mind control. The expansion is an evolutionary process that erodes the incentive urbanites have to care about and provide for their own welfare. This is a paradoxical by-product of democratic urban government. It is a by-product that is largely unintended and that is produced by a subtle process. It is a process, however, which can be observed. A closer examination of the dynamics of the public economy in cities will expose the logic of governmental indispensability and the consequent erosion of incentives.

Institutions in the Urban Public Economy: "Buchanan's Box" and the Paradox of Urban Service Provision

There are two central dimensions of the demand for urban service so far discussed. The first is the desire of the individual for the good provided by the service. If this desire is pervasive enough and if the community in question is relatively small, we can expect the good to be provided through voluntary, collective effort at a level considered satisfactory. This is the best of all possible urban worlds. The second dimension is the perceived need of the community for a certain benefit which, because of extensive external costs, requires collective effort, but does not stimulate individual participation. Once again, pollution provides a good example. Individuals may desire its elimination, but they have

[14]Direct General Expenditures of Local Governments in 74 Major SMSAs:

	1971–72	1972–73	1973–74	1974–75	1975–76
Millions	67,257	71,522	79,158	89,482	99,145
Per Capita	—	643.41	697.26	788.19	866.55

Source: U. S. Bureau of the Census, *Local Government Finances in Selected Metropolitan Areas and Large Counties* (1972–1973, 1973–1974, 1974–1975, 1975–1976, all separate reports).

little incentive to act voluntarily to clean up the environment. Most people would consider such individual effort to be futile, and usually the need for the coercive power of government will be recognized.

At this point we can return to our initial question: How is the public good determined in American cities? The answer is through the balance struck between the individual's desire for separable benefits from collective goods and the community's desire to eliminate external costs by providing collective goods that have *no* separable benefits. Community enterprises such as municipal governments have traditionally used "the greatest good for the greatest number" as a rule of thumb in planning ways to reduce external costs. This rule of thumb is often the most convenient way of producing the service and is also the best justification for collecting general tax revenues. However, before the individual will participate in a community enterprise, he must have an answer to the age-old question, "Where's mine?" The balance struck between providing the greatest good for the greatest number and providing a separable good for the individual will determine the position of a particular service along the continuum between pure public and pure private goods. The public good, the scope and quality of collective effort, will in large part be determined by the mix of *incentives* and *benefits* related to a particular position on the continuum. James Buchanan[15] explains the tension between individual desires and collective needs by constructing the "box" in Figure 8.2.

The best situation for a democratic city is represented by cell 1 in Buchanan's Box. In cell 1, as in Olson's intermediate group, the individual sees a connection between his own effort and the obtaining of a collective good from which he stands to benefit. Thus, in seeking individual benefits (i.e., personal security) the members of a community will collectively secure a public good (i.e., public safety). In this case (and it is obviously rare), no coercion is needed to ensure the individual's contributions. Each contributes because each prefers to do so.

In addition to defining the climate for noncoercive public service, cell 1 is also an economic definition of citizenship. The picture we get in cell 1 is of the model American frontiersman, building a life according to a personal design, and at the same time contributing to the commonwealth. The mission of government in cell 1 is completely defined by the needs and preferences of individuals. Citizenship, under such a system, does not imply a mere check on the authority of the state. Indeed, in cell 1 there is no central authority other than the collective, voluntary effort of individuals. This is the heavenly city, at last.

However, like any vision of redemption, cell 1 implies a broadly agreed upon moral value. Buchanan suggests two such values: the Judeo-Christian Ethic, which produces social harmony, and a social ethic drawn from the philosophy of Immanuel Kant. Under Kant's categorical imperative individuals are guided by a single rule: "Act only on that maxim whereby you can at the same time will

[15]James M. Buchanan, "Public Goods and Public Bads," *Financing the Metropolis,* John P. Crecine, ed., (Beverly Hills, Cal.: Sage Publications, 1970), p. 65.

Figure 8.2
"Buchanan's Box"

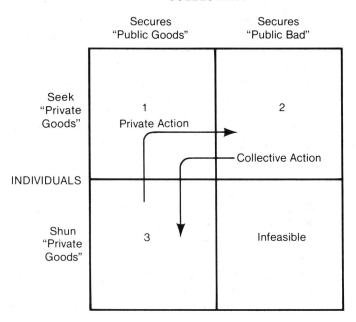

COLLECTIVITY

SOURCE: James M. Buchanan, "Public Goods and Public Bads," *Financing the Metropolis*, ed. by John P. Crecine (Beverly Hills, Cal.: Sage Publications, 1970), p. 65.

that it should become a universal law."[16] The implication of this maxim for the urban public economy is close to the Golden Rule: Contribute to the welfare of others as you would have others contribute to your own.

Kant makes a compelling argument for the necessity of such a rule. Goodwill, the impulse toward voluntary contribution, has an intrinsic value for Kant. Calculated short-term benefit and the prospect of a free ride are destructive of one's self-interest in the long run. If everyone rides free, no common "good" will be produced. Humanity, or the collective seeking of the public good, should be an end in itself, not only a means toward personal gain.

Kant's formulation of the *moral* public economy is an attractive ideal. However, the ideal is often compromised, since moral imperatives do not usually guide collective behavior. In cell 2 of the box, Buchanan describes the more usual situation, in which goodwill and humanity are not the ends and a separable, private benefit is the central purpose of collective action. In cell 2 there is little agreement on what the public good should be, and there is no agency to mediate

[16]Immanuel Kant, "Foundation for the Metaphysic of Morals," in *Philosophic Classics*, Walter Kaufman, ed. (Englewood Cliffs, N.J.: Prentice-Hall, 1961), p. 582.

differing perspectives or distribute benefits in a way that is considered just. In fact, a city in cell 2 may eventually slip into the warlike state in which individuals have made no common provision for either property or justice. Gang rule and privateering may be the result. From many reports, including the following excerpt, the public economy of the South Bronx in New York City around 1976 resembled the situation in cell 2.

> In the burned-out streets of the South Bronx, some thirty savage youth gangs grubbed like jackals around a corpse; they mugged and murdered, raped and robbed at random. The black and Puerto Rican residents called the gang kids predators and beasts and they likened the ghetto to a living hell.[17]

Cell 2 represents the dark side of rational choice. The individual chooses on the basis of preference and the calculation of cost and benefit according to the conventional economic model. However, choice in cell 2 is unimpeded by community norms, moral values, or public law. What common resources there are cannot last long in such an environment since the only "rational" course for the individual is to get as much for himself as possible. Instead of producing the public good, individual effort in a cell 2 society will produce public bads such as vandalism, looting, and widespread street crime.

Unfortunately, the South Bronx is not the only example of what may be called a decadent public economy. Most large American cities have "combat zones" where the police precinct station is referred to as Fort Apache. These zones, however, are generally distant from the commercial centers of urban areas and can be successfully isolated. But they do present extraordinary problems for the urban policy process.

The response of urban policy makers to the existence of combat zones has been tentative and erratic. In some cities they are ignored entirely. But in most cases the federal government becomes the first and last resort in dealing with the problem. And a focus on the *physical* deterioration of the combat zone is the most common prescription.

A second approach is to recognize that the social pathology that produces a combat zone is not susceptible to effective treatment by public policy; that it may be possible to rebuild an area but not a society. As James Q. Wilson puts it, "the issues that most concern a neighborhood are typically those about which politicians can do relatively little."[18] What Wilson seems to be saying is that governments cannot build communities. Edward Banfield comes to a similar conclusion in *The Unheavenly City Revisited:*

> Although there are many difficulties to be coped with, dilemmas to be faced, and afflictions to be endured, there are very few problems that can be solved. . . .[19]

---

[17]Jon Bradshaw, "Savage Skulls," *Esquire* (June 1977), p. 75.
[18]James Q. Wilson, *Thinking About Crime* (New York: Basic Books, 1975), p. 41.
[19]Edward C. Banfield, *The Unheavenly City Revisited* (Boston: Little, Brown, 1974), p. 285.

Why is it that government cannot solve the problem of urban combat zones? Or, to put it another way, why can't government direct the seeking of private goods in low income areas toward the attainment of the public good? Of course city governments try to provide such direction. But it is considered undemocratic to interfere very much with the individual's own determination of the common good. The best models of state direction of individual preference, such as the Soviet Young Pioneers, are considered to be unsuitable by most urban policy makers.

As Buchanan points out, urban governments do have options other than thought control and complete neglect. In the face of social disorder and the erosion of public goods, city governments may chose to impose strict usage rules.

> The user of a publicly supplied, commonly used facility or service has no privately valued incentive to protect and preserve the facility or service from deterioration, or at least this incentive tends to be grossly undervalued. The conservation of publicly supplied facilities may require the coercive implementation of rules of usage.[20]

The words "coercive implementation" do not harmonize with the American ideal of a democratic city. In making his argument, Buchanan shows us how far we are from the heavenly city of the colonial theocrat. In place of the communalism and consensus of the New England town meeting or the Quaker meeting style, we rely on the power of the state. This reliance is what makes the city truly unheavenly, and it is what places modern American urban life in the most pervasive of Buchanan's situations, cell 3.

The situation in cell 3 is what is often called the urban crisis. Large, rather than intermediate or community, groups dominate the policy process, so that the individual citizen is at best a constituent or client of some larger interest. The individual, therefore, sees little connection between any personal effort and the achievement of collective goods. This disconnection will stimulate an entrepreneurial spirit in some. The feeling is, "If the rules don't allow me to get what I want out of life, and if I can't change the rules, then I'll just have to take what I want." This attitude is recognizable as the healthy instinct of a self-interested, rational actor. However, in cell 3, healthy instincts can easily move urban society into the state of conflict in cell 2. The situation in cell 3 requires careful governmental scrutiny and continual maintenance, for no consensus on community principles can be assumed. The basic political question, "Where's mine?", which is the foundation of the public good in cell 1, becomes a public threat in cell 3. Self-interest must be carefully channeled by professional managers in cell 3, because definition of "the good" cannot be left to those who would define it in their own favor.

It is in cell 3 that the urban bureaucracy predominates; it has replaced "the community" as the maker and interpreter of the rules. In the bureaucrat's city, as it was explained in Chapter 7, the role of the citizen is redefined as the role of

[20]Buchanan, "Public Goods and Public Bads," p. 68.

urban government expands. The rough-hewn farmer in Norman Rockwell's well-known illustrations becomes either a constituent, a client, or a victim.

The paradox of urban service provision is the fall from cell 1 to cell 3 in Buchanan's Box. As urban society has opened up by growing in numbers and social diversity, it has at the same time closed the range of action allowed the individual in defining "the good." It seems as if the determination of the urban public good is a zero-sum contest between the prerogatives of the individual and the authority of government. A gain on one side appears to mean an equal loss on the other side.

Returning to the "Real" City

The real city, it can be argued, is not make up of intentions, incentives, and group classifications; it is made up of sewer lines, potholes, and badly run schools. What connection is there between the flesh-and-blood city and the abstract concepts we have discussed above? Can the fiscal crisis or public employee strikes be explained using the terms presented in this chapter? The argument here is that incentives and group characteristics are every bit as real as schools and potholes. However, the connection between the politics of urban service and the services themselves should be illustrated.

The next chapter will explore services in detail. By using the concepts developed in this chapter it will be possible to describe the workings of service provision and, in addition, to examine service provision in light of the urban public good.

Suggested Readings

Bish, Robert L., and Vincent Ostrom, *Understanding Urban Government* (Washington: American Enterprise Institute for Public Policy Research, 1973).

Buchanan, James M., "Public Goods and Public Bads," in *Financing the Metropolis,* John P. Crecine, ed. (Beverly Hills: Sage Publications, 1970), p. 65.

Crenson, Matthew A., *The Un-Politics of Air Pollution* (Baltimore: Johns Hopkins University Press, 1971).

Hirschman, Albert O., *Exit, Voice, and Loyalty* (Cambridge, Mass.: Harvard University Press, 1970).

Olson, Mancur, *The Logic of Collective Action* (Cambridge, Mass.: Harvard University Press, 1971).

Ostrom, Vincent, and Elinor Ostrom, "Public Choice: A Different Approach to the Study of Public Administration," *Public Administration Review* (March/April 1971), p. 203.

Ostrom, Vincent, Charles Tiebout, and Robert Warren, "The Organization of Government in Metropolitan Areas: A Theoretical Inquiry," *American Political Science Review* (December 1961), p. 839.

Wilson, James Q., *Thinking About Crime* (New York: Basic Books, 1975).

Chapter 9

The Architecture of Urban Service Delivery

A Public Sector Parable

The towns of Greenville and Crestmont lie outside a midwestern city of 150,000. The residents of each town have grown dissatisfied with the protection they are receiving from the county sheriff and have decided to hire police officers of their own. Both towns suffer from continuing juvenile delinquency, and irregular patrolling by overextended sheriff's deputies has not kept the kids in line.

The county allows local option for police protection by proportionally reducing the property tax so that taxpayers in communities that withdraw from the sheriff's jurisdiction will receive a rebate equal to the sheriff's proportion of the budget. Understandably, the sheriff would rather not "lose" a town. Each town that pulls out reduces the sheriff's budget and, he claims, "weakens the position of the country's best defense against crime"—his department.

Because Greenville and Crestmont can no longer rely on emergency support from the sheriff's department, they have negotiated a mutual aid pact. The pact provides that a call for help by either town will be given first-priority response by the other town. Not long after the pact was signed, a Greenville patrol unit received a call for help from the Crestmont unit and set off at high speed through the ten miles of cornfields between the two towns. En route, the Greenville patrol car was intercepted by a sheriff's deputy after a Hollywood-style chase. The Greenville car was forced off the road by the deputy and ticketed for speeding on a county highway. By the time the encounter was over it was too late for the Greenville officer to be of any help in Crestmont. He headed home but not before threatening to shoot the next deputy who interfered with the aid pact. The dispute over the legality of the pact was eventually resolved in favor of the two towns by the state attorney general.

The Greenville/Crestmont succession dispute is drawn from a real case (only names have been changed), and it is not as rare as it is absurd. The great number of independent political jurisdictions in metropolitan areas inevitably creates problems in the delivery of services. The most obvious problem is achieving efficient use of public resources. However, public efficiency, like any other aspect of the public good, is subjectively defined. Thus, for some, efficient use of resources means that services should be provided by one central metropolitan agency in order to eliminate waste. For others, the architecture of service delivery should remain as varied as possible in order to satisfy diverse consumer demand. The goal of this chapter is to explain these and other ideas about service architecture, both in terms of what is structurally possible and in terms of the distribution of benefits related to different designs.

The Structure of External Costs

It often seems that there is no rhyme or reason to urban government, much less an overall design or architectural style. In fact, one of our major contentions has been that nobody specifically governs American cities. If this is the case, can it be said that anyone *designs* American government? The answer is no, with very few exceptions. However, there *are* noticeable patterns and interconnections among services that deserve our attention, since they influence the allocation of resources and the quality of life in urban areas.

Like patterns of other kinds, the connections among urban services can be obvious or hidden. The obvious patterns usually involve connections between some demographic characteristic and the level of service provision. An obvious pattern, however, may be unintended, even if it is conspicuously discriminatory. (Just what constitutes "intent to discriminate" in the provision of a service is a matter of contention, which will be raised in Chapter 11.) A manifest pattern may also involve interdependence among services. For example, there is a subtle but noticeable connection between New York City's garbage barge operation and the regulation of parking on the city's residential streets. Ordinarily, parking is allowed on alternate sides of the street in the five boroughs so that the mechanical sweepers from the sanitation department can clean the streets. However, a strike of the drivers who haul the city's garbage to the harbor barges necessitates a shift in personnel from the street sweepers to the garbage trucks. Therefore the streets cannot be swept and the parking regulations can be suspended.

While a city government may not be designed in the same way as a piece of machinery or a building, there are a great many obvious connections of which the politician and the analyst should be aware. City governments do not conform to the first law of ecology, that everything is connected to everything else, but they do conform to the second law, that you can never do just one thing.[1] As fractioned and specialized as municipal bureaucracies are, a political act by any one of them

[1]Among other places, these ecological laws are explained in William Ophuls, *Ecology and the Politics of Scarcity* (San Francisco: Freeman, 1977).

will have both manifest and latent consequences in other policy areas. Educational policy has direct consequences for employment programs and juvenile justice policy. Transportation and housing policy are interdependent, as are health and sanitation services. This is inevitably the case in the provision of public goods. Such goods are provided in order to reduce external costs and, in the process of reducing some external costs, others will be created. You can't please all of the people all of the time, and urban governments are not likely to do so in the near future.

The interconnections among services makes for a critical irony in the way in which modern urban government is designed. As urban service bureaucracies have grown in size and complexity, the connections between them have become more intricate and also more significant to the quality of service that is produced. At the same time, however, each bureaucracy is developing a sense of turf by guarding its share of increasingly scarce public funds. The larger agencies grow, the more likely they are to generate external costs as they provide services. These external costs imply the need for more coordination between agencies—a need for a sense of governmental design. However, a parallel trend reduces the possibility of design just when it is most needed: the larger agencies grow, the more intense the competition is for scarce public funds.

Therefore, the pressure of fiscal constraints and interbureau rivalry tends to obscure the structure of external costs in the urban political system. This may occur to such an extent that significant changes in people's lives become the unanticipated consequences of fractional bureaucratic action. The people whose lives are changed this way, the people referred to above as victims, bear the heaviest external costs generated by public action. Of course the best way and possibly the only way to avoid victimizing citizens is to identify the structure of external costs. Public effort might then be organized and directed toward removing major external costs. Unfortunately, giving the problem a name does not always solve it, and the structure of external costs may be approached in at least three significantly different ways.

The first position on external costs proceeds from the assumption that government intervention is just as likely to increase any given cost as to reduce it. Those holding this position argue that there should be a *partition* between government provision of urban services and the impact of those services on urban society. According to the partitionists, the distribution of public benefits is unpredictable, especially where public goods are concerned. Therefore, if the distribution seems unfair or inadequate in some way, it is wiser to reduce or eliminate the service (or leave it to the private market) than it is to attempt achieving fairness or objective adequacy. Because fairness and adequacy do not invite careful measurement or scientific verification, it is often better to avoid them.[2]

[2]Examples of the partitionist position may be found in Edward C. Banfield, *The Unheavenly City Revisited* (Boston: Little, Brown, 1974) and, with respect to criminal justice policy, James Q. Wilson, *Thinking About Crime* (New York: Basic Books, 1975).

Another position on external costs is identified with the reform tradition discussed in Chapter 4. This position holds that the solution to the problem of external costs is the elimination of bureau competition and the consolidation of fragmented public authority. This approach tends to deemphasize the political aspect of externalities—the costs borne by those affected by a decision but who have no hand in it. Of course, political costs will not be reduced by consolidating municipal or metropolitan authority. But rather than being concerned about the scope of participation in service provision, the reformers pursue the public good almost as if it were separate from the demands and needs of individuals. The public good and the elimination of cost become a matter for specialized, professional planning. The centerpiece of structural reform, city/suburb consolidation, holds out a number of attractive promises. As Robert Lineberry puts it:

> Consolidation of metropolitan governments would accomplish, presumably, the same blessings as regionalizing brought the European Economic Community, shaking off the curse of fragmentation. It would facilitate intraregional migration by reducing land use barriers to mobility, rationalize economic growth by bringing regionwide economic resources to bear on pockets of underdevelopment, . . . and reduce political tensions by creating super-ordinate governing bodies.[3]

The third position on the structure of external costs is identified with the public-choice approach to political and economic analysis. While public-choice theorists recognize the need for some centralized authority to reduce certain costs such as the threat of disease and the spread of criminal activity, they emphasize the subjective nature of the public good and the need to consult individuals when assessing public costs. In fact, beyond consulting individuals, the goal of the public-choice approach is to return urban government to the neighborhoods through decentralization of service provisions. The need for this kind of architecture is explained by Robert Bish and Vincent Ostrom, two champions of urban public choice:

> Instead of assuming that fragmentation of authority and overlapping jurisdictions are the source of the contemporary urban crisis, we urge the opposite proposition be entertained—that the absence of fragmented authority and multiple jurisdictions in large central cities is the principle source of institutional failure in urban government. The absence of neighborhood governments makes it difficult for residents of urban neighborhoods to organize so that common problems can be handled in routine ways.[4]

Partitionists, reformers, and public-choice theorists agree on very little about the structure of costs or, even more basically, about the scope of urban government. How are we to discuss the architecture of urban service delivery in light of such fundamental disagreement about who should provide services and who

[3]Robert L. Lineberry, "Suburbia and the Metropolitan Turf," *The Annals of the AAPSS,* vol. 422 (November 1975), p. 7.
[4]Robert L. Bish and Vincent Ostrom, *Understanding Urban Government* (Washington, D.C.: American Enterprise Institute for Public Policy Research, 1973), p. 95.

should assess the cost and benefits that they produce? In order to proceed we should first consider the partitionists, reformers, and public-choice theorists to be of different schools of urban architecture, each of which solves certain design problems and neglects others. Second, we should focus our discussion not on approaches to design, but on those primary elements of service provision that establish the limits and constraints on the recommendations of *all three schools*. These elements, the macrovariables introduced in Chapter 1, and the combinations in which they are found, will have a strong influence on the kind of service design that is found in a city. These elements should also help us select the school of architecture that is most appropriate to solving both chronic and evolving design problems.

Elements of Urban Service Architecture

The greatest temptation in discussing the design of service provision is to rewrite history. A renewal or redesign of Utica, New York, would work best if the textile mills had not moved South. Detroit would be most easily rebuilt if a middle class still lived there. What we need to keep in mind when discussuing the basic elements of design is that although American urban history can be ignored, it cannot be changed. The defining characteristic of each metropolitan center is its peculiar historical inadequacy. Schools of architecture, including those mentioned above, start by assuming an empty lot. This is convenient but unrealistic. In order to be as realistic as possible in our discussion of service design, we will assume nothing more than the current social, economic, and political conditions of cities. These conditions vary from virtue to tragedy in different cities, and it is by using the elements of service design—or macrovariables, as they will be called—that the differences will be explained.

Approaching the question of design by assuming only the status quo seems short-sighted or at least unimaginative. Can we get out of the current situation unless we dream a little? We probably cannot. But too often in the past the dreamers and planners have not paused to understand what they were building on top of. The ideology of change requires a break with the old ways and a rejection of the old forms. Ideology, however, does not guarantee success, and it was the old ways and old forms that confounded the urban revolution of the 1960s.

Perhaps the best example of what happens when good intentions meet the status quo is the experience of the [Federal] Economic Development Agency in Oakland, California.

> Why, in their initial trips to Oakland, did Foley and Bradford (the administrators) neglect visiting City Hall? Foley offers this explantion: "I didn't want to alienate the black community by seeming to come in as part of the Establishment. I wanted to meet black people first." This strategy, however, did alienate Oakland's Mayor

John C. Houlihan, who complained bitterly about Foley's choice of initial contacts . . .[5]

The EDA approached Oakland as if its past were irrelevant, and as if it were possible to bypass the social and economic reality of the present. It is relatively easy to criticize a failure, and the EDA failed magnificently in Oakland. It is more difficult to say what might have been done to avoid failure. What should the EDA have taken into account in planning a redevelopment stragegy for Oakland? A general answer to this question brings us to the macrovariables. They can be used here to describe the context of urban service design and provision. However, these macrovariables are only the primary restraints on service design. There are three other, secondary categories of design elements that should be taken into account: political party and geographic region, state and federal influence, and the organization of public employees. Each of these categories expands on one or more aspects of either the extent of urban resources or the condition of urban infrastructure—the two broadest macrovariables. Next, the primary and secondary design elements will be defined and then applied to five metropolitan areas.

Primary Design Elements: Macrovariables in the Delivery of Urban Services

It is hard to know just what set of variables should be called primary design elements. If we take as a criterion those aspects of urban areas that determine the design of service delivery, we would have to include urban history prominently. However, while urban history is unavoidable and undeniably related to service provision, it is not a variable. Urban history will be considered in the case studies to follow, but as the context of service provision, not as an element in its design. By the same criterion, topography and climate should be included. While these aspects of urban areas do vary a bit more than does history (topography may change with jurisdictional expansion and climates may modify), it is also more accurate to consider them as contexts rather than as variable elements.

The two categories of design elements that we have chosen stand out for several reasons. First, they are prominent in the lives of all American metropolitan areas; they affect the quality of service provision and the quality of life in cities. Second, they are changeable, and none is invariable in the face of conscious human intervention. This last reason is especially important in light of the question of design. The macrovariables that will be discussed here are changeable, but they are so complex that they present the most difficult problems of design that the urban polity has to face. For this reason, they will be considered determinants of slightly less complex, more directly changeable urban services. It should be

[5]Jeffery Pressman and Aaron Wildavsky, *Implementation* (Berkeley: University of California Press, 1973).

kept in mind, though, that in principle, even these macrovariables can be affected by public policy.

Metropolitan Infrastructure

The usual interpretation of infrastructure confines it to the physical mechanisms that assist daily life, such as utility lines, roads, sanitation, and water supply lines. Our approach to the city as a social as well as a physical place allows us to define infrastructure more broadly. For our purposes, the infrastructure of a metropolitan area includes the physical and socioeconomic conditions that influence mobility and residential choice. Mobility and residential choice can be either facilitated or impeded by physical and socioeconomic conditions. For example, an old metropolitan area which is deteriorating physically will tend to be segregated socioeconomically, with the more affluent residents holding on to the better neighborhoods. Because of the marking of areas as "good," "bad," and "borderline"—familiar terms in almost all parts of the country—we would expect residential choice to be constrained. Public services in this metropolitan area could not be provided uniformly. The variety in the infrastructure of the area would require some distinctions in the provision of services. Police and social services will be concentrated in the poorer neighborhoods, and maintenance of physical facilities will be concentrated in the better neighborhoods.

This is not to say that infrastructure is immutable, but as we mentioned earlier, macrovariables like socioeconomic integration provide the structural contours to which service provision will inevitably conform. The next step in understanding the fit between services and macrovariables is to consider each macrovariable in turn.

SIZE AND DENSITY. The congestion of urban areas, the sheer force of numbers per acre, has been a factor in the quality of service for as long as there have been cities. For a few services, such as mail delivery, the more densely populated an area, the better. Mail can be delivered much more efficiently and quickly in Manhattan than in rural Arizona. For many other services as diverse as recreation, sanitation, and fire protection, a certain concentration of population is desirable, but extreme congestion overloads facilities and limits the possibility of rapid, effective response by emergency services. For this reason, the single-family dwelling has been the preferred alternative for most urban housing.

Single-family neighborhoods are generally dense, but not congested. They allow for the installation of public utility lines, which decreases external costs related to septic tanks and wells and to the special problem of their proximity. The moderate density of low-rise dwellings, it has been demonstrated, is also related to greater security. Neighborhoods in which private areas are easily identified and maintained, whether single-family or low-rise multifamily units, have a number of natural advantages against criminals. These advantages have been most clearly identified and described by Oscar Newman, a prominent student of urban design, who has turned the analysis of density into a theory of defensible space:

> "Defensible space" is a surrogate term for the range of mechanisms—real and symbolic barriers, strongly defined areas of influence, and improved opportunities for surveillance—that combine to bring an environment under the control of its residents. A *defensible space* is a living residential environment which can be employed by inhabitants for the enhancement of their lives, while providing security for their families, neighbors, and friends. The public areas of a multifamily residential environment devoid of defensible space make the act of going from street to apartment equivalent to running the gauntlet. The fear and uncertainty generated by living in such an environment can slowly eat away and eventually destroy the security and sanctity of the apartment unit itself.[6]

The size and density of an urban settlement can have a direct impact on public safety, according to Newman, and thereby on the quality of police service. Areas with natural protection require much less artificial protection. In such a case the police are an additional deterrent, not the last barrier between the citizen and chaos.

> The designs (of defensible space) catalyze the natural impulses of residents, rather than forcing them to surrender their shared social responsibilities to any formal authority, whether police, management, security guards, or doormen.[7]

At this point Newman's argument has implications for more than physical architecture. For Newman, physical and political architecture are part of the same enterprise. On a lower level, then, size and density and the quality of service are linked as well. The important point to learn from students of planning like Newman is that all cities are not equal in the value of their physical environments. Some cities are more naturally secure than others because of the historical artifacts of size and density. Once again, it should be remembered that although size and density have a significant impact on service quality, they are not strict limitations. In fact, the weight of Newman's argument is to demonstrate just how much difference the decisions of planners and other public officials can make through zoning laws, consolidation and annexation of other jurisdictions, the construction of public housing, and the enforcement and modification of housing codes.

EXPENDITURES ON PHYSICAL FACILITIES.   As noted previously, the physical deterioration of an urban area has significant social consequences. However, in addition to its direct impact on mobility and residential choice, deterioration

---

[6]Oscar Newman, *Defensible Space; Crime Prevention through Urban Design* (New York: Collier Books, 1973).
[7]*Ibid.*, p. 11.

has an important secondary effect on the quality of service provided by a municipality.

Crumbling highways and collapsing bridges are costly in the long and the short term. For example, New York City—which is now used instead of southern Kenya for rough road testing by British Leyland—must keep an annual budgetary reserve for the purpose of paying the inevitable damage settlements awarded by the courts to citizens who have been subject to injuries attributable to public neglect. This is lamentable, but unavoidable in a city as strapped for funds as New York.

But beyond the obvious broken axle or disconnected collarbone is the more subtle trade off with *other services* once repairs must be made or facilities must be completely replaced. Can the federal government be counted on to shore up the Brooklyn Bridge when the day comes? Uncle Sam has been an erratic benefactor at best and (unlike the mythical simpleton) he may be unwilling to buy the bridge. More likely, the bridge will either have to be closed, as the West Side Highway has been, or some other part of the city budget will have to be sacrificed.

The overall condition of a city's physical facilities is hard to assess. There have been attempts to measure the most obvious conditions, like road repair (with something called a rough-o-meter), but evolving costs, such as the New York City bridge problem, are not always apparent from budgets or even from on-site inspection. Therefore, a surrogate measure, *per capita expenditure for facilities maintenance,* will be used here. Although per capita maintenance costs do not present a picture of actual conditions, determining whether these costs have increased or decreased over the past decade will indicate the strain that physical facilities have put on a given city budget. The measure will indicate the degree to which it is likely that the condition of a city's physical facilities has influenced the condition or quality of other urban public goods.

SOCIOECONOMIC SEGREGATION.   There is an almost infinite variety of ways to segregate residential areas: by economic class, by occupational status, by race, by ethnicity, by sexual preference, and by age. Almost all American cities are segregated in almost all of these ways. In fact, this sort of separation is so pervasive that it is virtually a rule of urban settlement: people with significantly different social or economic characteristics do not live in the same areas in American cities. This will become more apparent when we consider five metropolitan areas in particular, below.

The social fabric of the city is a patchwork, but does that necessarily create any problem for service provision? As long as the Poles on the West Side do not get preferential treatment, the Italians on the East Side will be happy, and vice versa. But what if this ethnic distinction is also an economic and occupational one in which one group has achieved professional status while the other is still predominantly working class? We would expect to find some difference in demand between the two sides of town according to the difference in each group's collective ability to pay for services. The recent teachers' strike in Levittown, New

York, reflected just such a difference when the more affluent, Jewish part of town favored meeting the teachers' demands and the less affluent Italians held out against them. As public resources become scarcer, disagreements based upon the socioeconomic divisions in the urban polity will become more prominent.

The differences in demand for services presented by racial segregation are well known. In part, this is because of the correlation between race and population density. As was the case with earlier migrants to the city, blacks usually occupy the most densely populated part of town. However, another social distinction, sexual preference, has been a relatively unknown residential factor until recently. There are now identifiable homosexual communities in a number of American cities. Perhaps the most politically active one is in San Francisco, where the gay community has had an impact on the provision of certain services, most particularly, police protection. San Francisco provides a good example of the impact of this distinction. In addition to being sensitive to the problem of harassment of gays, the San Francisco police department has made a concerted, public effort to recruit homosexuals.

Communities also differ by age group, with a noticeable effect on service provision. The most obvious and expensive difference is in the school-age population. The more children between the ages of five and eighteen that there are, the greater is the need for large capital outlays for educational facilities and operating funds for personnel and materials. The growth of this sector of the population was a dominant service priority in most urban communities in the 1950s and 1960s. However, the school-age population is declining nationally, and the age group which is now presenting a challenge to urban service producers is the sixty-five and over cohort. As this group increases in size, city officials have been made aware of the inadequacy of transportation, health, and recreational services to the problems of the elderly. In addition, the special vulnerability of many older people to crime has become an issue in many cities.

What arrangement of socioeconomic characteristics in a metropolitan area will allow the provision of high quality service that corresponds to citizen demands? Homogeneity by political jurisdiction or complete integration block by block? Creating a city for each characteristic has its appeal. Service demand would be "single peaked," as the economists say, and the difficulty of satisfying diverse communities of interest would be greatly reduced. This approach is not without its defenders, and it is among the proposals of the public-choice school of service architecture. Complete integration is also considered by some to be a worthy goal for urban policy makers and the courts. The appeal of integration is the appeal of blind justice. If all areas of all cities in a metropolitan area were integrated along each of the divisions we have discussed, discrimination in the provision of public services would be virtually impossible. It would be extremely difficult to find a large enough group of the minority of your choice to provide with inferior service.

Given the current capacity of urban governments for social design, it is extremely unlikely that either complete integration or separation will come to pass very soon. Nonetheless, the *degree* and *kind* of separation that we do find in a metropolitan area and the socioeconomic characteristics that are being separated have a direct relevance to the provision of urban services.

SOCIOECONOMIC SPECIALIZATION. There are some metropolitan areas in which historical circumstances have conspired to emphasize single socioeconomic characteristic. This does not usually create a situation in which each area of the metropolis has a speciality—the case of complete separation mentioned above. What we find instead is one feature that comes to characterize an area larger than one or two neighborhoods, and in some cases the entire SMSA.

At least one metropolitan area among the illustrations we have selected is an excellent example of socioeconomic specialization: that is Tampa/St. Petersburg, Florida. Since World War II, what is now the Tampa/St. Petersburg SMSA has been among the more popular retirement locations in the country. One can observe the political influence of the retirement population everywhere in Florida, but it is especially strong in Tampa/St. Petersburg where the over sixty-five group is 21 percent of the population, more than twice the proportion nationally.[8] Some parts of the SMSA have an even higher concentration of citizens over sixty-five (31 percent in St. Petersburg). But whether a particular neighborhood is above the average for the SMSA or under it, the tone set by the older population is pervasive. Cities are not physical creatures, but they are organisms, demographically. The high concentration of the old-age characteristic in Tampa/St. Petersburg distinguishes it from most other American cities, and, as we shall see, it creates special problems for service delivery.

There are other kinds of socioeconomic specialization. Age, of course, has other dimensions, and there are cities in which the young hold sway. (Boston is one of these. Even though tens of thousands of college students do not appear in the Census, they are consumers of both public and private goods.) Quite apart from age, however, is one of the oldest and most formidable types of socioeconomic specialization, the company or industry town. Gary, Indiana, and Pittsburgh and Johnstown, Pennsylvania, are all steel cities. Anaconda, Montana, is dominated by the company of the same name, and the Balls of Ball Jar and Muncie, Indiana, is the famous family studied by the Lynds.

Are cities that are more specialized socioeconomically significantly different in anything other than tone or style? What political difference does socioeconomic specialization make? As we argued in the discussion of elitism, there is no single answer to this question. Some economic elites may choose to involve themselves in local politics but, by and large, powerful local industries will be interested primarily in the services provided to *them,* rather than in services provided to ordinary citizens. Nonetheless, heavy concentration of economic activity in one or two industries will have an influence on urban services.

[8]U. S. Bureau of the Census, *1977 County and City Data Book* (Washington, D.C.: U.S. Government Printing Office, 1977).

Social services is perhaps the area with the most direct connection to economic concentration. A major cutback at a plant or even a temporary layoff can increase welfare rolls and the demand for family services. An unfortunately graphic illustration of this is Seattle, Washington. When Seattle's major employer, the Boeing Corporation, lost federal support for development of the supersonic transport, and as other orders slowed down with the economy, 63,000 aircraft workers and engineers were laid off. Real estate values dropped, tax revenues dropped, and services had to be cut back just as the service demands of the newly unemployed were increasing. The brunt of Boeing's troubles hit Seattle in the early 1970s, but the effects can still be seen today.[9]

While it is rare to find even the most dominant industry in an urban area involved with day to day service provision, it is common to find them accorded a sort of feudal deference by service providers. What's good for Anaconda is good for Anaconda, Montana, to the point where the company influenced the city council to defeat an environmental quality ordinance regulating the level of arsenic produced by the local plant. The company did not need to buy votes or launch an extensive lobbying effort. All that was necessary was a public statement threatening to shut down the plant if the ordinance were passed. Anaconda, like other major urban industries, is a prime mover in the chain of events that eventually determines the level of service provided to the public.[10]

Public/Private Resources

Other things being equal, rich cities provide higher quality services than do poor ones. This alarming observation has captured the imagination of many urban economists as they attempt to go beyond mere fiscal constraints in their analyses of metropolitan political organization. According to one: "For a variety of reasons, fiscal diversity has traditionally been described as a problem. Among these reasons are that poor areas do not have sources to finance "needed" public services . . ."[11] It is possible to differ about what is needed in a poor area and the approach of some economists to the problem of scarcity has been to redefine need. Nonetheless, it is plain that no matter what level of service one prescribes for the poor, more money will make it more easily achieved.

The contrast in resources among cities and between cities and suburbs has caused the greatest political controversy in the area of education. It is well known among social scientists that the amount of money spent on education does not strictly determine the quality of schooling. However, this is not the first finding of social science to be widely ignored by the public. As a number of recent court cases demonstrate, differences in resources are taken very seriously by parents in

[9]"City of Despair," *The Economist,* May 22, 1971, vol. 239, pp. 57–58.
[10]*The New York Times,* May 22, 1971, p. 13.
[11]Robert L. Bish, *The Public Economy of Metropolitan Areas* (Chicago: Markham, 1971), p. 138.

school districts that do not have very much to spend. One case which challenged the constitutionality of the system of school financing based on the property tax was brought by Mexican-American parents in the Edgewood Independent School District in San Antonio, Texas. The argument made by the Edgewood parents is a classic statement of the connection between resources and the level of service.[12] At the time the case was brought, Edgewood was able to raise $26 per child at a 1 percent tax rate. Another district in the San Antonio area, Alamo Heights, was able to tax itself at a slightly lower rate and raise $333 per pupil after contributing to the Texas Foundation Program which provides a pool for redistribution to the state's poorer districts.

The San Antonio dispute reached the Supreme Court in 1973. The majority opinion, by Justice Powell, recognized the unevenness in resources, but found it to be constitutional:

> Appellees (the Edgewood parents) . . . argue that the Texas system is unconstitutionally arbitrary because it allows the availability of local taxable resources to turn on "happenstance." They see no justification for a system that allows, as they contend, the quality of education to fluctuate on the basis of the fortuitous positioning of the boundary lines of political subdivisions and the location of valuable commercial and industrial property. But any scheme of local taxation—indeed the very existence of identifiable local governmental units—requires the establishment of jurisdictional boundaries that are inevitably arbitrary. It is inevitable that some localities are going to be blessed with more taxable assets than others. Nor is local wealth a static quantity.[13]

The Court's decision in the San Antonio case is in line with the conventional wisdom of American politics about resource inequalities—the rules of local taxation are the same for everyone, and government should do no more than insure that they are not broken. Other than upholding the rules and providing some measure of subsidy, interurban inequalities are to be tolerated.

A more complete analysis of fairness in the provision of services will be taken up in Chapter 11. The question of fairness involves more than a consideration of the effect of resources on services. It also includes consideration of strategies in addition to legal actions available to citizens like the Edgewood parents. For the purpose of this discussion, however, community resources will be considered only as they confine or expand the possibilities of service provision. In this narrower vein, however, there are two additional elements of resource availability that should be included, pressure from public employee unions and the degree of home rule allowed to the city by the state.

PUBLIC EMPLOYEE UNIONS.   There are a great number of constraints on the fiscal resources of urban governments. The unionization of public employees, however, has proven to have the most immediate and potentially the most cata-

---

[12] *San Antonio Ind. School District* v. *Rodriguez,* 411 U.S. 1, (1973).
[13] *Ibid.*

strophic impact on public resources (with the possible exception of the wholesale emigration of private business). The primary effect of municipal unions is the most direct: "areas with a high degree of unionization are associated with higher public employee wages."[14] Higher wages, it is hoped, will attract more qualified workers. Municipal governments can then become competitive with the private sector in urban labor markets. There have been other positive aspects to unionization, such as job security and freedom for employees from the caprice of political management. However, there have also been significant costs for urban government associated with public employee unions.

One of the more comprehensive studies of the cost of unionization for local government, conducted by David T. Stanley, concludes that municipal employee demands have not been excessive, overall. Unions realize that breaking the city treasury benefits no one in the long run. But how much damage has been done already? The most important cost, according to Stanley and other observers, is the continual pressure exerted by the unions. Like a large diversified industrial corporation, municipal governments often face a whole series of labor negotiations, which requires the attention of a special agency in some cities. However, during periods of fiscal scarcity—which is more a chronic condition in some larger cities—unions are likely to press hardest just when government has least to give, or so government claims. Intense union pressure can bring the day to day business of city government to a halt:

> If a strike occurs or seems imminent, the mayor or manager and the city council pay little attention to anything else. With an eye on finances, public relations, political support, and the state capital, they are involved in day and night maneuvers. Furthermore, they must make detailed plans to administer the government under strike conditions.[15]

It is difficult to estimate the overall cost of public employee strikes, especially considering the drain on managerial energy that they cause.

HOME RULE.   In their classic study of political power in New York City, Sayre and Kaufman conclude that a loosely woven set of coalitions governs the metropolis in a pluralistic fashion. Even if this were the case at one time, the recent fiscal crisis has weakened its validity. When default and bankruptcy seemed imminent, New York State bypassed Sayre and Kaufman's coalitions and established indirect rule on the British Colonial model. The Municipal Assistance Corporation, created by the New York State Legislature to guide the city past default, was given broad authority to supervise New York's budgetary and spending policy.

> If the corporation (MAC) decided that the city was not living up to the contract terms, the director would first confer with the Mayor and seek an improvement. If

[14]Richard D. Gustely, *Municipal Public Employment and Public Expenditure* (Lexington, Mass.: Lexington Books, 1974), p. 33.
[15]David T. Stanley, *Managing Local Government Under Pressure* (Washington, D.C.: Brookings, 1972), p. 139.

that failed to help, the board could issue a "determination of noncompliance" and notify state and city officials and complain, in effect, to the public. The corporation also controls the reserve fund of city taxes to guard against board default.[16]

As Leonard Stavisky, Democratic State Assemblyman from Queens, put it, "This is very bitter medicine for New York City, a deprivation of home rule . . ." And so it was, but it is hardly unique. In other states, fiscal control of municipalities by state bureaucrats is the norm. Just across the river in New Jersey, strict regulation of urban finances has been in effect since 1938. There are strict limits on short- and long-term borrowing by local government based on a percentage of property tax revenues. In addition, each locality must submit its annual budget to the Division of Local Government Services, which may reject or question any program or line item. According to the division's director, "The state allows home rule just to a degree in financial affairs. The local governments don't like it, but they've grown up with it."[17]

Like any other kind of design, the architecture of urban service provision involves a certain amount of risk. Each of the "schools" discussed above, the partitionists, the reformers, and the public-choice theorists, requires a degree of autonomy or home rule at the local level in order to take the risks necessary to its own approach. The partitionists must be free from state mandates on spending levels and programs. The reformers and public-choice theorists generally require statutory permission from the state in order to make the structural changes they prefer, but thereafter a degree of independence is necessary. Whether it is more or less money that is in question, the area with more home rule will be better able to design service arrangements according to its own needs and desires. Autonomous control of the allocation of fiscal resources is a primary requirement of political independence. There is a variation on the Golden Rule that applies at this point—he who has the gold, rules.

A Comparison of Architectural Elements in Five Metropolitan Areas: Denver/Boulder, Fall River, Minneapolis/St. Paul, Philadelphia, and Tampa/St. Petersburg

Is There a Separate Urban Politics in the Urban Future?

The histories and modern problems of the five areas we have chosen probably do not cover the entire range for American urban areas. However, they are not unique. Tampa/St. Petersburg wants to control growth and Fall River wants to encourage it. Denver is troubled by pollution and Philadelphia by crime. Welfare,

[16] *The New York Times,* June 11, 1975, p. 26.
[17] *The New York Times,* June 8, 1975, p. 50.

taxation, and transportation are problems in all five. These areas are not microcosms or models, but they are representative of the range of problems confronting urban policy makers, service providers, and city dwellers.

The temptation is to consider urban problems and service provision, in particular, in light of national policy initiatives. After all, 70 percent of the American population lives in metropolitan areas, and at least since the 1960s, urban problems have been considered national problems by federal policy makers. But as true as this is, it is still important to keep a focus on individual cities. As we saw in the preceding section, separate cities have separable identities, politically. They provide different contexts for serving the public, and it may be argued that it is serving the public that should be the focus of urban public policy, not solving "national problems" of transportation, public safety, and social welfare. The realm of purely urban politics seems to be shrinking. The rising forms are state/urban politics and national/urban politics. The constitutional question for cities in the next generation is whether they themselves, not just their citizens, will become clients or even victims of broad-gauge state and federal urban policies. The macrovariables developed in this chapter help us address this question.

The macrovariables of service provision will be used to compare the five cities that have been selected as illustrations. The macrovariables are first of all indicators of the limits and possibilities of service provision—how much or how little service and for whom. In addition, the numerical portraits painted by these variables allow us to consider the shape of urban politics to come. A city with a declining resource base and a decaying infrastructure cannot be expected to survive independently, if it survives at all. A city with a healthy economy coupled with high socioeconomic segregation may not need financial aid from higher levels of government, but it may expect to be the target of state and federal social policies, such as court-ordered busing and subsidized housing.

Table 9.1 shows the relationship between the two categories or variables and service provision, and Table 9.2 shows the relationship between the variables and the potential dependence or independence of urban politics in each of the five areas. An area with a high position on most or all of the variables on the service table (9.1) will not have the social, political, or economic resources necessary to satisfy or even attend to citizen preferences for public services. A high position on the macrovariables is the worst case possible for a given city. A city or metropolitan area in this position would also be dependent on higher levels of government to a great extent in terms of both fiscal resources and the regulation of social and political life through the courts or state and federal bureaucracies. The architecture of service provision becomes all but moot in the worst case, because there is not enough slack in any of the critical resources to allow for local design. Such a city or area would likely become a client or victim in its relations with other governments. The best case, where an area enjoys a low position on most or all of the macrovariables, allows for a relative degree of independence from outside political control of urban politics and for a degree of experimentation, locally, in the design of public services. What Tables 9.3 through 9.7 show

Table 9.1
The Relationship of Urban Macrovariables to Service Provision

	Metropolitan Infrastructure				
	Size/Density	Expenditure on Central City Physical Facilities	Socioeconomic Segregation	Socioeconomic Specialization	Scarcity of Public and Private Resources
High	Lapses in emergency service response; Congestion in the use of public facilities, and difficulty in maintaining personal security.	Potential closing of facilities; Increasing number of tort claims; Tradeoff with other services for repair and replacement.	Disparities in service preferences by neighborhood; Racial and ethnic distinctions in housing and education; Conflict over level and quality of service.	Vulnerability of service quality to socioeconomic shifts; Influence of dominant economic or social group on the provision of services.	Cut-back in personnel and service levels; Increased pressure from public employees; Diversion of managerial attention.
Medium	Efficient service delivery; Possible design for "defensible space"; Expansion of utility services to new residential areas.	Bond issues and budgetary allocations to replace and repair deteriorating facilities, pressure vs. new capital expenditures.	Traditional distinctions tolerated with little conflict over any difference in service levels.	Shifting influence of several socioeconomic factors; No centralized dominance over service provision.	Pressure vs. taxing levels; Defeat of capital bond issues; Allegations of service erosion.
Low	Problems of service delivery and personal security over a large area; Higher transportation and information costs.	Possible expansion and improvement of physical plant; Retirement of capital construction bonds.	Consensus on desirable service level; Benefits from delivering service on a large scale.	Plural and conflicting demands on service providers; No locus of interest group influence.	Ability to satisfy diverse service preferences; Varied and expanding service sector; Potential for deliberate design of service arrangements.

Table 9.2
The Relationship of Urban Macrovariables to Metropolitan Political Independence

		Metropolitan Infrastructure			
	Size/Density	Expenditure on Central City Physical Facilities	Socioeconomic Segregation	Socioeconomic Specialization	Scarcity of Public and Private Resources
High	State and federal intervention in criminal justice, housing, and other public service planning and operation.	State guarantee of bond issues sought; Dependence on federal planning of roads and other facilities.	Intervention by state and federal social agencies and by the federal judiciary especially in housing and education.	Downturn in the dominant industry or increased demand from dominant group requires aid from higher levels of government.	Dependence on the annual largesse of state and federal government; Supervision of local budgeting and spending.
Medium	Planning aid coupled with pilot and incentive programs run by state and federal governments especially for criminal justice, transportation and welfare.	Independent bond issues for replacement and repair; Active grant activity to prevent further deterioration.	Potential for local adjustment of service level differences.	Some social and economic displacement in time of economic slump; Dependence on social services provided by higher governments.	Need for additional bonding authority and periodic loans from state government.
Low	Federal subsidy of intrametropolitan transport; State involvement in public safety if area is extensive.	Cultivation of grants for physical improvements; No chronic dependence on other governments for bonding authority.	No pressure from state and federal social agencies or courts; Local disputes adjudicated locally.	Diverse industrial and social base strengthens area against economic displacement.	Independence from the fiscal regulation of higher governments.

is the relative position of each of the five metropolitan examples between the best and worst cases.

Denver/Boulder

Introduction to the SMSA

Like the other mining and timbering centers of the West, Denver became an instant city. In little more than a decade, the late 1860s to 1880, Denver grew from a staging point for prospectors to a major mining and trading center. Growth was so rapid that it produced something like culture shock in the transplanted population.[18] Mansions were built along the city's unpaved, rutted streets, and the store-bought sophistication of the newly rich coexisted with the coarse atmosphere of the miners' quarter. The smell of money was in the air, and the spirit of the times placed a positive value on many modern problems, like explosive population growth and industrial concentration.

There is still a smell in the air around Denver, and it still means money for some. For others it is simply pollution. According to the Council on Environmental Quality, Denver has the second foulest air among American cities. Mile-high altitude, industrial concentration, and more automobiles per thousand population than any other city in the country have conspired to make the boom town an unhealthy place to live.[19] However, the area is still growing. Boulder and the suburban areas of both cities are experiencing the kind of growth that characterized Eastern metropolitan areas in the 1950s. But like the more recent history of the Eastern cities, it has been the oldest part of the area, the city and county of Denver, that has grown the least. While the Denver/Boulder SMSA grew nearly 33 percent between 1960 and 1970, Denver itself grew only 1 percent. Between 1970 and 1975 the area continued to grow, with trendy Boulder gaining by 18 percent, while Denver took a 6 percent loss (see Figure 9.1).

The sprawl that results from unidirectional growth (outward from Denver) has had some of the usual consequences. Prominently, Denver has more than twice the proportion of blacks, approximately 10 percent, as the rest of the SMSA. Metropolitan separation of the races is even more evident in the state of Colorado as a whole, where in 1970, the average metropolitan racial balance was 8.5 percent black in central cities and 2.2 percent black in the urban fringe. The decade since the last census has increased the segregation of the Denver/Boulder area as Denver lost white population to the suburbs. By 1973 the racial boundaries had

---

[18]The historical section on Denver is drawn from Caroline Bancroft, *Denver's Lively Past* (Boulder, Colo.: Johnson, 1959).
[19]"The Price of Denver's Auto Cult," *Business Week,* April 10, 1978, p. 42.

Figure 9.1
The Denver/Boulder SMSA

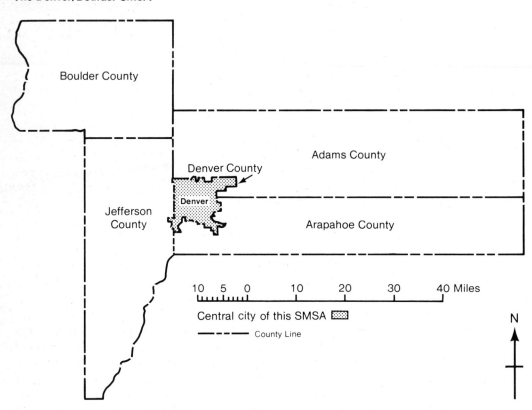

SOURCE: U.S. Department of Commerce, Bureau of the Census, Annual Housing Survey: 1976 Housing Characteristics for Selected Metropolitan Areas.

become so obvious that the U.S. District Court ordered the busing of schoolchildren to achieve racial balance.

The social problems attending sprawl and white flight often seem insoluble.
However, the Denver/Boulder area faces another problem that may put a final
limit on growth. Like Los Angeles and other cities to the southwest, Denver and
Boulder lie in a semiarid region with few natural sources of water. The height of
the region only adds to the problem. The scarcity of water in the Denver/Boulder
SMSA is a classic study of the conflict between the demand for private goods by
suburbanites—political autonomy and social homogeneity—and the need of the
collectivity for a critical resource. The water issue, particularly, has been used by
Denver politicians in arguing for regional government, which would sacrifice
suburban independence to a broader definition of the public good. Water is one
of the keys to regionalism in the Denver/Boulder SMSA because the Denver

Water Board controls the water supply in the entire metropolitan area. Nonetheless, the proposed regional board, the Urban Service Authority, was defeated at the polls in 1973 even though it carried in Denver proper.

The question of regionalism is likely to come up again as the next wave of growth hits the area. The attraction this time will not be silver or uranium, but more ordinary resources like coal and shale. The Denver region is rich in both, and both have been given priority by the Federal Energy Department and by the oil companies for immediate exploitation. The energy boom will be a mixed blessing for an area that has just caught its breath after a century of rapid development. However, no area could afford to turn away the jobs and capital that the energy boom will mean for Denver/Boulder. At the same time, a boom economy means a loss of controlled political development; that is, the loss of a considered approach to critical social problems like residential segregation and water supply. Politicians tend to make do for the short run during a boom, and pay for it later.

Urban Macrovariables in the Denver/Boulder SMSA: Table 9.3

METROPOLITAN INFRASTRUCTURE   The Denver/Boulder area is not densely settled. Among the five areas we are considering, Denver/Boulder has the lowest overall density at 304 persons per square mile. The increasing density of the two central cities, however, puts it near the middle of the list. In addition, we find that the area is divided into twenty-eight political jurisdictions. The diversity of political units along with medium density makes it possible for urban governments in Denver/Boulder to provide a wide range of private goods and satisfy broadly different communities of preference. Citizens who are dissatisfied with the school system in Denver for social or educational reasons, or with the police department, or with the recreational facilities can chose to live in a politically autonomous unit that is near the city and yet far from like it, and many have chosen to do so. The distinctions possible because of suburban fragmentation are reflected in the high degree of socioeconomic segregation in the area.

Just as diversity of political jurisdictions and medium density serve to assist service diversity, so can they inhibit collective effort in the SMSA. Public transportation has been one service that has suffered from the multiplicity of jurisdictions in the SMSA. Whether the area-wide need for water will prove to be the stimulus for metropolitan cooperation remains to be seen. For now, the Denver/Boulder area is a loosely connected series of political islands.

The largest of these islands, Denver and Boulder, has among the highest expenditures for physical facilities of the five areas. Once again, the area's semiarid climate comes into play. Per capita expenditures for water and sewerage service are higher in Denver and Boulder than in any other city in the five areas.

Table 9.3
The Denver/Boulder SMSA

	Metropolitan Infrastructure				
	Size/Density[a]	Expenditure on Central City Physical Facilities[b]	Socioeconomic Segregation[c]	Socioeconomic Specialization[d]	Scarcity of Public and Private Resources[e]
High		*66-67/75-76* Highways: $7.27/18.28 Sewers: $2.87/29.80 Public Buildings: $1.35/4.65 Water: $9.18/26.54	*1970* SMSA % black city/noncity: 8.2/4.0 SMSA % poverty families city/urban balance[2]: 9.4/4.6		*1974* SMSA per capita in- come: $5,386 *1972* SMSA local debt per capita: $403 *71-72* Property tax revenue, per capita: $227
Medium	*1977* Population of SMSA: 1,413,318 Gross Density: 304/sq. mi. City Density[1]: 5,371/sq. mi.				
Low				*1972* % Workforce . . . —in No. 1 industry: 11.9 —in top 3 industries: 38.4 *1970* % Population w/single significant characteris- tic[3]: 25.3	

[1] Combined, Boulder and Denver.
[2] "City" is Denver only.
[3] Black, foreign stock, over 65.
SOURCE: [a] County and City Data Book; [b] U.S. Census, City Government Finances; [c] U.S. Census, Census of Population; [d] U.S. Census, Census of Manufactures; [e] County and City Data Book; U.S. Census, Census of Governments.

The increase over the decade from 1966 to 1976 for water service alone has been startling. Per capita expenditure for water rose nearly 300 percent during this period, contributing to budgetary strain in Denver especially.

The pressure and demand on the public service system in the Denver/Boulder SMSA is not only related to water. The area has become nationally known for its racial problems. Denver has a small but well-segregated black population. Following suit, families below the poverty level are in a much higher concentration within the cities of the area than outside them. We must, therefore, classify Denver/Boulder as having a relatively high degree of socioeconomic segregation. The strain on the infrastructure of a metropolitan area caused by socioeconomic segregation is not strictly financial (although segregation certainly has economic consequences). The strain of segregation is, first, the difficulty it presents for the fair distribution of public services.

What happens due to segregation is akin to the neighborhood "red-lining" practices of some urban banks. If an inner-city neighborhood appears to be a relatively less secure risk than suburban areas or out-of-state developments, a bank will often refuse its residents mortgages and home-repair loans as a matter of course. This practice has been outlawed in several states, because it accelerates neighborhood deterioration. Similarly, a socially or economically homogeneous neighborhood presents an opportunity for public service red-lining. An area becomes a bad risk for public, capital improvements or even periodic maintenance. As we will see in Chapter 11, a broad justification for inequality in service provision often develops: neighborhoods should receive public goods and services corresponding to the life-style and property values of the neighborhood. By this logic, socioeconomic segregation and deteriorating living conditions become self-justifying.

The second problem facing a highly segregated metropolitan area is political pressure from higher levels of government. Denver has already experienced this with court-ordered busing. Like federal education policy, housing policy is also premised on integration. Funds for low-income housing are available with the condition that the new housing be placed where it will aid neighborhood integration.[20] (However, the opposition to integration is so strong in some cities that in some cases local politicians have simply forgone federal housing funds.) Some degree of socioeconomic segregation is found in all metropolitan areas in the United States. However, such segregation will compromise local political independence and block fair public service.

SCARCITY OF PUBLIC AND PRIVATE RESOURCES A city can survive social and political strain and perhaps even reduce the strain if it has enough money. The Denver/Boulder area is not wealthy enough to finance a social

[20]U.S. Commission on Civil Rights, *Equal Opportunity in Suburbia* (Washington, D.C., Government Printing Office, 1974).

revolution, nor does it have the slack resources that are necessary for major extensions of public service. Undaunted by its midrange fiscal capacity, the area has begun construction of a fixed-rail interurban transport system, scheduled for completion in 1982. Projects like metropolitan transport are based on the long-term ability of the area to bear public debt. The Denver/Boulder area should have a substantial ability to retire capital bonds based on the per capita income of local residents, which, at $5386 in 1974 is the highest among the five areas reviewed here. However, the area has not indebted itself as much as two other areas in our sample and its property tax rate per capita is moderate on the whole. What these indicators combine to tell us is that the Denver/Boulder area has considerable means that have not been overextended. This is not true for each separate town and city in the SMSA but, comparatively, urban governments in the Denver/-Boulder SMSA have been fairly conservative in their use of available resources. As of the mid-1970s, the public sector in the Denver/Boulder SMSA had some room to grow.

Fall River

Introduction to the SMSA

Unlike the Denver/Boulder SMSA, urban settlement in the Fall River area dates from the first era of English colonization in what became the United States. The early development of Fall River in Massachusetts is worthy of our attention because it is in many ways the model of the rise and fall of a number of other metropolitan areas in the Northeast (see Figure 9.2).

"A bud from Plymouth's Mayflower sprung . . ." is how a Fall River epitaph characterizes the early settlement, but the history of the first settlement is anything but poetic.[21] The attractive harbor and nearby string of fresh-water ponds were well occupied by the Wampanoag Indians by the time the English arrived. For nearly a generation, until the death of the Wampanoag Chief, King Philip, in 1676, the English and the Indians fought open battles and suffered massacres. As we know, the persistence of the outnumbered colonists triumphed. New England was won for the Europeans and the business of business could begin. Even before 1700, the area had a saw mill, a grist mill, and a mill for wool processing. Commercial development proceeded rapidly in the Bay Colony, and by the time of the Revolution, Fall River was a prosperous milling center ready for the advent of the textile mill at the turn of the century.

[21]Historical background on Fall River is drawn from Tercentenary Committee of Fall River, *Fall River in History* (Fall River, Mass.: Munroe, 1930).

Figure 9.2
The Fall River SMSA

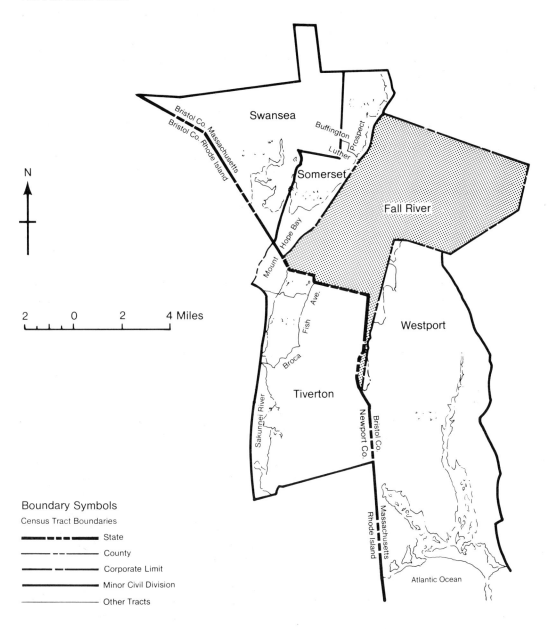

N

2 0 2 4 Miles

Swansea

Buffington

Prospect

Luther

Somerset

Bristol Co. Massachusetts
Bristol Co. Rhode Island

Mount Hope Bay

Fall River

Westport

Fish Ave.

Broca

Tiverton

Sakunnet River

Newport Co.

Bristol Co.

Rhode Island

Massachusetts

Atlantic Ocean

Boundary Symbols

Census Tract Boundaries

━━━━━━━━━━ State
───── ─ ─ ─── County
────── ─ ─ ────── Corporate Limit
━━━━━━━━━━━ Minor Civil Division
──────────── Other Tracts

SOURCE: U.S. Department of Commerce, Bureau of the Census, 1970 Census of Population and Housing (drawing modified).

Fall River's early involvement in the textile industry made it one of the top twenty-five manufacturing centers of the United States by 1860. However, this early prominence proved to be a mixed blessing for Fall River and the other textile centers of the Northeast. The second-generation technology in the textile industry did not rely on water power, nor, it seemed, did the new textile business-men need to rely on the skilled but increasingly organized labor of second-generation Irish- and Italian-Americans. In order to compete with the inexpensive textiles produced in European colonies such as Hong Kong, the textile industry went South after World War II, where it still enjoys the noninter-ference of local and state governments with its labor practices. Because of the migration of the mills, economic recession has been a long-term reality for cities like Fall River and other former textile centers like Utica, New York (which still has a bedsheet named after it even though the sheet is now manufactured in North Carolina).

**Urban Macrovariables in the Fall River SMSA:
Table 9.4**

METROPOLITAN INFRASTRUCTURE   The temptation is to place Fall River among the dead and dying in the urban life cycle. That would be premature. Although the area has relatively scarce public and private resources, it has managed to increase its level of spending on physical facilities, at least moder-ately. It would appear from the statistics in Table 9.4 that the increased spending has been made possible by cooling down the area's public economy. The area is sparsely settled for an Eastern metropolis, which increases the cost of emergency service delivery somewhat. However, the costs resulting from low density are off-set by the lack of governmental fragmentation in the area. Because it is an SMSA with relatively few political jurisdictions, it is able to coordinate service delivery easily—at the price of some diversity, of course.

Fall River has managed to cool down also because of its high degree of social homogeneity. The entire SMSA is less than 1 percent black. Because the racial distinction remains the most significant social distinction politically and residen-tially, the lack of a major black population in Fall River decreases the potential diversity of service demand; it also definitively decreases the potential for racial unfairness in the provision of services, including education. The less obvious unfairness there is in a metropolitan area, the less probable is social policy intervention by higher levels of government.

The trap waiting for the Fall River SMSA is a common one in the Northeast. As we see from the statistics on socioeconomic specialization, close to two-thirds of the metropolitan work force is employed by the top three industries in the area, which are still centered around textiles. A major shift in the market of any of these industries will have a direct and unavoidable impact on the economy of Fall River

Table 9.4
The Fall River SMSA

	Metropolitan Infrastructure				
	Size/Density[a]	Expenditure on Central City Physical Facilities[b]	Socioeconomic Segregation[c]	Socioeconomic Specialization[d]	Scarcity of Public and Private Resources[e]
High				*1972* % Workforce —in No. 1 industry: 40.3 —in top 3 industries: 62.6 *1970* % Population w/single significant characteristic: NA (49% foreign stock in central city).	*1974* SMSA per capita income: $4,034 *1970* SMSA local debt per capita: $135 *71–72* Property tax revenue per capita: $225
Medium		*66–67/75–76* Highways: $8.64/32.56 Sewers: $2.21/23.15 Public Buildings: $0.69/1.43 Water: NA/$11.73			
Low	*1977* Population of SMSA: 183,183 Gross Density: NA City Density: 3,043/sq. mi.		*1970* SMSA % black city/noncity: 0.5/0.1 SMSA % poverty families city/urban balance: 10.8/4.3		

SOURCE: [a]County and City Data Book; [b]U.S. Census, City Government Finances; [c]U. S. Census, Census of Population; [d]U. S. Census, Census of Manufactures; [e]County and City Data Book; U.S. Census, Census of Governments.

and on the provision of urban services. There is little that can be done about this in the short term by urban governments in the Fall River SMSA. Socioeconomic specialization is a key variable of metropolitan infrastructure, and when it is found to a high degree, as it is here, we must expect municipal governments to seek outside help. In this case, the Commonwealth of Massachusetts has taken steps both to attract new industry to declining urban centers through tax incentives and to aid urban governments in the renewal and preservation of core neighborhoods. Although help from the Commonwealth and the federal government will compromise the political integrity of the Fall River governments, aid from above is probably the only way in which depressed urban areas can revive their public economies.

SCARCITY OF PUBLIC AND PRIVATE RESOURCES   "The real trouble with the poor is that they have so little money." And so it is with the Fall River SMSA. Per capita income in the area is nearly $1200 lower than in the Minneapolis/St. Paul area, while per capita property tax revenue is comparable. This contrast indicates that relative to the other areas in our sample, the Fall River public economy has placed a strain on the economic power of the individual. While the city is served by public agencies (and we see the extent of service in the central city's expenditures on physical facilities), service comes at the expense of the citizen's ability to purchase private goods. Scarcity of resources such as it is found in the Fall River SMSA has a two-stage effect. First, it becomes likely that a significant segment of the population will require the services of urban bureaucracy, and the members of this segment will find themselves cast in the role of clients rather than constituents. Social workers, health service personnel, and public defenders become prominent on the city's political landscape. Second, just as the number of clients and their dependency is increasing, the public resources needed to deal with them are decreasing. This painful irony gives rise to another, one that we see evidence of in the Fall River area: the larger the client and victim population of an SMSA, the more likely it is that the urban governments in that area will themselves become clients and perhaps victims of state and federal agencies. If resources in an SMSA become especially scarce and the client interaction mode spreads, that mode comes to characterize the interactions of governments in the federal system.

The lesson to be learned from the Fall River SMSA, and one which may prove useful to metropolitan areas in similar straits, is that even a declining public economy can provide its citizens with an acceptable level of public service in the short term. This has been accomplished in the Fall River area because of the coincidence of small size, low density, and some strain on the individual taxpayer. The public economy in the Fall River SMSA has cooled down to the point where it can plan its way out of economic depression, year by year, without the immediate threat of fiscal collapse.

Minneapolis/St. Paul

Introduction to the SMSA

The Twin Cities SMSA has developed one of the more comprehensive regional planning and service systems in the United States, while at the same time retaining the separate identities of its cities and towns (Figure 9.3). The coincidence of similarity and distinction are well displayed by novelist and local observer Carol Brink in a slightly graphic metaphor.

> Let there be a single St. Minnehaha or a Minnepaulis, and be done with outmoded rivalry. To an outsider this may seem a sensible and logical idea. But I doubt if there is a resident of either city who would entertain it for a moment. Although our streets and suburbs are fantastically interlocked in a permanent embrace, each city retains an individuality which would be difficult to merge or to surrender.[22]

Although the issue may never have generated quite the degree of passion indicated, Ms. Brink is correct in saying that there has been neither merger nor surrender. The Metropolitan Council (Figure 9.4) was created by the Minnesota Legislature in 1967 to coordinate planning among the area's 7 counties, 140 cities, 49 townships, 6 metropolitan agencies, and 22 special districts.[23] However, as we see from the variety of functions depicted in Figure 9.4, the council now does a great deal more. The components of government in the Twin Cities area have achieved an unprecedented degree of architectural integration, even to the point of giving the Metropolitan Council the authority to coerce local governments on such issues as the location of low-income housing, environmental quality, and urban expansion.

The high degree of political integration in the Twin Cities area has not cost the area's local governments their independence. This is seemingly inconsistent, but it can be explained in terms of the special nature of the metropolitan infrastructure in the area. The figures in Table 9.5 tell part of the story, but for a more detailed picture we may refer to a study of the Metropolitan Council by John Harrigan and William Johnson:

> (T)he Twin Cities region experiences little of the suburban distrust and antagonism toward the central cities that was detrimental to metropolitan reform in Cleveland, St. Louis, and a number of other areas. Minneapolis and St. Paul share with their suburbs similar political styles and relative honesty in government. Like most of the older metropolises of the Northeast and Midwest, the suburbs tend to be more

[22]Carol R. Brink, *The Twin Cities* (New York: Macmillan, 1961), p. 6.
[23]John J. Harrigan and William C. Johnson, *Governing the Twin Cities Region* (Minneapolis: University of Minnesota Press, 1978), p. 4.

Figure 9.3
The Minneapolis/St. Paul SMSA

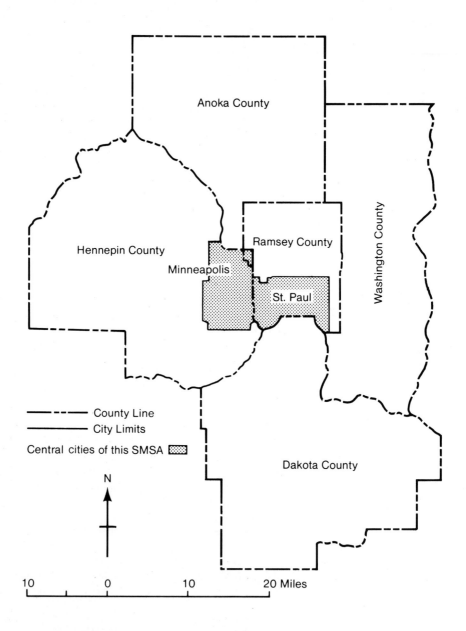

SOURCE: U.S. Department of Commerce, Bureau of the Census, Annual Housing Survey: 1974
Housing Characteristics for Selected Metropolitan Areas.

Figure 9.4
Twin Cities Metropolitan Council: Policy-Making Structure

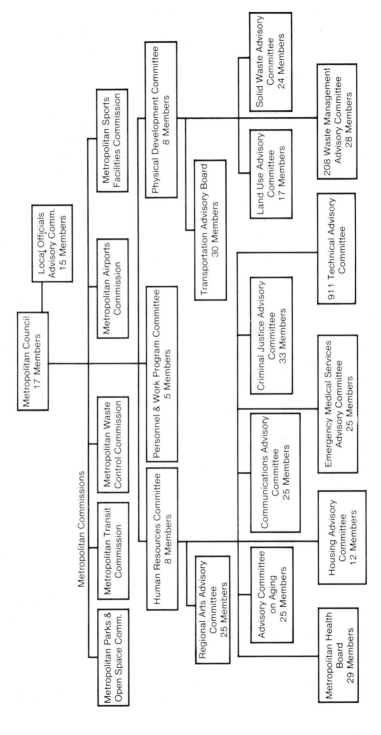

SOURCE: John J. Harrigan and William C. Johnson, *Governing the Twin Cities* (Minneapolis, Minnesota: University of Minnesota Press, 1978), p. 44.

affluent than the central cities, but the socioeconomic differences between the central cities and the suburbs are not as great as in many other metropolises. . . . As a result, the cleavages between the central cities and the suburbs have not been as detrimental to cooperation on regional service delivery problems as they have been in some other metropolitan areas. The people of the inner suburbs are becoming more socioeconomically similar to the populations of the central cities than they are to the outlying suburbs that are still growing and tend to be more affluent.[24]

Harrigan and Johnson recognize that the particular structures of metropolitan cooperation that have been developed in the Twin Cities area are probably not transferable. As they say in the conclusion to their study, it is more likely the "process of reform, rather than the total package of innovative structures" that will be imitated elsewhere with any success. We begin, then, with an innovative, vigorous metropolitan area; one which is successful perhaps because it is socioeconomically and politically unique. All the worse for those of us who do not live there. However, the elements of the local public economy that contribute to the area's good reputation can be observed in the urban macrovariables that we are using here to describe these five metropolitan areas.

Urban Macrovariables in the Twin Cities SMSA: Table 9.5

METROPOLITAN INFRASTRUCTURE The Twin Cities have always presented themselves candidly. Whether as timber merchant or flour mill, Minneapolis and St. Paul have always been commercial centers; they have done business with the rest of America and they have done well. The area has a reputation for political and fiscal frugality, much apart from what may be the modal images of American urban life—the romantic decadence of New York City and the indulgent affluence of Los Angeles. The Twin Cities are not like other cities; they are clean.

They are clean at least in part because of the moderate strain on their infrastructure. The Twin Cities SMSA has a population that is a model of moderation at around two million. It is large enough to attract and serve a talented work force and the industries to employ that force, yet, (again unlike New York and Los Angeles) it is not so large that it has the political integration problems of a Latin American country. The area is also moderate in population density. This aids the delivery of emergency services, especially. And, as Harrigan and Johnson point out, the socioeconomic distinctions that have riddled metropolitan politics elsewhere with divergent demands are relatively mild in the Twin Cities area. This is not to say that the area is free from social dissension, nor that it is particularly well integrated, economically or racially. What it does mean is that what segrega-

[24]*Ibid.,* p. 23.

Table 9.5
The Minneapolis/St. Paul SMSA

Metropolitan Infrastructure

	Size/Density[a]	Expenditure on Central City Physical Facilities[b]	Socioeconomic Segregation[c]	Socioeconomic Specialization[d]	Scarcity of Public and Private Resources[e]

High		*66–67/75–76*
		Highways:
		  $8.76/23.37
		Sewers: $13.31/24.61
		Public Buildings:
		  $1.68/4.19
		Water: $7.22/20.98			

Medium	*1977*
	Population of SMSA:
	  2,010,841
	Gross Density:
	  433/sq. mi.
	City Density[1]:
	  6,084/sq. mi.
			1970
			SMSA % black
			city/noncity: 4.0/0.2
			SMSA % poverty
			families
			city/urban balance
			M : 7.2
			SP: 6.4/2.9
				1972
				% Workforce
				—in No. 1 industry:
				  21.4
				—in top 3 industries:
				  43.3
				        1970
				% population w/single
				significant characteris-
				tic: 27.8	

Low					*1974*
					SMSA per capita in-
					come: $5,206
					        1972
					SMSA local debt per
					capita: $1,036
					        71–72
					Property tax revenue
					per capita: $271

[1] Combined, Mineapolis and St. Paul.
SOURCE: [a]County and City Data Book; [b]U.S. Census, City Government Finances; [c] U. S. Census, Census of Population; [d]U. S. Census, Census of Manufactures; [e]County and City Data Book; U.S. Census, Census of Governments.

tion one finds there is not politically significant and has not—at least not yet—influenced the provision of important urban services.

The social quiet in the Twin Cities is partially due to two factors, the historical dominance of Scandinavian and northern European stock in the area's demography and, more importantly, the concentration of wealthy industrial corporations willing to employ members of both majority and minority groups. Good jobs will reduce a number of social ills, and the Twin Cities area has more than its share of good jobs. In 1976 the area stood seventeenth nationally in population, but seventh in its share of corporations in the Fortune "500"—such as: Honeywell, Control Data, General Mills, Pillsbury, 3M, Green Giant, and IDS. Therefore, although a fairly high percentage of the work force in the Twin Cities SMSA—43.3 percent—is employed in the area's top three industries, the industries are not the kind whose time and place has passed, like cotton milling in the Northeast. They are industries like data processing and industrial mining, for which the area has developed a special talent and the rest of the country a need.

Our indicator of expenditures on central city physical facilities shows potential pressure on other items in city budgets in the area. Like the Denver/Boulder SMSA, each of the categories of facilities shows a large increase in expenditures per capita over the 1966–1976 decade. Both Denver/Boulder and the Twin Cities experienced rapid population growth during this period, and physical facilities budgets were pushed to keep pace. Consequently, both SMSAs closed out the 1970s by seeking to limit further growth, thereby better serving those already at the table. As mentioned above, Denver has been relatively unsuccessful in this so far. Because it already has a Metropolitan Council in place, the Twin Cities SMSA may be more successful.

SCARCITY OF PUBLIC AND PRIVATE RESOURCES   What we find in the last column of Table 9.5 is a dynamic, high-tension public economy. The Twin Cities metropolitan area is characterized by high per capita income, high per capita local indebtedness and high per capita property tax revenue. It all adds up to an abundance of public capital and an extensive public sector. It is an abundance that would be considered unstable in an area with more socioeconomic specialization or a higher degree of socioeconomic segregation. Public affluence depends on private affluence, and that means that the vigor of the Twin Cities public economy depends upon a stable and increasing per capita income coupled with a continued public acceptance of high taxes and relatively high local debt. Once again, we may point to social homogeneity to explain the legitimacy of high tax and public debt in such a large area. It may be that the Twin Cities SMSA, through historical accident and modern good fortune, resembles something like the "good city" in cell 1 of Buchanan's Box (Figure 8.2), where citizens, because of the commonality of their private interests, achieve public good by seeking private gain.

Philadelphia

Introduction to the SMSA

Although it is known as the "Cradle of Liberty," Philadelphia was not the first federal capital; in fact, it was New York City. Philadelphia was the banking and financial center of the new republic, but that distinction eventually went north also. Due largely to Hollywood's portrayal of it in the 1940s and 1950s (particularly through Grace Kelly), Philadelphia had the distinction of old money and the sophistication of a no-nonsense, civic-spirited upper class. But that portrayal has proven to be illusion (and Grace Kelly now reigns in Monaco). Philadelphia, like New York, its great rival to the north, is a city of "once was" and "thought to be." Of course, neither Philadelphia nor New York is thoroughly dead. However, it is fair to say that both cities have changed dramatically and perhaps irreversibly over the past generation, although not in the same ways that Denver/Boulder and the Twin Cities have changed. These newer cities have changed rapidly into growing commercial and industrial centers. The great eastern metropolis, like Philadelphia, showed growth mainly in its suburbs; the old city center slowed down, becoming something less than what it had been (see Figure 9.5).

From 1960 to 1970 the city of Philadelphia lost 123,000 of its two million inhabitants, while at the same time, its black community increased from 26 percent to 34 percent. By 1973 the population had declined by an additional 87,000, and the decline is not over. The suburban fringe of Philadelphia continues to gain population—white population—while the city declines and becomes increasingly poor and black. The increasing racial and socioeconomic distinction between central city and the rest of the metropolitan area makes the Philadelphia area perhaps the most representative of the five areas, demographically. In all SMSAs from 1960 to 1970, 14.6 million whites moved to the region outside central cities in metropolitan areas; there was an increase of only 64,000 whites in central cities over the same period. During a more recent period the change became dramatic. From 1970 to 1974, there was a net decline of 2.2 million whites in central cities.[25]

In one way or another, the Philadelphia SMSA has experienced all of the catastrophes associated with the "urban crisis": an 85 percent increase in reported crimes from 1969 to 1972 (and then, four years later, a charge by federal officials that the Philadelphia police had been undercounting serious crimes); near fiscal collapse in May 1976, when the city discovered an $86 million deficit; near bankruptcy of the city's school system coupled with a teachers strike; a steep

[25]U.S. Department of Commerce, Bureau of the Census, "Social and Economic Characteristics of the Black Population, 1974."

Figure 9.5
The Philadelphia SMSA

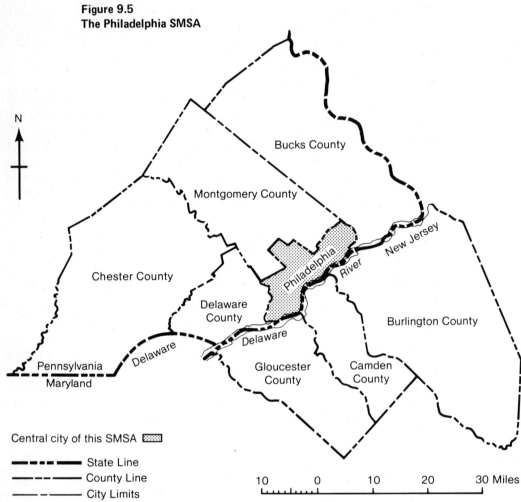

Central city of this SMSA ▨

▬ ▬ ▬ ▬ State Line
▬▬▬▬▬ County Line
▬ ▬ ▬ ▬ City Limits

10   0   10   20   30 Miles

SOURCE: U.S. Department of Commerce, Bureau of the Census, Annual Housing Survey: 1975
Housing Characteristics for Selected Metropolitan Areas.

increase in property taxes; and a divided electorate that cohered by race and
ethnicity.[26] Upon this list we must superimpose the name of Frank Rizzo, twice
elected mayor of Philadelphia. Rizzo, a former commissioner of police, stamped
his personality on the politics of a city as no one had since Mayor Daley of
Chicago. Unlike Daley, however, Rizzo found himself right in the middle of one
crisis after another. An interesting question at this point is: How much of the
tumult in Philadelphia was caused by Rizzo's brand of leadership and how much
was due to the condition of the city's public economy? It would be foolish to deny

[26] *The Economist,* May 29, 1976, p. 42.

that leadership as prominent and as forceful as Daley's or Rizzo's has a significant political impact and that it influences the quality of public services. However, a closer look at the service environment in the Philadelphia area reveals a severely strained public economy, one that presents a high degree of difficulty for any political executive.

Urban Macrovariables in the Philadelphia SMSA: Table 9.6

METROPOLITAN INFRASTRUCTURE   The Philadelphia SMSA is the most populous area in our sample, with its 4.8 million inhabitants placing it fourth among all SMSAs. It must be remembered in considering the problems of the SMSA that the city of Philadelphia is only one political jurisdiction among some three hundred in the metropolitan area, including two state governments, eight counties, and literally scores of cities, towns, special districts, and authorities. The Philadelphia SMSA does contain a few specialized regional councils, such as the Southeastern Pennsylvania Transportation Company, but there exists no formal basis for areawide coordination as we noted in the Twin Cities area.

The fragmented nature of the polity in the Philadelphia region is aggravated by two major factors, socioeconomic segregation and population density. The Philadelphia SMSA has the widest racial differential in our sample. The city is 34 percent black; the rest of the area is approximately 7 percent black. The difference in the location of families below the poverty level is also broad: 11.2 percent in Philadelphia and 3.9 percent in the balance of the urban region. When the city/suburb difference in population density is added to socioeconomic segregation, we find an explosive situation. The SMSA as a whole is moderately dense for a large metropolitan area at 1,353 inhabitants per square mile. The city of Philadelphia, however, is more than ten times as dense as the area as a whole.

These figures conspire against even the most carefully planned and equitably designed service provision scheme. We must expect emergency services, especially, to be overloaded and charges of unfair treatment to recur. Social tension and political dissent follow inevitably and may be expected to stimulate intervention by state and federal government. For example, in August, 1979, the U.S. Justice Department brought suit against the city, in the person of the mayor and other officials, for police brutality due to "internal administrative policies, practices and procedures which directly contribute to and result in physical abuse and other denial of rights."[27] While the Justice Department has not yet proved a connection between administrative behavior and brutality on the street, the significance of the suit for this discussion is its recognition of the disproportionate number of complaints and charges from Philadelphia's black and Hispanic neigh-

[27] *Sarasota Herald Tribune*, August 14, 1979, p.1. The suit was rejected in U.S. District Court on October 30, 1979: *U.S.* v. *City of Philadelphia*, 482 F. Supp. 1248 (1979).

Table 9.6
The Philadelphia SMSA

	Metropolitan Infrastructure				
	Size/Density[a]	Expenditure on Central City Physical Facilities[b]	Socioeconomic Segregation[c]	Socioeconomic Specialization[d]	Scarcity of Public and Private Resources[e]
High	*1977* Population of SMSA: 4,807,001 Gross Density: 1,353/ sq. mi. City Density: 14,131/sq. mi.		*1970* SMSA % black city/noncity: 33.6/6.6 SMSA % poverty families city/urban balance: 11.2/3.9		*1974* SMSA per capita income: $4,877 *1972* SMSA local debt per capita: $664 *71–72* Property tax revenue per capita: $182
Medium				*1972* % Workforce —in No. 1 industry: 9.2 —in top 3 industries: 28.0 *1970* % Population w/single significant characteristic: 47.9	
Low		*66–67/75–76* Highways: $6.98/17.10 Sewers: $2.50/8.81 Public Buildings: $2.97/10.61 Water: $6.32/10.93			

SOURCE: [a] County and City Data Book; [b] U.S. Census, City Government Finances; [c] U. S. Census, Census of Population; [d] U. S. Census, Census of Manufactures; [e] County and City Data Book; U.S. Census, Census of Governments.

borhoods. The Philadelphia that we "see" in Table 9.6 is a social tinderbox. When an inflammatory political leader is added to the picture, one who bases his fortunes on the racially divided nature of the electorate, we can predict protest and factional conflict to lead to anything from civil disorder to the present federal case.

But not everything about the metropolitan infrastructure works against the Philadelphia SMSA. It has a well-diversified industrial base, which employs only 28 percent of the work force in the top three industries. This provides the local public economy with a shield against unemployment and social service costs in the event of serious failure in any one industry, a shield that is notably lacking in Fall River and other old eastern cities. In addition, the pressure put on municipal governments in the area for expenditures on physical facilities has been relatively low. On the average, Philadelphia spends less on the facilities we have considered here than any other central city in our sample. As we will bring out in the next section, this is due to what was, until recently, moderate taxation and moderate local indebtedness.

SCARCITY OF PUBLIC AND PRIVATE RESOURCES   The Philadelphia area has modest private resources, indicated by an income per capita of $4,877. What makes public resources scarce, however, is the moderate debt level and low per capita property tax level. All of this might indicate an SMSA that demands and needs less than other areas, and therefore makes less of a collective effort. What seems closer to the facts of the case is that expenditures, debt, and taxes were kept artificially low during the first half of the 1970s, the years from which we draw most of our data. By 1976 it became difficult to support the illusion. The city faced the aforementioned $86 million deficit, the school board at the same time claimed a $100 million deficit, and the public transportation system came up $13 million short in current operating expenses. These deficits came on the heels of a 13 percent pay raise for the city's 20,000 public employees. Something had to give, and the show of moderation was first. At the beginning of his second term, Mayor Rizzo announced a 29 percent hike in property taxes, a 30 percent increase in city wage taxes, and a 33 percent increase in the local business tax. Further, just when the city needed to borrow, it became most difficult. Early in 1976, Moody's, the credit rating agency, dropped Philadelphia to a BAA, a rating low enough to take Philadelphia out of the market so effectively that a $25 million bond offering went begging.[28]

Because of the socioeconomic strain on its infrastructure and the scarcity of public and private resources, Philadelphia will have to or will be made to surrender some of its independence as a political jurisdiction. This will be necessary for the economic survival of the central city and for the welfare of suburban areas as well. However, it is evident from the experience of the recent past that increasing the local authority of state and federal agencies does not compensate for

[28] *The Economist,* May 29, 1976, p. 42, and *Nation,* October 30, 1976, p. 423.

weaknesses in metropolitan infrastructure, nor does it substantially reduce resource scarcity. Law suits, guaranteed loans, and last minute concessions are likely to characterize the public economy of the Philadelphia area for some time. Unfortunately, there will probably be little time or energy for humane social innovation in the city that gave America the municipal fire brigade and the public library.

Tampa/St. Petersburg

Introduction to the SMSA

The Tampa/St. Petersburg (or Tampa Bay) SMSA (Figure 9.6) is the last metropolitan area in our sample, alphabetically. However, it is first among the five

Figure 9.6
The Tampa/St. Petersburg SMSA

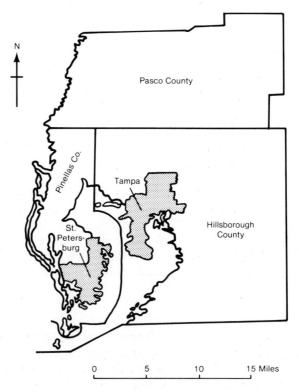

SOURCE: U.S. Department of Commerce, Bureau of the Census, 1970 Census of Population and Housing (drawing modified).

SMSAs in the strength of its public economy, as demonstrated by our macrovariables. Not coincidentally, it is also one of the major metropolitan areas of America's expanding Sunbelt. The Sunbelt phenomenon deserves some mention here, because it accounts for a substantial share of the healthy, growing, urban economies in the United States today. What was optimistically called the New South in 1960 has, by the early 1980s, developed an industrial and financial base that rivals and in some ways outstrips the older centers of the Northeast and Midwest. The demographic and economic changes that constitute the challenge are nicely summarized in an anthem to the Sunbelt by Kirkpatrick Sale titled, *Power Shift:*

> Slowly there grew up a rival nexus, based in the Southern and Western parts of the country that stand in geographical—and to a large degree cultural, economic, and political—opposition to the Northeast, specifically in the *Southern Rim*, the broad band of America that stretches from Southern California through the Southwest and Texas, into the Deep South and down to Florida. Here a truly competitive power base took shape, built upon the unsurpassed population migrations that began to draw millions from the older and colder sections of the Northeast to the younger and sunnier sections of the South and Southwest . . . upon an authentic economic revolution that created the giant new postwar industries of defense, aerospace technology, electronics, agribusiness, and oil-and-gas extraction. . . . Over the last thirty years, this rival nexus, moving on to the national stage and mounting a head-on challenge to the traditional Establishment, has quite simply shifted the balance of power in America away from the Northeast and toward the Southern Rim.[29]

The Tampa/St. Petersburg area has played an important part in the sectional rivalry that Sale describes. However, like the other Sunbelt cities, Tampa and St. Petersburg are relatively recent phenomena. Tampa Bay was first colonized by whites as a fortification against the Seminole Indians. By 1880 there were still fewer than one thousand settlers. However, over the following four decades, the population seemed to double every few years:[30] first with the coming of the railroad in the 1890s and the discovery of vast deposits of phosphate in the surrounding area; and later with immigrations from the Caribbean and South America, the beginning of the cigar industry, the land boom of the 1920s, and the rapid development of beef processing based on cattle ranching in the central peninsula. Each of the early industries grew and thrived, but it was a little-noticed trend that began around 1925 that was to change the character of the Tampa Bay SMSA most profoundly. Tourism in central and southern Florida began with ragtag caravans of cars from the North forming "Tin Can Camps" on open land in the winter months. It was not long before the economic potential of this trend became apparent, and tourism developed into one of Florida's major industries.

[29]Kirkpatrick Sale, *Power Shift: The Rise of the Southern Rim and Its Challenge to the Eastern Establishment* (New York: Random House, 1975) p. 6.
[30]The historical sketch of Tampa/St. Petersburg is drawn from Charlton W. Tebeau, *A History of Florida* (Coral Gables, Fla.: University of Miami Press, 1971).

However, it was not tourism that changed the Tampa Bay area; it was the number of tourists, their friends, relatives, and others who found Florida, or just the idea of Florida, so attractive that they left their northern homes after their sixty-fifth winter and moved to the Sunshine State:

> No segment of Florida's population has grown as rapidly as the older age groups. Prior to 1940, elderly people in Florida accounted for less than 5 percent of the population; by 1970 the proportion had reached 14.6 percent, and since 1950, the number of persons over 64 years of age has more than tripled (317%). Of the total additions to Florida's population over the past twenty years (4,010,000), 19 percent (715,900) were 65 years or older.[31]

The Tampa Bay SMSA typifies the age shift. As we mentioned earlier, 21 percent of the Tampa Bay area population is over sixty-five, and along with the Hispanic population, they set the social tone of the area and have substantial influence on the provision of public services.

Urban Macrovariables in the Tampa Bay SMSA: Table 9.7

METROPOLITAN INFRASTRUCTURE   The Tampa Bay area has shared in the Sunbelt boom, but it is not without social and economic problems. It is moderately, but definitively segregated. Table 9.7 shows a disproportionate share of the area's black and poor residing in the two central cities. The Hispanic community is also well concentrated, as it has been since the turn of the century, in the Ybor City area. These concentrations have produced the predictable fairness disputes, in this case over primary services, education, and police and fire protection. The demands of minority communities have focused most recently on the selection of a city manager in St. Petersburg. As chief political and administrative officer, the St. Petersburg city manager is responsible for setting public service priorities in the form of a budget each year. The previous city manager had been less than successful in minority neighborhoods, so by the summer of 1979 a number of black and Hispanic groups were pressing their interests in the selection of a successor. Whether they will succeed is open to question; both groups together are outnumbered by nearly two to one in St. Petersburg and in the area at large by the sixty-five and over cohort. Although there is naturally some overlap in the memberships of the minority and elderly factions, each tends to live in a different part of the SMSA, and each tends to have different preferences for particular services. The racial and ethnic minorities have pressed for improved educational facilities and enlarged school and family-service budgets; they have

---

[31]T. Stanton Dietrich, *The Changing Patterns of Florida's Population: 1950–1970* (Tallahassee: Florida State University Press, 1974), pp. 35–37.

Table 9.7
The Tampa/St. Petersburg SMSA

	Metropolitan Infrastructure				
	Size/Density[a]	Expenditure on Central City Physical Facilities[b]	Socioeconomic Segregation[c]	Socioeconomic Specialization[d]	Scarcity of Public and Private Resources[e]
High					*1974* SMSA per capita income: $4,751 *1972* SMSA local debt per capita: $346 *71–72* Property tax revenue per capita: $131
Medium			*1970* SMSA % black city/noncity: 17.5/4.4 SMSA % poverty families city/urban balance T : 14.9 SP: 10.8/8.1	*1972* % Workforce —in No. 1 industry: 17.2 —in top 3 industries: 43.3 *1970* % Population w/single significant characteristic: 48.8	
Low	*1977* Population of SMSA: 1,347,677 Gross Density: 659/sq. mi. City Density[1]: 3,748/sq. mi.	*66–67/75–76* Highways: $9.74/16.25 Sewers: 4.19/15.86 Public Buildings: 0.44/3.90 Water: $7.24/14.24			

[1] Combined, Tampa and St. Petersburg.

SOURCE: [a] County and City Data Book; [b] U.S. Census, City Government Finances; [c] U.S. Census, Census of Population; [d] U. S. Census, Census of Manufactures; [e] County and City Data Book; U.S. Census, Census of Governments.

also complained about inadequate police protection. The elderly faction, which is increasingly well organized, also wants better police protection, but in their own neighborhoods; and to some degree, it is the minority groups against whom they want protection. As for the schools, one cannot expect too much enthusiasm for increased expenditures from a group that has already educated an entire generation with its property taxes.

However, as we found in the Twin Cities, social conflict can be relieved by a healthy, diversified urban economy. The Tampa Bay area has not attracted the number of national corporate headquarters that the Twin Cities have, but the Gulf Coast of Central Florida has a strong manufacturing and commercial base that continues to expand. This has kept unemployment down, although the lower, local wage rate puts 8 percent of the area's families below the federal poverty level.

Two other aspects of metropolitan infrastructure in the Tampa Bay area have contributed to the strength of its public economy: low density and low expenditures on central city physical facilities. Philadelphia, a highly dense, highly segregated city also has low physical facility expenditures, but we found them to be artificially restrained. The low expenditures in Tampa and St. Petersburg are probably closer to actual demand. We should also keep in mind the lower construction and maintenance costs allowed by the Florida climate. Without freezing temperatures and road salt to worry about, road construction and repair dollars go further in Tampa than in Philadelphia.

SCARCITY OF PUBLIC AND PRIVATE RESOURCES   Because the Tampa Bay economy is still expanding, and because the public demands that have been made on it so far have been relatively modest, we consider public and private resources in the area to be less scarce than they might appear from Table 9.7. The area's per capita income is not outstanding, but then neither are the area's per capita debt or property tax. From many indications, the Tampa Bay public economy has considerable room to grow, yet one of the area's major political issues during the past decade has been that of imposing legal limits on growth. Like their fellow planners in the Denver/Boulder SMSA and the Twin Cities region, zoning officials, budget officers, and city managers in the Tampa Bay area are concerned that the area's gains of the past twenty years will erode and disappear if the area is subject to unrestrained subdivision and growth. With this in mind, the St. Petersburg Council voted a population ceiling of approximately 250,000 inhabitants, a figure that represents the peak capacity of utility lines already in place.[32] There have been constitutional challenges to such laws in other cities. Nevertheless, the council's action illustrates the desire of the fiscally sound cities in our sample to walk away from the game while they are ahead.

[32] *The New York Times,* March 26, 1974, p. 24.

Perspectives on the Urban Service State

The argument that we have made in this and the preceding chapter is that public services are the bottom line in urban politics. All the commotion of elections, protests, factional lobbying, and budget hearings boils down to the demand for services. And it is services, increasingly, that stimulate citizen participation in the urban political system. Services—whether they are the right kind or in the right quantity—have come to define the relationship of the urbanite to urban government. Economically, this relationship is that of service producer to service consumer; politically, it is that of service administrator to service constituent, service client, or just plain victim.

What we have learned by reviewing five rather different metropolitan areas is that there are two categories of variation that seem to affect the relationship of citizen to government urban areas: metropolitan infrastructure and the scarcity of public and private resources. By constraining or expanding the options available to cities for the provision of services, these variables will constrain or expand the competition among groups for services as well as the possibility of individual citizens becoming clients or victims. In other words, the more that the macrovariables restrain the variety and quality of urban services, the more likely it is that clients and victims will be created by service policy. Less variety in service design means more dissatisfaction among those with preferences that differ even slightly from the current norm. In turn, this dissatisfaction will increase the number of unintended consequences resulting from the actions of urban governments. There are, as we indicated in the first section of this chapter, three schools of service architecture that speak to the problems of clientelism, victimization, and the possibility of planned, intended, consequences of urban service policy. Let us reconsider each of these schools in light of what we have learned from the five metropolitan illustrations.

The Partitionist School

The position that nothing much can be done to change the basic social imbalance in urban communities seems to characterize the urban service strategy in the Philadelphia area. One way to reduce unanticipated consequences and squabbling over who gets what is to simply attempt less. The object of partitionist policy making is to keep order and provide only those public goods that eliminate the worst and most widespread external costs. This makes for a situation very like that in cell 3 of Buchanan's Box: because of the scale and isolation of the collective enterprise, individuals lose a sense of connection between themselves and government. The individual's search for comfort and security and the government's attempt to provide public services become separate, discontinuous efforts. The

government's effort to provide useful public goods and services satisfies some but
not others, and the individual's search for private benefit may be satisfactory but
it often imposes a cost on others. The neighborhood security patrols and block-
long chain-link fences that we find in Philadelphia are the results of private action
for private, not collective, gain.

What Buchanan, Banfield, and other partitionists are saying is that a city like
Philadelphia, faced with serious fiscal problems and a factional polity, will be
throwing good money after bad if it tries to satisfy everyone by expanding services
and solving social problems. The most prudent and honest course of action,
according to this school, is to partition what urban government can do from what
it cannot do. For the partitionists, the public good is to be defined as narrowly
as possible. This may stimulate discussion at the neighborhood level to determine
which services and goods are worthy of collective effort. The ultimate effect of
partitionism, if it is severe enough, is the establishment of neighborhood governments by withdrawal and neglect. Like nature, urban politics abhors a vacuum.
However, what develops to fill the neighborhood power vacuum can be anything
from a civilized system of cooperative services to a gang of gun-toting thugs. The
uncertainty of the result and the potential for feudalistic, urban conflict has been
well known in this country at least since Madison wrote, and it is the reason for
being of state-chartered municipalities in a federal system.

The Reformist School

Professional, centralized service provision has an intuitive appeal for many urbanites. The economies of large-scale service production can be taken advantage of,
and the greatest good for the greatest number can be calculated by those specially
trained to make such calculations. Recognition can be taken of special interests
by providing special services if the need arises. Senior citizens get their own
transportation system, disadvantaged minorities get their special housing subsidies and family services, and the business community can argue for tax incentives.
This combination of majority service design and minority consideration can make
for a noble polity. However, as we have learned from our sample of SMSAs, the
noble polity can be created and sustained only under particular circumstances.

As much as we would like to think otherwise, metropolitan communities are
not basically the same. Faction reigns when it has the chance, but there are a few
metropolitan areas where factional conflict is significantly less than elsewhere.
One of these is the Twin Cities SMSA and, oddly enough, Fall River is another.
But social harmony is only half of the equation. The other half, the one that
distinguishes the Twin Cities from Fall River, is money. In all likelihood, Fall
River could develop a high degree of consensus as to how to expand services and
improve physical facilities. All that is missing is the means. The Denver/Boulder
SMSA also lacks half of the equation. It is an area with substantial fiscal means,

but no broad social consensus. Of the five areas in our sample, the Twin Cities SMSA is the only one with the right combination of social consensus and fiscal means to fit the reformist model.

The trouble with the sound ideals of the reformist school and of the other schools as well is that their adherents are unwilling to admit to the limited application of their schemes. The Metropolitan Council works in the Twin Cities because it is built on a *strong public economy and a history of relatively little socioeconomic conflict.* These factors appear to us as nothing less than preconditions for the kinds of reforms accomplished in the Twin Cities. In essence, the Metropolitan Council in the Twin Cities was not really a reform at all, but a natural development in a metropolitan area that has a tradition of social and political cooperation. Centralization of public service authority would be a genuine reform in an SMSA like Philadelphia or Denver/Boulder; they are also the kinds of metropolitan areas where reform is least likely.

The Public-Choice School

One way to solve the problem of diverse, conflicting service preferences is to take each identifiable "community of preference"—neighborhoods defined by age, race, ethnicity, or whatever—and turn it into an urban government. This would maximize public choice and public satisfaction. What the public-choice school does is recognize the very special nature of successful reform experiments, like the Twin Cities Metropolitan Council, and then argue that for most other cities, neighborhood government is the only democratic alternative to partitionism. Cities have gotten too big and their governments too bureaucratic and remote, the argument goes; metropolitan governments should take a page from the suburban experience and perform only a few coordinating functions, leaving the others to neighborhood communities.

At first reading, the public-choice school looks a great deal like the partitionist school, and several theorists like James Buchanan seem to have a foot in each camp. The more one learns about public-choice theory, however, the more it differs from partitionism. The public-choice school is highly rationalist; individuals pursuing private interest will take an interest in their own communities if they are provided with the appropriate incentives. These incentives will make them aware of the connection between their own effort, building a better community, and attaining better public service. This chain of logic is quite distinct from the partitionists' withdrawal from the realm of social welfare and concentration on order maintenance.

The public-choice school would create a federated, "polycentric" service state for the metropolitan area. Once again we have a plan for a noble city, but unlike the reformists, public-choice theorists have no successful experiments with which to confront the cynical. There are several attractive analogies to be found in the suburban experience and in the ideal of the federal system at large, but America has yet to produce a decentralized yet integrated metropolis.

The Bully in the School Yard: The Politics of Intergovernmental Revenue

Our strong suspicion is that each of these schools will become irrelevant to the future of urban politics. We have indicated the strengths and weaknesses of each, but it should be clear that the debate over the structure and functions of the urban service state is a positive contribution of social science to the governance of the city. Conscious design of institutions in the urban political system is to be encouraged. The trouble is that the scope of institutional design has narrowed, and the possibility of long-range design and planning, suited to the special problems and strengths of the SMSA, is decreasing. This is largely due to the increased dependence of *all* governments in metropolitan areas on revenues distributed by state and federal government.

In 1967 governments in the Denver/Boulder SMSA received over one-fourth (27 percent) of their general revenue from the State of Colorado and the U.S. Government. Five years later, the proportion was up to 33 percent. No figures are available for the more recent period in Fall River, but in 1967 local governments in the Fall River SMSA received 42 percent of their revenue from other governments. Over the same five-year period, the proportion of intergovernmental revenue (the usual term for state and federal contributions) increased from 32 percent to 43 percent in the Twin Cities; from 25 percent to 33 percent in the Philadelphia SMSA; and from 24 percent to 37 percent in the Tampa Bay SMSA.

Rich and poor, large and small, reformed and unreformed, American metropolitan areas are taking a great deal of money from their state governments and from the federal government. It is already a remarkable proportion and it is increasing. When we actually see how large the proportions are, we can understand the weight of a new federal or state regulation that has attached to it the sanction of suspending or withdrawing aid. Federal civil rights regulations, housing and hiring regulations, pollution standards, and law enforcement assistance funds all carry this sanction, as do state education regulations, which usually include both curricular and personnel standards. In this way (and it has been an incremental process) federal and state bureaucrats make urban service policy. Like their citizens, cities themselves have become clients in some realms.

The loss of local control implied by an increase in intergovernmental revenue reduces the influence of each of the schools of service architecture at the local level. What is likely is a shift in the argument which will follow the shift in control. If urban policy is made by state and federal agencies, then the debate over urban service design will have to be conducted with these agencies in mind. Indications of a shift in the debate can already be seen in the scholarly literature on urban public policy.[33] The reduction or elimination of intergovernmental revenue is the single most threatening contingency facing local politicians and administrators. It is only natural that some of the supporters of the three schools will try to influence the use of this threat so that it serves the public good—at least as they have defined it. In order to consider the threats and promises of federalism more fully, we turn next to the politics of intergovernmental relations.

Suggested Readings

Bish, Robert L., *The Public Economy of Metropolitan Areas* (Chicago: Markham, 1971).

Bish, Robert L., and Hugh Nourse, *Urban Economics and Policy Analysis* (New York: McGraw-Hill, 1975).

Frieden, Bernard J., *The Politics of Neglect: Urban Aid from Model Cities to Revenue Sharing* (Cambridge, Mass.: Massachusetts Institute of Technology Press, 1975.)

Harloe, Michael, ed., *Captive Cities: Studies in the Political Economy of Cities and Regions* (London: Wiley, 1977).

Kaufman, Herbert, and Wallace Sayre, *Governing New York City* (New York: Russell Sage, 1960).

Lineberry, Robert L., "Suburbia and the Metropolitan Turf," *The Annals of the AADSS,* vol. 422 (November 1975).

Smerk, George M., *Urban Mass Transportation: A Dozen Years of Federal Policy* (Bloomington: Indiana University Press, 1974).

[33]Examples of the tendency in urban scholarship to focus on federal and state institutions are George M. Smerk, *Urban Mass Transportation: A Dozen Years of Federal Policy* (Bloomington: Indiana University Press, 1974); Paul Terrell, "Competing for Revenue Sharing: The Role of Local Human Service Agencies," *Urban Affairs Quarterly,* vol. 12, no. 2 (December 1976), pp. 171–196; Bernard J. Frieden, *The Politics of Neglect: Urban Aid from Model Cities to Revenue Sharing* (Cambridge: Massachusetts Institute of Technology Press, 1975); and for an international perspective on this tendency, Michael Harloe, ed., *Captive Cities: Studies in the Political Economy of Cities and Regions* (London: Wiley, 1977).

Chapter 10

The Politics of Intergovernmental Relations

Introduction: Unacknowledged Offspring

As we argued earlier, there is a traditional bias in American politics against cities. Cities themselves are the offspring of industry and commerce, but they are largely unacknowledged offspring. By the early twentieth century, cities were already parts of a complex, national economic system. Whether engaged in wheat milling, iron forging, or meat packing, each city and region had increased its dependence on all others.

The precise degree of economic dependence is difficult to measure, although it becomes evident when the economy falters. However, in good times or bad, an indicator of mutual dependence can be found in the formal definition of "interstate commerce" used by the Congress in regulatory legislation and by the federal judiciary in reviewing commercial arrangements. The definition of interstate commerce is interesting to the observer of modern urban politics because it has been used in American history to answer several key questions about the political nature of cities:

To what extent do local governments stand alone in their ability to tax and regulate economic activity?

Are local governments to be given a free hand in the arrangement of formal and informal political activities?

Is determination of the public good in cities a matter of legitimate state and federal concern?

Since the impetus behind the U.S. Constitution was at least partially commercial, it is not surprising that the answers to these questions come in terms of the "free flow of commerce" and the distinction between "national and local" industry.[1] The evolution of these terms and of federal power over local affairs can be traced in three basic steps.

Localities as Free Agents

For the purpose of federal law and constitutional litigation cities are considered to be agents of states. The Constitution makes no mention of cities as discrete entities. And while cities have been parties to federal cases, their pleas are made in terms of the prevailing interpretation of state authority. The earliest interpretation of state authority over commerce and local political activity was quite broad. Alexis de Tocqueville, who observed American political structure during this early period, reflected on the autonomy of local government by referring to the states as the "American Republics."[2] The earliest Supreme Court interpretations of the clause giving the Congress power "to regulate Commerce with foreign Nations and among the Several States" reflected the same autonomy. Even the great "Federalizer," Chief Justice John Marshall, deferred to the states by holding in 1819 that "the mere grant of a power to Congress did not imply a prohibition on the States to exercise the same power."[3]

Marshall's early statement might be called the "Sink-or-Swim Doctrine." In giving states and cities such wide berth the Court was allowing or, rather, insisting that localities bear the burden of external costs alone. So that even if an officially supported industrial price in State A imposes the external cost of unemployment in the cities of neighboring State B, the cities of State B are left to their own devices to deal with the problem. Similarly, demographic and social overflows related to foreign immigration and domestic migrations may be construed as local problems. Under the "Sink-or-Swim Doctrine," the public good is defined according to artificial political boundaries without reference to the social and economic origin of local costs and benefits.

Localities in the National System

As a general doctrine the free-agent approach to local government did not even last until the middle of the nineteenth century. However, as a political perspective on the city it has never been completely abandoned. The current notion that cities must "live within their means" conveniently ignores the difficult question of

[1]The terms used to characterize the national-local relationship in constitutional law are clearly defined by Gerald Gunther in "The Commerce Power," in *Cases and Materials on Constitutional Law,* 9th Ed. (Mineola, N.Y.: Foundations Press, 1975), pp. 127–228.
[2]Alexis de Tocqueville, *Democracy in America,* vol. 1, chap. 8, "The Federal Constitution" (New York: Harper & Row, 1966), pp. 101–155.
[3]*Sturges* v. *Crowninshield,* 4 Wheat. 122, 193 (1819).

interdependence and the extent of local responsibility, but it is popular nonetheless. As soon as five years after Marshall issued the holding quoted above, he set out a much broader standard for federal scrutiny of local action in *Gibbons* v. *Ogden* (1824).[4] In his justly famous decision upholding federal regulation of domestic navigation, Marshall takes official notice of the external effect of local policies and practices:

> The genius and character of the whole government seem to be, that its action is to be applied to all the external concerns of the nation, and to those internal concerns which affect the States generally; but not to those which are completely within a particular State, which do not affect other States, and with which it is not necessary to interfere, for the purpose of executing some of the general powers of the government.[5]

This seemingly innocuous statement is the driving wedge of federal control over local government. From this beginning flows a remarkable number of regulations designed to deal with "internal concerns which affect the States generally," including wage and hour regulation, labor-management relations, air and water pollution, and civil rights. Each of these areas, once the province of local government or the private sector, is now grist for the federal bureaucratic mill. As the Court held in the modern era, federal concern is appropriate, "if it is interstate commerce that feels the pinch . . . [no] matter how local the operation that applies the squeeze."[6]

Localities as a Necessary Burden

The year 1937 is often indicated as a turning point in American political history. It marks the watershed of the New Deal and the point at which the Roosevelt programs were validated by the Supreme Court. It also marks the point at which the power to regulate interstate commerce was transformed from a sanction against state obstruction into a charter for social and economic reform. The federal government, beginning in 1937, took the pose of a benevolent patron toward local governments. What had been a partnership was all but dissolved by the Great Depression. Just as we would no longer trust the market to order economic relationship, so we would no longer trust the principles of federalism to order intergovernmental relationships.

Perhaps the most prominent example of federal patronage is *Maryland* v. *Wirtz* (1968)[7] which tested the constitutionality of amendments to the Fair Labor Standards Act seeking to extend protection "to the fellow employees of any employee who would have been protected by the original act." The State of

---

[4]*Gibbons* v. *Ogden,* 9 Wheat 1, (1824).
[5]Gunther, *Cases and Materials on Constitutional Law,* p. 131.
[6]*U.S.* v. *Women's Sportswear Manufacturers Association,* 336 U.S. 460, 464 (1949).
[7]*Maryland* v. *Wirtz,* 392 U.S. 183 (1968).

Maryland argued that such a broad, vague classification effectively eliminated any control that local government might have over labor standards and practices. To which Justice Harlan for the majority replied that congressional regulation of commerce "may override countervailing state interests whether these are described as 'governmental' or 'proprietary' in character." State and local interests may be sacrificed in order to obtain a valued public good—an unimpeded national market system. Justice Douglas did not agree and asked a pointed rhetorical question in dissent: "Could the Congress virtually draw up each State's budget to avoid 'disruptive effect(s) on . . . commercial intercourse'?"

Justice Douglas's point has been obscured by the growing demand for federal assistance from local governments of all sizes and descriptions. It is interesting to compare Douglas's words with a comment by Mayor Richard Hatcher of Gary, Indiana, whose only concern about "disruptive effects" stems from a *decrease* in federal contributions to his city's budget:

> Even if an estimated $3.5 million in special revenue sharing materializes for Gary, we will have about 42 percent of what we had previously expected, and less than 40 percent of what we received in 1973.[8]

Those who are supposed to be victims in Justice Douglas's dissent turn out to be petitioners. It might be argued that their petitions result from addiction to federal help, but the actual, fiscal distress of many cities is hard to ignore. Plainly, cities receiving aid from the federal and state governments have come to depend on such aid; it is also plain that some of this aid is badly or inappropriately used. However, when one considers the proportion of local revenue derived from higher levels of government, it is apparent that aid from above—whether it is a waste or a luxury—is an organic part of urban public finance. As we see in Table 10.1, the average proportion of intergovernmental aid in recent budgets of America's forty-eight largest cities was 42 percent.

A 42 percent share would be more than enough to control the policies and direction of a privately held corporation. However, like other kinds of political power, fiscal control must be concerted in order to be effective. The proportion of large-city budgets that higher levels of government contribute is not controlled in a concerted fashion. Federal aid to states and cities came to about $60 billion in Fiscal Year 1976 (Table 10.2). However, data from an earlier year show that only about a fifth of this money goes to cities and other local governments, and that fifth is only about a quarter as much as most states contribute to local revenue (Table 10.3).

"Intergovernmental aid" is a phrase, not an institution. In addition to the division between state and federal control, there is a multiplicity of programs in each category. The gross federal aid figures in Table 10.2 show eleven categories of federal aid under the category labeled "Education, Employment, Training, and Social Services." The number of categories is factored further by the number of

[8]G. R. Wheeler, "New Federalism and Cities—Double Cross," *Social Work,* vol. 19, no. 6, p. 662.

Table 10.1
Intergovernmental Aid as a Source of Municipal Revenue,
the 48 Largest U.S. Cities, 1973–74

| City | Per Capita General Revenue | Per Capita Intergovernmental Revenue | | | | Total Inter-governmental Revenue as Percent of General Revenue |
		Total	From Federal Government	From State Government	From Local Government	
Atlanta	$ 453	$142	$101	$ 19	$22	31
Baltimore	945	572	91	473	7	61
Birmingham	265	70	44	15	11	26
Boston	893	266	91	173	3	30
Buffalo	640	376	52	264	60	59
Chicago	319	102	56	36	6	32
Cincinnati	736	224	86	114	24	30
Cleveland	370	117	71	41	6	32
Columbus	235	65	38	24	3	28
Dallas	260	40	31	6	3	15
Denver	565	204	110	94	1	36
Detroit	486	186	100	72	15	38
El Paso	161	35	31	3	2	22
Fort Worth	223	54	43	10	1	24
Honolulu	282	62	41	21	—	22
Houston	185	31	27	2	2	17
Indianapolis	312	123	50	74	—	39
Jacksonville	302	107	50	57	—	35
Kansas City	371	82	64	16	3	22
Long Beach	330	68	14	43	10	21
Los Angeles	311	76	34	38	3	24
Louisville	423	178	153	14	11	42
Memphis	425	250	33	122	94	59
Miami	234	83	29	47	7	35
Milwaukee	327	155	45	107	3	47
Minneapolis	349	146	50	88	8	42
Nashville-Davidson	510	170	60	109	1	33
Newark	783	408	56	349	3	52
New Orleans	338	115	72	42	—	34
New York	1,378	664	66	595	2	48
Norfolk	676	347	128	218	1	51
Oakland	338	84	41	40	4	25
Oklahoma City	227	62	49	13	—	27
Omaha	222	78	42	31	5	35
Philadelphia	457	137	69	66	2	30
Phoenix	239	98	47	50	1	41
Pittsburgh	282	120	87	30	3	43
Portland	270	88	54	29	5	53

City	Per Capita General Revenue	Per Capita Intergovernmental Revenue				Total Inter-governmental Revenue as Percent of General Revenue
		Total	From Federal Government	From State Government	From Local Government	
St. Louis	$ 418	$106	$ 60	$ 45	$ 1	25
St. Paul	320	134	39	82	13	42
San Antonio	140	40	36	2	2	29
San Diego	220	74	30	32	11	34
San Francisco	884	324	98	225	1	37
San Jose	209	60	25	33	3	29
Seattle	365	135	69	41	25	37
Toledo	250	90	64	25	1	36
Tulsa	265	76	65	11	—	29
Washington, D.C.	1,520	680	680	—	—	45
Largest Cities	597	249	71	171	6	42

SOURCE: U.S. Bureau of the Census, *City Government Finances in 1937–74*, Series GF74, No. 4, U.S. Government Printing Office, Washington, D.C., 1975, Table 7.
NOTE: A dashed entry (—) indicates less than $0.50.

Table 10.2
Federal Grants to State and Local Governments, by Function and for Selected Major Programs, FY 1976 Estimates

Program		FY 1976 Outlays ($ millions)
National Defense		77
Natural Resources, Environment, and Energy		3,088
Environmental Protection Agency	2,532	
Agriculture		499
Commerce and Transportation		8,227
Airport trust fund	375	
Highway trust fund	6,170	
Urban Mass Transportation Administration	1,276	
Community and Regional Development		4,008
Appalachian development programs	338	
Economic Development Administration	204	
Community development block grants	750	
Urban renewal	1,375	
Other categorical programs replaced by community development block grants	444	

Table 10.2, Continued

Program		FY 1976 Outlays ($ millions)
Community Services Administration	478	
Education, Employment, Training, and Social Services		14,422
Elementary and secondary education	2,277	
School assistance in federally affected areas	438	
Emergency school assistance	232	
Occupational, vocational, and adult education	674	
Work incentives	330	
Social services	2,358	
Child development	466	
Youth, aging, and vocational rehabilitation programs	1,122	
Employment and training assistance	3,050	
Temporary employment assistance	2,331	
Unemployment trust fund: training and employment	434	
Health		10,032
Health Services Administration	595	
Alcohol, Drug Abuse, and Mental Health Administration	508	
Health Resources Administration	613	
Medicaid	8,184	
Income Security		11,212
Agricultural Marketing Service	294	
Food Stamps—administration	230	
Child nutrition and special milk programs	2,225	
HEW: Public assistance maintenance	5,898	
HUD: Housing assistance	1,609	
Unemployment trust fund: administration of payments	939	
Veterans Benefits and Services		73
Law Enforcement and Justice		838
Law enforcement assistance	750	
General Government		145
Revenue Sharing and General-Purpose Fiscal Assistance		7,166
Customs receipts for Puerto Rico and the Virgin Islands (shared revenue)	216	
General revenue sharing	6,272	
Federal payment to the District of Columbia (shared revenue)	254	
Total		59,787

SOURCE: *Budget of the United States Government, Fiscal Year 1977, Special Analyses,* Washington, D.C., pp. 268–273.

Table 10.3
Intergovernmental Grants to Local Governments,
1973—74

Function	Direct Federal Grants ($ millions)	Grants from State Governments ($ millions)
Total, All Functions	12,122	45,600
Education	892	27,107
Welfare	(a)	7,028
Highways	(a)	3,211
Health and Hospitals	(a)	948
Housing and Urban Renewal	2,290	163
General Support	4,286[b]	4,804
All Other	4,654	2,339

[a] Some items in these categories may be included under "All Other."
[b] Includes General Revenue Sharing payments ($4,098 million) and payments to the District of Columbia ($188 million).
SOURCES: U.S. Bureau of the Census, *Governmental Finances in 1973–74*, GF74, No. 5, Washington, D.C., November 1975; U.S. Bureau of the Census, *State Government Finances in 1974*, GF74, No. 3, Washington, D.C., August 1975.

state programs. Far from depicting an overlord or controlling shareholder, a closer look at intergovernmental aid reveals a political realm that is noncentral and fragmented. However, given the fragmented nature of political control in cities themselves, it would be illogical to expect aid from other governments to be a great deal more rational and comprehensive. What we contend and hope to demonstrate in the rest of this chapter is that, *in general, intergovernmental aid reinforces the influence of the macrovariables in determining expenditure patterns in a given urban area.* In other words, instead of being a force for social and political reform in the city, intergovernmental aid encourages *systems maintenance* by reinforcing existing patterns. To explore this contention, we will first consider the policies of the New Federalism and then the influence of state and regional policies on urban areas.

The Rise and Fall of Creative Federalism

The complex scheme of federal grants-in-aid to cities built up by the 1960s had its historical origin in the public philosophy of the New Deal. The programs themselves, however, had their origins in the demographic and social push of the post-World War II era. The millions of new families formed in the late 1940s put pressures on metropolitan public economies that changed cities permanently. The most immediate and drastic effect of demographic explosion was the expansion and relocation of the urban residential community. As John Brooks put it in a retrospective on the boom:

> The amount of such expansion, familiar as it must be to everyone from both reading and personal observation, is almost beyond belief when shown statistically. Of the thirteen million dwelling units erected in nonfarm areas during the period of 1946 through 1958, about eleven million, or 85 percent, were outside central cities—which, to all intents and purposes, means in suburbs. Between 1952 and 1962 a million and a half people left New York City alone for the suburbs.[9]

Meanwhile, downtown there was a "faded grandeur and grace almost reminiscent of a classic ruin." Due to the war and the Great Depression before that, American cities were in suspended animation for a generation. The postwar era did not revive them. The two major federal policy initiatives of the 1950s in metropolitan areas served to foster suburban development rather than redevelopment of the central city. First, federally subsidized road construction made the automobile a second home and stimulated residential development farther from the urban core. The effect of the Federal Highway Act of 1956 (Table 10.4) was to increase urban highway mileage by 55 percent in thirteen years, and while the expansion slowed in the 1970s it has not stopped completely.

The second major federal initiative was in the home mortgage market. While the 1980s opened with the federal government trying to slow growth in the mortgage markets, a generation earlier federal programs backed the housing boom. As a historian and critic of suburban expansion, Robert C. Wood has documented the extent of federal involvement:

> (T)he Federal Housing Administration emerged in 1934 to insure over 35 million mortgages and housing loans in the next twenty years, covering 30 percent of all the dwelling units started since then, and to make possible 17 million property improvement loans as well. It was joined after World War II by the home guarantee programs of the Veterans' Administration, which independently underwrote 4 million loans on 13 billion dollars' worth of property.[10]

By the 1960s many of America's great cities had become little more than "convenience nodes," as urban economists put it. They were "used" for a variety of economic and social purposes—they became places where the middle-class citizen worked, but probably did not choose to live; locations of business headquarters and manufacturing plants, but less likely locations for plant expansion or industrial construction; and residences for the high and low extremes on the economic scale. The federal government seemed to awaken to these facts with a start. By the time of Lyndon Johnson's administration, the slow joining of consequences was inescapable. Whether earlier federal policies had caused the "urban

[9]John Brooks, *The Great Leap* (New York: Harper & Row, 1966), p. 108.
[10]Robert C. Wood, *Suburbia* (Boston: Houghton Mifflin, 1958), p. 62.

Table 10.4
Increase in Urban Highway Mileage

	1956	1969
Urban highway mileage, total	36,222	55,980
Percent	100	100
(a) State primary system, 4-lane divided (miles)	2,596	13,112
Percent	7.2	23.4
(b) State primary system, full-access control (no grade crossing)	355	6,247
Percent	1.0	11.2
(c) Remaining urban highway mileage	33,271	36,621
Percent	91.0	65.4

crisis" became a moot point. Something had to be done, and it would be done in the grand style of the New Deal, but with a crucial and unavoidable difference that proved fatal.

The major initiatives of the New Deal were designed to bring major, preexistent groups and constituencies into the policy arena. Legislation such as the National Labor Relations Act of 1935 dealt with a crisis—lockouts, wildcat strikes, and industrial disruption—by establishing a statutory balance between the combatants and placing a federal agency between them as referee. Similar tactics were used to "federalize" crises in agriculture, commerce and transportation, and rural development. These tactics succeeded, by and large, because each side in a policy area pursued its interests vigorously, so that the role of the National Labor Relations Board or the Federal Trade Commission was by design judicial, not administrative. As the New Deal programs have matured, the role of federal regulatory agencies has become more and more administrative. But even those New Deal agencies that now seem to *make* policy in a particular arena retain the role of mediator because of the different perspectives of organized groups in their environments. That is to say that while there is much less industrial violence in the United States now than there was in the 1920s and 1930s, there is a natural conflict between organized labor and organized capital that would exist with or without federal involvement.

The problem with applying the New Deal to the urban crisis is that there were no natural conflicts to mediate, no embattled organizations to coopt. Instead, the key agencies of urban revival, like the Federal Housing Administration and the Office of Economic Opportunity, were faced with the perverse task of creating policy arenas by identifying problems and then organizing competing constituencies which the agency would then proceed to regulate. Sufficient time has passed since the days of the great urban initiative to make it possible to abstract a few principles from the politics of the period. Broadly stated, there were two rules that guided the enactment and administration of federal urban programs:

> *The Rule of Objective Perception* The condition of urban areas by the mid 1960s was mute testimony to the incompetence or malicious neglect of state and local officials with respect to urban affairs. Thus, only the federal government could be trusted to discern the needs of cities objectively and to administer remedies justly.

> *The Rule of Maximum Feasible Participation*[11] While other government officials, even city officials, might not be appropriate agents of renewal, the people of urban areas themselves must be allowed to speak and to participate in each phase of the programs designed to help them.

There are several points of conflict between these two rules. First, contrary to the intent of The Rule of Objective Perception, state and local officials are unlikely to allow federal officials to restructure their political and social environment unimpeded. In several cases, the local prerogative proved too strong to ignore or to flout. In Chicago, for instance, Mayor Richard Daley, unlike most of his counterparts, had substantial control over the allocation of antipoverty and housing funds to his constituents. Second, the supposed beneficiaries of federal intervention were not organized. The unemployed, the ill-housed, and the chronically poor have traditionally had only their numbers as a resource. An empty block or gutted building is no constituency. The federal programs applied to the urban crisis were quite creative in their attempts to give the poor an organizational base. Most prominent among these efforts were the Community Action Programs (CAPs) required by the Economic Opportunity Act of 1964. The CAPs were models of participatory democracy complete with community elections and consensual decision making. But as the CAPs found out, they were late in joining a well established game. If the issue was housing, real estate developers and building contractors were interested. If the issue was education, the school bureaucracy and teachers' unions had a vested interest.

In order to even the score and give the poor a chance against established interests—something that was not necessary for the preexistent organizations of the New Deal—federal agencies loaded the dice with subsidies and compliance regulations to be enforced against any private groups seeking to profit from the urban crisis. But loading the dice created a third conflict, this time between the agencies' artificial constituencies and the agencies themselves. The more the agencies tried to even the odds, the more control they took of administering the programs. Consequently, the participation fostered by the CAPs and advisory councils gave way to frustration. The agencies were faced with the choice of supporting democratic administration of ineffective programs or of making the programs effective by narrowing participation. The tension caused by the shifts

---

[11]For a description of maximum feasible participation see: Daniel P. Moynihan, *Maximum Feasible Misunderstanding* (New York: Free Press, 1976).

between these two choices grew in intensity to the point that strong criticism of the federal urban programs began as early as the late 1960s and came from diverse quarters. Early supporters of federal intervention were government advisors like Daniel Patrick Moynihan, who turned away from the idea of a larger federal presence as did academics like Theodore Lowi who put the case pungently in the following comparison:

> The Harlem program, upon which so many hopes were pinned precisely because the makings of a good group process were available, was something of a disaster. Not a tenth of originally expected federal and local funds became available, and for a time new money was stopped and leadership was totally in abeyance while the executive director took a leave to trace the whereabouts of an unaccounted-for $400,000. One leader and one element of the black community, in Harlem and elsewhere in New York, was set off against another, culminating in strenuous battles to create peace. A real culture of poverty was in the making.
>
> Chicago represents the other extreme. Here the experience was minimum feasible participation and maximum appropriation of funds to the poor. In New York the sense of futility come (*sic*) from stalemate. In Chicago it came from paternalism.[12]

It was not only the poverty programs that were criticized. The urban renewal programs initiated by the Housing Act of 1949 had, in fifteen years, turned toward those parts of the renewal mission which were most strongly defended by established constituencies: revitalizing central business districts and general community planning. As Scott Greer puts it in his study of the period:

> The older goal of increasing low-cost housing, of eliminating and preventing slums, is mixed with the newer goal of revitalizing the central city; to both has been added the more recent goal of creating the planned American city through the community renewal program. But as these goals are translated into actions of municipal bodies, based on local interests, they seem to be moving rapidly toward a program concerned only with revitalizing the central business district.[13]

With respect to the highly touted, richly funded urban policy goal of "decent housing" in central cities, Greer concludes the following:

> The urban renewal program has done little to increase low-cost housing. In fact, the policy of destroying housing without providing any compensating new housing, has had the effect of decreasing the supply of low-cost housing.[14]

The consensus growing in the academic and policy making communities by 1970 was that the major federal initiatives in aid of local governments in the postwar period had been ineffective in restructuring and rebuilding American urban areas. In some cases, the effect of the initiatives had been perverse or entirely unintended. In 1970 Edward Banfield published a broad injunction to

---

[12]Theodore Lowi, *The End of Liberalism,* 2d ed. (New York: Norton, 1979), p. 217.
[13]Scott A. Greer, *Urban Renewal and American Cities* (Indianapolis: Bobbs-Merrill, 1965), p. 165.
[14]*Ibid.,* p. 166.

policy makers about the strictly limited scope of their activities. The controversy that resulted, and it was considerable, was actually the shock of recognition felt among his readers.[15] Lowi, Greer, Moynihan, and many others had been saying the same thing for several years, but no one before Banfield had summed it up and put it so bluntly: urban areas like urbanites are imperfectable—the extent of the possible must be debated and agreed upon. Banfield makes a number of arguments about race and class that have been considered in depth elsewhere and which are still open topics for some. However, it is his statement of the "partition-ist" position as we described it in Chapter 9 that was the heart of his thesis. It now appears that while Banfield's tone was often strident, he was merely stating the piecemeal verdict on at least the federal contribution to urban policy in the 1960s. The explosion of federal grant-in-aid programs from 100 in 1960 to 600 in 1972 had shaken the American system of intergovernmental relations to its foundations by channeling resources literally from the level of the President's office (where OEO was seated) to street level. However, what the federal explosion had not managed, according to many critics, was any real change in the anticity demographic trends of the postwar era. "Creative Federalism," as it had been called, was clearly losing support. It was time for something new.

Old Problems and the New Federalism

The notion that those who know best about local problems are local officials was counter to a cardinal rule of the Creative Federalism, *The Rule of Objective Perception,* but this rule was discredited as the grant-in-aid programs were judged failures. Since the city is "unheavenly," immaculate perception of its problems is unlikely. Since allocation of resources in urban policy making is inevitably tainted by political circumstance, it is the better part of democracy to choose a local taint. The opposite and equal reaction to Creative Federalism was the New Federalism with its reliance on local decision making in aiding urban areas (and all other state and local governments) through general revenue sharing.

The bill signed into law by President Nixon in October 1972, the "State and Local Fiscal Assistance Act," proclaimed the new era by setting out a formula for returning $30.2 billion to state and local governments during the five-year life of the program. Revenue sharing was extended in 1976 for an additional three years with an additional $25 billion. Thus a significant amount of relatively unencumbered money has fallen upon state and local governments.

The formula stated in the 1972 Act required the funds to be "divided between each state and its local governments on a one-third, two-thirds basis, and among eligible local governments according to . . . population, general tax effort,

---

[15]Edward C. Banfield, *The Unheavenly City Revisited* (Boston: Little-Brown, 1974), chaps. 11 and 12.

and relative income."[16] Therefore, within a specified range, those localities with the fewest resources and the heaviest tax burden would get a relatively larger allotment. This, on paper, seems to be the kind of redistribution that many social scientists have prescribed as a cure for the "cycle of poverty" that had not been broken by the programs and grand rhetoric of the 1960s. However, it must be noted that revenue sharing did nothing to disturb the politics of allocation at the local level. As an explanatory note in *The Congressional Record* put it, there are "no special requirements" on the allocation of revenue-sharing money "other than use of funds in accordance with state and local laws."[17] The political position of the poorest members of the metropolitan areas as described in Chapter 9, is that the poor seldom have control of any of a metropolitan area's political jurisdictions. Rather, the poor are usually a community within the area's central city. While the intent of revenue sharing was both distribution and redistribution, it left untouched the most important elements of local resource distribution, the administrative machinery of urban government. Nonetheless, it is still possible that the money was spent in such a way as to accomplish some of what the antipoverty and urban renewal programs could not. Where has the money gone?[18]

The most detailed study of the use of federal general revenue sharing funds has been done by two political scientists, Richard L. Cole and David A. Caputo. Table 10.5 from their book *Urban Politics and Decentralization* shows how cities with populations over 50,000 used the new discretionary federal aid. In brief, they found that the money has gone where it traditionally goes when it leaves city treasuries—to security and maintenance services. Cole and Caputo conclude that whatever the intentions of the 1972 Act, its effect so far has been to support municipal business-as-usual:

> First, general revenue sharing obviously has not been responsible for bold, new, and innovative programs at the local level. Although we found that in some areas (such as social services) a larger proportion of general revenue-sharing funds have been spent for innovative programs than in others, for the most part general revenue sharing funds have been used to support on-going programs.[19]

One additional finding from Cole and Caputo's study, considered along with their general conclusion, tends to confirm our position on the influence of large-

---

[16]Deil S. Wright, *Understanding Intergovernmental Relations* (North Scituate, Mass.: Duxbury Press, 1978), pp. 370–371.

[17]*Ibid.,* p. 371.

[18]The question, "Where has the money gone?" raises the basic issue of federalism and fiscal structure; works concerned with this topic include Samuel H. Beer, "Federalism, Nationalism, and Democracy in America," *American Political Science Review,* 62 (March 1978), pp. 9–21; Wallace E. Oates, *Fiscal Federalism* (New York: Harcourt 1972); and D. B. Walker, "A New Intergovernmental System in 1977," *Publius,* 8 (1978), pp. 101–116.

[19]Richard L. Cole and David A. Caputo, *Urban Politics and Decentralization* (Lexington, Mass.: Heath, 1974), p. 154.

Table 10.5
Prior Budgetary and General Revenue-Sharing Expenditures (%) in Cities over 50,000

Expenditure Category	General Revenue-Sharing Expenditures 1973 (N = 213) %	Prior Budgetary Expenditures[a] 1971 (N = 213) %	General Revenue-Sharing Expenditures 1974 (N = 216) %	Prior Budgetary Expenditures[a] 1971 (N = 216) %
Law Enforcement	11.3	13.3	16.3	12.6
Fire Prevention	10.3	10.0	15.3	9.4
Building and Code Enforcement	1.4	NA	.7	NA
Environmental Protection	12.6	11.9	13.2	11.8
Transit Systems	1.9	NA	2.9	NA
Street and Road Repair	11.6	11.9	12.5	11.6
Social Services	1.7	1.0	2.8	1.1
Health	1.5	3.5	2.8	3.7
Parks and Recreation	7.2	7.4	10.9	6.9
Building Renovation	4.0	3.8	3.9	3.7
Libraries	1.4	2.0	2.2	1.9
Municipal Salaries	4.3	NA	1.1	NA
Other	12.0	35.2	11.3	37.3
Undetermined	18.8	NA	4.1	NA
Totals	100.0	100.0	100.0	100.0

[a] Analysis, in addition to that reported here, was done by removing education from total expenditures and then dividing the new expenditure total into the amount spent in each category. There were no significant differences when this was done.
SOURCE: 1971 budgetary expenditures calculated from data in Table 5, U.S. Bureau of the Census, *City Government Finances in 1970–1971* (Washington, D.C.: Government Printing Office, 1972).

scale bureaucracy on urban governments. We argued in Chapter 6 that decisions made by professional administrators in hierarchical agencies were "likely to be favorable to the powers that be." Smaller organizations with more resources, such as suburbs, might be more flexible and innovative. Cole and Caputo present support for this thesis in general terms in Table 10.6. The distinction between the two classes of cities—"less wealthy, large central cities" and "more wealthy, small suburban cities"—makes sense intuitively, and it seems to have a clear effect on the use of revenue-sharing funds. While the larger cities have used the new federal money for existing programs and to lower taxing levels, smaller, wealthier cities have applied the new funds to new programs rather than to tax rates.

Overall it is difficult to consider the New Federalism either a failure or a success. It is not that the jury is still out. There is plenty of evidence on fiscal behavior at each level of the federal system in the past ten years. It is just that a retreat is difficult to evaluate. The dominant idea of fiscal federalism over the past decade has been "phased withdrawal." In some ways the retreat has been very successful. Cole and Caputo report growing satisfaction among local officials at all levels with the New Federalism. It is also, at the very least, a battle won for the partitionists. Deil Wright, an eminent scholar of the question, characterizes the current phase as "picket fence" federalism in Table 10.7. The notion that between intra- and intergovernmental rivals "good fences make good neighbors" is a charming one, but it seems somewhat inadequate in portraying the connection of billions of dollars with millions of citizens that modern local government has become. Perhaps a more accurate (though possibly overdramatic) metaphor for current intergovernmental aid is "Vietnamization," which was the policy of aid to the government and army of South Vietnam adopted by the Nixon Administra-

Table 10.6
Consequences of Revenue Sharing: A Summary of Overall Trends, by Categories of Cities

	Categories of Cities	
Consequences	Less Wealthy Large Central Cities	More Wealthy Small Suburban Cities
Use of Funds?	Existing Programs	New Programs
Public Hearings?	Yes	No
Support of OEO and Model City Activities?	Yes	No
Impact on Taxing Levels?	Lowered Taxing Levels	No Effect
Effect on Receipt of Federal Funds?	Decrease	Increase

NOTE: This table represents overall trends and is not necessarily indicative of any single city.

Table 10.7
Phases of Intergovernmental Relations

Phase Descriptor	Dominant Policy Issues	Participants' Perceptions	IGR Mechanisms	Federalism Metaphor	Approximate Climax Period
Conflict	Defining boundaries Proper spheres	Antagonistic Adversary Exclusivity	Statutes Courts Regulations	Layer cake	19th century–1930s
Cooperative	Economic distress International threat	Collaboration Complimentarity Mutuality Supportive	National planning Formula grants Tax credits	Marble cake	1930s–1950s
Concentrated	Service needs Physical development	Professionalism Objectivity Neutrality Functionalism	Categorical grants Service standards	Water taps (focused or channeled)	1940s–1960s
Creative	Urban-metropolitan Disadvantaged clients	National goals Great society Grantsmanship	Program planning Project grants Participation	Flowering (proliferated and fused)	1950s–1960s
Competitive	Coordination Program effectiveness Delivery systems Citizen access	Disagreement Tension Rivalry	Grant consolidation Revenue sharing Reorganization Regionalization	Picket fence (fragmented)	1960s–1970s

SOURCE: Deil S. Wright, *Understanding Intergovernmental Relations* (North Scituate, Mass.: Duxbury Press, 1978).

tion in the early 1970s to encourage local resolution of local problems while allowing the United States to disengage.

State Aid: The Survival of Urban Home Rule in Times of Scarcity

Home Rule is the ability of local government to independently allocate resources toward self-specified goals—or more simply, the ability of self-government. All states compromise this ability to some degree, most often by setting taxing and debt limits, but in some cases, such as Indiana, by reviewing local budgets line by line before any local money is committed. The confinement or expanse of Home Rule is usually considered to be a question of formal governmental structure requiring analysis of state constitutions and municipal charters. But structure is at best half the story. We must also consider the flow of money from the state capital to localities and especially the increasing need for that money in many municipalities. *Home Rule is a function of scarcity as much as it is a function of formal structure.* The most extreme example of the effect of scarcity on local autonomy, New York City's near-bankruptcy, is discussed in some detail earlier in the book. The conclusion to be drawn from the New York experience is that even if formal protection of Home Rule is available (as it was in New York State, which has a high degree of structural Home Rule) Home Rule will dissipate when met with a serious shortage of local funds. In such cases, local citizens are substantially disenfranchised as state governing boards and emergency bonding agencies supersede the authority of local officials.

However, the great majority of American cities are far from broke. At the same time, a majority of city officials are firmly persuaded that the quality of urban services and municipal fiscal health are responsibilities of state government as well as of their own. An effort by President Carter's Urban and Regional Policy Group to get states to plan for declining cities and aging suburbs indicated that states are willing to help benighted cities but on the condition that the states set priorities for urban growth. Three states studied by Rochell Stanfield, California, Michigan, and Massachusetts, reported a willingness to increase aid to urban government, but only if the current growth pattern in metropolitan areas was altered. Each of these states, in a slightly different way, is planning to encourage central city revitalization and development at the cost of additional fringe area and suburban growth.[20]

The Massachusetts case provides the most graphic demonstration of the trials of a state government attempting to reverse the trend of urban sprawl in economic and population growth. As it was put by the economic development chairman during the administration of Governor Michael Dukakis, a clear message went out to real estate and manufacturing interests:

[20]Neal R. Pierce, "Some States Are Putting Their Urban Strategies to Work," *National Journal* (October 15, 1977), pp. 1605–1607.

We'll bust our backsides to help you develop in a city industrial park, to rehabilitate an old mill building, to engage in a downtown recycling project. But it's counterproductive for us to spend money extending a sewer line or highway to your development out in the middle of nowhere.[21]

This state policy has helped cities like Fall River, which we discussed in Chapter 9. Fall River has a wealth of unused or abandoned industrial and commercial space, and at the same time, it is an excellent transport and distribution point for several of the country's largest markets. However, while the cities themselves may welcome the new state policies favoring them, private interests have been more difficult to persuade. For example, state policy ran aground when a developer in western Massachusetts decided to place a major new shopping complex in the rural fringe area outside Lenox, a classic New England village. At the same time older, larger Pittsfield was making a bid for commercial revitalization of its downtown. When push came to shove, the state bureaucracy used its control over public services to block the site outside Lenox:

Dukakis came down squarely for Pittsfield. His message to the would-be Lenox developer: "There will be no access to the state highway. Forget about your development. We just won't permit it."[22]

States play a critical mediating role in metropolitan development, particularly when local officials agree that basic service and fiscal problems neither begin nor end within their own jurisdictions. During the suburban boom of the 1950s and 1960s it was possible for state governments to ignore the problems of older cities since the glow of health could be seen almost everywhere else. The late 1970s and the 1980s present a much different problem. Older suburbs now have the same problems cities did fifteen years ago and growth in all but the most affluent communities has slowed to a crawl. The health of the metropolitan areas taken as a unit is now recognized as being synonymous with the health of the entire state. The recognition of mutual dependence between metropolitan areas and state governments has brought with it a focus on "metroregion" planning. What the new regional focus will bring is a matter of conjecture. However, the popularity of regional planning is shared at the federal level and may well come to dominate Washington's aid priorities in the future. One forecast of the change is the proposal of the Carter Administration for the revised 1981 budget that the portion of revenue-sharing funds going to state governments be eliminated. Local governments are to be considered independently and in the context of their metropolitan regions.[23]

[21] *Ibid.,* p. 1606.
[22] *Ibid.*
[23] "States Face Uphill Battle in Revenue Sharing Debate," *Congressional Quarterly Weekly Report* (February 23, 1980), pp. 531–535; "House Democrats Seek Truce in Budget Rift," *Congressional Quarterly Weekly Report* (March 29, 1980), pp. 844–845. The truce was eventually achieved, and the states kept their portion of revenue sharing funds.

Federalism and the Redress of Local Grievances

The city itself, we have found, has no clear center of power, but is instead a series of disconnected, bureaucratic networks. We have not been very optimistic about the possibility of individuals—particularly poor individuals—influencing these networks without substantial organization behind them. The conclusion of this chapter is not very much more optimistic.

The fiscal influence of the federal government is largely reinforcement and support of the status quo in American cities. Given the lessons of the interventionist programs of the 1960s, it is probably just as well that the federal government has attempted less fiscal direction of urban affairs. But the federal government has not withdrawn from urban social conflict entirely. The following chapter, which deals with the question of equity in public service provision, focuses on the most active agent of urban social change in the postwar era, the federal judiciary.

Suggested Readings

Banfield, Edward C., *The Unheavenly City Revisited* (Boston: Little, Brown, 1974).

Cole, Richard L., and David A. Caputo, *Urban Politics and Decentralization* (Lexington, Mass.: Heath, 1974).

Greer, Scott, *Urban Renewal and American Cities* (Indianapolis: Bobbs-Merrill, 1965).

Wood, Robert C., *Suburbia* (Boston: Houghton Mifflin, 1958).

Wright, Deil S., *Understanding Intergovernmental Relations* (North Scituate, Mass.: Duxbury Press, 1978).

Chapter 11

The Question of Equity

A Persistent Embarrassment

In the late 1960s a reform group called the Urban Coalition sponsored a poverty-awareness campaign with a pointed slogan: "In Harlem, it's still 1935."[1] The sentiment expressed by the slogan was widely shared at the time. Somehow black neighborhoods were being overlooked by the affluent 1960s. This was evident in the broadest terms from statistics on annual income. In 1962 the average income of white Americans was $7,070; for blacks it was $3,280, and the situation improved only marginally in the following decade.[2] But what the slogan was really referring to were the decayed, inhuman living conditions in the ghetto. In *Dark Ghetto,* Kenneth Clark describes the standard of living in Harlem in the 1960s:

> Harlem houses 232,792 people within its three and one half square miles, a valley between Morningside and Washington Heights and the Harlem River. There are more than 100 people per acre. Ninety percent of the 87,369 residential buildings are more than thirty-three years old, and nearly half were built before 1900. . . . The condition of all but the newest buildings is poor. Eleven percent are classified as dilapidated by the 1960 census; that is, they do "not provide safe and adequate shelter," and thirty-three percent are deteriorating. . . . There are more people in fewer rooms than elsewhere in the city. Yet rents and profits from Harlem are often high, as many landlords deliberately crowd more people into buildings in slum areas, knowing that the poor have few alternatives. . . . The multiple use of toilet and water facilities, inadequate heating and ventilation, and crowded sleeping quarters increase the rate of acute respiratory infections and infectious childhood diseases. . . . The best single index of a community's general health is reputed to be its infant mortality rate. For Harlem this rate in 1961 was 45.2 per 1,000 live births compared to 25.7 for New York City.[3]

[1]For a general description of the organization see: "Leaders of Urban Coalition Optimistic Amid Difficulties," *The New York Times,* 28 October 1969, p. 49.
[2]Edward C. Banfield, *The Unheavenly City Revisited* (Boston: Little, Brown, 1974), pp. 81–82.
[3]Kenneth B. Clark, *Dark Ghetto* (New York: Harper & Row, 1965), pp. 30–31.

258

By 1974 the rate for blacks in Manhattan was 32.1 per 1,000, and the rate among whites in Manhattan was 17.4.[4]

Harlem is America's most famous ghetto. And although it has been romanticized in song, its very name is shorthand for the worst in American urban life. It has become so notorious that groups of foreign tourists in New York usually include it on their itineraries along with a newer abomination, the South Bronx. It might seem that if any ghetto could be eliminated by federal and local governments it would be Harlem, America's biggest urban embarrassment. But Harlem is still there, largely unchanged. Worse still, it is far from an exception. Slum conditions in black neighborhoods appear to be immune to government treatment.

However, government has not failed from lack of trying. From the mid-1960s to 1974, the federal government alone had spent $12 billion on an extraordinary variety of programs designed to aid the poor and minorities in one way or another (Table 11.1).[5] These programs, as well intentioned as they were, did not eradicate poverty or even improve urban public services very much. Several students of government assistance to the poor argue that the federal effort should not be discounted because many of the expenditures will pay off only in the long term.[6] By and large, programs like manpower training and special education for the disadvantaged have been investments in the future. Such programs, and they dominated the federal effort in the war on poverty, were future oriented for good reason. The future can always be put off until tomorrow. The here and now of urban public services is a very different proposition, as federal poverty bureaucrats quickly discovered.

The war on poverty bypassed the machinery of the present—that is, the local governments that provide routine public services to the urban poor. The poverty bureaucrats had a grander vision. The idea was to establish programs and structures that would be the basis of a social and economic renaissance for the black community. However, between the idea and reality were a number of obstacles, not the least of which was local government. A classic example of the gap between idea and reality was the large-scale intervention by the Economic Development Administration into the problem of minority unemployment in Oakland, California. That intervention has become a classic case study largely due to a book by two political scientists, Jeffrey Pressman and Aaron Wildavsky, which they titled, *Implementation: How Great Expectations in Washington Are Dashed in Oakland; Or, Why It's Amazing That Federal Programs Work At All This Being a Saga of the Economic Development Administration as Told By Two Sympathetic Observers Who Seek To Build Morals on a Foundation of Ruined Hopes.*

---

[4]U.S. Department of Health, Education and Welfare, *Vital Statistics of the United States, 1974,* vol. 1, pp. 2–47; vol. 2, pp.7–46.

[5]Robert Plotnick and Felicity Skidmore, *Progress Against Poverty* (New York: Academic Press, 1975), p. 8.

[6]*Ibid.,* p. 61.

Table 11.1

Office of Economic Opportunity Budgets, by Program Obligation, 1965–1974 (in millions of dollars)

Program	1965	1966	1967	1968	1969	1970	1971	1972	1973	1974
Adult Education	4.4	34.1	*	*	*	*	*	*	*	*
College Work-Study	54.9	.8	*	*	*	*	*	*	*	*
CAP (Local initiative)	137.8	364.1	353.0	411.1	416.1	416.9	452.4	393.0	469.4	209.5
Concentrated Employment Program	*	*	50.7	73.0	83.0	139.0	*	*	*	*
Emergency Food & Medical Services	*	*	*	12.8	23.2	46.1	48.6	3.5	28.6	9.4
Family Planning	*	*	*	9.0	13.8	22.1	18.8	23.9	15.4	*
Follow Through	*	*	*	14.6	32.0	70.3	68.4	*	*	*
Foster Grandparents	*	5.1	5.7	9.5	9.1	*	*	*	*	*
Head Start	96.4	198.9	349.2	316.2	333.9	325.3	360.0	*	*	*
Health Programs	*	*	50.8	33.2	58.3	89.1	127.4	129.8	121.5	*
Job Corps	165.0	289.9	190.1	260.2	257.3	158.2	*	*	*	*
JOBS	*	*	*	60.1	113.0	47.0	*	*	*	*
Legal Services	*	24.8	25.2	35.9	47.3	54.7	61.2	67.7	77.2	71.5
Migrant Program	14.9	25.5	33.0	25.0	28.5	33.3	36.1	36.5	38.6	*
Neighborhood Youth Corps (In-School)	*	68.4	58.9	49.0	59.2	*	*	*	*	*
Neighborhood Youth Corps (Out-of-School)	*	92.8	147.6	96.3	123.7	97.9	*	*	*	*
Neighborhood Youth Corps (Summer)	130.0	104.3	132.9	113.8	140.5	124.1	*	*	*	*
Operation Mainstream	*	10.3	30.3	22.3	41.0	51.0	*	*	*	*
Public Service Careers	*	*	15.6	7.6	18.5	46.9	*	*	*	*
Rural Loans	17.2	32.3	31.9	27.7	12.1	4.1	4.0	*	*	*
Special Impact	*	*	*	19.9	22.4	36.2	37.1	26.8	36.6	38.1
Upward Bound	2.5	24.9	28.2	31.6	30.8	*	*	*	*	*
VISTA	1.8	14.8	20.3	22.4	25.4	27.3	29.6	*	*	*
Work Experience	*	112.0	112.5	100.0	44.3	6.4	*	*	*	*
Total	737.0	1403.6	1623.4	1695.5	1896.1	1824.9	1285.5	681.2	465.4	328.5

*Denotes years when there was no OEO budget item. The programs were not necessarily disbanded. Many were transferred to other agencies.
SOURCE: Robert D. Plotnick and Felicity Skidmore, *Progress Against Poverty* (New York: Academic Press, 1975), pp. 8, 9.

Oakland, like most cities, cannot be understood at a glance, but that is what was required of the EDA administrators, as Pressman and Wildavsky explain it:

> The struggle of EDA officials to comprehend the divided city of Oakland reads like a replay of the dilemmas of foreign aid officials almost any place around the world. They need official contact and approval to get their projects ratified; but they fear being labeled with the stigma of status quo, so they point first in the direction of the powers that be and then to their opponents and end up, naturally, satisfying neither one. No one knows for certain whether the city is as explosive as claimed. No one knows who, if anyone, can really speak for the black people of the city. . . . Visitors to EDA headquarters in Washington report always being asked for information on what Oakland was really like, questions that did not vary from the first visit to the last. It is not easy to grab hold of a shifting and volatile environment, particularly when the people in it do not agree on what is there, who is responsible for it, how it might be remedied or who speaks for them.[7]

Responsibility, remedy, and representation in urban areas were once thought to be the exclusive preserve of urban governments. It can be argued that federal agencies like the old EDA and the committees of the Congress that supervise aid to failing municipalities have indeed become urban governments. But they do not provide the vital and routine services for which chartered municipalities are responsible. It is only logical that municipal government should have some influence on the quality and *equity* of municipal service. But how much influence, and to what degree should municipal government be held responsible for *bad service* and *inequities?* The way this question is answered—and by whom—will determine whether the quality or urban life is considered something government ought to work to influence and improve or whether it is considered an environmental factor like the weather—beyond the range of human effort.

Whichever position is preferred, its supporters at some point will have to indicate whether or not there exist any substantial inequities in the provision of urban services. The inequity may then be rejected as trivial or accepted as too massive, but first it must be demonstrated.

Arguing About Equity

There is no general body of data on the relative equity of service provision in American cities. However, the question of equity has attracted a number of social scientists. Their attempts to validate or reject the complaints of minority citizens constitute the evidence we have on the equity of service provision in particular settings.

[7]Jeffrey L. Pressman and Aaron Wildavsky, *Implementation: How Great Expectations in Washington Are Dashed in Oakland; Or, Why It's Amazing That Federal Programs Work At All, This Being a Saga of the Economic Development Administration as Told By Two Sympathetic Observers Who Seek To Build Morals on a Foundation of Ruined Hopes* (Berkeley: University of California Press, 1973), p. 140.

Almost without exception, the studies of urban service equity have focused on one or two services in a single city or metropolitan area. This is a distinct drawback. Are services provided more equitably under one form of representation than another? Is one region of the country more equitable than another? Does party competition matter? None of these questions can be answered given the current extent of research. What these studies do give us are some concrete situations in which services are discussed against the background of race and ethnicity. We should need to rely less on rhetoric, charges, and countercharges, if we have at least a few tests of service equity.

One prominent analyst of urban politics, Robert Lineberry, studied several services in San Antonio, Texas. Lineberry's study tested the racial and ethnic equality (he does not use the term equity) in the provision of facilities like public libraries and services like police protection. The measure of equality he uses is based on the *effort* applied by the government of San Antonio in terms of resources dedicated to various neighborhoods in the city. Lineberry's analysis of police service is a good example of his technique.

The minority neighborhoods of San Antonio, which are largely Mexican-American, appear to be "overpoliced" according to Lineberry's measures. As Table 11.2 shows, there is little variation in police service effort as the minority portion of a neighborhood increases. This finding, together with similar analyses of the other services he has selected, allows Lineberry to conclude that:

> Neither neighborhood ethnicity, nor political power, nor socioeconomic status are very satisfactory predictors of service allocations. . . .[8]

Table 11.2
Lineberry's Analysis of Police Service Allocation

Distribution of Sampled Police Man-Units, by Percentage Minority				
Percentage Minority	Man-Units per Sector	Man-Units per Capita	Man-Units per Sector/Number Major Crimes	Man-Units per Sector/Number Radio Calls
100%–75%	7973.70	.09	1.80	.20
74%–50%	6990.48	.17	1.13	.17
49%–25%	6894.72	.08	1.17	.18
24%–0%	7359.84	.08	1.31	.23

SOURCE: Robert L. Lineberry, *Equality and Urban Policy* (Beverly Hills, Cal.: Sage Publications, 1977), p. 141.

[8]Robert L. Lineberry, *Equality and Urban Policy* (Beverly Hills, Cal.: Sage Publications, 1977), p. 183.

Therefore, as he puts it, the "distribution of urban public service provision can be characterized as one of 'unpatterned inequality.' "[9] So inconsistencies exist, but no single group in the city has been singled out, intentionally or unintentionally, for inadequate service. But do Lineberry's measures really deal with the adequacy of service? Does he tell us anything about the equity of service in San Antonio as well as equality? Not really. Lineberry does not presume to say anything about adequacy, and he is modest about the extent of his analysis:

> Obviously, there is much to which these data do not speak. They say nothing about the *quality* of police protection, as opposed to its quantity, nothing about the conduct of police officers, and nothing about the efficacy of police patrol.[10]

As we use "equity" here it comprehends quality, conduct, and efficacy since each of these elements contributes to the fairness of service distribution. Lineberry, however, is not satisfied that good measures can be developed to test for these elements. He is not alone. Another important work on the question of equity comes to a similar conclusion. From their study of school and other services in Oakland, California, Frank Levy, Arnold Meltsner, and Aaron Wildavsky conclude that *effort* is as much as social science is likely to measure in the foreseeable future:

> There is no theory for relating educational resources to results, and we are just beginning to learn the effects of air pollution. Moreover, as the study of impacts is pushed further down the chain of cause and effect, too many antecedents enter the picture, antecedents which we understand little and can control less.[11]

However, there is one additional set of studies that has attempted to consider the impact and results of service provision, undiscouraged by the warnings of Levy et al. These studies, conducted by Elinor Ostrom and her colleagues, have measured impact in terms of citizen experience and evaluation of particular services, especially public safety. Their method is described by Ostrom and Gordon Whitaker:

> Because of our interest in services provided to citizens, we have utilized survey methods to obtain two types of indicators of police output. The first type of indicator is the police-related experiences which respondents have had. Levels of criminal victimization and the quality of variety of police actions are assessed in this way. The second type of indicator consists of citizens' evaluations of service levels. In eight items, citizens were requested to evaluate various aspects of police service (among them; office demeanor, community relations and overall quality of service).[12]

[9]*Ibid.*
[10]*Ibid.,* p. 141.
[11]Frank Levy, Arnold Meltsner, and Aaron Wildavsky, *Urban Outcomes* (Berkeley: University of California Press, 1974), p. 21.
[12]Elinor Ostrom and Gordon P. Whitaker, "Community Power and Governmental Responsiveness: The Case of Police in Black Neighborhoods," *Improving the Quality of Urban Management,* Ed. by Willis D. Hawley and David Rogers (Beverly Hills, Cal.: Sage Publications, 1974), p. 322.

In their studies of service quality in the St. Louis and Chicago areas, Ostrom et al. do not analyze the differences between neighborhoods according to racial and ethnic composition. However, using their data on police output in St. Louis it is possible to piece together a racial comparison that will give us a more detailed picture of service equity than those mentioned above.

Demonstrating Service Inequity

The two St. Louis neighborhoods that provide the comparison are Baden, which was approximately 98 percent white at the time of the study (1972), and Penrose, which was approximately 98 percent black. Both neighborhoods are served by the same district of the St. Louis Metropolitan Police Department. They are alike in other important respects as well. In both areas a majority of dwellings are owner occupied; in Baden, 68 percent and in Penrose, 64 percent. In addition, the median value of housing in the two areas is comparable: $15–20,000 in Baden and $10–15,000 in Penrose. In short, though they are each racially homogeneous, they are both fairly ordinary middle-class neighborhoods.

According to one effort measure, at least, it would appear that Penrose, the black area, was getting more than its fair share of police service. Survey respondents in both areas were asked, "How many times do you think the police patrol this neighborhood during an average eight-hour shift . . . once every shift, twice, or how often?" Respondents in the black community, Penrose, perceived a significantly higher frequency of patrol than did the citizens of predominantly white Baden. If we compare the percentage of those in each area perceiving a frequency of three or more times per shift, we find 17.2 percent (n = 19) in Baden and over twice that proportion, 38 percent (n = 19), in Penrose. This has been the case in other studies of racial difference in the delivery of police service. But does more effort mean better effort and better service? Not according to the residents of these two neighborhoods.

As we see in Table 11.3, the experience and evaluation of the white residents in this comparison was measurably more favorable than that of the black residents. On the evaluative measures, 48 percent of the Penrose sample felt that crime was increasing in their neighborhood, compared with 29.8 percent of the sample in Baden. The overall rating of police showed an even sharper discrepancy between the areas, with 61 percent of the Baden sample rating police services better than average compared to 20 percent in Penrose. Police-community relations received the same rating in Penrose as police service overall, while 70.4 percent of the Baden sample rated police-community relations above average.

The three measures of citizen experience with public safety and the police also showed a more positive rating in the white community. Thirty-two percent of the Penrose sample had been victims of criminal activity as opposed to 23.8 percent in Baden. With respect to perception of police-response time, an element that the police in most jurisdictions regard as an important measure of the service

Table 11.3
Measures of Police Service Output in Two St. Louis City Neighborhoods

Variable[a]	Baden (1.4% black pop.)		Values[b]	Penrose (98.4% black pop.)	
	%	(N)		%	(N)
Crime Trend	29.8	(31)	Increasing	48.0	(24)
	38.5	(40)	Same	30.0	(15)
	21.2	(22)	Decreasing	18.0	(9)
	1.0	(1)	No Crime	—	
Q = −.33	6.7	(7)	Don't know	4.0	(2)
Overall Rating of Public Service	14.3	(15)	Outstanding	2.0	(1)
	46.7	(49)	Good	18.0	(9)
	26.7	(28)	Adequate	54.0	(27)
	2.9	(3)	Inadequate	6.0	(3)
	—		Very Poor	10.0	(5)
Q = .76	6.7	(7)	Don't know	8.0	(4)
Rating of Police-Community Relations	13.3	(14)	Outstanding	2.0	(1)
	57.1	(60)	Good	18.0	(9)
	12.4	(13)	Adequate	30.0	(15)
	3.8	(4)	Inadequate	10.0	(5)
	1.0	(1)	Very Poor	10.0	(5)
	—		Non-Existent	2.0	(1)
Q = .83	10.5	(11)	Don't know	22.0	(11)
Response-Time Rating	26.9	(28)	Very Rapidly	14.0	(7)
	39.4	(41)	Quickly Enough	38.0	(10)
	9.6	(10)	Slowly	26.0	(13)
	3.8	(4)	Very Slowly	8.0	(4)
	1.0	(1)	Not at all	2.0	(1)
Q = .52	16.3	(17)	Don't know	8.0	(4)
Victimization	23.8	(25)	Yes	32.0	(16)
Q = −.20	76.2	(80)	No	68.0	(34)
"Police use too much force"	16.7	(11)	Yes	26.5	(13)
	77.3	(51)	No	57.1	(28)
Q = −.37	6.1	(4)	Don't know	16.3	(8)

Table 11.3, Continued

Variable[a]	Baden (1.4% black pop.)		Values[b]	Penrose (98.4% black pop.)	
	%	(N)		%	(N)
Satisfied with Police Response to Specific Situations	88.9	(24)	Yes	64.3	(9)
Q = .63	11.1	(3)	No	35.7	(5)

[a]Broken lines indicate the points of dichotomy drawn in the computation of Yule's Q.
[b]Values often do not sum to 100% due to a number of noncategorical responses.

they provide, 36 percent of the black respondents perceived the police as respond-ing "slowly" or "not at all," compared to 14.4 percent in the same category in the Baden sample. Once the police responded, 88.9 percent of those who had called them in Baden reported being satisfied with the action taken by the police. The comparable figure among those having called for service in Penrose is some-what lower, 64.3 percent. One more evaluative measure was included as an indicator of police officer manner toward citizens; that is a question of whether the police in the respondent's neighborhood use "more force than is necessary." There was a 10 percent difference between the two communities on this question, with a larger portion of the Penrose sample evaluating the police negatively.

The degree to which the neighborhoods differ—the extent of difference in output—is hard to determine from the percentage alone. An additional measure, Yule's Q, is included in Table 11.3. Yule's Q gives us the relationship between the racial difference and the differences in service evaluation and experience. The statistic was computed by dividing each set of responses into two categories (indicated by the broken lines), *favorable* and *neutral to unfavorable*. The compu-tations were done so that a perfect positive score (+1.0) would mean that there was a perfect correlation between being a resident of Baden (and thereby white) and giving a "favorable" response. So we see that the highly positive Q scores for overall rating of police, rating of police community relations, rating of response time, and satisfaction with specific response, all indicate a strong association between being a resident of Baden and having positive evaluations of or favorable experiences with the police. Conversely, the negative scores on the crime trend, victimization, and police demeanor variables show some association between being a resident of Penrose and giving the unfavorable answers in the top half of each of those categories; that is, perceiving an increase in crime, having been victimized, and finding that the police use too much force.

Laying the Blame

If we accept these measures of police output as valid indicators of the quality of service provided by the St. Louis city government, we should then raise the question of equity. But as we have noted, according to a measure of effort, the frequency of police patrol, the black neighborhood Penrose is getting more than its share of city resources, even if the residents of Penrose find that more is less. The measure of equity that should be used in this case is not clear. What is clear is the political nature of the choice. The choice that is made will define the nature of the public good in question: public safety. "Public safety" will either turn out to be the quantity of resources distributed among the population, or it will be the quality of the product delivered to citizens.

There is no single point of reference that allows us to choose between *effort* and *output* as indicators of equity, no matter how they are defined. The defenders of effort as a standard argue that the responsibility of government must be limited; that some outside line should be drawn. Otherwise, they argue, there is little to protect citizens from a benevolent but total government that must be with them at all times in order to better serve them. The defenders of output measures argue that urban government is meaningless if it is not responsible for the quality of a service as it is used by citizens. Without reference to output, urban government, it is argued, is like an aircraft firm with no responsibility for fatal defects in the manufacture of its product, as long as it expends adequate effort in design and engineering.

In the case of industrial production, federal trade regulations have established that corporations engaged in interstate commerce must be held responsible for the quality of their products. If a similar standard were to apply to urban governments and *their* products, who, exactly, would be held responsible? This question is another form of one that recurs in the study of urban areas—who governs? It is the government of a city that *should be* responsible for the quality of service provision, but who is the government? The answer we arrived at above is that nobody governs. Specialized, professional bureaus are responsible for providing services in most municipalities, but those agencies cannot be held responsible for output *or* effort individually. Each bureau competes for the resources that will determine its level of effort and each has some effect on output as well. Can a municipal sanitation department be held accountable for inferior service if it has received inferior funding from the city council?

Perhaps the city council and other elected officials, such as the mayor or the comptroller, ought to answer for the quality of urban services provided under their administration. However, just as the service bureaus are not engaged in setting budgetary priorities, political executives and legislators are not engaged in the day to day decision-making that determines the quality of service for city dwellers. For instance, the sanitation department has a number of ways it may choose to respond to a budget reduction. It may reduce the number of trash collections citywide from five to three per week, or it may attempt to identify those areas of the city that "require less frequent collection" and cut their service to once or twice per week. Although this is far from the most subtle, professional area of administrative discretion available to city bureaucrats, it is the type of decision that most mayors and council members are usually willing to leave to the department in question.

Who should be sued, hoisted, or picketed in the case of identifiable inequity in the provision of a service? Theoretically, the answer is not clear. Although it seems that an *effort* standard of equity might apply more directly to the primary allocators, the executives and the legislators, an *output* standard would include bureaucrats as well. In either case, the web of responsibility is complex and elusive. The convention that has been adopted by the courts indicates what is perhaps the only practical solution—a legal fiction. Thus we find service equity suits inventing or assuming executive responsibility, e.g., *Citizens for Garbage Equity* v. *J. Jones, Mayor of Dimsdale.* Such a fiction is necessary, given the fragmented nature of service provision. However, as we shall see shortly, the fiction does not eliminate the problem of responsibility once the equity question reaches the picket line or the courtroom.

Of Potholes and the Quality of Urban Justice

It is usually easier to define equity by saying what it excludes. Equity is not prejudice, favoritism, or fraud. When a positive definition is ventured, it usually equates equity with fairness and justice. The problem with either approach is in applying it to a concrete example of service delivery and being able to answer the question, "Is it equitable?" This question is usually answered by individuals with reference to a personal moral code. A more general, "public" definition cannot rely on a personal code, but must have reference to some standard or principle. Finding an "equity principle" in legislation and in case law is an eminently political enterprise. The equity principle becomes a political boundary between those who can legally demand resources to compensate them for inequitable treatment and those who must do the compensating. The narrower the definition, the fewer the legitimate demands for redress. It is also possible to define equity so broadly that almost everyone appears to be a victim of municipal injustice.

The key to the political debate over equity in urban service provision is the Equal Protection Clause of the Fourteenth Admendment to the U.S. Constitution:

> No State shall make or enforce any law which shall . . . deny to any person within its jurisdiction the equal protection of the laws.

The Equal Protection Clause, like other parts of the Constitution, depends on the federal judiciary for its application and interpretation. Therefore, using the clause to raise the question of service equity usually involves legal action. But is it worth "making a federal case" out of complaints about potholes and dirty parks? Isn't there a less expensive, more direct way to deal with such eminently local problems? The traditional democratic mechanism of electoral choice is suggested by pluralist analysts as a route to the correction of inequity. Protest, both violent and nonviolent, is prescribed by some and acknowledged by many as the most direct way for a relatively powerless minority to present its demands. In addition, a number of discussions of equity over the past decade have centered around the idea of neighborhood political control. An important exercise in the consideration of equity and its place in the urban political system is an evaluation of each of these strategies in terms of its characteristic worth and its practical payoff for urbanites.

The Politics of Protest

A situation in which a group has to resort to protest to present its claim for service bodes ill. It indicates a group that lacks the political resources to confront policy makers directly. A situation in which a group has to resort to violent protests is worse yet. Although a riot may be political and may be based in frustration over inequity, it is a very diffuse, nonspecific demand. So diffuse is it that in a number of municipalities civil disorder has been used to justify increased expenditures for police and fire services, rather than for any effort toward service equity.

As Michael Lipsky found in his study of rent-strikers in Harlem, the most that protesters can achieve for themselves is symbolic benefit. Material benefits —improved plumbing and the extermination of rats—can be achieved, but they require the charitable intervention of a well-positioned third party or reference group. Some sort of "front" is needed to translate the demands of the protest group into the language of specialized service bureaus. As Lipsky puts it:

> (A)dmission to policy-making councils is frequently barred because of the angry, militant rhetorical style adopted by protest leaders. People in power do not like to sit down with rogues.[13]

The poorer and less-educated that petitioners are, the more roguish they will look to urban service bureaucrats. In the case of the Harlem rent strike, the great majority of discussion with housing bureaucrats and court officers was conducted by a civic group, Call-for-Action, which acted in behalf of the protesters. Unfortunately, all those protesting service inequity cannot count on the support and advocacy of groups like Call-for-Action. Most often, protests over inequity simmer and occasionally boil up into public confrontations in which both sides have so much to lose that the original protest goal gets lost in the commotion. The longer an issue takes to receive public attention—and such attention is the only capital available to protesters—the more likely it is that all kinds of subsidiary

[13]Michael Lipsky, *Protest in City Politics* (Chicago: Rand-McNally, 1970), p. 174.

and residual demands and frustrations will be raised as well. So what starts out as protest over police harassment in one black neighborhood can easily become a broad debate over the political influence of the black community. This happens as the volume of protest is raised in order to attract the media and as the battle is joined by other, sympathetic groups with slightly different interests. By the time the protest group has enough public power to warrant a meeting with the police commissioner, almost anything that the commissioner offers will be rejected as too little, too late.

The increasing pitch and scope of protest as it travels to the councils of power provides policy makers with a way out. The first and last refuge of the bureaucrat is his specialty. Unless the protesters can talk police-talk in terms of shift schedules, patrol routes, and personnel practices, they are likely to get redirected to the office of the deputy mayor for community (read: noisy minority) affairs. This will not be an appropriate scenario in all cases, however. At least as often, the protest group will never develop the momentum necessary to get a hearing in the first place.

Neighborhood Political Control

The major works in social science on minority (particularly black) community control are more than a decade old. Alan Altshuler's *Community Control* and Milton Kotler's *Neighborhood Government* are filled with the optimism of an idea whose time has come.[14] A completely new "constitution" for metropolitan areas was predicted. The same kind of political control available to suburbanites would be given to ghetto residents. The diverse preferences of different constituencies in the metropolis would finally be satisfied by diverse service arrangements. The city would become a better place in which to live. It is difficult to argue with these sentiments, but they should be considered in context. Despite arguments, demands, and careful plans for minority control of city neighborhoods, community control has not happened anywhere in the past decade. Even its most constant supporters must begin to doubt its practicability.

However, there is an interesting question apart from practicability which is raised by the community control proposal. Can ghetto residents ever have as much political control as middle-class suburbanites? Clearly, they cannot. The large difference in resources means that the government of a low-income ghetto neighborhood will be able to accomplish much less, collectively, than a relatively affluent suburb. The ghetto neighborhood government has a good deal less money to buy, hire, and build. In fact, it is possible that the quality of urban services in a neighborhood may decline with the introduction of community control. It is also possible, in the long term and with help from other levels of government, that

[14]See Alan Altshuler, *Community Control* (New York: Pegasus, 1970); Milton Kotler, *Neighborhood Government* (Indianapolis: Bobbs-Merrill, 1969).

minority communities may improve the level of public services. But like protest politics, community control is not directed at specific service inequities. To the contrary, under a system of complete political control for urban neighborhoods, the question of inequity becomes pointless, because the new neighborhood government is the *only* agency responsible for the quality of services in that neighborhood. Under a system in which neighborhoods provide their own services, the Equal Protection Clause cannot be used to compare service levels among neighborhoods. The city government is off the hook. The neighborhood has become the "state" for purposes of constitutional legal action.

Municipal Electoral Politics

During the heyday of the urban political machine, the ward heeler was held directly responsible for the level of public services provided to his constituents. The machine, as we argued in Chapter 3, established a linkage between citizen demand and service quality that has been missing since the machine's death in some cities (and which may never have existed in others). It is the model of the urban machine, together with the belief that electoral power means political power, that has persuaded black community leaders in many cities to focus their energies on mayoral and councilmanic elections. But is the election of blacks and other minorities to key municipal offices likely to have an effect on existing service inequity?

The problem with an electoral strategy for service equity in many cities is that the ward system is largely a thing of the past. Instead of competing for neighborhood leadership, city-council candidates are more likely to be running in multicommunity districts or for citywide (at-large) seats. The linkage between the citizen's vote and the quality of neighborhood service delivery is broken if there is significant diversity in a councilmanic district, and the trend has been toward larger, more diverse districts. In addition, unless a particular minority group constitutes a citywide majority, it is unlikely that one of its number will be elected under an at-large or multicommunity district system.

Nonetheless, there is a recent series of federal court cases that challenges the constitutionality of the district systems that have made it difficult for minority-group members to be elected. By making such an argument, blacks in Dallas, Texas, were able to have the at-large district system in that city declared unconstitutional. In *Lipscomb* v. *Wise*, the U.S. Court of Appeals ordered the District Court to "require the city to reapportion itself into an appropriate number of single-member districts for the purpose of holding City Council elections."[15] Upon review, the U. S. Supreme Court differed with the Appeals Court's requirement that only single-member districts be used. Instead, the majority of the high Court let stand a District Court-approved plan of the Dallas City Council that

[15] *Lipscomb* v. *Wise,* 551 F. 2d 1049 (1977).

provided for eight council members from single-member districts and three council members, including the mayor, to be elected at-large.[16] (The operating rule
for federal court plans is to "employ only single-member districts." The Dallas
plan, however, comes from a legislative body, so the variation is allowed.)

The federal judiciary (and especially the Fifth Circuit Court of Appeals) has
shown its willingness to invalidate discriminatory schemes of representation at
the local level, but will court intervention improve the equity of service delivery?
Perhaps the best that can be said is that it cannot hurt. This is largely because
control over the quantity, quality, and distribution of urban services has shifted
away from elected officials, whether they are from at-large or single-member
districts. For many important services, key allocation and delivery decisions are
made by appointed officials and hired professionals. Of course, these officials will
respond to significant shifts in the composition of the city council, but each
bureaucrat's authority is bounded and specialized, so that the response to a
demand will be bounded likewise. For example, a black council member demanding more equitable transportation service for his district might get any one of a
number of responses from transit bureaucrats. Bus circulation might be increased,
a usage study might be required, some stops might be shifted to other areas, or
the approach might be to change personnel policy by hiring more black drivers
and maintenance workers. Any one of these might serve as a response to a
demand for more equitable service. Some responses will be closer to the community idea of equity than others. The point is that single-member districts are not
equivalent to community control of services. As long as services are provided by
specialized bureaucracies, any idea about equity or redistribution of services will
be interpreted and carried out by specialized bureaucrats.

Nonetheless, the value of minority representation on city councils should not
be discounted. A council seat gives minorities a bargaining position that allows
them to compete for public benefits and to at least challenge bureaucratic interpretation of equity. But we should remember that service equity is at least one
step removed from the electoral process, and it is the electoral process that is the
target of cases such as *Lipscomb* v. *Wise.*

Suing for Service Equity

Any law, policy, or budgetary allocation made by a local government must
protect all *persons* (not just citizens or adults) *equally.* But there is room for
interpretation here, and the meaning of the individual words in this clause has
shifted over time. These shifts are significant because *"equal protection" is the
ultimate principle of equity used in the United States.* A slight change in emphasis
in the way the federal courts read the clause can eliminate or expand the possibil-

[16]*Wise* v. *Lipscomb,* 98 S. Ct. 2493 (1978).

ity of relief for thousands of people who feel they are receiving an insufficient public benefit or bearing an undue public cost.

By and large, the groups that have used the Equal Protection Clause to seek remedy have been racial and ethnic minorities. For urban minorities, the question of service equity is a matter of basic resources. Public services like education, police protection, health, and transportation have perhaps the greatest influence on the poorest neighborhoods. If a low-income, minority area is receiving inferior urban service, the quality of life will tend to deteriorate. This is not to say that city governments are solely responsible for the quality of life within their jurisdictions. It is impossible to defend such a notion in a democracy. However, it would be difficult to defend *any* notion of the public good that permitted selective inferiority in the provision of public services. Urban governments are inevitably held responsible for the fairness of their actions, and there will always be a portion of the population that claims it has not gotten its fair share at the public trough. The question that we must deal with is what do the courts consider a fair share, or, in more specialized language, what is the judicial definition of equal protection in the provision of urban services? As we will see in the following cases, the definitional argument over equity as effort or equity as output is not just a scholar's knot, but is alive in the courtroom.

Beal v. *Lindsay,* a service equity case that sheds light on the definitional controversy, was decided by the Federal Court of Appeals in New York in 1970. The suit, which involved the quality of a public park, was brought by "black and Puerto Rican residents living in the neighborhood of Crotona Park alleging that New York City unconstitutionally discriminated against (them) by failing to maintain the park in a condition equivalent to that of other multicommunity parks in the Bronx."[17] What constitutes equal protection in the provision of park facilities? What level of service should the city be held responsible for? The Beal case provides answers to these questions, answers which provide a working definition of equity.

Beal and his neighbors argued that the court's answer should define equal protection as equality of condition. The city, according to Beal's argument, should be held responsible for maintaining the park at a level of cleanliness and repair equal to that of municipal parks in predominantly white neighborhoods.

A significant aspect of Beal's argument was the absence of any claim of intentional discrimination. No charge was made that any officer or agency of the city government had selected Crotona Park for inferior treatment. What Beal was counting on was the court's recognition of the situation as a *"prima facie* case of forbidden discrimination."[18] If plaintiffs, in this case, Beal, can show that

---

[17] *Beal* v. *Lindsay,* 468 F. 2d 287 (1972).
[18] For a complete explanation of the *prima facie* case see Daniel Fessler and Charles Haar, "Beyond the Wrong Side of the Tracks: Municipal Services at the Interstices of Procedure," *Harvard Civil Rights—Civil Liberties Law Review,* 6 (1971).

residential distinctions by race correspond with disparities in the level of public service, then the distribution of service violates the Equal Protection Clause, *prima facie*—on its face. In such a case, the burden of proof shifts to the government to show that it has not discriminated. The *prima facie* case is the most desirable one for minority-group plaintiffs because it puts urban governments on the defensive. Equally important, the *prima facie* case eliminates the need to prove a specific intent on the part of government to discriminate.

Whether or not the federal courts require plaintiffs to show that they have been discriminated against intentionally by urban governments is of primary significance, politically. Recourse to the federal judiciary in the face of local discrimination is the last resort for minority communities because of the blind spot urban governments have for service inequity. Patterns of service provision develop a permanence over time. The level of service *provided to a neighborhood* comes to be considered the level of service *required by that neighborhood.* Ghetto neighborhoods, it has been argued, require a lower level of service than middle-class areas because of differing "living standards." Assumptions like this become historical artifacts which generally cannot be attributed to any individual municipal officer or agency. In most cases, no one can be found who actually "intended" that a minority area receive inferior service; that's just *the way things are.* Given the widely spread nature of responsibility for patterns of service provision, requiring a showing of governmental intent would discourage all but the most obvious cases of service discrimination from reaching court.

In the Beal case, the Crotona Park community did not allege that the city had *intended* that their park be inferior, but simply that it *was* inferior. It was then up to the court to decide whether the inferior results of governmental effort was enough to make it unconstitutional. In his decision for the court, Chief Judge Friendly found that it was not:

> Implicit in plaintiff's case is the proposition that the equal protection clause not merely prohibit less state effort on behalf of minority racial groups but demand the attainment of equal results. We very much doubt that when, as here, the factor requiring added effort is not the result of past illegal action. . . . In a case like this, the City has satisfied its constitutional obligations by equal input even though, because of conditions for which it is not responsible, it has not achieved the equal results it desires.[19]

Judge Friendly was convinced by the city's argument that the park had deteriorated because of a certain degree of vandalism and misuse, not because of official neglect. This made a substantial change in the meaning of the *prima facie* case under the Equal Protection Clause. It was now not enough to show that a dissimilar level of services corresponds to a racial distinction. The disparity must be in the level of service *effort,* not only in the level of service result.

An additional qualification is implied in the Beal decision and was made

[19] *Beal* v. *Lindsay,* 468 F 2d 286 (1972).

explicit by the U.S. Supreme Court a few years later: it is necessary to show that an alleged inequity was intended by a governmental official or agent. This does more than modify the *prima facie* case; it effectively eliminates it. Intention simply does not appear "on the face" of most cases.

But the intention requirement does not apply equally to all aspects of municipal government. In the city council cases noted earlier, the Court of Appeals has ruled that it is enough to "infer" discriminatory intention from a long history of black exclusion from the municipal policy process. Another prominent exception to the intention requirement is for the one service that seems to be "preferred" in court decisions on Equal Protection—education.

The best illustration of the special status accorded to education is the U. S. Supreme Court's ringing declaration in *Brown* v. *Board of Education:*

> We conclude that in the field of public education the doctrine of "separate but equal" has no place. Separate educational facilities are inherently unequal. Therefore, we hold that the plaintiffs . . . are, by reason of the segregation complained of, deprived of the equal protection of the laws guaranteed by the Fourteenth Amendment.[20]

There is no need to prove intention here. Federal District Courts have ordered citywide busing in cities from coast to coast. This has been done without the need to consider discriminatory motive. What distinguishes education and city council districting from other aspects of municipal government? Why should minority communities have to show that public officials have intended discrimination in order to claim inequity in police or utility services, but not in order to claim inequity in education or urban representation? There is no detectable judicial doctrine that clarifies the distinction, but there are several potential explanations. One explanation might be that Equal Protection legal action is simply too confused to be considered a body of law. Those who hold to this position are waiting for the Supreme Court to ride in and clean up the mess. But there is more logic to this litigation than may at first appear.

A second explanation begins by noting the similarities between the two major exceptions to the intention requirement. Both education and representation are *means to benefits in urban society, but not benefits in and of themselves.* The federal courts seem to be saying that they will at least defend the equity of minority access to the traditional routes of upward social mobility—electoral politics and schooling.

This approach might be justified constitutionally if it were true that access to these time-honored routes also meant access to other public goods. Unfortunately, there is no necessary connection between a seat on the city council and the equity of other services. Nor do racially integrated schools necessarily provide minority children with an acceptable education. Equal access is not the same as equal protection, although the federal courts often read it that way. The guiding

[20] *Brown* v. *Board of Education,* Topeka, Kans., 346 U.S. 483 (1954).

belief seems to be that a couple of key structural changes will cause changes in the substance and functioning of urban government and, further, in the quality of urban life. This allows the courts to neglect the quality of life, day to day, in minority communities—mundane things like decaying parks and police hostility—because these communities have been provided with eventual redemption. This puts the federal courts in the mainstream of the reform tradition, a tradition marked by a faith in the effectiveness of public institutions, a reliance on the school's ability to socialize the lower class, and a vision of the public interest that prevails over ordinary misfortunes. The position of the federal courts on service equity was expressed by Fifth Circuit Judge Clark in a dissenting opinion that has been vindicated by later decisions and by the Supreme Court. Judge Clark's dissent in *Hawkins* v. *Town of Shaw* argued that black grievances about service equality were properly electoral issues, not constitutional questions. Further, a degree of inequality is justified, in Judge Clark's terms, "because the people of the Town of Shaw had living standards that varied according to their individual financial condition and social values, some of them occupied properties which required and permitted a lower level of municipal service than other properties."[21]

This position may very well be the only politically realistic option open to the federal courts. The alternative is to broaden the Equal Protection Clause to include every sewer system, every police force, and every parks department in the country. Intervening in the delivery and organization of these other services in the way that the courts have intervened in the delivery and organization of education would require an enormous expansion of the federal judiciary. This is not likely to occur. However, as we have argued above, recourse to the courts is probably the most direct and effective way to identify and remedy inequity in urban services. Now that this "superior" alternative has receded, the question of equity may recede as well.[22]

If equity should become less important in the analysis and planning of service provision, we will be left with a notion of the urban public good that has no center. Obviously, this would challenge the ideal of democratic community in an urban setting. Is it possible to provide public services democratically with an ill-defined notion of equity? More generally, what type of community is implied by the urban service state? Our concluding chapter considers the definition of community implied by the arguments we have made up to this point.

---

[21]*Hawkins* v. *Town of Shaw, en banc,* 461 F. 2d 1183 (1972).

[22]The "superior" alternative of constitutional equity receded a bit further with the Supreme Court's decision in *Mobile* v. *Bolden* (64 L Ed 2d 47, 1980). The *Bolden* decision narrowed the holding in *Wise* v. *Lipscomb* (noted above) by requiring, as Justice Stewart put it for the majority, "that the disputed (electoral district) plan was 'conceived or operated as (a) purposeful device . . . to further racial discrimination.' " (at 58). Since many minority plaintiffs will be unable to meet the Court's requirement, achieving equity through electoral reform will become less likely.

Suggested Readings

Althshuler, Allan, *Community Control* (New York: Pegasus, 1970).

Clark, Kenneth B., *Dark Ghetto* (New York: Harper & Row, 1965).

Kotler, Milton, *Neighborhood Government* (Indianapolis: Bobbs-Merrill, 1969).

Levy, Frank, Arnold Meltsner, and Aaron Wildavsky, *Urban Outcomes* (Berkeley: University of California Press, 1974).

Lineberry, Robert L., *Equality and Urban Policy* (Beverly Hills, Cal.: Sage Publications, 1977).

Lipsky, Michael, *Protest in City Politics* (Chicago: Rand-McNally, 1970).

Ostrom, Elinor, and Gordon P. Whitaker, "Community Power and Governmental Responsiveness: The Case of Police in Black Neighborhoods." *Improving the Quality of Urban Management,* ed. by Willis D. Hawley and David Rogers (Beverly Hills, Cal.: Sage Publications, 1974).

Chapter 12
City of Despair,
City of Hope

Growth, Decline, and Displacement

For most of their history, Americans built cities only to abandon them for the great westward trek. Yet few ghost towns resulted from this process. Seemingly endless waves of immigration kept cities populated, and there have always been multiple and highly valuable uses to which cities could be put by successive and evolving generations of capitalists, industrialists, merchants, and traders.

Thus an eastern port city might be depopulated in the early nineteenth century by westward migration, only to be repopulated as industrialized activity requiring large amounts of labor began to arise. Central banking and administrative functions might replace the factories when these latter declined or were moved to cheaper labor markets. River cities, port cities, and then railroad cities grew and declined with the introduction and deterioration of transportation and communication technologies. Today we live in an age of "truck cities" and "airport cities," some of which are direct descendents of earlier transportation centers.[1]

Our tendency has been to view cities in a semi-Darwinian sense. Once some cities can no longer compete with other cities as industrial, mining, or agricultural centers, we have as a nation tended to ignore them, letting them slip into decline unless some new technology revitalizes them in new form. This process of growth, affluence, and decline has been dominant since the late seventeenth century. Often cities become multifunctional and cosmopolitan, thus in effect defending themselves from decline through diversification, much as might a modern corporate enterprise.

But always there was a sense of coming growth and change in the urban place as the country went from an agrarian backwater to an international giant of commerce and industry. Today, however, there are some good reasons to suspect that the older cities are no longer attracting new economic forces and technologies

[1]Edgar M. Hoover and Raymond Vernon, *Anatomy of a Metropolis* (Cambridge, Mass.: Harvard University Press, 1959).

to replace what has spread to the suburban fringe or migrated to the South and West. Cites large and small, from New York to Cleveland to Detroit, are in decline. Certainly the key to this decline can be largely explained by the flight to the suburbs of the 1950s and 1960s and by the tendency of older industries not to replace antiquated facilities at the old locations.[2]

As we have suggested, the latest wave of immigration to the cities has consisted of blacks and Hispanics from the back country in search of realization of the dream that has drawn millions to the urban place: jobs and a chance of upward mobility. But the necessary employers and capital have not been drawn to the declining cities. The results have been very serious indeed. For the longest period yet in our history, we have allowed central cities to decline and become the warehouses of the unemployed, the unemployable, and the underaged and elderly poor. Instead of the typical periodic renovating and renewal of the stock of urban housing, we have seen the wholesale destruction of housing in many cities. New York City's South Bronx, constantly referred to in the press as a "bombed-out" hell of anarchy and waste, serves as a symbol of this new period of decline. Dozens of other cities now have their no-man's land, their "Fort Apaches" and "combat zones."

We have lived in an era of increasing "gray areas," blight, and dilapidation now for nearly a generation and the pattern seems to be spreading from the East to the Midwest and into the Middle Atlantic states. Accompanying this decline has been the commonly heard complaint that nothing in cities works anymore. Trains don't run on time, kids don't learn to read, write, and calculate any longer, streets are unmaintained, crime is rampant, and the entire fabric of urban life seems to some to have been torn apart.

How Could This Have Happened?

What answers we can provide to this question and to related ones are in the body of this text. By way of summary, we go back to some of these answers as the basis for some speculation that concludes the book.

Certain brute facts of urban political economy demand repetition. Federal and state policies of the past thirty years have directly encouraged the particular economic forces that led to the decline-without-replacement situation in which many cities find themselves. One must begin with the phenomena that are partially captured by the term "suburbanization." The celebration of the rural over the urban and the idealization of the ruggedly individualistic pioneer have been, as we noted earlier, persistent themes in American culture for at least two

[2]Richard V. Knight and Thomas M. Stanback, Jr., *Suburbanization and the City* (Montclair, N.J.: Allanheld/Osmun, 1976).

centuries. We have long believed in the biblical evil of the city and in the city's harmful moral and physical effects on the rearing of the young.[3]

While the city functioned as a place of fortune, sin, commerce, and amenity, it was to the countryside that we looked when we thought of mom and home and apple pie. The frontier died in the late nineteenth century, and the romance of farming in the twentieth century followed suit—except for the country gentleman who, with his excess wealth, could afford to maintain a rural squire fantasy. Today, some highly educated people abandon city life for the simplicities of rural small-town life in hopes of a more "basic" or "real" pattern of existence. But the great romance of the present era was and still is to be found in suburbia, that approximation of the homestead minus the hardship from which the vast majority of modern college students have sprung, often swearing never to return.

Single-family dwellings surrounded by a patch of green on which the kids could romp became the object of aspiration pushing countless husbands in their drive to the top in the past thirty years. Family life reminiscent of an idealized countrified past was promised by such settings. The popular taste reflected in television shows of the past generation illustrated the "truth" of this idealization to millions. From "Ozzie and Harriet" to "Life with Father" to what seems to have been the entire life cycle of Lucille Ball as suburban housewife, America lived and hoped for a material and cultural existence epitomized by the idea of the suburb.

Although the suburban ideal as the culmination of the American dream stirred the souls of millions, the stirring had "help" from a set of political and economic actors with whom the reader should by now have more than passing familiarity. Billions of federal and state dollars went into highways ringing the central cities and fanning out spokelike to the hinterlands where tract-house builders created near-identical versions of split-level happiness. More billions were spent on automobiles and even more on keeping them running, insured, and free from harm in garages. The houses, or more specifically the mortgages which made possible the purchase of those houses by the middle and working classes, were underwritten by Uncle Sam in several ways. Through the FHA and through the Veterans Administration, the federal government directly guaranteed bankers' loans to new house buyers. Federal highway subsidies were as crucial as guaranteed loan programs in making the creation of the suburbs possible.

The suburbs were also legal and governmental units capable of walling off "undesirables" from the central cities in any number of ways. They walled off the cities through restrictive housing covenants and zoning regulations, by refusing to cooperate in the sharing of services, and through their increasing power in state

[3]Josef J. Barton and Jeffrey K. Hadden, "An Image That Will Not Die: Thoughts on the History of Anti-Urban Ideology," *The Urbanization of the Suburbs,* ed. by Louis H. Masotti and Jeffrey K. Hadden (Beverley Hills, Cal.: Sage Publications, 1973); Morton and Lucia White, "The American Intellectual versus the American City," *American Urban History,* ed. by Alexander B. Callow, Jr. (New York: Oxford University Press, 1969).

legislatures.[4] The latter have been writing prosuburb legislation for decades now. To this day for instance, one can still discover funding formuli which award state funds for (K through 12) school districts on the basis of the per capita local tax figures for education. Thus, if I live in a suburb where I pay $500 per year in school taxes, my school district might receive an additional $250 per capita in state aid. If you live in the central-city school district and pay $100 per capita, your district will receive $50 per capita in state aid *no matter your district's need or quality.* Such policies can be discovered in nearly every area of public activity.[5]

Capital construction needs in the form of public buildings and roads were underwritten by special federal and state bond issues, grants, or loans. Consumption and personal debt rose to dizzying heights as suburbanization became the life-style of America. Business boomed in lawn care and recreational products. Automobiles were produced and consumed with such rapidity that the idea of a disposable car seemed "just around the corner," as did the fully automated kitchen and home laundry. Soon the new industrial plants of a new industrial era began to spring up in something called "industrial parks," created by suburban municipalities to lure large-property taxpayers into their nets.

In the 1970s the "heads" followed the bodies as dozens of central-city world and national administrative headquarters moved to where all the commuters lived. Suburban New York and Connecticut corporate headquarters, for instance, began to resemble feudal cities with their walled towers and elaborate landscaping. Left behind by the new American society of the suburbs were the traffic, the congestion, the pollution, and the crime of the city. True, urban renewal funded by more billions of federal dollars has been creating new downtowns of glacial office towers while various housing agencies attempt to house the millions living in the deteriorating residential areas. But in few cases has there been an attempt to recreate the positive aspects of the city that had been.

Throughout the years that the suburbs were being created, little thought was given to the consequences that might follow. A key, but unarticulated, major assumption of the creation of the suburbs was that energy costs would remain relatively stable over time. A correlative assumption was that there was sufficient energy at some price to maintain the spread city which was willy-nilly being built. Both of these assumptions are now beginning to haunt us. If it is true that gasoline, heating oil, and electricity are about to become as scarce as they are costly, then the suburban dream is in serious danger of being shattered. The material conditions of life, wrapped in the automobilization of the culture and sustained by huge and distant shopping malls, is due for a horrendous shock. The journey to work, which requires the consumption of billions of gallons of gasoline,

[4]Anthony Downs, *Opening Up the Suburbs* (New Haven, Conn.: Yale University Press, 1973); Michael N. Danielson, *The Politics of Exclusion* (New York: Columbia University Press, 1976).
[5]For more on school finance see Robert D. Reischauer and Robert W. Hartman, *Reforming School Finance* (Washington, D.C.: Brookings Institution, 1973); Joel S. Berke and Michael W. Kirst, *Federal Aid to Education* (Lexington, Mass.: D.C. Heath, 1972).

will be curtailed by price or scarcity or both. The dependency of the suburban household on highly mobile plumbers, exterminators, and repairmen of all sorts is likely to be revealed in starkest fashion.

The crises of the suburbs are upon us. The great social movement of suburbanization may very well be the last rung on the ladder of expansion. For generations now Americans have created social distance from one another through physical mobility. The richer we got, the further we moved away from the city. The move beyond the city's rim was fueled by advances in technology, cheap and seemingly endless energy supplies, and a set of government programs and policies. These elements made the suburbs possible. Some of them are about to become constraints to suburban growth and may turn the eyes of many suburbanites toward that which they or their parents abandoned.[6] When that reflective glance occurs, the suburbanites will find, in effect, two cities, one of despair and one of hope.

The City of Despair

The city of despair is that residual place where poverty, inequality, racism, and crime are to be found. It is the city of pollution and decay left nearly paralyzed by the migration of a generation of citizens who were productive of wealth and political activity.

The city of despair can no longer rely upon its citizens or its political system for renewal and change. As we have repeatedly noted, the great federal and state bureaucratic presence has in effect replaced many of the aspects of local self-determination as cities have become increasingly dependent upon such agencies for their very survival. The political integrity of cities as units both of a larger system and a self-contained one is beginning to disappear. The city of despair is the last stop for the socially undesirable, the economically weak, and the politically impotent. Core notions of common interest and need have fallen to the greed of organized interests and to the hegemony of bureaucratic agencies which themselves have begun to approximate sovereign entities.

We have suggested that these "new sovereignties" tend to create constituencies, clients, and victims, as distinct from citizens represented by elected legislative bodies and chief executives. The quality and quantity of dependency upon the dollar and service outputs of special districts and bureaucratic agencies of the federal and state governments have led to a city of residents, claimants, and dependents. For most of them, the city as a political entity does not exist. Alienation, despondency, and anger are the expressions of the breakdown of urban social and political culture.

Fear is pervasive in the city of despair. Fear of crime, of pollution, of traffic

[6]See David Goldfield, "The Limits of Suburban Growth," *Urban Affairs Quarterly*, vol. 12, no. 1, September 1976, pp. 83–102.

and noise, and of incivility in its many forms underpins the stereotype of the city of despair. The idea of the city as a community or as a collection of communities seems nearly to have vanished in our time. We believe the city to be ungovernable and even unmanageable. Of course, some older cities and many new ones still provide the zest of possibility and life, particularly for the very rich and for the young college graduate. But this means only that, for some, the city continues to be a place either to enjoy the fruits of having "made it" or to set off on the road of economic promise. Thus we can visit that part of the city which is the locale for the few and never see much of the city of despair in which the many live.

If we extrapolate present conditions and look to the future of the city of despair, the picture is bleak indeed. We can see abandoned central-city shopping areas, hotels, restaurants, and the like, surrounded by crisscrossing expressways delivering commuters to home, work, and shopping on the city's rim. Neighborhoods will be packed with the displaced, the despised, and the hopeless, and held together by dependencies on agencies of the state whose power and influence rests in part on the very misery they seek to eliminate. No-man's land will be a familiar sight as housing is destroyed by neglect and by the insurance fires landlords employ to close out their operations in the black.

The city of despair is the dark side of the urban service state. The fiscal crisis of the city will lead to the reduction of services provided locally, thus further speeding the decline. Increasingly, teachers, firemen, policemen, and other urban service workers will become suburbanites who look upon the city of despair as a place of hazardous employment, much as foreign service officers face remote and dangerous international outposts. The city of despair, then, will be gutted, surrounded, and dependent on the greater society for its very existence. Its political system will be inactive, its communal life a cruel joke.

There are excellent reasons to believe that the city of despair is with us now in some of our older, poorer cities.[7] Yet to project such a future is surely to overstate the case. This book has suggested repeatedly that in the past cities have had enormous potential for providing key aspects of civilized life. It is to these aspects that we now return in hopes of synthesizing some dissimilar notions that might combine to create the possibility of a city of hope.

The City of Hope

There are several reasons to look upon the urban service state as the city of hope. The reasons are varied and as yet not fully articulated into the potentially powerful union they could create. The first of these is the question of community. Cities have in recent decades been pointed to as the source of nearly every social ill imaginable, from the breakdown of the nuclear family to the increase in homicide

---

[7]See sections in Chapter 9 about Philadelphia and Fall River.

rates. Whatever one makes of such charges, the fact remains that cities have provided the basis for those social and cultural ties with which we associate the oft-used term "community."

Indeed, the glorification of the small town in the American past has led to seeing the suburb as the natural successor. Without discounting the many aspects of social solidarity found in the suburb, we believe that the city neighborhood still deserves the consideration of those who seek community in American life. By community we mean more than the vital neighboring functions that the city block can and does afford. We also wish to imply the ideas of sharing, sympathy, understanding, and compassion for those who surround us when we speak of community. Although simple physical space cannot create such feelings for others, the city with its density and compelling requirement that at least we live in recognition of one another, has offered more promise of community than nearly any other public living arrangement. Shared cultural, religious, ethnic, and class identity can reemerge as groups begin to repopulate the abandoned urban core. But why should such groups repopulate the cities from which they so recently departed? Why would the "missing middle," which consists largely of those over twenty-five who are white, married, and child-rearing, return to the city?

The search for community can easily be misinterpreted to suggest a romantic, utopian ideal reminiscent of a past that never was. But there is no ideological transformation or revolution in consciousness implied by our use of the term "community." On the contrary, there are good sociological as well as economic reasons to believe that such a search might typify the struggle to create the "city of hope." An entire generation of middle-class Americans has lived in the suburbs, safe from the ills and joys of city life. There is little reason to believe that they are less likely than their parents or ancestors to move to places of new possibility and opportunity. There are excellent reasons to suspect that the economics of city life will enhance movement toward the urban core in the coming decades.

Two factors seem to point toward an economic renaissance in cities. The first of these is the relatively small cost of urban housing and land. The rapid departure for the suburbs left the cities relatively depopulated, housing undervalued, and much vacant land available for the construction of new housing. The second factor is the increasing cost of commuting by automobile and maintaining the single-family dwellings (see Figure 12.1). Cities are the efficient and economical sites for housing, schools, amenities, and commercial institutions when energy costs increase rapidly. The economies of scale which brought the nineteenth-century city into existence resulted not only from the centralization of industry, but also from the centralization of transportation and communication infrastructure.

The irony of ironies for the future city of hope in fact may be that cities may once again become relatively cheaper places to live and to enjoy the "good life" of material well-being and community—the same promise which the suburbs once held out to previous urbanites. The sheer cost of automobiles and their

Figure 12.1
Cost of the Journey to Work in One City

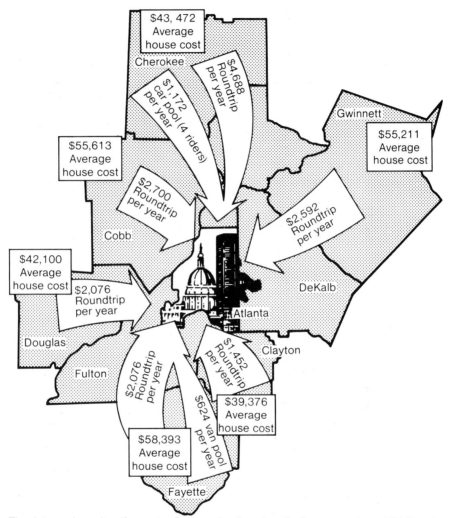

$43, 472
Average
house cost

Cherokee

$1,172
car pool (4 riders)
per year

$4,688
Roundtrip
per year

Gwinnett

$55,211
Average
house cost

$55,613
Average
house cost

$2,700
Roundtrip
per year

Cobb

$2,592
Roundtrip
per year

$42,100
Average
house cost

$2,076
Roundtrip
per year

DeKalb

Atlanta

Douglas

Clayton

Fulton

$2,076
Roundtrip
per year

$1,452
Roundtrip
per year

$624 van pool
per year

$39,376
Average
house cost

$58,393
Average
house cost

Fayette

The data are based on the costs of commuting in a six-cylinder compact car at 21.6 cents per mile for one year. The current average price of gasoline in Atlanta is $1.26 a gallon for full-service, unleaded gas.

SOURCE: AAA Atlanta in *Atlanta Constitution*, March 23, 1980, p. 1.

operation and maintenance may act as an incentive for the creation of the city of hope. Scarcity of energy resources, gas lines, and periodic failure to deliver services and goods to distant suburbs will be further incentives to move to the city with its relatively cheap housing and its mass-transit possibilities.

We have repeatedly noted that despite good intentions and huge dollar expenditures, the interventions of national and state bureaucratic agencies have on the whole been less than successful. Moreover, we have associated the decline of local politics with this growing domination of scarce public resources by external agencies. We have also suggested that part of the problem of external intervention results from scale and source of policy direction. This should be fairly clear: the more distant and bureaucratic the source of policy making, the greater the scale of the organization; and the greater the organizational scale, the less the likelihood that (a) programs will be appropriate to a given city, and (b) that those affected will have an opportunity to influence any given program.

The widespread suspicions (and agreements) that the above relationships are correct provides yet another possible source of political action for the city of hope. It is something of a cliché to point out that increasing numbers of citizens are hostile to remote political and bureaucratic actors over whom they seem to have little or no influence. This view once characterized those who called themselves political conservatives. Today such views can be discovered in nearly every shade of political opinion. Indeed, the incumbent president of the United States repeated his "anti-Washington" campaign litany despite the fact that for nearly three years he was supposed master of that which he condemned.

There is promise in this shift in public attitudes for the city of hope. Local control of local matters could easily become a slogan with sufficient drama to activate passive local politicians, mass media, and the soon-to-be-returning middle classes from the suburbs. This, of course, is pure speculation, but the coming together of energy scarcity, widespread disaffection with large-scale bureaucratic domination, and the tarnishing of the suburban dream might bring about the rebirth of a set of ideas.

These ideas are as old or older than America itself. The city of hope is one of diversity, conflict, and cooperation where people join together to solve common problems. The city of hope is one of bustling economic and commercial life, bringing together talent, innovation, and capital in productive and useful ways. The city of hope is cosmopolitan and eclectic in its taste and in its vulgarity. Above all, as much as possible its future is determined by politicians elected by and responsive to the people of the city.

Modern man's lust to consume will never be eliminated by the city of hope, nor will crime, pollution, racism, and poverty. What could happen, however, is the development of a city that begins to recognize the interdependency of all conditions within its physical and moral span. Humane treatment of the unfortunate and a concern with the kinds of questions dealt with here under the heading of "public economics" are neither improbable nor idealistic in the coming age of retrenchment and resource scarcity.

The city of hope has an asset of great significance, one that was unavailable to earlier architects of city planning and politics. We now possess a stock of experiential knowledge on a number of vital questions that were simply unavailable to our forefathers. We now know what *not* to do in a wide range of public policy areas from welfare to zoning. We now know the cost of failing to invest in pollution-control schemes. We may even have learned a few things about policing, teaching, solid-waste disposal, and delivery of health services.

Perhaps it is true that this is the age of narcissism, brought about partially in reaction to the decline in belief, trust, and hope in the idea of community. Economic upheaval, periods of artistic ferment, and a desire to find or create "ties that bind" can combine in the rediscovery of the city. The city can once again be that place where civilization is reborn. The city of hope can contain the push and pull of appropriate politics and humane concern for community members less fortunate than the rest of us. The ancient concerns for equity, equal treatment, and, above all, self-rule are far from forgotten.

Such concerns have arisen repeatedly in cities throughout the history of the modern world. American cities have made their own vital contributions to those concerns. Public resources were mobilized on behalf of radical innovations in the day-to-day life of the urban citizen for generation after generation. From free libraries, public education, and police forces to public lighting and transportation, cities have been a key public force down through the years. Our society has recently treated the city as though it were a disposable soft-drink can to be thrown aside on the highway to progress. That highway has, for the past two generations, led us away from the city. One ought not forget that the same road leads back to the city as well.

Still in Search of the City

We set out in search of the city twelve chapters ago and we must conclude with the admission that the search is far from over. Certainly, others might legitimately complain about areas of the urban political system only briefly mentioned or excluded completely. More fundamentally, we have failed to formulate a model or a paradigm of urban politics. But our key failure is to authoritatively define the "city" in such a manner that one can readily "see" it. In part this is a failure of intellect, imagination, and scholarship. Yet it also reflects a profound societal confusion about the spiritual and material meanings that people attach to the idea of the city. After years of neglect and mindless incremental change, the city of American life no longer enjoys even the unspoken shared meanings of the past, meanings which contributed so much to the ties that bind us. Even as we disagreed and fought over the city in its variable reality, Americans implicitly assumed that it was worth fighting for.

The city of hope is that emergent protean idea that accommodates all manner of activity and life; the city of despair only warehouses misery and unenlight-ened self-interest. All cities are to some extent both cities. Which ones will tend toward the city of hope and which toward the city of despair we can hardly predict. We do believe that the concepts, issues, and analyses presented in these pages are, and will continue to be, pertinent to the complex processes that will bring us closer to the city of hope—or the city of despair.

Suggested Readings

Bell, Daniel, *The Coming of Post-Industrial Society* (New York: Basic Books, 1973).
Ellul, Jacques, *The Meaning of the City* (Grand Rapids, Mich.: Eerdmans, 1970).
————, *The Technological Society* (New York, Knopf, 1964).
Stobaugh, Robert, and Daniel Yergin, *Energy Future* (New York: Random House, 1979).
Wildavsky, Aaron, *Speaking Truth to Power* (New York: Random House, 1979).

Index